AF361578

PREACHING APOCRYPHA
IN ANGLO-SAXON ENGLAND

Preaching Apocrypha in Anglo-Saxon England

BRANDON W. HAWK

UNIVERSITY OF TORONTO PRESS
Toronto Buffalo London

© University of Toronto Press 2018
Toronto Buffalo London
utorontopress.com
Printed in the U.S.A.

ISBN 978-14875-0305-5

♾ Printed on acid-free, 100% post-consumer recycled paper
with vegetable-based inks.

Library and Archives Canada Cataloguing in Publication

Hawk, Brandon W., author
Preaching apocrypha in Anglo-Saxon England / Brandon W. Hawk.

(Toronto Anglo-Saxon series ; 30)
Includes bibliographical references and index.
ISBN 978-1-4875-0305-5 (hardcover)

1. Apocryphal books – Criticism, interpretation, etc. – England – History –
To 1500. 2. Sermons, English (Old) – History and criticism. 3. England – Church
history – 449–1066. I. Title. II. Series: Toronto Anglo-Saxon series ; 30

BS1700.H39 2018   229.00942'09021   C2018-900766-4

This book was published with the generous assistance of a Book Subvention
Award from the Medieval Academy of America.

University of Toronto Press acknowledges the financial assistance to its
publishing program of the Canada Council for the Arts and the Ontario
Arts Council, an agency of the Government of Ontario.

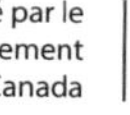

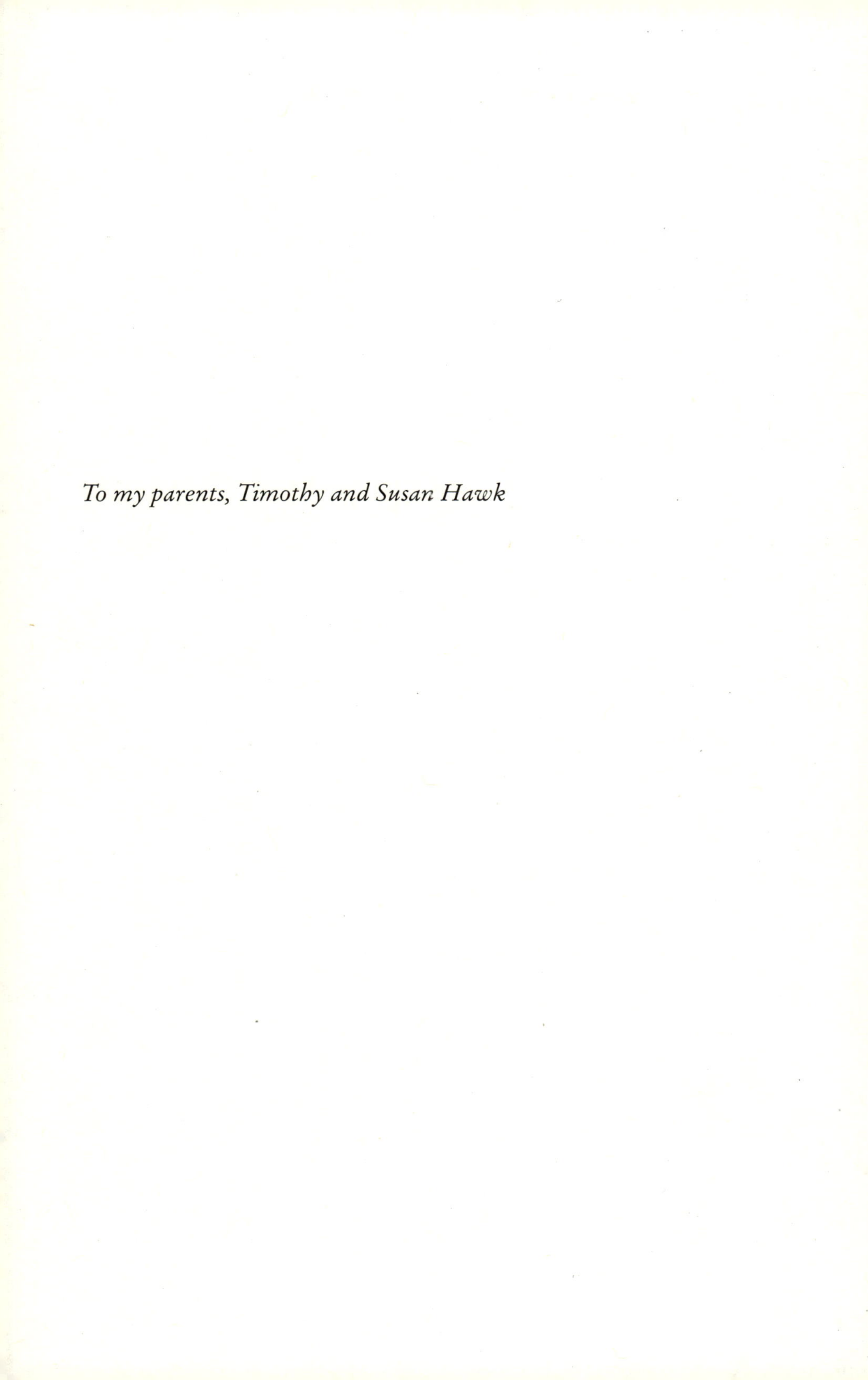

To my parents, Timothy and Susan Hawk

Contents

Figures

Acknowledgments

While I have amassed much debt to many who have supported me over the years, offering my thanks is not a burden but a pleasure. The core of this book began at the University of Connecticut, and my thanks, first and foremost, go to Fred Biggs and Clare Costley King'oo. Fred's influence may be seen throughout this book in many ways – likely even more than I can consciously acknowledge – and he has continually, generously read and discussed the project over the years; I hope that I have honoured his foundational work by extending it in fresh ways. Clare has consistently been a critical reader, often prompting me to clarify my readings, methodologies, and arguments in ways that have certainly strengthened my work in this book and beyond. I also thank my other mentors at UConn: Bob Hasenfratz, who encouraged me to sow the first seeds of my interest in this project in his Vercelli Book course; Sara Johnson, who helped me to situate my work in connection with late antiquity; Sherri Olson, who spurred me toward serious historiographic study (and frequently reminded me to keep peasants in view); and Fiona Somerset, who asked to read my work-in-progress only weeks after she arrived at UConn, and has continued to do so.

I owe more than I can express to the greater academic community for support of this project. In particular, I am deeply grateful to Mark LaCelle-Peterson for opening up the rich world of Anglo-Saxon England to me when I was an undergraduate, and for continuing our conversations since. I want to thank a number of colleagues who have shared their own work as well as discussed, read, and commented on various parts of this project, especially Lindy Brady, Tony Burke, Aidan Conti, Lorenzo DiTommaso, Mary Dzon, Helen Foxhall Forbes, Martin Foys, Micah Goodrich, Stephen Harris, Laura Howes, Brendan Kane, Kathleen Kennedy, Bre Leake, Roy

Liuzza, Kathryn Lowe, Nicola McDonald, Britt Mize, Els Rose, Winfried Rudolf, Don Scragg, Alison Shonkwiler, Elaine Treharne, Nicholas Watson, Lauren Whitnah, Christina Wilson, Charlie Wright, Stephen Yeager, Samantha Zacher, and the anonymous reviewers for the University of Toronto Press. I also owe many thanks to Suzanne Rancourt for seeing this book through to print. Any remaining mistakes are my own.

My fellowship at the University of Connecticut Humanities Institute in 2013–14 was instrumental to my project: I spent the year discussing my work with a wonderful community who helped me to rethink my project, reframe key issues, and begin reimagining the whole as a book. The critical and probing questions that I received stretched my thinking, and the discussions that arose from my presentations were vital for shaping the finished project into what it is now. This book is all the better for every conversation with the other fellows.

I am also appreciative for the financial and institutional support that I have received over the years. I have benefited from the generosity of the Medieval Studies Program at UConn, which awarded me a number of fellowships for research and travel to present parts of this project. I am grateful to the Medieval Academy of America for a Graduate Student Travel Bursary that allowed me to attend the 2013 Annual Meeting and present an early version of chapter 2, and for a generous Book Subvention Award to help publish this book. For travel support for archival research at Princeton University in 2013, I am thankful to the University of Connecticut Humanities Institute. While at Princeton, the helpful staff of the Rare Books and Special Collections welcomed me; I am most thankful to Paul Needham for arranging my time with the Blickling Homilies. I enjoyed the kindness and conversations of the staff at the Index of Christian Art, where I spent many hours and learned much that informed chapter 4. I am also indebted for the support of my colleagues at Rhode Island College, where I revised much of this book into its present form. I am especially appreciative of financial and research support from Daniel Scott, Chair of the English Department; Earl Simson, Dean of the Faculty of Arts and Sciences; and Ron Pitt, former Vice President for Academic Affairs.

A version of part of chapter 4 appears in *Fakes, Forgeries, and Fictions: Writing Ancient and Modern Christian Apocrypha, Proceedings from the 2015 York University Christian Apocrypha Symposium*, edited by Tony Burke (Eugene, OR: Cascade, 2017); I thank Cascade for permission to incorporate that material into this book. For images and permissions to print them, I would like to thank the Master and Fellows of Corpus Christi College, Cambridge, and the Institut de recherche et d'histoire des textes.

I would be remiss not to mention my family members. It is difficult to put my gratitude into words for Judy, my wife, since she has supported me in myriad ways. I owe her thanks for first entertaining many of my ideas (even in half-baked form), accompanying me from blank pages to finished chapters, and for her constant encouragement. I wrote several parts of this book, and revised much of it, while holding my daughter Catie asleep in one arm, or while she played nearby. I am happy for her companionship over the first year of her life as this book took its final shape, and I look forward to both of us sharing much together in years to come. Finally, my longest-standing debt is to my parents, Timothy and Susan Hawk, who first fostered my love of learning and imagination – especially in their stalwart defence of my creative choice to colour elephants purple as a child. I dedicate this book to them for their many years of support and encouragement.

Brandon W. Hawk
Feast of Corpus Christi, 2017

Abbreviations

ASE	*Anglo-Saxon England*
ASL	Michael Lapidge, *The Anglo-Saxon Library* (Oxford: Oxford University Press, 2006)
ASM	Helmut Gneuss and Michael Lapidge, *Anglo-Saxon Manuscripts: A Bibliographical Handlist of Manuscripts and Manuscript Fragments Written or Owned in England up to 1100*, Toronto Anglo-Saxon Series 15 (Toronto: University of Toronto Press, 2014), cited by item no.
ASPR	*Anglo-Saxon Poetic Records*, ed. George Philip Krapp and Elliott van Kirk Dobbie, 6 vols. (New York: Columbia University Press, 1931–53)
BH	*The Blickling Homilies*, ed. Richard Morris, EETS os 58, 63, 73 (London: Oxford University Press, 1874–80; repr. in 1 vol. 1967)
BHL	*Bibliotheca Hagiographica Latina Antiquae et Mediae Aetatis*, 2 vols., Subsidia Hagiographica 6 (Brussels, 1898–1901)
CANT	Maurits Geerard, *Clavis Apocryphorum Novi Testamenti* (Turnhout: Brepols, 1992), cited by item no.
CC	Corpus Christianorum
CM	Continuatio Mediaevalis (Turnhout: Brepols, 1966–)
SA	Series Apocryphorum (Turnhout: Brepols, 1983–)
SL	Series Latina (Turnhout: Brepols, 1953–)
CH Introduction	*Ælfric's Catholic Homilies: Introduction, Commentary and Glossary*, ed. Malcolm Godden, EETS ss 18 (Oxford: Oxford University Press, 2000)

CH I	*Ælfric's Catholic Homilies: The First Series, Text*, ed. Peter Clemoes, EETS ss 17 (Oxford: Oxford University Press, 1997)
CH II	*Ælfric's Catholic Homilies: The Second Series, Text*, ed. Malcolm Godden, EETS ss 5 (Oxford: Oxford University Press, 1979)
CLA	E.A. Lowe, *Codices Latini Antiquiores: A Palaeographical Guide to Latin Manuscripts Prior to the Ninth Century*, 11 vols. and Supplement (Oxford: Oxford University Press, 1934–71), cited by vol. and item no.
CSASE	Cambridge Studies in Anglo-Saxon England
EETS	Early English Text Society
es	Extra Series
os	Original Series
ss	Supplementary Series
Fontes	*Fontes Anglo-Saxonici: A Register of Written Sources Used by Anglo-Saxon Authors*, http://fontes.english.ox.ac.uk
LS	*Ælfric's Lives of the Saints*, ed. Walter W. Skeat, 4 vols., EETS os 76, 82, 94, 114 (London: Oxford University Press, 1881–1900; repr. in 2 vols. 1966)
MGH	Monumenta Germaniae Historica
MRTS	Medieval and Renaissance Texts and Studies
N&Q	*Notes and Queries*
NRK	N.R. Ker, *Catalogue of Manuscripts Containing Anglo-Saxon* (Oxford: Clarendon Press, 1957; repr. with supplement, 1990), cited by item no.
NTA	*New Testament Apocrypha*, ed. Edgar Hennecke and Wilhelm Schneemelcher, trans. R. McL. Wilson, revised ed., 2 vols. (Louisville: Westminster John Knox Press, 1991–2)
PL	*Patrologia cursus completus, series Latina*, ed. J.-P. Migne, 221 vols. (Paris: Migne, 1844–64), cited by vol. and col.
PUEM	Orietta Da Rold, Takako Kato, Mary Swan, and Elaine Treharne, *The Production and Use of English Manuscripts 1060 to 1220*, University of Leicester, 2010, http://www.le.ac.uk/ee/em1060to1220/
RES	*The Review of English Studies*

SASLC	*Sources of Anglo-Saxon Literary Culture*
SASLC 1	*Sources of Anglo-Saxon Literary Culture, Volume One: Abbo of Fleury, Abbo of Saint-German-des-Prés, and Acta Sanctorum*, ed. Frederick M. Biggs, Thomas D. Hill, Paul E. Szarmach, and E. Gordon Whatley, with the assistance of Deborah A. Oosterhouse (Kalamazoo: Medieval Institute Publications, 2001)
SASLC Apocrypha	*Sources of Anglo-Saxon Literary Culture: The Apocrypha*, ed. Frederick M. Biggs, Instrumenta Anglistica Mediaevalia 1 (Kalamazoo: Medieval Institute Publications, 2006)
SASLC Trial	*Sources of Anglo-Saxon Literary Culture: A Trial Version*, ed. Frederick M. Biggs, Thomas D. Hill, and Paul E. Szarmach, with the assistance of Karen Hammond, MRTS 74 (Binghamton, NY: Center for Medieval and Early Renaissance Studies, 1990)
VH	*The Vercelli Homilies and Related Texts*, ed. D.G. Scragg, EETS os 300 (Oxford: Oxford University Press, 1992)

PREACHING APOCRYPHA
IN ANGLO-SAXON ENGLAND

Seeking Out Gold in the Mud

This book is an examination of Christian apocrypha in Anglo-Saxon England, focused specifically on the use of these extra-biblical narratives in Old English sermons. Throughout this study, I challenge normative assumptions about the use of non-canonical gospels, acts, and apocalypses in preaching texts by suggesting that they are a substantial part of the apparatus of Christian tradition inherited by Anglo-Saxons. I explore uses of apocrypha as, on the one hand, hermeneutic in expanding and explaining biblical and doctrinal knowledge, and, on the other hand, ideological responses to local pedagogical needs. While these texts have been marginalized in scholarship, I argue that they are part of a corpus of orthodoxy that speaks to a plurality of beliefs and practices in Anglo-Saxon culture. Situated in relation to the general pervasiveness of apocrypha, Old English sermons should be understood as participating in the widespread transmission of Christian materials in the period. These Old English sermons are not isolated, but part of more general cultural trends. I account for the broader prevalence of apocrypha by studying Old English sermons as significant witnesses to Anglo-Saxon religious attitudes within a wider media network encompassing the afterlives of texts, manuscripts, and visual arts. In other words, I argue that extra-biblical media did not merely survive on the margins of culture, but thrived at the heart of mainstream Anglo-Saxon Christianity.

One specific passage in a letter by the famous biblical scholar Jerome (347–420) serves to introduce several of the issues to be dealt with in this study. Around the years 401–2, Jerome corresponded through letters with a Roman noblewoman named Laeta about the best way to provide her daughter Paula with a Christian education. In addressing Laeta's questions about Paula's education, Jerome outlines a program of Christian learning rooted in the Scriptures and other Christian writings.[1] He recommends beginning with the Psalms, then Proverbs, Ecclesiastes, Job, the Gospels, Acts of the Apostles, and the New Testament Epistles, followed by the Old Testament Prophets, Heptateuch (the first seven books of the Hebrew Bible), historical books, Ezra, Esther, and, finally, the pinnacle of biblical spiritual allegory, the Song of Songs. After this outline of Scripture, Jerome continues:

> Caueat omnia apocrypha et, si quando ea non ad dogmatum ueritatem, sed ad signorum reuerentiam legere uoluerit, sciat non eorum esse, quorum titulis praenotantur, multaque his admixta uitiosa et grandis esse prudentiae aurum in luto quaerere.

> (Let her take care with all apocrypha and, if ever she wishes to read them, not for the truth of their doctrines but for respect for miracles, let her know that they are not by those to whom they are ascribed, that many faults are interspersed in them, and that it demands great discretion to seek out gold in the mud.)[2]

Although this passage includes Jerome's warning about the false authority of apocrypha, it also reveals that he does not wholly denounce reading these texts. On the contrary, by acknowledging that apocrypha may indeed belong within a program of personal education – even as valuable as gold – Jerome admits that there may be great benefits to sifting through these narratives.

This anecdote serves as an introduction to *Preaching Apocrypha in Anglo-Saxon England* for several reasons, not least of which is that it provides an authoritative starting point to which Anglo-Saxon intellectuals also looked. One major theme that may be gleaned from examining such critical comments is that apocrypha occupied a tenuous place in Christian

---

1 Unless otherwise noted, biblical citations and quotations are according to Weber, ed., *Biblia sacra iuxta vulgatam versionem*, and translations are from *The Holy Bible: Douay Version Translated from the Latin Vulgate*. For quotations of other texts, I have occasionally modernized capitalization and punctuation, and accepted editorial emendations as appropriate. Translations are my own, except where noted.

2 *Epistula* 107.12 (*Ad Laetum*), in Hildberg, ed., *Sancti Eusebii Hieronymi Epistulae*, 55:303, lines 5–9.

tradition.[3] But they did at least occupy a place. By expressing his view, Jerome continues the convention of recognizing a tripartite approach to canonical and extra-canonical materials inherited from previous Christian writers,[4] which François Bovon suggests with the categories "canonical, rejected, and useful books."[5] As I argue throughout this book, Anglo-Saxons clearly valued certain apocrypha for their usefulness in preaching, even if they understood them to be outside of the biblical canon. As Bovon convincingly establishes, "from the beginning Christian communities used more than two categories and respected several degrees of authority for their texts."[6]

For matters of biblical canon, reading, and interpretation, Jerome's place in the medieval period was central, and his criticism exemplifies the general vacillation that pervades many statements about apocrypha during the patristic and medieval periods. Jerome's attitude towards apocrypha was well known throughout the early Middle Ages, and similarly ambivalent sentiments may be found in the writings of his contemporaries, like Augustine of Hippo (354–430) – whose opinion differs somewhat from Jerome's – as well as later Anglo-Saxon writers, like Aldhelm, bishop of Sherborne (c. 639–709), Bede of Monkwearmouth-Jarrow (672/3–735), and Ælfric, abbot of Eynsham (c. 955–c. 1010). Yet, at the same time, Old English sermons also betray a fascination with Christian apocrypha that demonstrates that Anglo-Saxon authors were, indeed, busy seeking out gold in the mud.

Apocrypha and Their Preaching Afterlife

My project primarily rests at the intersection of scholarship on Old English sermons, apocryphal sources, and transmission studies. In recent years, there has been a growing interest in both sermons and apocrypha in Anglo-Saxon England. Regarding sermons, the most prominent studies are a series of essays collected in *The Old English Homily: Precedent, Practice, and Appropriation*, edited by Aaron J Kleist, as well as Samantha

---

3 On the concept of tradition, see esp. Stock, *Listening for the Text*, and Lees, *Tradition and Belief*.

4 On treatments of the biblical canon in the patristic period, see Gallagher, *Hebrew Scripture in Patristic Biblical Theory*.

5 See Bovon, "Canonical, Rejected, and Useful Books," and "Beyond the Canonical and the Apocryphal Books, the Presence of a Third Category."

6 Ibid., 126.

Zacher's *Preaching the Converted: The Style and Rhetoric of the Vercelli Homilies*, Joyce Tally Lionarons's *The Homiletic Writings of Archbishop Wulfstan: A Critical Study*, and Hiroshi Ogawa's *Language and Style in Old English Composite Homilies*. In addition to these books, both Elaine Treharne and Stephen M. Yeager pay attention to preaching texts and manuscripts in recent studies emphasizing the endurance of Anglo-Saxon traditions beyond the Norman Conquest of 1066.[7] While these studies reveal a recent upsurge in attention to Anglo-Saxon preaching, the fact that Zacher's and Ogawa's studies are the only monographs of the past twenty years to focus on anonymous Old English sermons also reveals the need for further in-depth work on this subject. Furthermore, while both Zacher and Ogawa largely focus on rhetorical and stylistic examinations, I look outward to cultural contexts and ideological implications surrounding Old English sermons more generally.

Similarly, attention to apocrypha in Anglo-Saxon England is evident in essays collected in *Apocryphal Texts and Traditions in Anglo-Saxon England*, edited by Kathryn Powell and Donald G. Scragg, as well as the collaborative bibliographic volume *Sources of Anglo-Saxon Literary Culture: The Apocrypha*, edited by Frederick M. Biggs. Els Rose has offered a monumental study of the reception of apocryphal acts of the apostles in early medieval liturgy, mainly focused on the Continent but also including some English materials.[8] No scholar, however, has yet offered a full-length examination of apocrypha in Anglo-Saxon England that situates the significance of this subject within the history of Christianity. Individual articles and source work have done much to enhance our knowledge of apocrypha in early England, but they often show the trees rather than the forest. Putting various previous work into conversation creates a greater sense of extra-biblical media in the landscape of Anglo-Saxon culture. In *Preaching Apocrypha in Anglo-Saxon England*, I present a sustained study of the subject, synthesizing disparate studies and historical contexts, offering a bird's-eye view that allows for the reconsideration of previous assessments that have marginalized apocrypha.

Bringing the fields of apocrypha and sermon studies together, I explore authorial reshaping of apocryphal sources into texts useful for preaching within the particular cultural contexts of late Anglo-Saxon England. At the core of this study are compositions that I call "preaching texts,"

---

7 Treharne, *Living through Conquest*, and Yeager, *From Lawmen to Plowmen*.
8 Rose, *Ritual Memory*.

encompassing a range of literary types such as sermons and homilies in both Latin and Old English (see my "Excursus on Terminology").[9] All of these texts are, in some way, related to preaching. As Carolyn Muessig observes, "Defining medieval preaching is a difficult task. There are a variety of explanations that one could give, yet a concise definition obscures its multifaceted character."[10] I assume as expansive a definition as possible, since a broad view of preaching cuts across its potential roles as speech act, textual composition, social practice, liturgical ritual, and literature for lay devotion.[11] A working definition, then, is that preaching comprises a religious exposition to an audience (ecclesiastical, lay, or both) by a recognized authority of the Christian community. All of the specific compositions or collections I examine bear the generic conventions of the discourse of preaching as didactic teaching.

While traditional source studies emphasize antecedents, and stylistic sermon studies emphasize rhetorical conventions, I am concerned with the *processes* undertaken by sermon authors using apocrypha. By situating these sermons in their historical contexts, I seek to highlight their significance not only as *products* of culture but also as *interventions*. In many ways, my approach to preaching texts as cultural artefacts is indebted to the work of predecessors like Clare A. Lees, who acknowledges that "late Anglo-Saxon vernacular religious writing … is evidence for a cultural practice that constitutes itself as traditional and is constitutive of social practice."[12] Similarly, I examine Old English sermons not as fixed texts, but as witnesses to the processes by which Anglo-Saxon authors used apocrypha to think through and address contemporary issues. As adaptations, they are refashionings of the materials at hand – in this case, cultural sources usefully appropriated for teaching (from the pulpit, for private devotion, or other purposes). One way of understanding this notion is through the suggestion of cultural critic Raymond Williams, who remarks on "apparent continuations or even conscious revivals of older forms, which yet, when they are really looked at, can be seen to be new."[13] Old English sermons drawing

---

9 For general introductions to medieval preaching, see esp. Kienzle, ed., *The Sermon*, and studies by Muessig: "What Is Medieval Monastic Preaching?," "Preacher, Sermon and Audience in the Middle Ages: An Introduction," "Sermon, Preacher and Society in the Middle Ages," and "Medieval Preaching."
10 Muessig, "What Is Medieval Monastic Preaching?," 3–4.
11 See Muessig, ed., *Preacher, Sermon and Audience in the Middle Ages*.
12 Lees, *Tradition and Belief*, 5.
13 Williams, *Marxism and Literature*, 189. Cf. Lees, *Tradition and Belief*, esp. 12–18.

on apocrypha portray precisely this quality, as they are new in language (vernacular rather than Latin), adapted in contents (through the handling of sources), and meant to address the particular concerns of Anglo-Saxon preachers.

The canonical Bible offered stories about Jesus, his family, his apostles, and the imminent Judgment, but many other para-biblical narratives also circulated from the early Christian period onward. Because terms *apocrypha* and *apocryphal* have been much debated in reference to biblical and early Christian studies, my use of them requires some clarification at the outset.[14] The related terms *pseudepigrapha* and *apocrypha* are often distinguished in modern scholarship, to denote those works associated with the so-called Old Testament or Hebrew Bible (pseudepigrapha) or with the so-called New Testament (apocrypha).[15] Generally and historically speaking, the term *pseudepigrapha* (singular *pseudepigraphon*) was used to signify works "falsely attributed" (Greek *pseudo* and *graphos*) to authors who historically did not write them, while the term *apocrypha* (singular *apocryphon*) was used to signify works as "hidden" or outside of the biblical canon.[16] In the early Christian church, these terms were variously used and debated along with the development of the biblical canon as it came to be established. Also significant is the three-part distinction, arising out of post-Reformation criticism, concerning so-called Jewish pseudepigrapha, Christian apocrypha, and deuterocanonical Apocrypha. The last of these – Jewish works included in the Septuagint but not accepted as canonical by Protestants – may be set aside for the medieval period, since the issue is irrelevant for pre-Reformation Christians.

With the aim of casting a wide net for the study of apocrypha, my working definition fosters an inclusive understanding of extra-biblical texts. Eric Junod offers the most cogent definition:

> anonymous or pseudepigraphal texts of Christian origin, which stand in some relation to the books of the [New Testament] or the [Old Testament], because they are devoted to events which are narrated or mentioned in these

---

14 For a useful overview, see Burke, *Secret Scriptures Revealed*. For specific apocrypha, I refer throughout this study to entries in *CANT*, cited by item no., and *SASLC Apocrypha*, both with further references. A growing bibliography on apocrypha in general and specific texts may be found at *e-Clavis*.

15 See, for example, Charlesworth, ed., *The Old Testament Pseudepigrapha*, and *NTA*.

16 On pseudepigraphy generally, see Ehrman, *Forgery and Counterforgery*, esp. on terms at 29–68.

books, or because they are devoted to events which can be understood as a continuation of events presented or mentioned in these books, because they concentrate upon persons who appear in these books, or because their literary *Gattung* is related to those of the biblical writings.[17]

In this sense, apocrypha are works generally biblical in character that were traditionally excluded from the canonical Bible in Western Christianity. While I deal mainly with Christian materials, I also occasionally refer to Jewish pseudepigrapha, and employ the term *apocrypha* throughout to encompass both as extra-biblical traditions. Yet the scope remains focused on apocryphal media related to Christian subjects, especially Jesus, Mary, and the earliest disciples.

One of my major claims in this study is that, while apocrypha are not formally part of the biblical canon, they were central to Anglo-Saxon culture as part of the Christian traditions that they inherited and valued. The prevalence of apocryphal influences in Anglo-Saxon media generally – and in Old English sermons specifically – is ample enough to suggest as much, though scholarship has been hindered from this perspective because of modern biased views of apocrypha as "heterodox," even "heretical," due to their extra-canonical status. It is a common assumption that the corpus of anonymous Old English sermons represents a heterodox tradition in need of reform, while Ælfric of Eynhsam is often heralded as the pinnacle of Anglo-Saxon conservative orthodoxy.[18] The two collections of sermons known as the Vercelli and Blickling Books are often considered illustrative of the types of literature against which Ælfric levelled his condemnations of "mycel gedwyld on manegum engliscum bocum" ("much error in many English books")[19] and the circulation of certain "dwollican bec" ("erroneous books").[20]

---

17 Originally in French, in Junod, "Apocryphes du Nouveau Testament ou apocryphes chrétiens anciens?," 412; translation from *NTA*, 60.

18 Cf. remarks in Treharne, "The Form and Function of the Vercelli Book," and Zacher, *Preaching the Converted*, 44–51.

19 *CH* I, Old English Preface: 174, line 51.

20 *CH* II.29: line 125. Many examples of scholarly rhetoric about these condemnations may be cited, but several prominent examples suffice: Godden, "Ælfric and the Vernacular Prose Tradition"; Greenfield and Calder, *A New Critical History of Old English Literature*, 77; Fulk and Cain, *A History of Old English Literature*, 72; Scheil, *The Footsteps of Israel*, esp. 200–2.

Yet such false assumptions rest on two problems. First, there is no evidence that Ælfric had even a passing familiarity with the Vercelli and Blickling collections, or that they were the objects of his exasperations. Second, while "gedwyld" and "dwollican" are often taken to mean "heresy" and "heretical," these and related terms are used across the Old English corpus to signify various meanings, such as "error," "foolishness," "ignorance," "uncertainty," and "doubt," as well as "perverse," "erroneous," "wrong," "foolish," and "false."[21] While these more diverse meanings leave no room for reading Ælfric's comments positively, they do provoke a more nuanced view (as I discuss in chapter 3). For modern scholars, evaluations of anonymous Old English sermons have long been dominated by predisposed attitudes about the underlying apocryphal sources. But dichotomies established by associating "canonical" with "orthodox" and "apocryphal" with "heterodox" are false binaries. Apocryphal narratives embedded within Old English preaching texts may be seen as central to Anglo-Saxon Christianity rather than exceptions.

By concentrating on anonymous Old English sermons as representative of apocryphal influences in Anglo-Saxon England, this project seeks to avoid assumptions associated with documents that are often read as normative. It is not surprising that Ælfric – a figure embroiled in tenth-century institutionalized reforms – enjoys a status of authority, and that his pronouncements against certain apocrypha have greatly influenced scholarly assessments.[22] But scholarly assessments that accept Ælfric's valuations without question fail to do justice to the reality of medieval Christianities. The danger is that historians might misrepresent the past by accepting certain documents as more important than others. For example, Ælfric is often seen as of paramount importance because he is a known, named author associated with Benedictine reform movements, while the Vercelli and Blickling sermons are viewed as lesser because they are earlier, anonymous, and not clearly associated with any particular movement.[23] As John Blair

---

21 See Momma, ed., *The Dictionary of Old English*, s.v. *dwol, gedwol, dwola, gedwolen, gedwolenlic*, and *dwollic*.

22 On tenth-century Benedictine reforms and Ælfric's role, see, recently, Stephenson, *The Politics of Language*.

23 From another perspective, Charles D. Wright has argued for situating at least some anonymous sermons in the Vercelli and Blickling collections in relation to Benedictine reforms, in "Vercelli Homilies XI–XIII and the Benedictine Reform" and "A New Latin Source for Two Old English Homilies (Fadda I and Blickling I)." Similarly, Treharne has argued that the Vercelli Book was compiled in relation to early Benedictine reforms at St Augustine's Canterbury, in "The Form and Function of the Vercelli Book."

points out, those sources attributed to the most institutionalized, influential authorities (like Ælfric and other Benedictine reformers) "possessed a virtual monopoly of record" among the many documents from Anglo-Saxon England.[24]

Furthermore, throughout his works, Ælfric did much to construct a self-fashioned persona imbued with special authority that lends strength to his condemnations and pronouncements about correct doctrine (as I discuss in chapter 3). Modern scholars accepting this persona of self-made authority without acknowledging a more complex situation leads to folly. In relation to evidence about tenth-century England, Blair contends, "The [Benedictine] reformers used their considerable powers of communication and dissemination to form a homogeneous national religious culture, embodying carefully selected elements from the past, beneath which the religious culture of the localities sank to near-invisibility."[25] The institutionalization and dissemination of such reformers' legacies continue to affect our understandings of late Anglo-Saxon England.

Unfortunately, sources that have become normative continue to be used as the basis for inquiries about aspects of religion in the Middle Ages. The *Pseudo-Gelasian Decree*, for instance, remains an authoritative document used as a starting point for discussions of the Bible and orthodoxy in the medieval period, as it provides a codified list of accepted and rejected works; anything falling outside of the prescribed norms of this document is, for scholars, often considered part of heterodox trends.[26] Even taking its wide transmission into account, the *Pseudo-Gelasian Decree* is only one prescriptive document, not descriptive of actual practices regarding apocrypha. Indeed, the author of the decretal creates an imposing voice for the document in much the same way as Ælfric does for himself, establishing the document as orthodox in distinction to competing claims in a way that lends the decree authority for future readers. M.R. James identifies that many of the references to books listed in the *Decree* are collected from patristic authors, especially Jerome.[27] To accept the *Pseudo-Gelasian Decree* as normative, in fact, is indeed ironic, given that the document is clearly a pseudonymous forgery (likely from the sixth century) and not a genuine decretal of Pope Gelasius I (492–6).

---

24 Blair, *The Church in Anglo-Saxon Society*, 353.
25 Ibid., 353–4.
26 Dobschütz, *Das Decretum Gelasianum de libris recipiendis et non recipiendis in Kritischem Text herausgegeben und untersucht*. See also *NTA*, 1.38–40.
27 James, *The New Testament Apocrypha*, 21.

It is also important to acknowledge that any study of the reception of Christian apocrypha is closely related to the study of the received canonical Bible. As Julie Sanders points out, adaptations are closely linked with some "shared community of knowledge" or "textual communities," in which texts "operate within the parameters of an established canon, serving indeed to reinforce that canon by ensuring a continued interest in the original source text."[28] This concept raises significant points central to this study: that medieval adaptations of apocrypha not only revolve around the biblical canon but also further perpetuate their continued transmission as part of the intellectual heritage related to that canon. In this regard, it is telling that so many apocryphal influences have been identified alongside biblical influences in Anglo-Saxon literature; the two are hardly separable.[29] Michael E. Stone acknowledges the circularity of this aspect of biblical and apocryphal interactions, but has singled out the subject for special attention: "What was transmitted to the present was for the most part such as reinforced the claims and positions of the eventually dominant varieties of Christianity and Judaism"; after all, "The preserved data are themselves selected by the orthodoxies of a period later than that of their creation."[30] In other words, the sustained use of apocryphal materials by medieval writers essentially embedded them within the received corpus of authoritative texts that continued to be transmitted. While this view of apocrypha is contrary to modern attitudes, it is nevertheless borne out by the myriad medieval sources influenced by extra-biblical texts, both inside and outside of Anglo-Saxon England.

I am not the first or the only one to call into question modern scholarly claims about apocrypha, either in Anglo-Saxon England or more generally. For example, Mary Clayton, Aideen O'Leary, Nancy M. Thompson, and Biggs have recently helped to reassess the significance of apocrypha not on the margins of Anglo-Saxon belief but within mainstream Christianity.[31] Particularly poignant are Clayton's demonstrations that the cult of

---

28 Sanders, *Adaptation and Appropriation*, 97–8. On "textual communities," see esp. Stock, *The Implications of Literacy*.

29 See *SASLC Apocrypha* for an extensive overview of scholarship.

30 Stone, *Ancient Judaism*, 11. Stone also admits that, in using the terms "orthodox" and "orthodoxy," they essentially "designate the *eventually* dominant forms of Judaism and Christianity"; see ibid., 4–16, quotation at 4 n. 7, emphasis added.

31 Clayton, *The Apocryphal Gospels of Mary in Anglo-Saxon England*; O'Leary, "An Orthodox Old English Homiliary?"; Biggs, "An Introduction and Overview of Recent Work"; Thompson, "'Hit Segð on Halgum Bocum'" and "Anglo-Saxon Orthodoxy"; summaries of scholarship in *SASLC Apocrypha*; and further references in chapter 3.

the Virgin Mary and Marian apocrypha that contributed to it were central to Anglo-Saxon devotion.[32] Thompson aptly summarizes one assumption that I use as a starting point for my own study: "scholars have tended to read backwards, approaching the anonymous homilies with a set of assumptions about what Anglo-Saxon Christians should have believed, rather than looking at what they did believe."[33]

Scholars examining early Christianity have also challenged normative histories that marginalize apocrypha against canonical biblical texts. This work rests largely on theories developed by Walter Bauer, claiming that diversity is a key feature in the early history of Christianity,[34] which has been repeatedly refined and supplemented with more recent evidence.[35] While much of the scholarship on Christian apocrypha – by scholars such as Tony Burke, Bart D. Ehrman, Helmut Koester, and Elaine Pagels – focuses on the first four centuries of Christianity for evidence (especially constrained by the more solidified form of the canon in the fourth century),[36] more recent work has called for casting wider nets.[37] My intervention, therefore, should be understood as part of a larger conversation about the diversity of Christian belief across cultures, and the ways in which medieval apocryphal media fit into that history. One goal is bringing ideas of early Christian studies forward in time, to address similar concerns about the diversity of Christianity in the medieval period. This type of work means incorporating concepts from the history of reception, following work by Els Rose (early medieval), Irena Backus and Annette Yoshiko Reed (early modern), Pierluigi Piovanelli (modern), and Philip Jenkins (transhistorical).[38] As all of these studies have demonstrated,

---

32 Clayton, *The Cult of the Virgin Mary in Anglo-Saxon England* and *The Apocryphal Gospels of Mary in Anglo-Saxon England*.

33 Thompson, "Anglo-Saxon Orthodoxy," 40.

34 Bauer, *Rechtgläubigkeit und Ketzerei im ältesten Christentum*; the second edition, ed. Georg Strecker, was translated as *Orthodoxy and Heresy in Earliest Christianity*.

35 See, for example, Ehrman, *Lost Christianities*; and Hartog, ed., *Orthodoxy and Heresy in Early Christian Contexts*.

36 For the state of the field, see Burke, ed., *Forbidden Texts on the Western Frontier*.

37 See, for example, Junod, "Apocryphes du Nouveau Testament ou apocryphes chrétiens anciens?" and "'Apocryphes du Nouveau Testament'"; Piovanelli, "What Is a Christian Apocryphal Text and How Does It Work?"; and Shepherd, "Early Christian Apocrypha."

38 Rose, *Ritual Memory*; Backus, *Historical Method and Confessional Identity in the Era of the Reformation (1378–1615)*; Reed, "The Afterlives of New Testament Apocrypha"; Piovanelli, "What Is a Christian Apocryphal Text?"; and Jenkins, *The Many Faces of Christ*.

Christian apocrypha did not disappear, but have remained a vital part of faith and belief up until the present. *Preaching Apocrypha in Anglo-Saxon England* is a contribution to scholarship tracing the longer history of these afterlives of apocrypha.

At the heart of this study is my contention that the uses of apocrypha in Old English sermons were based upon a certain narrative impulse of the authors to retell these stories as ways of expressing core doctrinal concerns. For this reason, I focus mainly on Anglo-Saxon uses of longer, sustained narratives, rather than apocryphal motifs explored elsewhere, for example, by Charles D. Wright in *The Irish Tradition in Old English Literature*.[39] In other words, one of the assumptions in this study is that the desire for narrative is crucial to the role of apocrypha in the imaginative landscape of Christianity in the medieval period. Could it be that narrative impulse was more important for Anglo-Saxon authors than questions about the boundaries of canonicity and orthodoxy? The success of apocrypha in popular media from the Anglo-Saxon period suggests as much, and I follow this argument throughout the project.

The literary texts that I discuss are primarily found in Old English preaching collections.[40] Four of these are especially prominent: the anonymous sermons of the tenth-century Vercelli Book (Vercelli, Biblioteca Capitolare CXVII; s. x^2)[41] and Blickling Book (Princeton, University Library, W.H. Scheide Collection 71; s. x/xi);[42] Ælfric's two series of *Catholic Homilies* (*CH* I and II), composed between about 989 and 992;[43] and the late twelfth-century collection Oxford, Bodleian Library, Bodley 343 (s. xii^2, West Midlands).[44] While the corpus of Old English sermons

---

39 Many examples of specific motifs are also discussed in *SASLC: Apocrypha*.

40 Throughout this study, manuscript dates and origins are based on NRK, cited by item no.; Gameson, *The Manuscripts of Early Norman England (c. 1066–1130)*, cited by item no.; *PUEM*; and *ASM*, by item no. I have also consulted Scragg, *A Conspectus of Scribal Hands Writing English, 960–1100*, and *DigiPal*.

41 NRK, 394; and *ASM*, 941. See *VH*.

42 NRK, 382; and *ASM*, 905. See *BH*.

43 See esp. Clemoes, "The Chronology of Ælfric's Works." See *CH* I and *CH* II, as well as *CH Introduction*.

44 NRK, 310. Bodley 343 remains unedited in whole, but some vernacular sermons are edited by Irvine in *Old English Homilies from MS Bodley 343*, and some Latin sermons are edited by Conti in "Preaching Scripture and Apocrypha."

extends beyond these collections,[45] these manuscripts are representative of Anglo-Saxon preaching for several reasons. First, the Vercelli and Blickling compilations contain the earliest surviving witnesses to vernacular preaching in England, while Bodley 343 contains the latest. Second, they are the largest collections of Old English preaching texts: the Vercelli Book contains twenty-three sermons; the Blickling Book contains eighteen; Ælfric's *Catholic Homilies* comprise eighty in total; and Bodley 343 contains around seventy sermons, including versions and adaptations of works by earlier anonymous authors, Ælfric, and Wulfstan, archbishop of York (d. 1023). This selection is thus not meant to marginalize other Old English sermons, but to focus this study on a representative set of Anglo-Saxon preaching materials. Despite this focus, chapter 1 addresses a much wider range of Anglo-Saxon sermons – including Latin and Old English, in both Continental and English manuscripts, from the eighth to twelfth centuries – in order to show the widespread prevalence of apocrypha and the interconnectedness of media across geography and temporality.

Sermons represent what have been punningly called the "mass media" of the medieval period, serving as a major arbiter between intellectuals and popular culture.[46] While the divide between learned and unlearned has often been emphasized – in medieval sources as well as modern scholarship – Old English sermons serve to bridge this seeming gap, as they both taught and were influenced by the beliefs of common people. In terms of cultural and media studies, vernacular preaching may be understood as embedded within popular culture because, to borrow a framework established by Mikita Brottman, "it fits in with a phase of general understanding," "it is familiar to the most widely shared manners and tastes prevalent in … culture," and "it effects and is ordinarily understood, shared and enjoyed by a large proportion of the general population."[47] Composed from the

---

45 More generally, see esp. Scragg, "The Corpus of Vernacular Homilies and Prose Saints' Lives before Ælfric." For lists of surviving preaching collections and their contents, see "Homiliaries" and "Homilies" in "Index I" of NRK; Kleist, "Appendix"; and, for the periods c. 1050–1100 and c. 1100–1220, Treharne, *Living through Conquest*, 99–101 and 125–6.

46 See, for example, d'Avray, "Introduction," *Medieval Marriage Sermons*; and, more recently, Rosen, "The Last Time a Pope Resigned Mass Media Was Called … Mass." See more on this notion, below.

47 Brottman, *High Theory/Low Culture*, xiii. On medieval popular culture, see esp. Gurevich, *Medieval Popular Culture*; Le Goff, *The Medieval Imagination*; and, recently, Somerset, "Introduction," with further references there. For extended discussion, see my Conclusion.

materials of Latin intellectual culture, written in the accessible English of the people, preached in public, and circulated widely for later reuse, Old English sermons fit well into this framework. This is all the truer since sermons and the collections they comprise make up a large portion of the surviving vernacular literature from the Anglo-Saxon period. In this, "popular and 'high' culture are virtually interchangeable – or at least, the distinction between them is blurred"[48] – and vernacular sermons exist in the smudges of these blurred lines, representative of cultural currents.[49] As I contend throughout this book, apocryphal sermons fit into a range of contexts, purposes, and uses for diverse groups in Anglo-Saxon society: cloistered religious, secular clergy, laity, both men and women. Based on the evidence, in fact, these categories are not mutually exclusive, as apocryphal narratives appeal to a multiplicity of possible audiences simultaneously.

Transmitting Media

Much of this book deals with what may be broadly called transmission studies. I am particularly interested in what Walter Benjamin calls the "afterlife" (*Überleben*) of a text,[50] which Jacques Derrida, following Benjamin, evokes as "sur-vival" (*survie*).[51] While both of these critics discuss their ideas in relation to textual translation, the notion of a text's "afterlife" may also be expanded to consider its transmission and influence more broadly. Benjamin insists that the afterlife of a text is a meaningful continuation of its existence, since in later iterations, "the life of the originals attains its latest, continually renewed, and almost complete unfolding";[52] indeed, he insists that "in its afterlife – which could not be called that if it were not a transformation of something living – the original undergoes a change."[53] With this idea in mind, the significance of apocrypha within medieval

---

48 Brottman, *High Theory/Low Culture*, xxvi.

49 I borrow the concept of "cultural currents" from cultural studies, especially the work of Raymond Williams, such as *Culture and Society, 1780–1950* and *Marxism and Literature*. Although Williams does not explicitly use the phrase (to my knowledge), he uses the terms *current* and *currents* in this sense in *Culture and Society*, at 10 (quoting Edmund Burke), 11, 129 (quoting Matthew Arnold), 130, and 186.

50 Benjamin, "The Task of the Translator."

51 Derrida, "Des Tours de Babel," esp. 178ff; cf. "Living On/Border Lines," 102–3. Derrida cites the French translation of Benjamin's essay, "La tâche du traducteur."

52 Benjamin, "The Task of the Translator," 255.

53 Ibid., 256.

Christianity may be understood by paying attention to their afterlives in manuscript circulation, intertextualities, translations, adaptations, and interrelationships between them. This scope includes Latin and vernacular preaching collections from the Continent as well as England; Latin prayers in liturgical anthologies like the *Book of Cerne*; Old English poetry such as *Andreas*, Cynewulf's *Fates of the Apostles*, and *The Dream of the Rood*; legal documents like the laws of Alfred, Æthelred, and Cnut; as well as visual arts in the forms of manuscript miniatures, ivory and metal engravings, and sculptures. These artefacts constitute a complex network of media engaged with apocryphal narratives that attest to their vivacious afterlives in early English culture.

Following these notions of afterlives, I engage media by looking beyond conventional assessments of one-to-one source identifications to understand transmissions of apocrypha in a broader sense. Indeed, we find that some of the most significant witnesses to apocrypha are formed not from discrete relationships between a single source and the product at hand, but from traditions of materials that are accumulated and adapted over time. I argue that such accumulative, adaptive, and fluid characteristics are distinct features of apocryphal narratives and their transmissions in later media. This is the case with narratives about the apostles (chapters 2 and 3), the Holy Rood (chapter 3), Jesus' deeds (chapter 4), his mother Mary (chapter 4), and even the general transmission of apocrypha as they collect together with other media (chapters 1 and 5). In all of these, accumulative traditions are more important than distinct, identifiable sources. An Anglo-Saxon author did not open up a single book and begin working from it; instead, Anglo-Saxons looked towards whole libraries of writings and myriad other media to inform their own productions. Many of the books in Anglo-Saxon libraries contained apocryphal narratives or texts (in both Latin and Old English) that adapted these narratives.[54] Other authors perhaps found inspiration in wall paintings, stone sculptures, or other material artefacts depicting apocryphal imagery (as discussed in chapter 4). All of these media contributed to the apocryphal traditions that circulated in Anglo-Saxon England and influenced vernacular preaching.

Turning towards developments in translation and adaptation studies helps to address some of these complications and reassessments. The history

---

54 Curiously, this fact is all but neglected by Lapidge in *ASL*, focused almost exclusively on classical and patristic texts, with only a few brief mentions of apocryphal acts of apostles.

of translation in the West is fraught with anxiety. For writers theorizing translation, from antiquity to the present, anxieties have revolved around a cluster of problematic notions, particularly assumptions based on seeming dichotomies: the theory versus practice of translation; "word for word" versus "sense for sense" renderings; the fidelity versus infidelity of translations to their sources; the importance of form versus content; the relevance versus irrelevance of translations for intended readers; and, overall, the notion of "good" versus "bad" translations.[55] Underlying all of these assumptions, in fact, is the essential dichotomy of source set against translation. In discussions of translation centred on Christianity – especially taking into account assumptions about the Bible – these anxieties are all the more pronounced.[56] It is clear that these anxieties and dichotomies are long-standing, deriving ultimately from the earliest explicit statements about translation from classical authors (most significantly Cicero) and transmitted to the medieval period by patristic authors (such as Jerome and Augustine).[57] These concepts influenced later writers, remaining central issues even with the advent of translation studies as an institutionalized discipline in the twentieth century, and they continue to linger in current theories of translation.[58]

Recent studies of translation in Anglo-Saxon England similarly rely on the Ciceronian dichotomy of "word for word" and "sense for sense," since they largely report on how Anglo-Saxons conceived of their own efforts. For example, in *The Culture of Translation in Anglo-Saxon England*, Robert Stanton provides an important study of the subject through close literary examinations of Latin and Old English texts, but he establishes a divide between glosses ("literal" and "word for word") and fuller prose ("sense for sense") translations.[59] Similarly, in *Reversing Babel: Translation among the English during an Age of Conquests, c. 800 to c. 1200*, Bruce

---

55 For an overview, see Bassnett, *Translation Studies*; for a selection of primary sources, see Venuti, ed., *The Translation Studies Reader*.

56 See esp. Noss, ed., *A History of Bible Translation*.

57 The classic work on medieval translation (though largely focused on the later period) is Copeland, *Rhetoric, Hermeneutics, and Translation in the Middle Ages*; for more recent bibliography (though often also focused on the later medieval period), see esp. Batt, "Introduction"; Campbell and Mills, "Introduction"; Rikhardsdottir, *Medieval Translations and Cultural Discourse*; and annual volumes of *The Medieval Translator* (1991–).

58 For a necessarily general but useful overview from antiquity to the twentieth century, see Bassnett, *Translation Studies*, 45–78.

59 In contrast, cf. Stanton, "The (M)other Tongue."

R. O'Brien offers a historical overview encompassing translation from the ninth through twelfth centuries in not only Old English but also Latin, Anglo-Norman, and a host of other languages; yet, throughout this study, O'Brien emphasizes the influence of "word-for-word, sense-for-sense commonplaces that marked both [classical and Christian] traditions [which] appear throughout the period."[60] O'Brien does complicate this foundation by acknowledging that authors referred to translation for a spectrum of meanings, but even this spectrum is based on the Ciceronian extremes.[61] In situating their examinations in conjunction with these conceptions of translation, scholars run the risk of passively taking Anglo-Saxon accounts at face value, leading to the acceptance of normative readings rather than critical engagement with texts.

My approach to translation naturally resonates with scholarship within adaptation studies.[62] Combining mutual interests from translation and adaptation studies has other recent theoretical precedents. For example, scholars like Lawrence Venuti and Souad Hamerlain Amara have pointed out helpful ways in which the two fields can learn from and talk to each other.[63] Indeed, scholars of translation studies generally have moved towards embracing more inclusive concepts of translation and wider methodologies from various disciplines.[64] In examining the style and rhetoric of the Vercelli Book sermons, Zacher has shown that anonymous Old English sermons often present "considerable sophistication by their authors in the manipulation and combination of (primarily Latin) source-texts."[65] She further goes on to argue that these sermons challenge "a modern preference for 'original' composition over that which is borrowed, inherited, or otherwise reiterated, ignoring perhaps the very different tastes of authors (or in this case collectors) towards 'found' materials."[66] She has emphasized

---

60 O'Brien, *Reversing Babel*, 44.

61 Ibid., 45.

62 For overviews, see esp. Hutcheon, *A Theory of Adaptation*; and Sanders, *Adaptation and Appropriation*.

63 Venuti, "Adaptation, Translation, Critique"; and Amara, "Towards a Model of Tradaptation."

64 This is particularly true of the cultural turn in translation theory; for summaries of scholarship, see esp. Bassnett, "Culture and Translation" and "Translation Studies at a Cross-Roads."

65 Zacher, *Preaching the Converted*, 49.

66 Ibid., 65.

similar issues in studying biblical poetry, which she argues create adaptive translations that speak to ideological concerns of the moment for each poet.[67] Zacher's studies set a precedent to follow as I consider the processes that sermon authors undertook in translating apocrypha into new forms for their own purposes.

By eschewing classical and problematic dichotomies often set up around translation, I seek to show how translation and adaptation are mutually informative – both in medieval practice and for scholarly examination. If scholarship has taught us anything, it is that medieval translators actually understood the notion of "translation" (Latin *translatio*, a carrying across) as encompassing a variety of practices and possibilities – not only textual but also cultural more generally. More often than not, throughout this study I discuss translation and adaptation as overlapping practices, which cannot be understood apart from each other; it is my assumption that all translations are fundamentally adaptations. For my purposes, then, the more valuable inquiries lie in asking what is being adapted, what the extent of those changes is, and why they mattered for authors and contemporary readers. While considering adaptive translation as one facet of the afterlife of texts through transmission, I also seek to recognize how the concept of translation (again, *translatio*, in the sense of transferring) may be theorized beyond literature. I approach the transmission of apocrypha by examining not only written texts but also material culture – including manuscript codices, illuminated miniatures, ivory and metal inscriptions, and stone sculptures. While Old English sermons are the central media of this study, they may be best understood by recognizing that they are part of the entire "culture of translation" that Stanton has observed, encompassing the wide variety of artefacts that participated in the afterlives of apocryphal narratives in Anglo-Saxon England.

For my approach to these artefacts, as a way to draw together the threads of transmission, translation, and adaptation with an overarching methodology, I draw on work in media archaeology, an emerging subfield of media studies.[68] Contributions to the field of media studies often focus either on "new media," such as video games and developments on the internet, or

---

67 Zacher, *Rewriting the Old Testament in Anglo-Saxon Verse*.
68 The classic work of media studies is McLuhan, *Understanding Media*. The field is vast, but I have benefited esp. from recent formulations in Mitchell and Hansen, eds., *Critical Terms for Media Studies*, and Foys, "Media."

on media of modernity, such as telephones and films.[69] The field of media studies rarely takes account of premodern cultures. With *Preaching Apocrypha in Anglo-Saxon England*, I pose an intervention in scholarship, demonstrating how media across centuries are ineluctably connected and mutually help us to make sense of past and present – and especially how considering a variety of media situates apocrypha in Old English sermons within a larger network of relationships at the heart of early English culture. Media archaeology in particular has opened up new possibilities for theorizing premodern media, since scholars in this field are concerned with examining artefacts of the past as part of the layers leading up to current media.[70] After all, "The very concept of media is thus both a new invention and a tool for excavating the deepest archaeological layers of human forms of life."[71] Medievalists have facilitated work with these methods by way of sustained critiques of medieval manuscripts in terms of media specifically and directly.[72] Conceptualizing apocrypha and preaching materials with the help of media studies methodologically ties together the various threads that run through this book.

While media archaeology offers new ways forward, it also poses difficulties, since this emerging field should be viewed not as a distinct discipline but as an outgrowth of various pursuits. By titling his recent introduction to the subject *What Is Media Archaeology?* Jussi Parikka poses a poignant but difficult question. Perhaps his most definitive answer appears in the introduction:

Media archaeology is introduced as a way to investigate the new media cultures through insights from past new media, often with an emphasis on the forgotten, the quirky, the non-obvious apparatuses, practices, and inventions. In addition ... it is also a way to analyse the regimes of memory and creative

---

69 Among many examples, see esp. Kittler, *Gramophone, Film, Typewriter*; Bolter and Grusin, *Remediation*; Gitelman and Pingree, eds., *New Media, 1740–1915*; Gitelman, *Always Already New*; Kirschenbaum, *Mechanisms*; Manovich, *Software Takes Command*; Gitelman, *Paper Knowledge*; and Kirschenbaum, *Track Changes*.

70 See Huhtamo and Parikka, eds., *Media Archaeology*; Parikka, *What Is Media Archaeology?*; and Goddard, "Opening Up the Black Boxes."

71 Mitchell and Hansen, "Introduction," ix.

72 Recent examples include Foys, *Virtually Anglo-Saxon*; Treharne, "The Architextual Editing of Early English" and "Fleshing Out the Text"; Bredehoft, *The Visible Text*; Kennedy, *Medieval Hackers*; Somerset, "Introduction"; and Foys, "Medieval Manuscripts."

practices in media culture – both theoretical and artistic. Media archaeology sees media cultures as sedimented and layered, a fold of time and materiality where the past might be suddenly discovered anew, and the new technologies grow obsolete increasingly fast.[73]

Media archaeology, in other words, puts materials in dialogue across history, so that past media might speak to current media, and vice versa.

Especially relevant are two claims for the consequences of media archaeological approaches. First, as Erkki Huhtamo and Parikka claim, "Media archaeologists have challenged the rejection of history by modern media culture and theory alike by pointing out hitherto unnoticed continuities and ruptures."[74] Second, Michael Goddard points out that "another effect of an archaeological approach [is] to extend the temporal layers of media back beyond their usually circumscribed periodization as artefacts of recent modernity."[75] If, as Lisa Gitelman has suggested, "there must be other such histories" leading up to our digital present, then media archaeology seeks to excavate artefacts that help to construct those narratives beyond the presentism of our own media.[76]

A central methodological assumption of this book is that media facilitate transmission. Media are the conduits of communication across time and space. More to the point, translations and adaptations across media allow Anglo-Saxon authors to engage with the apparatus of tradition inherited from the Christian past, as well as to influence contemporary and future audiences. In his classic work on the subject, Marshall McLuhan acknowledged technologies of translation as part of the larger conceptual media ecology and devoted a brief chapter to the metaphor of "Media as Translators."[77] More recently, Kathleen E. Kennedy has written about how language and translation are central to considering medieval media; as she argues, "in a manuscript culture, texts were part of an information commons."[78] In this sense, texts and manuscripts (and many other media) were circulated, read, annotated, copied, translated, adapted, appropriated, remixed, mediated and remediated, combined and recombined – in

---

73 Parikka, *What Is Media Archaeology?*, 2–3.
74 Huhtamo and Parikka, "Introduction," 3.
75 Goddard, "Opening Up the Black Boxes," 7.
76 Gitelman, *Paper Knowledge*, 56.
77 McLuhan, *Understanding Media*, chapter 6.
78 Kennedy, *Medieval Hackers*, 20.

other words, used, and reused; as Kennedy says, medieval people worked to "assess, modify, and disseminate" media.[79] Conceptualizing sermons as conduits of communication from this perspective encourages understanding the afterlives of apocryphal narratives as part of the cultural network of Anglo-Saxon media.

Given the nature of evidence from Anglo-Saxon England, I discuss many examples of representative media not necessarily contemporary with specific Old English sermons – especially since some artefacts are difficult to date to exact cultural moments, while others exerted strong influence throughout the period. This wide-ranging discussion, however, lends further support to my overall arguments, since uses of apocryphal materials are found across a variety of different settings and time periods within early England. While discussing these cultural artefacts, I rely on an assortment of examples, embracing the concept of "intermediation" – that is, the interconnectedness of media.[80] Ted Striphas observes three main guiding aspects of this concept: "first, media shouldn't be isolated analytically from one another; second, the relationships among media are socially produced and historically contingent rather than given and necessary; and, third, media rarely if ever share one-dimensional, causal relationships."[81] These same notions are also true for Anglo-Saxon England, where cultural artefacts subsisted in complex relationships with each other. Within this media ecology, influences of apocryphal materials may be found across a wide range of media that drew on and interacted with shared cultural currents from an array of Christian traditions, just as they drew on and informed each other.

Even with a limited scope, the production of manuscripts like homiliaries and other preaching collections poses a case to make my point about the complex nature of media. After all, the production of medieval manuscripts often employed the labour of collective workers: authors, scribes, rubricators, illuminators, binders, even patrons with specific requests or others who might oversee projects within a scriptorium. Even individual preaching texts often draw on multiple (or myriad) sources – particularly in compositions that might be called "composite" or "scissors and paste"

---

79 Ibid., 25.
80 Acland uses the terms "intermedia" and "intermedial" in *Screen Traffic*, and Striphas adopts this concept from Acland by using the term "intermediation" in *The Late Age of Print*, esp. 15–16; Hayles also uses the term in *My Mother Was a Computer*.
81 Striphas, *The Late Age of Print*, 16.

sermons.[82] These all speak to the complexity, fluidity, and intermediality of influences in sermons, preaching collections, and manuscripts more generally (as will be discussed further in chapters 1 and 5). Looking beyond manuscripts and their contents multiplies these intermedial associations as further relationships may be traced across the wider media ecology.

Examining the medieval transmission of apocrypha by way of media studies reveals an idea already evoked that runs like a thread throughout this study: networks.[83] Medieval media – like all media, in all cultures – never existed in a vacuum: to borrow Lees's words, "Preaching thus participates in the constitution of, while also being constituted by, historical sociocultural concerns specific to late Anglo-Saxon England."[84] Indeed, as the core arguments of this book make clear, understanding apocryphal media in Anglo-Saxon England means accounting for wider cultural contexts, just as attention to apocryphal media reveals more about the social milieu from which they come. Media must be considered as part of larger social networks. Preaching texts are especially pertinent cases for investigating social networks, as David d'Avray has claimed that the transmission and circulation of medieval sermons "can fairly be described as a kind of mass communication" across a variety of manuscripts and textual communities.[85] As the following chapters demonstrate, the corpus of preaching texts discussed in this book constitutes a sophisticated network of media. Combining methodologies that consider transmission, media, and networks facilitates recognizing and analysing this network of associations at the heart of the medieval afterlives of apocrypha in preaching materials.

Considering literature with the help of network theory is one way in which digital methods can feed back into well-established modes of inquiry, as well as pose new methods for literary history. One major question for both practitioners and critics of digital humanities alike is how digital tools and methods contribute new questions for pursuing traditional,

---

82 See esp. Scragg, *Dating and Style in Old English Composite Homilies*; Thompson, "'Hit Segð on Halgum Bocum'"; Szarmach, "The Vercelli Prose and Anglo-Saxon Literary History," 32–7; and Ogawa, *Language and Style in Old English Composite Homilies*, passim.

83 For overviews of networks and graph theory, see esp. Watts, *Six Degrees*; Galloway, "Networks"; and Barabási, *Linked*. For another recent conception of networks in relation to culture and literature, see Levine, *Forms*, esp. 112–31.

84 Lees, *Tradition and Belief*, viii.

85 D'Avray, "Printing, Mass Communication, and Religious Reformation," 50; see also his *Medieval Marriage Sermons* and *Medieval Marriage*.

humanistic study.[86] After all, contemporary network theory is a product of possibilities for analysing large corpora of data brought about by computers. Despite emergent uses of network theory in the digital age, often for analysing so-called new media, I suggest that this means of conceptualizing associations is also applicable more generally in the long history of old media. In other words, I assume that new methods in network theory made possible by recent inquiries in digital humanities may be brought together with traditional humanistic hermeneutics for fruitful analysis of medieval media.

The rise of network theory (or graph theory) in literary studies provides a well-suited approach for conceptualizing relationships between media, particularly as a social web.[87] This way of viewing texts has been fruitfully used for text mining, which Franco Moretti calls "distant reading" and Matthew L. Jockers calls "macroanalysis" – using computers to analyse large corpora of literature for relationships between texts.[88] I seek to consider this type of analysis with a large corpus of data from a different perspective, to ask how these methods contribute to Anglo-Saxon cultural history. My goal is to look at both the literary history of apocrypha in sermons and their relatedness to larger cultural currents. As Caroline Levine cogently states, "All networks afford connectivity; all create links between disconnected nodes"; and "it is the relation of networks and wholes that allows us to grasp culture as an object of study."[89] In this book, network theory helps to situate the study of preaching collections within contextual relationships to each other and to the wider media ecology of Anglo-Saxon England.

In his book about networks, Albert-László Barabási argues for the success of ideas because "Our biological existence, social world, economy, and religious traditions tell a compelling story of interrelatedness."[90] For example, he points out that the success of the early spread of Christianity

---

86 See, for example, recent collections of essays such as Gold, ed., *Debates in the Digital Humanities*; Burdick et al., eds., *Digital_Humanities*; Berry, ed., *Understanding Digital Humanities*; and Terras, Nyhan, and Vanhoutte, eds., *Defining Digital Humanities*.

87 For recent studies combining network theory and literary studies that have influenced my thinking, see, for example, Moretti, *Graphs, Maps, Trees* and *Distant Reading*, 211–40; Jockers, *Macroanalysis*, 154–68; and Levine, *Forms*, esp. 112–31.

88 Moretti, *Graphs, Maps, Trees* and *Distant Reading*; and Jockers, *Macroanalysis*.

89 Levine, *Forms*, 114 and 117.

90 Barabási, *Linked*, 5.

was due in part to Paul's social network.[91] Two of Barabási's points are poignantly applicable to apocrypha in early England: extra-biblical narratives were well connected to a vast array of other media; and the success of their survival seems to be related to this interconnectedness throughout Anglo-Saxon social networks. This book examines one part of this network, the relationships of apocrypha to preaching. Within this smaller network, I aim to show the interconnectedness of extra-biblical stories about Jesus, Mary, and his earliest followers with the canonical Bible, patristic texts, Old English poetry, laws, liturgy, visual arts, and, above all, sermons at the heart of mainstream Anglo-Saxon Christianity.

Many studies of sermons and preaching necessarily focus on literary analysis: editing texts, analysing them rhetorically, and examining the relationships between them. But recent work has also demonstrated that we gain much from situating sermons within their cultural contexts. A media studies approach helps with this, as it affords viewing sermons as just one facet of the network related to the transmission of apocrypha in a larger media ecology. "[M]edia are unique and complicated historical subjects," Gitelman says, continuing with the assertion, "Their histories must be social and cultural, not the stories of how one technology leads to another, or of isolated geniuses working their magic on the world."[92] With this perspective in mind, it is clear that preaching texts are fundamentally intermedial, encompassing oral speech acts, textual artefacts, and liturgical rituals, as well as social circumstances. They are, simultaneously, able to shift across all of these roles, to be extracted and remediated in other contexts, across boundaries that might be seen to distinguish media. In each of these media contexts, preaching accompanies other, related forms like oral performances, written discourses, ritual practices, and social signifiers. In this book, I aim to highlight these intermedial relationships and leverage these associations to open up new understandings about the uses of apocrypha in Anglo-Saxon preaching texts.

Chapter Organization

The organization of this book reflects an increasingly expansive notion of the media network for the transmission of preaching apocrypha that

---

91 Ibid., 3–5.
92 Gitelman, *Always Already New*, 9.

I want to highlight throughout. The overall study comprises a series of examinations around this concept; each chapter broadens the theoretical understanding of how apocrypha relate within the wider media network, as either individual texts or groups. Chapter 1 encompasses the big picture of the network of Anglo-Saxon preaching texts that draw on apocrypha. I suggest that Latin and vernacular preaching collections from both the Continent and England provide a key example of a media network in the early medieval period – and prime evidence for how apocryphal narratives circulated. This approach allows for reconciling multiple layers of media, remediation, and intermediation: sermons, preaching collections, and manuscripts all constitute distinctive but related media within the larger media ecology. Concepts about media networks drawn from recent work in digital humanities thus allow for considering complex associations between texts in Latin and Old English as Anglo-Saxons engaged with them from the tenth to the twelfth centuries.

In chapter 2, I examine Blickling 15, a text most closely representing traditional scholarly understandings of media through a one-to-one relationship between source and translation. This sermon has previously been read as a close translation of the Latin *Martyrdom of Peter and Paul*, yet Blickling 15 differs from its source in significant details as the author deliberately emphasizes apostolic speeches to teach Trinitarian doctrine. This chapter, then, establishes resistance to normative notions of translation fidelity as well as distinctions between "word for word" and "sense for sense" renderings. In this chapter I also open up the concept of translation to the significance of examining differences beyond words, phrases, and even sentences, in order to situate the meanings of texts in relation to the ideologies of translators. In this way, Blickling 15 is best understood as a reflection of tenth-century reforms affecting vernacular preaching.

The third chapter broadens my conception of media to discuss a small network of interrelated apostolic apocrypha in Ælfric's *Catholic Homilies*. For all of the differences established by scholarship regarding anonymous and Ælfrician sermons as distinct, recent work has questioned the fissure, partly regarding apocrypha. Addressing Ælfric's use of apocryphal acts in the first part of this chapter, I suggest that scholars have too often read the author's few explicit statements about apocrypha as normative, and have subsequently constructed an exaggerated view of his condemnations. Instead, like anonymous authors, Ælfric also found use for apostolic acts in his preaching. In the second part of this chapter, I examine another, broader network of media related to the transmission of the *Catholic Homilies*: relationships to other Old English sermons with apocryphal content. By looking at the afterlives of these sermons in eleventh- and twelfth-century manuscripts, we are able to see that Anglo-Saxon compilers also acknowledged associations between Ælfric's works and other apocryphal preaching texts – in manuscript contexts as well as thematic intertextual connections with Old English sermons.

An expanding notion of the media network encompassing apocrypha is further pronounced in chapter 4, in which I discuss apocryphal narratives related to the life of Christ in both textual and visual examples. Vercelli 6 and Blickling 7 offer representative witnesses, since they respectively draw on the *Gospel of Pseudo-Matthew* and traditions surrounding the Harrowing of Hell. My interdisciplinary methodology opens up the concept of intermedial translation to consider how narratives travel across various media. Besides adaptive and combinatory methods in sermons, this chapter also addresses how visual images serve as translations of apocrypha, and therefore key contexts for the culture surrounding Old English sermons based on the same sources. In particular, I focus on material artefacts like the Sacramentary of Robert of Jumièges, the *Book of Cerne*, and ivory and metal engravings used by ecclesiasts. This multimedia consideration allows for conceiving of the transmission of stories beyond verbal representations, to encompass the many cultural currents that surrounded and affected Anglo-Saxons in their engagements with apocrypha.

In the final chapter, I focus on the late twelfth-century preaching collection Oxford, Bodleian Library, Bodley 343, suggesting that this codex represents in microcosm the media network of apocrypha for preaching as it existed in Anglo-Saxon England. Since this single collection contains both Latin and Old English sermons – anonymous as well as Ælfrician and Wulfstanian productions – it survives as a key representative of preaching traditions accumulated from the tenth through twelfth centuries. Starting with an examination of the Latin Homiliary of Angers contained in Bodley 343, I take a sermon based on the *Martyrdom of Peter and Paul* as my launching point to trace connections outward to other apocryphal content included in the collection. Following associations between preaching texts reveals a sophisticated network of apocryphal media at the centre of Anglo-Saxon Christian teaching as represented between the covers of this single book.

In the conclusion, as a way to synthesize my arguments, I address how examinations of preaching with apocrypha in this book help to reconceptualize sermons as media. This approach allows for confronting binaries such as "orthodox" and "heretical" as well as "high" and "popular" cultures. At a more fundamental level, relationships between apocrypha, sermons, and media explored in this study also prompt a more fundamental question: What do apocrypha tell us about sermons? As part of the ideological apparatus of tradition inherited and engaged by medieval authors, apocrypha reveal the very fundamentals of interpretation at play in preaching. Considering a McLuhanesque approach to the medium of preaching as the message for understanding religious doctrine reveals significant payoff for recognizing the role of sermons in Anglo-Saxon England.

Preaching, Worship, and Audience

Running through this book are a number of thematic threads tying together key points that may be foregrounded here. One of these threads is the role of worship and liturgy in relation to preaching. This should not be surprising, given the ways in which sermons themselves are integrally linked to the liturgical cycle and mass, although the contexts I discuss in this study make this all the more pronounced. While such associations will be brought out most obviously in discussing liturgical media related to apocryphal gospels in chapter 4, this theme also occurs in other sections of the study. For example, the place of feast days for apostles in the liturgical year is important background for discussions of apostolic apocrypha in chapters 2, 3, and 5; in chapter 2 I connect Trinitarian preaching with ecclesiastical reforms focused especially on liturgical practices; and in chapter 4 I discuss devotion to both Jesus and Mary in relation to material artefacts for liturgical use. Furthermore, preaching collections like those discussed in chapters 1 and 5 are often structured with the liturgical calendar in mind. Considering liturgy, mass, and other ritualized observances generally, Christian worship as a broad cultural practice involves many of the media examined in this book. At the core of such practices, sermons with apocryphal narratives remain a key feature of Anglo-Saxon worship and devotion in a multiplicity of settings.

Considering regularly performed worship also highlights another thread running through this study: the role of sermons for many different audiences. There is not abundant evidence that Old English sermon collections were meant for reading specifically in mass (and it is likely that the Vercelli Book was meant for private devotional reading),[93] but generically sermons were certainly written with the idea of performance in worship in mind.

---

93 See esp. Zacher, *Preaching the Converted*, 32–42, with further references there.

In a practical sense, the sermons I discuss in this study represent actual Old English preaching. Even more, the vernacularity of these sermons is telling for their accessibility in the mass for men and women, commoners and elites, cloistered and lay people, regardless of social class or standing. Apocrypha in these sermons could reach many audiences. Following some scholars who have studied Carolingian preaching, I adopt the "maximalist" view of preaching, "that sermons were the main medium of teaching" and "To this end, bishops and priests preached regularly to their flocks in the vernacular using Latin exemplars."[94]

I address the potential audiences of sermons and collections throughout this study, but it is important here to mention the implications of their vernacularity. We may be partly hindered by what Milton McC. Gatch has called "the unknowable audience" of some sermons or collections,[95] yet the composition of Old English sermons in the vernacular provides an implicit clue that they were meant for wider reception – unlike Latin, which only the educated could understand with proficiency. Even if wider accessibility were not the intention of authors or compilers of vernacular preaching texts, the actuality is that Old English sermons could be preached to anyone who could hear. Old English sermons that could be preached to audiences in their own native language thus demonstrate the pervasive transmission of apocrypha across social strata in Anglo-Saxon England. It is for this reason that we should be more attentive to these media as vibrant witnesses to the heritage of Christian apocryphal narratives.

Like our own society, in which we are inundated with media through various sensory experiences, medieval people also lived in a world of multimedia. Christian apocrypha were present in many of the experiences that Anglo-Saxons encountered: at least through the aural, visual, and tactile features of media relating narratives about Jesus, Mary, and the earliest disciples. Resituating apocryphal sermons within this multimedia ecology at the heart of Anglo-Saxon culture also re-centres our sense of medieval Christian traditions, not with extra-biblical media on the margins, but with apocrypha alongside the Bible in the wider network of the apparatus of mainstream Christianity.

---

94 McCune, "The Preacher's Audience, c. 800–c. 950," 283. On the "maximalist" and "minimalist" interpretations of early medieval preaching and audiences, see d'Avray, *Medieval Marriage*, 21–37.
95 Gatch, "The Unknowable Audience of the Blickling Homilies."

Chapter One

Homiliaries, Apocrypha, and Preaching Networks

In this chapter, I discuss Latin and vernacular preaching collections that represent one major way in which Anglo-Saxons encountered apocrypha. Previous studies of Old English sermons alongside Latin preaching collections known as homiliaries have brought about substantial discoveries for understanding and contextualizing Anglo-Saxon preaching. For instance, examinations of homiliaries by Continental ecclesiasts like Alan of Farfa (d. 769), Paul the Deacon (d. 799), Smaragdus of Saint-Mihiel (c. 760–c. 840), and Haymo of Auxerre (d. 878) have illuminated knowledge of Anglo-Saxon libraries, sources, and composition techniques.[1] The exploration of the Pembroke Homiliary of Saint-Père de Chartres led J.E. Cross to identify the sources of passages for at least eight anonymous Old English sermons.[2] More recently, Aidan Conti's identification of the Homiliary of Angers in a twelfth-century Anglo-Saxon manuscript has sparked studies of its influence on Old English preaching from as early as the tenth century.[3] Such collections remain significant witnesses for the

---

1 For overviews with further bibliography, see Clayton, "Homiliaries and Preaching in Anglo-Saxon England"; Kleist, ed., *Old English Homily*; Joyce Hill, "Ælfric and Haymo Revisited" and "The Context of Ælfric's Saints' Lives." For a case study, see Richards, *Texts and Their Traditions in the Medieval Library of Rochester Cathedral Priory*, esp. 86–120.

2 Cross, *Cambridge Pembroke College MS. 25*.

3 See Conti, "Preaching Scripture and Apocrypha" and "The Circulation of the Old English Homily in the Twelfth Century"; and further discussion and references in chapter 5.

circulation of preaching both on the Continent and in England, and for representing transmissions of texts picked up by Anglo-Saxon authors.[4]

In many ways, this chapter serves to introduce readers to the general world of early medieval sermons and homiliaries as well as apocryphal media that will be addressed more specifically in the following chapters. The Latin homiliaries discussed comprise texts that have been identified as sources for Old English sermons as well as texts not definitively linked to Anglo-Saxon England but nonetheless useful as representatives. In the latter category, we find collections with versions of texts that the Anglo-Saxons read and used, though perhaps not the specific iterations that they encountered. What these homiliaries demonstrate, however, is the extent to which apocrypha circulated in early medieval preaching collections, many of which Anglo-Saxon authors actually used: in other words, apocrypha in preaching collections were both prevalent and interconnected.

While scholars have often looked to Ireland to explain transmissions of apocrypha to early England,[5] I suggest that Latin homiliaries from the Continent are key to reconceptualizing our knowledge of extra-biblical narratives in Anglo-Saxon libraries. This does not preclude Irish influences, of course, but more attention to Continental collections allows us to acknowledge a wider network of related texts across Western Europe. After all, early medieval networks of transmission between the Continent, England, and Ireland were much more sophisticated than often acknowledged. Studies of Hiberno-Latin and Irish-influenced texts and manuscripts prove the point, since it is often difficult to distinguish "Insular" and "Irish" features, as well as whether a text or manuscript originated in Ireland, England, or a Continental scriptorium with Insular associations.[6]

---

4 On the contents of several homiliaries, including those of Alan of Farfa and Paul the Deacon, see Grégoire, *Homéliaires liturgiques médiévaux*; and Étaix, *Homéliaires patristiques latins*; on the contents of the Homiliary of Angers, see Étaix, "L'homéliaire carolingien d'Angers." The homiliaries of Smaragdus and Haymo (misattributed to Haymo of Halberstadt) are printed (though not as critical editions) in *PL* 102.13–552 and 118.11–746.

5 For overviews with further bibliography, see esp. Wright, "Hiberno-Latin and Irish-Influenced Biblical Commentaries, Florilegia, and Homily Collections"; "Hiberno-Latin Writings in *Sources of Anglo-Saxon Literary Culture*"; and *The Irish Tradition in Old English Literature*.

6 See Bischoff, "Wendepunkte in der Geschichte der lateinischen Exegese im Frühmittelalter," repr. with rev. in his *Mittelalterliche Studien*, 1:205–73 (trans. O'Grady as "Turning-Points in the History of Latin Exegesis in the Early Middle Ages"); as well as Gorman, "The Myth of Hiberno-Latin Exegesis"; Wright, "Bischoff's Theory of Irish Exegesis and the Genesis Commentary in Munich Clm 6302"; and Ó Cróinín,

The following discussion highlights some of these nuances. Since others have concentrated more on the possibilities of apocryphal influences from Hiberno-Latin and Irish sources, I focus on the less well studied associations to be drawn out of Continental sources.

Studying these associations has become more possible in recent years, with an increase in digital facsimiles, a return to manuscripts in light of rising online accessibility, and examinations and editions of specific manuscripts and texts. Thus, digital tools open up new avenues for situating Anglo-Saxon sermons and apocrypha within the wider scope of Western Europe beyond the British Isles. Media studies in the digital age offer methods of conceptualizing intersections between Latin and Old English preaching collections containing apocrypha through not only bibliographic description but also methodological theory and practice. Foremost, the possibilities of media archaeology and network theory reveal significant implications for understanding the production, circulation, and use of preaching collections. In this investigation, I pay particular attention to surviving manuscripts of preaching collections, accounting for transmissions between the Continent and England as well as their circulation and uses at significant centres of book production.

Anglo-Saxon preaching materials may thus be understood as media artefacts within a widespread and interconnected network of shared texts – a textual culture of preaching encompassing Latin alongside Old English, ranging across geographic borders. It is a salient reminder that the etymology of the term *network* is, for the English language, fundamentally rooted in the Anglo-Saxon period.[7] The compound term, after all, derives from the independent Old English words *nett* and *weorc*, brought together in the early modern period to signify the collective substance holding constituent parts together.[8] Alexander R. Galloway writes that, from different perspectives, networks constitute both "communication technologies" and "social and cultural contexts," and I mean to invoke both aspects in this study.[9] Thus, media networks consist of communications and cultural ideologies

---

"Bischoff's Wendepunkte Fifty Years On." For a recent discussion of one example, with further bibliography, see Hawk, "A Fragment of Colossians with Hiberno-Latin Glosses in St. Gall, Stiftsbibliothek, Cod. Sang. 1395."

7 Cf. Galloway, "Networks," 283; and Levine, *Forms*, 113–14.

8 See Toller, ed., *An Anglo-Saxon Dictionary, Based on the Manuscript Collections of the Late Joseph Bosworth*, s.v. *nett* and *weorc*; and *Oxford English Dictionary Online*, s.v. *network* (n. and adj.), http://www.oed.com/view/Entry/126342.

9 Galloway, "Networks," 283.

entwined and inextricable. Such networks should be understood and considered as including both the *net* (structure) and the *work* (content) within them. In terms of the apocryphal sermons of this study, such a media network includes both the means, as hermeneutic expositions for preaching, and the meaning, as ideological products that speak to their culture.

This approach allows for reconciling multiple layers of media, remediation, and intermediation: sermons, preaching collections, and manuscripts all constitute distinctive but related media. These media do not exist in seclusion, but overlap, with some forms remediating others. As Galloway writes, invoking Marshall McLuhan, "any new medium contains within it older media: film contains still photographs as frames, a Web page contains images and text, and so on."[10] We might imagine such relationships with the example of an iTunes library containing Beethoven's collected symphonies, in which digital files remediate the original, raw, recorded sound files, which remediate the particular orchestra on the recordings from performances which, in turn, remediate printed sheet music. In this analogy, we must take account of all of the symphonies as a collective whole and each symphony on its own, in addition to every individual file for each component part of the whole collection (broken into symphonies, movements, and so on), as well as how they all relate to each other. The result is a complex of intermedial relationships.

In a similar sense, a manuscript might contain much more material than a homiliary, which is itself a collection of individual sermons; and a whole manuscript should be considered as a more encompassing type of medium that remediates both individual texts and collective assemblages. Conversely, not all sermons circulate in homiliaries, but they do survive in forms accessible to us in manuscript codices. While layers of media overlap, they do so in multifaceted relationships with each other. Each medium is distinct, but might also rely on other media for circulation and use. McLuhan's famous dictum that "the medium is the message" becomes rather important when dealing with manuscripts: as assemblages of related media, their contents should be considered not only for individual texts but also as collections in wider contexts.

This chapter is divided into three sections, each one meant to introduce a different aspect of this media network and the contextual backgrounds that help to situate Old English apocryphal sermons discussed

---

10 Ibid., 290.

in subsequent chapters. In the first section, I demonstrate the prevalence and interconnectedness of apocrypha in representative Latin preaching collections that moved between the Continent and England in the early medieval period and influenced Anglo-Saxon authors. In the next section, I introduce the primary vernacular collections examined throughout this study, claiming connections to and parallels with Latin homiliaries in their structures, contents, and purposes. In the third section, I examine a number of Old English sermon collections containing apocrypha, suggesting how their contents may be understood within a textual network similar and related to that of Latin homiliaries. Taken together, these collections represent mainstream Anglo-Saxon Christianity: not only what Anglo-Saxons read and wrote but also which sermons survive because they were useful for local preaching needs. The overarching argument is that apocrypha need to be considered not in isolation, but as part of larger media networks that reveal their proximity to and associations with the apparatus of Christian tradition used by Anglo-Saxon preachers.

Network theory draws on applied mathematics to understand relationships between elements in graphs.[11] The basic features of this type of graph theory are the related elements, called *nodes* or *vertices*, and the connections between them, *edges* or *lines*. In the simplest graph visualization, then, two related nodes are connected by a single edge, and these elements are considered *adjacent*. In what follows, network associations are presented in both conceptual overviews as well as visualizations. Conceptually, this chapter explores the associations that range across texts and manuscripts containing apocrypha. In the accompanying graphic visualizations, each text and each manuscript represents a single node or vertex, with edges or lines representing the affinities discussed. If one text is related to another, those textual nodes are connected to each other with a line; if a text survives in a particular manuscript collection, that textual node is connected to the manuscript node with a line to represent the relationship. The resulting web of associations from adjacent elements – relationships between texts and manuscripts together – constitutes the network under discussion, visually demonstrating how prevalent and interrelated apocryphal media were across early medieval preaching collections related to Anglo-Saxon England.[12]

---

11 See the Introduction, with further references there.

12 Visualizations in this chapter were generated using *Palladio*, developed by Humanities + Design at Stanford University; links to data sets used for this chapter may be found online at Hawk, "Preaching Apocrypha in Anglo-Saxon England."

Circulating Latin Sermons

In the eighth and ninth centuries, Continental ecclesiastical authorities undertook distinct efforts to cultivate effective preaching by compiling, copying, and circulating homiliaries.[13] Moreover, as Anglo-Saxons in the next few centuries looked to the Continent for models – particularly models for ecclesiastical reform – they also looked to these collections. It is also during this period that Anglo-Saxon scriptoria became key to the transmission of texts in Western Europe, as more books began to be transported from England (as well as Ireland) to Continental centres, and vice versa.[14] In some cases, English and Irish missionaries and pilgrims on the Continent reintroduced texts, feeding into the upsurge of the transmission of classical and patristic texts at the time.[15] These centuries saw a dramatic increase in the movement and subsequent transmission of manuscripts in Western Europe. As we will see, these developments brought about what we might think of as, in Rosamond McKitterick's words, "the maintenance of a wide network of communication and the preservation of religious and intellectual links from the seventh century well into the Carolingian period and beyond."[16]

In what follows – and throughout this book – it is imperative not to view early England as isolated because of its insular status. Anglo-Saxon culture was well connected in the international landscape. The international and boundary-crossing nature of Anglo-Saxons may be seen from the surviving material culture of manuscripts alone, which are diffuse across early medieval Europe. Medieval manuscripts may be understood as *portable objects*, following the concept posed by Eva R. Hoffman:

> [T]he circumstances of portability, [shift] the emphasis from "production" to "circulation." Portable arts are innately characterized by their potential for movement and indeterminacy ... While portability destabilized and dislocated works from their original sites of production, it also re-mapped

---

13 For a collection of recent studies, see Diesenberger, Hen, and Pollheimer, eds., *Sermo doctorum*.

14 This is a general trend in the manuscript evidence in *CLA*; see also Bischoff, *Manuscripts and Libraries in the Age of Charlemagne*, esp. 11–15; and Buringh, *Medieval Manuscript Production in the Latin West*, esp. 254–314, with further references there.

15 See McKitterick, "The Diffusion of Insular Culture in Neustria between 650 and 850," with further references there.

16 Ibid., 430.

geographical and cultural boundaries, opening up vistas of intra- and cross-cultural encounters and interactions … Portability and circulation highlight the active "lives" of objects; their openness and permeability; how objects referred to and merged with their makers and users, the people and cultures that exchanged them, and the relationships that they defined.[17]

Through the lens of media archaeology, tracing "pathways of portability" and their effects matters. Manuscripts tell a major part of the story of how culture circulated, and, as Hoffman points out, they need to be considered within "a network of portability extending well beyond fixed geographical sites of production to include the geographical and cultural arenas in which the works were circulated and viewed."[18] This chapter attempts to do just this by situating Old English sermons in relation to Latin homiliaries containing apocrypha. To do this means acknowledging the wider landscape in which manuscripts accessible to Anglo-Saxons circulated, and the range of transmission across international contexts in which sermons were used. First, it is helpful to consider the broad scope of manuscript production in the early medieval period.

In terms of statistics according to the monumental catalogue *Codices Latini Antiquiores* (*CLA*) begun by E.A. Lowe, 257 manuscripts containing Anglo-Saxon scripts survive from before 800, which constitute around 12.5 per cent of 2,047 identified Latin manuscripts surviving from Western Europe from that period.[19] Rolf H. Bremmer, Jr provides a list of 108 manuscripts that survive as witnesses to Anglo-Saxon missionaries on the Continent in the eighth century.[20] Similarly, Michael Lapidge lists 112 eighth-century manuscripts from the area of the Anglo-Saxon mission

---

17 Hoffman, "Pathways of Portability," 17.

18 Ibid., 21.

19 A link to the full data set may be found online at Hawk, "Preaching Apocrypha in Anglo-Saxon England." I have obtained this data by searching *Earlier Latin Manuscripts*, compiled by Mark Stansbury; cf. *Leuven Database of Ancient Books*. Both databases rely on *CLA*; Bischoff and Brown, "Addenda to *Codices Latini Antiquiores*"; and Bischoff, Brown, and John, "Addenda to *Codices Latini Antiquiores* (II)."

20 Rolf H. Bremmer, Jr, "The Anglo-Saxon Continental Mission and the Transfer of Encyclopedic Knowledge," 39–50. On Anglo-Saxon missions and English contributions to Continental manuscript production, see McKitterick, "Anglo-Saxon Missionaries in Germany" and "The Diffusion of Insular Culture in Neustria between 650 and 850"; Palmer, *Anglo-Saxons in a Frankish World*; Scharer, "Insular Mission to the Continent in the Early Middle Ages"; and Lifshitz, *Religious Women in Early Carolingian Francia*.

in Germany (compiled from *CLA*), and another 80 ninth-century manuscripts that originated on the Continent and had an English provenance before 1066.[21]

Beyond statistics based on material evidence, however, are the ways in which the presence of Anglo-Saxons is a vital part of the history of the production and transmission of books in the early medieval period more generally. Bernhard Bischoff continually emphasizes the contributions of Anglo-Saxons throughout his *Manuscripts and Libraries in the Age of Charlemagne*, which represents the fruits of his spending a career with Latin manuscripts across Western Europe:

> It was the Anglo-Saxons who bequeathed to the Carolingian era the ideal of a well-balanced library organized for study. Classical authors even appear in their libraries, and it is certain that some Anglo-Saxon books became the progenitors of manuscript traditions in the ninth century.[22]

Before and during the Carolingian period, Anglo-Saxon influences thus stretched across a wide geographical area and many centres: Tours in the Loire region; Chelles, Corbie, and other centres around Paris in northeast France; Echternach (founded by Anglo-Saxons) and Werden in Austrasia; the Germanic-Insular region in the upper Rhine, and along the Main, such as at Hersfeld, Fulda, Hesse, Mainz, Lorsch, Amorbach, Karlburg, and Würzburg, as well as the court library of Charlemagne that originally developed in this region; Anglo-Saxon missionary foundations like Eichstätt, Heidenheim, and Solnhofen; Regensberg, Freising, and Salzburg in southeast Germany; Nonantola in northwest Italy; and, finally, Rome, where scribes not only visited on pilgrimage but also established a "schola Saxonum."[23] During the ninth and tenth centuries, many of these influences continued, through the survival of early manuscripts in various libraries as well as Anglo-Saxons travelling to and from the Continent with new manuscripts.[24] Through all of this, the transmission of intellectual culture, manuscripts, and texts went both ways across the Channel.

---

21 *ASL*, 155–66 and 167–73.

22 Bischoff, *Manuscripts and Libraries in the Age of Charlemagne*, 15.

23 Ibid., passim, esp. 14–15, 17–18, 19, 22–3 (n. 8), 30–1 (n. 49), 36, 40–4, 49, 51–2 (n. 155), 66–7, 139–40, and 149. See also provenances of manuscripts in *ASL*, 155–66 and 167–73; and Rolf H. Bremmer, Jr, "Anglo-Saxon Continental Mission," 39–50.

24 See entries listed under "Libraries outside the British Isles" in *ASM*.

The evidence of surviving books from this period also raises challenges, giving pause to consider questions about manuscript production and survival. How many Latin manuscripts from Western Europe survive from the sixth through tenth centuries? What might have been lost from these centuries? How do preaching collections and apocrypha fit into these contexts? Fortunately, the work of paleographers and bibliographers has done much to illuminate our knowledge of the wider questions about manuscript production and survival in the early medieval period. As already stated, around 2,047 Latin manuscripts survive from Western Europe dated to before about 800.[25] For the ninth century, the *Katalog der festländischen Handschriften des neunten Jahrhunderts* compiled by Bischoff and edited by Birgit Ebersperger accounts for around 8,200 surviving Continental manuscripts, a number that increases to around 8,500 when Visigothic and Anglo-Saxon evidence is included.[26]

Using a database of information about medieval manuscripts, Eltjo Buringh has confirmed these figures and more data up to 1900, and through statistical analysis he has generated estimated numbers of manuscripts produced and lost from the medieval period.[27] Marilena Maniaci has raised some warranted criticisms about the scope (temporal and geographic) and construction of the database;[28] but, despite these concerns (and Buringh's own hesitations to use his data for concrete conclusions from estimated numbers), Buringh provides estimates that may be used for illustrative purposes. He suggests that around 405,252 manuscripts from the Latin West were produced between the sixth and tenth centuries: 13,554 in the sixth, 10,640 in the seventh, 43,697 in the eighth, 201,728 in the ninth, and 135,633 in the tenth.[29] Of these, only 18,010 survive: 242 from the sixth, 253 from the seventh, 1,383 from the eighth, 8,512 from the ninth, and 7,620 from the tenth.[30] In other words, the surviving manuscripts make up only 4.4 per cent of the total estimated to have been produced between the sixth and tenth centuries.[31]

---

25 See *CLA*; and Stansbury, *Earlier Latin Manuscripts*.

26 See also Buringh, *Medieval Manuscript Production*, esp. 259–61.

27 Ibid. Buringh's study is from the perspective of a data analyst rather than a medievalist, and thus focuses on statistical analysis.

28 Maniaci, "Quantificare la produzione manoscritta del passato."

29 Buringh, *Medieval Manuscript Production*, esp. table 5.5.

30 Ibid., esp. tables 5.4 and 5.5.

31 For more detailed discussion of loss estimates, see ibid., 179–251.

Given the misfortunes of time and intentional destruction of books in the medieval and early modern periods, every manuscript survival is a happy accident. Like all texts from the Middle Ages (particularly the early period), apocrypha among the survivals speak to the many more that have been lost. This might be further pronounced in the case of apocrypha, considering the attitudes of Protestants who might have sought to destroy these documents – especially if they were viewed as associated with Catholics – in the early modern period.[32] We must approach our evidence with these issues in mind, knowing that extant texts and manuscripts constitute only representative survivals, not the full range of medieval artefacts produced at the time. Nonetheless, survivals from the eighth and ninth centuries provide key evidence for the growing network of apocrypha in preaching collections from the Continent and England, which we can see further extended in Anglo-Saxon witnesses from the tenth, eleventh, and twelfth centuries.

A few notes about surviving apocrypha are useful for broad context. Of the 1,291 surviving manuscripts known in Anglo-Saxon England before 1100,[33] forty-one include Latin apocryphal texts.[34] To this number may be added another ten manuscripts excluded from Helmut Gneuss and Michael Lapidge's *Anglo-Saxon Manuscripts* because either they post-date 1100,[35] or they were known by Anglo-Saxons on the Continent without ever travelling to England (two of which I discuss in this chapter).[36]

---

32 See esp. Backus, *Historical Method and Confessional Identity in the Era of the Reformation (1378–1615)*; Reed, "The Modern Invention of 'Old Testament Pseudepigrapha'" and "The Afterlives of New Testament Apocrypha."

33 See *ASM*, in which Gneuss and Lapidge give this number in the "Preface," x.

34 Numbers are based on manuscripts listed in *SASLC Apocrypha*, with some updates based on my own work as noted.

35 Like *ASM*, the scope of *SASLC* does not usually account for manuscripts post-dating 1100. For example, although copies of Peter Damian's version of the *Fifteen Signs before Judgment* survive in London, British Library, Cotton Faustina A.v (s. xi/xii or xii; *ASM*, 330.5) and Oxford, St John's College 17 (c. 1110–11), they are not discussed in "Fifteen Signs before Judgment" in *SASLC Apocrypha* (76); cf. Hawk, "The *Fifteen Signs before Judgment* in Anglo-Saxon England." Similarly, cf. "Psalm 151" in *SASLC Apocrypha* (16–17) and Hawk, "Psalm 151 in Anglo-Saxon England," esp. manuscripts listed at 810–11.

36 Vatican City, Biblioteca Apostolica Vaticana, Pal. Lat. 220 and Würzburg, Universitäts-bibliothek, M.p.th.f. 28, with details below. See also Munich, Bayerische Staatsbibliothek, Clm 6433 (s. viii[ex.], Freising; *CLA* 9.1283) and Munich, Bayerische Staatsbibliothek, Clm 19410 (s. ix[med.], Passau); and, on their relevance to Anglo-Saxon England, A. diPaolo Healey's second entry for "Apocalypse of Paul" as well as Charles D. Wright's entries on "Apocrypha Priscillianistica," and "Three Utterances Apocryphon," in *SASLC Apocrypha*, at 70, 73–4, and 80–3.

Some of these fifty-one total manuscripts contain multiple texts, and all told they include seventy-five copies of Latin apocrypha: twenty-six associated with Old Testament subjects and forty-nine associated with New Testament subjects, which may be subdivided into eight gospels, twenty-four acts, three epistles, five apocalypses, and the rest miscellaneous. Yet, as recognized in previous observations about production, loss, and survival of medieval media, these texts and manuscripts are only the tip of the iceberg. This fact is made all the clearer when we consider that no manuscript with an English provenance before 1100 survives for some of the most popular Latin apocrypha, such as the *Gospel of Pseudo-Matthew*, *Acts of Andrew and Matthias*, *Martyrdom of Peter and Paul*, *Martyrdom of Thomas*, *Apocalypse of Paul*, and *Apocalypse of Thomas* – all of which clearly circulated and were used by Anglo-Saxon authors, especially since they were all translated into Old English. The point is that we must look farther afield to understand the whole range of apocrypha that permeated Anglo-Saxon media, as well as where they came from, and Continental preaching collections constitute one major avenue for this study.

The following section focuses primarily on three Latin preaching collections representative of and significant for both Continental and Anglo-Saxon associations. For reasons to be discussed in more detail in the following analysis, each collection is represented by a single manuscript most closely connected to Anglo-Saxon England:

1) Homiliary of Burchard, in Würzburg, Universitätsbibliothek, M.p.th.f. 28 (s. viii[4/4], Bavaria?)[37]
2) Palatine Homily Collection, in Vatican City, Biblioteca Apostolica Vaticana, Pal. lat. 220 (c.800, Middle or Upper Rhineland)[38]
3) Homiliary of Saint-Père de Chartres, in Cambridge, Pembroke College 25 (s. xi[ex.] or xi[2], Bury St Edmunds)[39]

---

37 *CLA*, 9.1408. Description and digital facsimile at *Universitätsbibliothek Würzburg*, 2015, http://vb.uni-wuerzburg.de/ub/mpthf28/index.html. See Thurn, *Die Handschriften der Universitätsbibliothek Würzburg*, vol. 3, part 1, 19–21; and Lapidge, *ASL*, 162, no. 69.

38 Description and digital facsimile at *Bibliotheca Laureshamensis Digital*, http:// bibliotheca-laureshamensis-digital.de/bav/bav_pal_lat_220. See Stevenson, ed., *Codices Palatini latini Bibliothecae Vaticanae descripti praeside I.B. cardinali Pitra*, 1:46–8; and Reifferscheid, *Bibliotheca patrum latinorum Italica*, 1:229–32.

39 *ASM*, 131. See Cross, *Cambridge Pembroke College MS. 25*.

The Latin apocrypha presented in these collections are many of the same texts used for Old English sermons. In some cases, they survive as direct sources, and in others they serve as representatives. Other similar collections could be included for suggestive parallels (and some will be cited as appropriate), but these remain some of the most relevant witnesses to the issues discussed here, since all of these manuscripts have established or plausible connections to Anglo-Saxons. These manuscripts survive as valuable witnesses to the types of collections and texts accessible to authors of Old English sermons.

The Homiliary of Burchard comprises an eighth-century collection of sermons and ecclesiastical texts on a range of subjects, surviving solely in the Insular manuscript Würzburg M.p.th.f. 28. The homiliary has been traditionally associated with the Anglo-Saxon missionary Burchard, the first bishop of Würzburg (d. 753), as Germain Morin, McKitterick, and Yitzhak Hen have claimed.[40] Whether or not Würzburg M.p.th.f. 28 (or perhaps its exemplar) actually belonged to Burchard, previous studies have highlighted the associations between this collection and Anglo-Saxon missionaries on the Continent.[41] This is all the more striking since the single surviving manuscript was produced in a German scriptorium with lasting Anglo-Saxon influences. The most substantial connection is the material evidence, since the original, ninth-century binding contains a fragment of an eighth-century copy of the *Regula pastoralis* of Gregory the Great in an Anglo-Saxon hand.[42] McKitterick, who sees this book fitting into the international character of eighth-century missionary work and the library at Würzburg, comments that "historically and textually there is a lot to be said for this book being Burchard of Würzburg's own compilation of sermons from an earlier Caesarian collection."[43] Building on these contexts, Hen has convincingly argued that the contents fit into the Christianization program of Anglo-Saxon

---

40 See Morin, "L'homéliaire de Burchard de Würzburg"; McKitterick, "Anglo-Saxon Missionaries in Germany," 302–3 and 307–8, and "The Diffusion of Insular Culture in Neustria between 650 and 850," 414–15; and Hen, "The Content and Aims of the So-Called Homiliary of Burchard of Würzburg."

41 For recent accounts of Anglo-Saxon influences in Francia, see Palmer, *Anglo-Saxons in a Frankish World*; and Lifshitz, *Religious Women in Early Carolingian Francia*.

42 *CLA*, 9.1400. See Hen, "The Content and Aims of the So-Called Homiliary of Burchard of Würzburg," 129.

43 McKitterick, "Anglo-Saxon Missionaries in Germany," 302.

missionaries on the Continent spurred on by Boniface and his followers, including Burchard himself.[44]

From the turn of the ninth century, the Palatine Homily Collection is another compilation focused on Christianization.[45] The most relevant witness for this study survives in Pal. lat. 220, with most of the contents copied in an Anglo-Saxon script around the turn of the ninth century.[46] The collection likely reflects the teachings of Insular missionaries on the Continent in the ninth century,[47] and Tomás O'Sullivan has demonstrated that it was created to preach to lay Christians in Germany, using catechetical, didactic, and eschatological subjects.[48] Furthermore, he argues for close connections between the Palatine Collection and Anglo-Saxon England based on the overlap of texts in this homiliary with the sources of Old English sermons. O'Sullivan's examination leads him to claim that "the balance of evidence would seem to favor the suggestion that the Palatine Collection itself may have been assembled in early medieval England."[49]

From slightly later, the Homiliary of Saint-Père de Chartres was compiled between the middle of the ninth century and the middle of the tenth century, as established by its datable contents and earliest known influences.[50] A number of manuscripts survive (Cross identifies five), but the closest witness to the original collection, and most relevant for early English connections, is Pembroke 25. Copied at the abbey of Bury St Edmunds in the late eleventh century, this manuscript was likely meant as a companion to the two-volume Homiliary of Paul the Deacon in Cambridge, Pembroke College 23 and 24 (s. xi[2], France), which was at the abbey by the end of the eleventh century.[51] As previously mentioned, a number of Latin texts in the Homiliary of Saint-Père provide identified sources for Old English

44 Hen, "The Content and Aims of the So-Called Homiliary of Burchard of Würzburg."
45 See O'Sullivan, *Predicationes Palatinae.*
46 Three other witnesses also survive: Berlin, Staatsbibliothek zu Berlin-Preussischer Kulturbesitz, Phillipps 1716 (s. ix, poss. Holland); Munich, Bayerische Staatsbibliothek, Clm 6293 (s. ix, Freising); and Vatican City, Biblioteca Apostolica Vaticana, Pal. Lat. 212 (s. ix, prob. Lake Constance). See O'Sullivan, *Predicationes Palatinae.*
47 See Meens, "Christianization and the Spoken Word," 217–18; and O'Sullivan, *Predicationes Palatinae.*
48 Ibid.
49 Ibid., 136.
50 See Cross, *Cambridge Pembroke College MS. 25,* esp. 88–90.
51 *ASM,* 129–30.

preaching.[52] This homiliary, then, should be understood within the general tradition of early medieval preaching on the Continent that was imported to England and exerted strong influences on vernacular sermons.

In addition to their associations with Anglo-Saxon subjects, these homiliaries also serve to represent the range of common stock of texts for early medieval preaching. Their contents draw on sermons attributed to Augustine of Hippo, Jerome, Gregory the Great, Caesarius of Arles, and Bede – all authoritative exegetes whose work pervaded medieval religious literature. Many of these preaching texts explicate gospel pericopes used throughout the liturgical year in masses and monastic services during the seasons of Advent, Christmas, Epiphany, Lent, Easter, Pentecost, and the Ordinary Time in between them. The Latin homiliaries included here also present appropriate readings for saints' feast days that punctuate this ecclesiastical calendar, providing details about the lives of Mary, the apostles, and major holy men and women venerated in Western Europe. In other words, these collections ordered the year around common readings from authoritative patristic and early medieval voices.

Apocryphal texts contained in these homiliaries range across the varieties discussed throughout this study. They include narratives about Jesus, his family, and disciples (related to the canonical gospels); narratives about the earliest apostles (related to the canonical Acts of the Apostles); letters (related to the canonical Pauline and Catholic epistles); and apocalyptica (related to the canonical Apocalypse of John). In addition, a number of sermons in these homiliaries rely on apocrypha as sources for brief passages, motifs, or commonplace imagery. Within these collections are represented versions or extended passages based on the following apocrypha given in the order of gospels, acts, letters, and apocalypses:

Protevangelium of James (Homiliary of Saint-Père)[53]
Gospel of Pseudo-Matthew (Homiliary of Saint-Père)[54]
Pseudo-Melito *Transitus Mariae* (Homiliary of Saint-Père)[55]
Martyrdom of Andrew (Homiliary of Saint-Père)[56]

---

52 For details, see Cross, *Cambridge Pembroke College MS. 25.*
53 *CANT*, 50.
54 Ibid., 51.
55 Ibid., 111.
56 Ibid., 226.

Pseudo-Melito *Martyrdom of John* (Homiliary of Saint-Père)[57]
Acts of John (Homiliary of Saint-Père)[58]
Martyrdom of Peter and Paul (Homiliary of Saint-Père)[59]
Letter of Pseudo-Titus (Homiliary of Burchard)[60]
Three Utterances Apocryphon (Palatine Collection)[61]
Apocalypse of Paul (Palatine Collection)[62]
Apocalypse of Thomas (Homiliary of Burchard, Palatine Collection)[63]

These apocrypha (with the exception of the *Letter of Pseudo-Titus*, surviving uniquely in Würzburg M.p.th.f. 28) enjoyed widespread popularity
in the medieval West generally and in early England in particular. Several
of these apocrypha will reappear in later chapters, occurring in many instances related to the Old English sermons at the heart of this book.

To the homiliaries already discussed, we may also add other collections
copied at Continental centres with Anglo-Saxon affiliations, particularly
those with apocryphal acts of apostles. Especially pertinent are two collections of *passiones apostolorum* in Brussels, Bibliothèque Royale, II. 1069,
fols. 59–97 (s. viii²)[64] and Würzburg, Universitätsbibliothek, M.p.th.f. 78
(viii², Karlburg?),[65] both written in Anglo-Saxon scripts and from the area
of eighth-century missions on the Continent. The Brussels manuscript is
a palimpsest fragment, with the bottom layer preserving the *Martyrdom
of Thomas* and *Martyrdom of Peter and Paul*.[66] Given the present state of
the manuscript, there is no way of knowing how many other acts were included, although it is plausible that the manuscript (like similar contemporary witnesses) comprised a larger collection of apostolic lives. Würzburg

---

57 Ibid., 220.
58 Ibid., 215.
59 Ibid., 193.
60 Ibid., 307.
61 The *Three Utterances* is not included in *CANT*.
62 *CANT*, 325.
63 Ibid., 326.
64 *CLA*, 10.1551. See *ASL*, 164, no. 91.
65 *CLA*, 9.1425. Description and digital facsimile at *Universitätsbibliothek Würzburg*,
    http://vb.uni-wuerzburg.de/ub/mpthf78/index.html. See Thurn, *Handschriften der
    Universitätsbibliothek Würzburg*, 65; Lapidge, *ASL*, 162, no. 75; and Lifshitz, *Religious
    Women in Early Carolingian Francia*, esp. 41–9 and 112–47 (esp. on the possible
    Karlburg origin).
66 For the *Martyrdom of Peter and Paul*, see *CANT*, 193; the *Martyrdom of Thomas*
    is not included in *CANT*.

M.p.th.f. 78 contains the martyrdoms of John (Pseudo-Melito), James the Great, Thomas, Bartholomew, Matthew, Simon and Jude, and Philip.[67] These manuscripts survive as two of the earliest witnesses to the collection now known as the *Virtutes apostolorum*,[68] containing the popular Latin acts of apostles that circulated widely throughout the medieval period.[69] As will be seen throughout this book, the *Virtutes apostolorum* contained the same apostolic acts used by anonymous Old English sermon authors, Ælfric of Eynsham, and Wulfstan of York.

The collection of apostolic acts in Würzburg M.p.th.f. 78 also reveals the appeal of these stories for a range of audiences. Recently, Felice Lifshitz has argued for the connection of this manuscript to the use and production of religious texts by educated women in the Rhineland area of Francia with close connections to Anglo-Saxon missionaries and culture.[70] In the late eighth and early ninth centuries, religious women produced, used, and circulated a number of books that attest to their beliefs and practices.[71] Among these, Lifshitz argues, the apostolic *passiones* of Würzburg M.p.th.f. 78 were especially appealing to women, since prominent females appear throughout these apocryphal narratives about early Christian missions of conversion. In addition to the points already mentioned, Lifshitz also poses further connections between the contents of Würzburg M.p.th.f. 78 and Anglo-Saxon England. She claims that the exemplar for the *Martyrdom of Bartholomew* came from England, where connections to Guthlac were particularly striking; that the *Martyrdom of Simon and Jude* originated in England (where Bede knew it) before being taken to Francia; and that the exemplar for the *Martyrdom of Philip* (which Bede also knew) came from England.[72] Resting on connections between England and the Continent in the eighth and ninth centuries, Lifshitz's claims provide implications for the interrelated circulation, transmission, and use of apostolic *passiones*

---

67 See Lifshitz, *Religious Women in Early Carolingian Francia*, 41–9.

68 *CANT*, 256.

69 See esp. O'Leary, "By the Bishop of Babylon?"; Backus, *Historical Method and Confessional Identity in the Era of the Reformation (1378–1615)*, 292–321; as well as essays by Rose, "*Virtutes apostolorum*: Editorial Problems and Principles"; "*Virtutes apostolorum*: Origin, Aim and Use"; "*Abdias scriptor vitarum sanctorum apostolorum?*"; and "The Apocryphal Acts of the Apostles in the Latin Middle Ages." See also "Pseudo-Abdias Apostolic Histories," *SASLC Apocrypha*, 38–40, and entries for individual acts at 40–54.

70 Lifshitz, *Religious Women in Early Carolingian Francia*, 112–47.

71 See ibid.; McKitterick, "Nuns' Scriptoria in England and Francia in the Eighth Century" and "Women and Literacy in the Early Middle Ages."

72 Lifshitz, *Religious Women in Early Carolingian Francia*, 41–9.

between and across these cultures. Indeed, the uses of these stories for feminist religious aims also speak to the varied beliefs and practices to which apocryphal narratives contributed in the early medieval world.

Considering these Continental Latin homiliaries as nodes of an interconnected network of preaching media presents myriad associations between them and other manuscripts. Comparing the contents of homiliaries discussed in this chapter, it is easy to multiply connections, as medieval authors and compilers extracted individual sermons and groups of texts from collections for use in others. O'Sullivan highlights a set of Continental manuscripts related to the Palatine Collection in Pal. lat. 220, including Karlsruhe, Badische Landesbibliothek, Aug. perg. 254 (s. viii/ix, Northern Italy),[73] Munich, Bayerische Staatsbibliothek, Clm 14446B (s. ix$^{1/4}$, Regensburg), Munich, Bayerische Staatsbibliothek, Clm 28135 (s. ix$^{1/4}$, prob. Freising) – containing the so-called *Three Utterances Apocryphon* and *Apocrypha Priscillianistica* – and Vatican City, Biblioteca Apostolica Vaticana, Pal. lat. 556 (s. ix) – the last copied in an Anglo-Saxon script in a German centre with missionary affiliations.[74] Cross points out relationships between the Pembroke Homiliary of Saint-Père and another set of Insular-influenced sermons in Munich, Bayerische Staatsbibliothek, Clm 6233 (s. viii^2, Tegernsee).[75]

Further manuscripts could be cited for parallels, amounting to at least dozens of interconnected collections. As already mentioned, Lifshitz has demonstrated associations between Würzburg M.p.th.f. 78 and several other eighth-century manuscripts from the Rhineland region with close Anglo-Saxon ties.[76] Among these books is Würzburg, Universitätsbibliothek, M.p.th.f. 69 (s. viii^2, Würzburg?), a collection of Paul's epistles copied from an English exemplar.[77] This manuscript includes a Crucifixion miniature (fol. 7r), which Lifshitz analyses through cultural connections with various media such as the version of the *Apocalypse of Paul* in Pal. lat. 220 (among other visionary texts) and the *Acts of Paul and Thecla*.[78] Charles D. Wright has identified fifty manuscripts containing versions

---

73 *CLA*, 8.1110.

74 O'Sullivan, *"Predicationes Palatinae,"* 35–46.

75 Cross, *Cambridge Pembroke College MS. 25*, 62–3 and passim.

76 Lifshitz, *Religious Women in Early Carolingian Francia*, esp. 112–47.

77 *CLA*, 9.1424. See also Lifshitz, *Religious Women in Early Carolingian Francia*, 36–8.

78 Ibid., 73–5. For the *Apocalypse of Paul* and *Acts of Paul and Thecla*, see *CANT*, 325 and 211.

of the *Three Utterances Apocryphon*, which multiplies the associations well beyond the scope of the present study.[79] Especially significant among these is the so-called *Florilegium Frisingense* in Munich, Bayerische Staatsbibliothek, Clm 6433, copied at Freising in the late eighth century by an Anglo-Saxon scribe conveniently named Peregrinus.[80] Yet even with the handful of manuscripts discussed so far we find an impressive network. Visualizing a graph with lines (edges) between intersecting texts (nodes) across the Latin homiliaries discussed so far creates an impressive web of associations in which these collections and their constituent apocrypha are well connected (see figure 1).

To this media network we may add a handful of other relevant Latin compendia closer to home for the Anglo-Saxons, those modelled on Continental collections but copied in England or brought there soon after compilation. Foremost among these are copies of the Homiliary of Paul the Deacon and the so-called Cotton-Corpus Legendary. The popular Carolingian Homiliary of Paul the Deacon was in use by Anglo-Saxon vernacular writers from at least the period of tenth-century Benedictine reform movements onward. Ten versions of this homiliary (some complete, others only partial) survive in English manuscripts from before 1100, with contents varying between them.[81] Among these, a tenth- or eleventh-century revision of the *Gospel of Pseudo-Matthew* known as *De nativitate Mariae* appears in two of these collections:[82] Durham, Cathedral Library A.III.29 (s. xi[ex.], before 1096, Durham) and Salisbury, Cathedral Library 179 (s. xi[ex.], Salisbury).[83] In addition, a copy of the *Martyrdom of Philip* appears in Cambridge, Pembroke College 24, copied in France (perhaps Saint-Denis) in the late eleventh century but in England (Bury St Edmunds) by the turn of the twelfth century.[84]

The Cotton-Corpus Legendary is the only surviving collection of saints' legends from before the twelfth century to be organized according to

---

79 For a list, see Wright, "Latin Analogue for *The Two Deaths*," 128–37. More recently, see also idem, "More Latin Sources for the Old English 'Three Utterances' Homilies."
80 *CLA*, 9.1283. See also Wright, *The Irish Tradition in Old English Literature*, 56; and, on Peregrinus, Bischoff, *Die südostdeutschen Schreibschulen und Bibliotheken in der Karolingerzeit*, I, 61–3 and 73–5.
81 See a descriptive list in Joyce Hill, "Ælfric's Manuscript of Paul the Deacon's Homiliary."
82 *CANT*, 52.
83 *ASM*, 222 and 753.
84 *ASM*, 130.

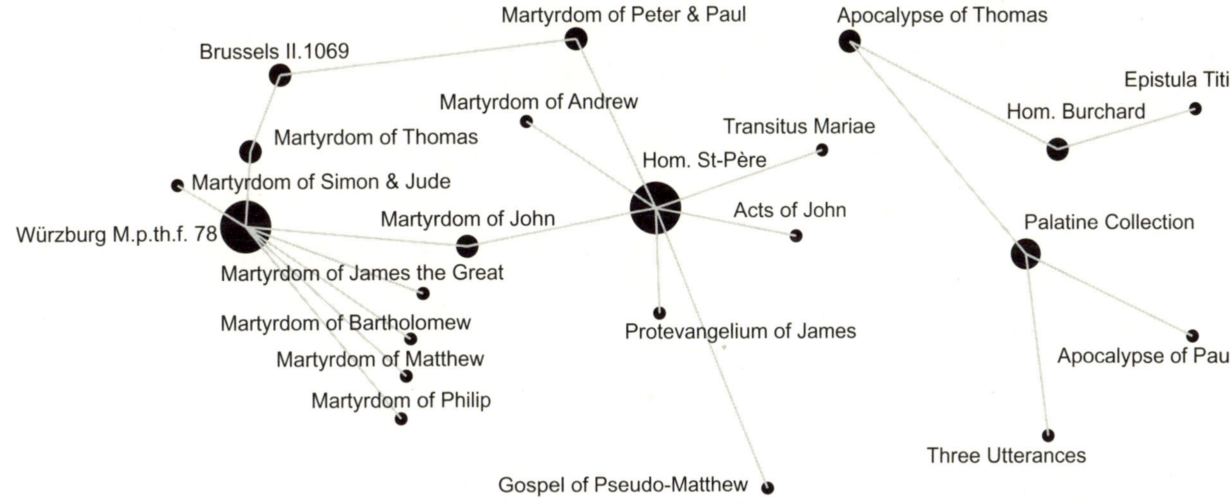

Figure 1 Network visualization of apocrypha in Continental Latin preaching collections with Anglo-Saxon associations.

the liturgical calendar.[85] Surviving manuscripts of the Cotton-Corpus Legendary come from the late eleventh and twelfth centuries, but they represent collections that circulated earlier in the Anglo-Saxon period. While the collection was not necessarily intended for preaching, evidence shows that its contents were certainly used as sources for vernacular sermons. For example, Patrick H. Zettel brought greater attention to this legendary by demonstrating that many of Ælfric's works on saints derive from texts in this collection. The presence of passions of apostles in early versions of the Cotton-Corpus Legendary is difficult to parse, yet certain representatives of the legendary help to situate apostolic acts among collections accessible to Anglo-Saxon preachers. Particularly significant in this respect are London, British Library, Cotton Nero E.i, fols. 1–155 (s. xi$^{3/4}$, Worcester) and the two-part compendium of Salisbury, Cathedral Library 221 and 222 (s. xi$^{ex.}$, Salisbury).[86] Both of these collections contain apocryphal martyrdoms of Bartholomew, James the Great, James the Less, Mark, Matthew, Paul (Pseudo-Linus), Peter, and Philip – representing a majority of apocryphal acts from the *Virtutes apostolorum*. In addition, Nero E.i also contains an account of the birth of Mary from the *Gospel of Pseudo-Matthew*, chapters 1–6.3.

Finally, apocrypha concerning New Testament figures appear in at least two other collections that would have been useful for preachers in late Anglo-Saxon England. One is a Latin homiliary, though with a more specific cycle than some of the others discussed in this chapter. Cambridge, St John's College 35 (s. xi$^{ex.}$, prov. Bury St Edmunds) contains Gregory the Great's series of *Homiliae in Hiezechielem* as well as an added homiletic rendering of a text known as the *Trinubium Annae* (s. xi/xii).[87] This apocryphal account about the Virgin Mary's family lineage derives from sources like the *Protevangelium of James* and *Gospel of Pseudo-Matthew*, mediated through Continental authors like Haymo of Auxerre. Ælfric also makes reference to similar subjects, indicating that versions of this tradition were already in use in tenth-century England before the composition of the text in St John's College 35.[88] Finally, to this web of English preaching

---

85 See Zettel, "Saints' Lives in Old English"; and Jackson and Lapidge, "The Contents of the Cotton-Corpus Legendary."

86 *ASM*, 344 and 754.5–6.

87 *ASM*, 147. See Hall, "The Earliest Anglo-Latin Text of the *Trinubium Annae* (*BHL* 505zl)."

88 See Frederick M. Biggs and Thomas N. Hall, "Trinubium Annae," *SASLC Apocrypha*, 83–4.

collections with Latin apocrypha may be added Paris, Bibliothèque nationale de France, lat. 10861 (s. ix[1/4] or ix[1], S England), containing nineteen saints' passions, among which are martyrdoms of James the Great and Philip.[89] Like the Cotton-Corpus Legendary, this collection was not necessarily compiled for preaching, although its contents represent sources used for sermons on saints' feast days.

Adding these English manuscripts and their texts to others discussed so far expands the preaching media network significantly, particularly in relation to apocryphal gospels and saints' lives for the apostles (see figure 2). These collections from England also provide evidence that Continental homiliaries with Anglo-Saxon associations are not the only representatives of these texts in Latin. Copies of Paul the Deacon's Homiliary, the Cotton-Corpus Legendary, and other passionals helped to transmit this material, further demonstrating the widespread and interconnected nature of these types of apocrypha. In other words, this network of collections and apocryphal texts established a basic model for Anglo-Saxon writers composing sermons in the vernacular, to which I now turn.

The Oldest Vernacular Preaching Collections

Around fifty manuscripts containing Old English sermons survive from the tenth through twelfth centuries, encompassing single texts or groups mixed with other types of works, as well as larger and even complete preaching collections.[90] It is clear from this abundance of evidence that neither Old English sermons nor collections of them were created *ex nihilo*. While Anglo-Saxon literary history reveals an early and large vernacular corpus

---

89 *ASM*, 898.

90 For the range of vernacular sermons and manuscripts, see "Homilies" in "Index I: Index of the Contents of the Manuscripts," NRK, at 527–36; as well as lists under "Ælfric of Eynsham" (esp. *Catholic Homilies* and "Homilies and Sermons"), "homilies and sermons in Old English, anonymous," and "Wulfstan the Homilist, bishop of Worcester and archbishop of York" (esp. "Sermons and homilies in OE") in the "Index of Authors and Texts," *ASM*, at 888–9, 914, and 936. See also Scragg, "The Corpus of Vernacular Homilies and Prose Saints' Lives before Ælfric"; Kleist, "Appendix"; and, for the periods c. 1050–1100 and c. 1100–1220, Treharne, *Living through Conquest*, 99–101 and 125–6. These lists do not, however, include all manuscripts, such as more recent discoveries like the Latin and Old English bilingual collection (now fragmentary) in Taunton, Somerset County Record Office, DD/SAS C/1193/77 (s. xi[?med., ?2, ?3/3], SE England, Kent?); see *ASM*, 756.8 (though not listed in the previously cited section of the index).

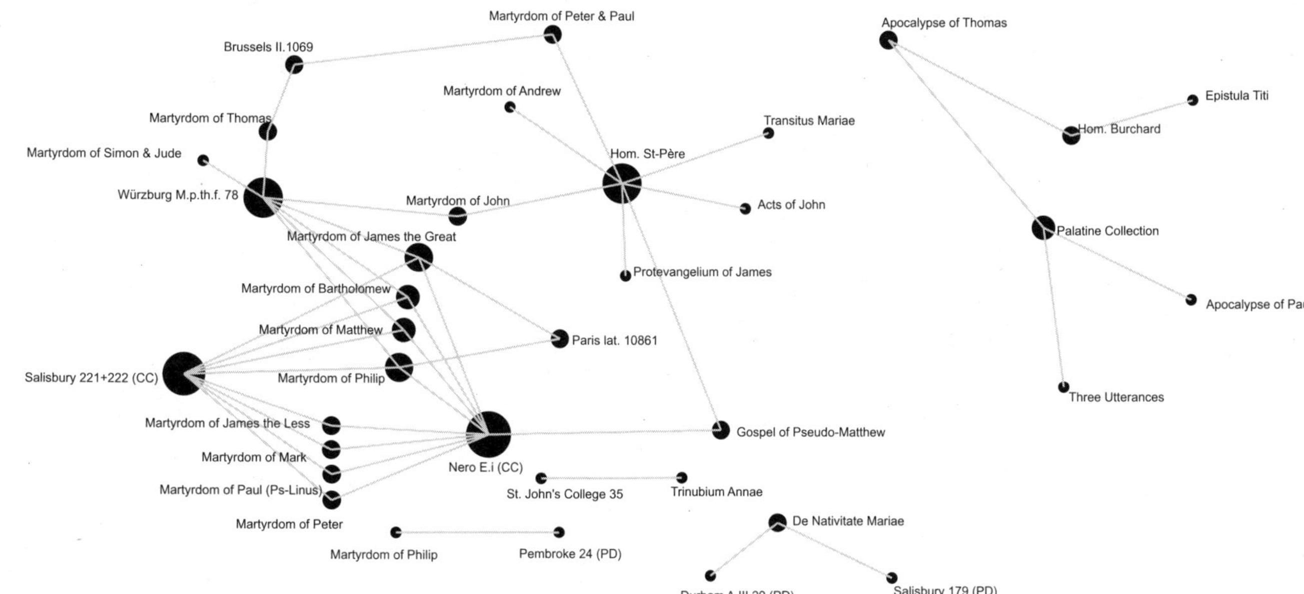

Figure 2 Network visualization of apocrypha in Continental and English Latin preaching collections with Anglo-Saxon associations.

compared to other Western European cultures, most of their works are modelled on Latin literature.[91] In her overview of homiliaries in Anglo-Saxon England, Mary Clayton presents evidence for close links between Latin and Old English preaching collections, pointing towards the former as models for the latter.[92] M.J. Toswell presents different evidence, based on codicological examinations and Pamela Robinson's claims that some vernacular collections were first made up of booklets of material rather than wholesale compilations.[93] While working from booklets was not standard practice for creating complete Latin homiliaries, it is clear that scribes sometimes created vernacular collections in this way. Nonetheless, Anglo-Saxon scribes did compile these booklets into whole codices at some point, organizing them into contiguous assemblages as they survive up to the present.

Old English sermons seem to have been compiled in many different ways: for example, copied into a single volume all at once; as booklets at first, then combined later; added into the margins of manuscripts; and in miscellanies, copied over time; in all cases, texts could have been copied by a single scribe or multiple, sometimes even several. My point here is not to argue against Robinson and Toswell, who present cogent codicological evidence. Instead, I seek to extend Clayton's work on Latin homiliaries as models for Old English sermon collections in order to consider the contexts of apocrypha in vernacular preaching materials as they circulated in surviving manuscripts. In this section, I introduce collections that will feature most prominently throughout this book, with discussion of several more to follow in the next section.

The two earliest manuscripts containing Old English sermons are the collections known as the Vercelli Book (Vercelli, Biblioteca Capitolare CXVII) and the Blickling Book (Princeton, University Library, W.H.

---

91 Generally, see Curtius, *European Literature and the Latin Middle Ages*. For Anglo-Saxon England, see, for example, Allen and Calder, *Sources and Analogues of Old English Poetry*; and Wright, "Old English Homilies and Latin Sources," with further references there. Many more individual associations between Latin and Old English literature may be gleaned from entries in *Fontes* and volumes published by *SASLC*.

92 Clayton, "Homiliaries and Preaching in Anglo-Saxon England."

93 See Pamela Robinson, "Self-Contained Units in Composite Manuscripts of the Anglo-Saxon Period"; and Toswell, "The Codicology of Anglo-Saxon Homiletic Manuscripts, Especially the Blickling Homilies."

Scheide Collection 71), both dated to the second half of the tenth century.[94] As already discussed, these are two of the most important witnesses for this study because of their apocryphal content, although they should be understood as only the earliest surviving representatives of a longer tradition of preaching in Anglo-Saxon England. As D.G. Scragg points out, "Since no manuscript containing Old English homilies survives from before the end of the tenth century [before c. 950], our knowledge of the early development of the homily in English is limited."[95] Yet vernacular preaching began earlier than this period, and sermons certainly continued to be copied until the end of the twelfth century.[96] Many of the surviving manuscripts containing vernacular sermons (including the Vercelli and Blickling collections) are copied from earlier sources, creating a picture of a complex network between witnesses very much like that found among Latin homiliaries. To begin unravelling this network, the following presents a number of collections that prove significant for situating apocrypha in vernacular preaching contexts.

The Vercelli Book was compiled sometime in the second half of the tenth century, likely 959–88 in St Augustine's Canterbury, although its precise origins, rationale for its creation, full provenance, and circumstances of its arrival in Vercelli remain ambiguous.[97] This collection contains twenty-nine texts, which traditionally have been distinguished from each other as "anonymous homilies" and "religious poetry,"[98] although they are included together without noticeable distinction by the single scribe. The Old English poems include *Andreas* and Cynewulf's *Fates of the Apostles* (items 6–7), *Soul and Body I* and *Homiletic Fragment I* (items 21–2), *Dream*

---

94 See references in the Introduction.

95 Scragg, "The Corpus of Vernacular Homilies and Prose Saints' Lives before Ælfric," 223.

96 See Gameson, *The Manuscripts of Early Norman England*; *PUEM*; and Scragg, *A Conspectus of Scribal Hands Writing English, 960–1100*; as well as recent discussions in Swan and Treharne, eds., *Rewriting Old English in the Twelfth Century*; Treharne, Da Rold, and Swan, eds., *Producing and Using English Manuscripts in the Post-Conquest Period*; and Treharne, *Living through Conquest*.

97 For summaries of scholarship, see Zacher, *Preaching the Converted*, 3–29; essays and bibliography in Zacher and Orchard, eds., *New Readings in the Vercelli Book*; Leneghan, "Teaching the Teachers"; and *ASM*, 941. On date, origin, and contexts, see Scragg, *VH*, xxxviii–ix; idem, "The Vercelli Homilies and Kent"; and Treharne, "The Form and Function of the Vercelli Book."

98 See, for example, Scragg, "The Corpus of Vernacular Homilies and Prose Saints' Lives before Ælfric," 225.

of the Rood (item 23), and Cynewulf's *Elene* (item 28). Further blurring the lines between poetic and homiletic genres and forms, scholars have examined alliterative verse embedded within the sermons, as well as homiletic characteristics within the poetry.[99] There is ample evidence for considering all of the Vercelli Book contents – regardless of genres and forms – as preaching texts: "preaching was a subject pervasively on the mind of the compiler."[100] There is no identifiable order to these contents, and they do not adhere to the order of the liturgical year. The contents were not copied consecutively but presumably as exemplars were available. Various purposes for the collection have been put forward, and the most accepted theory is that it was meant as a devotional book for personal reading, although this is uncertain.[101] Nonetheless, in its inclusion of various types of texts, the Vercelli Book reveals the many possibilities that Anglo-Saxon preachers had to hand.

Apocryphal materials pervade the Vercelli Book contents.[102] Vercelli 6 includes a translation of chapters 17–24 of the *Gospel of Pseudo-Matthew* (discussed in chapter 4). In terms of apostolic lives, the *Acts of Andrew and Matthias* rests behind *Andreas*, while Cynewulf's *Fates of the Apostles* is indebted to a number of details ultimately derived from apocryphal acts. The *Apocalypse of Thomas* makes up the source of Vercelli 15. The *Dream of the Rood* provides an elegant and expansive reflection on Jesus' Crucifixion, and perhaps (if we compare it to Junod's definition provided in my introduction) should be regarded as an apocryphal revelation in its own right. The book has been perceived as particularly focused on eschatological subjects, since it includes a number of sermons about Judgment Day, in which many details ultimately derive from apocryphal motifs and exempla.[103] All of these examples paint a picture in which apocrypha play

---

99 For recent examples, with further bibliography, see Wright, "More Old English Poetry in Vercelli Homily XXI"; and Randle, "The 'Homiletics' of the Vercelli Book Poems."

100 Zacher, *Preaching the Converted*, 274.

101 See esp. Treharne, "The Form and Function of the Vercelli Book."

102 Convenient lists of sources for the sermons may be found in Gatch, "Eschatology in the Anonymous Old English Homilies," 138–42; and McCoy, "The Use of the Writings of English Authors in Old English Homiletic Literature," 180–2; although these source identifications are superseded by introductions in *VH*. For sources of the poetry, see Allen and Calder, *Sources and Analogues of Old English Poetry*; and bibliography in *SASLC Apocrypha*.

103 For a classic formulation, see Gatch, "Eschatology in the Anonymous Old English Homilies"; see also Wright, *The Irish Tradition in Old English Literature*, passim.

a key part in the contents of the Vercelli Book, alongside sources by or attributed to figures such as Augustine, Caesarius of Arles, Gregory the Great, Isidore of Seville, Alcuin of York, and Felix of Crowland.

The Blickling Book presents another unique case, somewhat closer in kind to the Latin homiliaries previously discussed.[104] Compiled in the last few decades of the tenth century – probably as booklets first, then as a whole compilation – this collection contains eighteen sermons arranged according to the liturgical year. The first twelve items represent an abbreviated *temporale* (from Annunciation through Pentecost), and items 13 through 18 represent a brief *sanctorale* (from the feast of the Assumption of Mary through the feast of Saint Andrew). With this structure, the most obvious models are Latin homiliaries organized according to liturgical cycles, with selections of sermons appropriate for various occasions. Like the Vercelli Book, however, many details of its origins and early history remain unknown. Since the sermons are written in the vernacular, the logical assumption is that the Blickling Book was meant as a collection for preaching to the laity, although it also could have plausibly been used for private devotional reading or in a monastic setting.

Apocrypha in many forms also underpin the contents of the Blickling Book.[105] An account of the Harrowing of Hell and the eschatological *Apocalypse of Thomas* features in Blickling 7 (discussed in chapter 4). Apocryphal sources are especially prominent in sermons in the latter section of the book, meant for saints' feast days: Blickling 13 consists of a translation of a version of the Pseudo-Melito *Transitus Mariae*; Blickling 15 consists of a translation of the Pseudo-Marcellus *Martyrdom of Peter and Paul* (discussed in chapter 2); and Blickling 18 (like the Vercelli Book *Andreas*) consists of a translation of the *Acts of Andrew and Matthias*. These examples of reliance on apocrypha for narratives about biblical saints like Mary and the apostles suggest that these sources were perceived by medieval readers and authors as useful for understanding Christian

---

104 No useful summary of scholarship exists, but see Clayton, "Homiliaries and Preaching in Anglo-Saxon England," 167–71; Scragg, "The Homilies of the Blickling Manuscript"; Gatch, "The Unknowable Audience"; Thompson, "The Carolingian *De festiuitatibus* and the Blickling Book"; Toswell, "The Codicology of Anglo-Saxon Homiletic Manuscripts, Especially the Blickling Homilies"; Jonathan Wilcox, "The Blickling Homilies Revisited"; and *ASM*, 905.

105 Convenient lists of sources may be found in Gatch, "Eschatology in the Anonymous Old English Homilies," 119–22; and McCoy, "The Use of the Writings of English Authors in Old English Homiletic Literature," 177–9.

history extended beyond the narratives of the New Testament. Again, as in Latin homiliaries and the Vercelli Book, apocrypha are as much a part of the fabric of the Blickling sermons as sources by or attributed to figures like Augustine, Sulpicius Severus, Peter Chrysologus, Caesarius of Arles, Gregory the Great, Adomnán, Paulinus of Aquileia, and anonymous histories.

Working at the end of the tenth century and the beginning of the eleventh was one figure about whose life and works we know much more: Ælfric of Eynsham.[106] Although his works are often presented as somehow set apart from anonymous sermons, one of my aims in this book is to demonstrate that his reliance on apocrypha (particularly acts of apostles) is in some ways strikingly similar – and certainly connected – to the practices of contemporary anonymous sermon authors. While this notion will be discussed at length in chapter 3, it is useful here to provide an overview of Ælfric's major sermon cycles and the apocrypha on which he relied. His most ambitious project of vernacular sermons comprises the First and Second Series of the *Catholic Homilies*, together totalling eighty-five sermons meant for use throughout the full liturgical cycle of the church year. Composed in 989 and 992, when Ælfric was still a monk and masspriest at Cerne, the whole enterprise remains the magnum opus of his career.[107] It is clear that he modelled his vernacular collections on Latin homiliaries, especially since he relied for many of his sources on the three major collections of Paul the Deacon, Smaragdus of Saint-Mihiel, and Haymo of Auxerre.[108] In presenting these series of homilies in the vernacular, however, Ælfric provided primarily monastic sources for preaching to the laity in a move closely linked to his ideals of reforming Anglo-Saxon Christian beliefs and practices.

Between 992 and 1002, Ælfric composed another monumental collection of primarily monastic material translated into the vernacular, his *Lives of Saints*. This collection contains thirty-seven texts for saints' days and other occasions not covered by the *Catholic Homilies*. While not all of the *Lives of Saints* are obviously stylized as sermons, the collection has been regarded as a sort of third series – a companion collection to the two series of *Catholic Homilies* – with contents appropriate for preaching. As

---

106 On Ælfric's life and works, see esp. Magennis and Swan, eds., *A Companion to Ælfric*, with further references there.

107 For the dating of Ælfric's works, see Clemoes, "The Chronology of Ælfric's Works"; Kleist, "Ælfric's Corpus"; and Joyce Hill, "Ælfric: His Life and Works."

108 See entries for "Aelfric" in *Fontes*; and *CH Introduction*.

with his two previous collections, Ælfric relied on Latin models like homiliaries and legendaries, and the vernacular product reveals his desire to provide the laity with access to these materials.

Ælfric is often hailed as an orthodox preacher in a landscape of heterodox teachings, but this claim is only possible from the perspective of modern assumptions.[109] It is true that he most often relied on identifiable authorities like Augustine, Jerome, Sulpicius Severus, Caesarius of Arles, Gregory the Great, and Bede, but as already seen, many of these same authors' works lie behind anonymous sermons in the Vercelli, Blickling, and other collections. Ælfric also turned to certain anonymous apocrypha that were perceived to be authoritative in their own way. In particular, he used acts of apostles for his sermons commemorating the first disciples' feast days. While the so-called Cotton-Corpus Legendary has been identified as a major collection containing many of the same texts that Ælfric used, questions still remain about the particular version he may have consulted. The possibility therefore remains that he also turned to collections like the *Virtutes apostolorum*, or found versions of the apocryphal acts in other legendaries or preaching collections. The parallels of contents between Ælfric's sermons, Latin homiliaries, and anonymous Old English sermon collections open up many more possibilities for thinking about the complexities of Anglo-Saxon preaching as interrelated and cohesive in some ways, rather than establishing artificial boundaries between certain figures and texts.

Vernacular Networking

The eleventh and twelfth centuries produced a large upsurge in the amount of preaching media copied and preserved in England. Among these may be counted anonymous sermons (many composed decades earlier than surviving copies), Ælfric's *Catholic Homilies* and *Lives of Saints*, as well as Wulfstan's sermons. Scribes continued to use earlier Latin and Old English works at the same time that they composed, compiled, circulated, and copied new sermons and collections. Both old and new compositions coalesced in English libraries, sometimes within the covers of a single manuscript. Indeed, a survey of the corpus of surviving sermons in Latin and Old English – as with much Anglo-Saxon literature – shows that more

---

109 See further discussion and references in chapter 3.

texts survive from the eleventh century onward than before. Anglo-Saxons continued to include apocrypha within these assemblages. The final set of media considered in this chapter represents a handful of related vernacular preaching collections containing apocrypha within eleventh- and twelfth-century contexts. The following is not meant to be comprehensive, but representative of the connective tissues that may be found linking apocrypha across the surviving manuscripts bearing witness to the corpus of Old English preaching.

I begin with Cambridge, Corpus Christi College 162 (s. x[ex.] or xi[in.], SE England), a near-contemporary to the Vercelli, Blickling, and Ælfrician collections, compiled at the end of the tenth or beginning of the eleventh century.[110] The contents of this manuscript represent part of a *temporale* collection, including forty-five sermons for Sundays and certain special occasions from the second Sunday after Epiphany to the second Sunday in Advent. Twenty-eight of these are from Ælfric's *Catholic Homilies*, while the other seventeen are anonymous. Among these are Old English translations of the *Apocalypse of Thomas* and a version of a text known as the *Sunday Letter*. Both of these sermons form parts of complex textual associations, since versions of the *Apocalypse of Thomas* and the *Sunday Letter* comprise the two most copied apocryphal sources in the Old English corpus.[111] Surviving in the vernacular are five texts of the *Apocalypse of Thomas* and six texts of the *Sunday Letter*. Associations with these two apocryphal sermons contribute further to the overall network of media under discussion, as the connections bring together many of the subjects discussed in this chapter. Indeed, it is notable that each related apocryphon and manuscript context is another significant node for understanding the wider network of extra-biblical media in Anglo-Saxon England.

Arguably the most prevalent apocryphal tradition in Anglo-Saxon England, the *Sunday Letter* shares associations with many texts and manuscripts – many even beyond the scope of this study.[112] Dorothy Haines has edited all of the Old English versions, as well as five Latin versions, delineating the text types circulated and translated in Anglo-Saxon England.[113] In addition to CCCC 162, Old English versions survive in Cambridge, Corpus Christi College 140 (s xi[1]–xii, Bath), Cambridge, Corpus Christi

---

110 NRK, 38; and *ASM*, 50.
111 See entries in *SASLC Apocrypha*, 58–61 and 71–2.
112 *CANT*, 311.
113 Haines, *Sunday Observance and the Sunday Letter in Anglo-Saxon England*.

College 419 (s. xi[1], prob. SE England) – which includes two different versions consecutively – London, British Library, Cotton Tiberius A.iii (s. xi[med.], Canterbury, Christ Church), and London, Lambeth Palace 489 (s. xi).[114] Most of these manuscripts constitute sermon collections, with two aberrations: in CCCC 140, the *Sunday Letter* is the only sermon, added in a late eleventh-century script; and Tiberius A.iii is a large collection of diverse texts in Latin and Old English (further discussed below), with the *Sunday Letter* part of a series of vernacular sermons copied together. Numerous Latin versions survive up to the fifteenth century, although no single manuscript has been acknowledged as directly related to Anglo-Saxon England.[115]

Also noteworthy are the links between the *Sunday Letter* and a large number of texts known as *Sunday Lists*, which enumerate significant holy events said to have occurred on Sundays. Passages from *Sunday Lists* are appended to five of the surviving Old English *Sunday Letter* sermons (excepting only the version in CCCC 140). Another noteworthy connection is to the Latin Homiliary of St Père in Pembroke 25, which includes an expanded version of a *Sunday List*. While clear relationships between variant lists, versions of the *Sunday Letter*, and earlier Latin versions remain ambiguous, they seem to derive from a common tradition for explaining the veneration of Sunday as the Christian holy day.[116] Furthermore, as with many apocrypha, developments and transmissions of *Sunday Lists* are closely related to writings by or attributed to authoritative late antique and early medieval authors such as Augustine, Pope Leo I, Isidore, Alcuin, and Hrabanus Maurus.

The *Apocalypse of Thomas* survives in both Latin and vernacular forms, in a sophisticated array of manuscripts and text types. Wright has most extensively studied the Old English texts and their relationships between each other and the Latin versions, illuminating the details of the various texts.[117] In focusing on the network encompassing this apocryphon, we encounter three Old English versions already mentioned, in Vercelli 15,

---

114 NRK 35, 48, 186, and 283; and *ASM*, 44, 108, and 363.

115 Haines provides a list of all identified manuscripts containing Latin versions in *Sunday Observance and the Sunday Letter in Anglo-Saxon England*, 211–14.

116 For some possible explanations, see Whitelock, "Bishop Ecgred, Pehtred and Niall," 62–4; and Haines, *Sunday Observance and the Sunday Letter in Anglo-Saxon England*, passim – but further work remains.

117 See Wright, "Vercelli Homily XV and *The Apocalypse of Thomas*," with further references there.

Blickling 7, and CCCC 162, as well as two others in Cambridge, Corpus Christi College 41 (s. xi¹, additions s. xi¹⁻ᵐᵉᵈ·, prob. S England)[118] and Oxford, Bodleian Library, Hatton 116 (s. xii¹) – the latter closely related to the text in CCCC 162.[119] CCCC 41 will be further discussed below. Hatton 116 survives as a collection of twenty-six sermons with a *sanctorale* section for saints' feast days from 24 June to 30 November (mainly from *Catholic Homilies*) as well as an assortment of other sermons mainly from Ælfrician sources. Beyond Old English texts, twelve Latin texts have been identified, surviving in three versions of varying lengths and types: interpolated, non-interpolated, and abbreviated.[120] Among these are the previously mentioned versions of the *Apocalypse of Thomas* in the Latin Palatine Collection and Homiliary of Burchard. All of these witnesses to Latin and Old English versions comprise a far-reaching array of texts, languages, and manuscripts, across a widespread temporal and geographic scope – from the fifth to fifteenth centuries, from Italy to England.

Associations between the *Apocalypse of Thomas* and the Latin Palatine Collection (however close or distant they might be) also elicit discussion of another set of relationships between this continental homiliary and Old English literature related to the *Apocalypse of Paul* and the so-called *Three Utterances Apocryphon*.[121] All three of these apocrypha come from common traditions – and ultimately common late antique sources – of Christian eschatological apocalyptica.[122] As the *Apocalypse of Paul* offers fantastic tours of heaven and hell, and the *Three Utterances* narrates a contest between angels and devils for newly departed souls, both feature subjects, themes, and imagery parallel to the *Apocalypse of Thomas*. It is not surprising that these apocalyptica would circulate together in both Latin and vernacular contexts. Indeed, they would collectively make up a

---

118 NRK, 32; and *ASM*, 39.

119 NRK, 333.

120 See summary in Wright, "Vercelli Homily XV and *The Apocalypse of Thomas*," 152–5.

121 On these apocrypha in the Palatine Collection and relationships to other versions, including Old English sermons, see O'Sullivan, "*Predicationes Palatinae*," esp. 103–28.

122 Scholarship on late antique apocalyptica is vast; for an overview with extensive bibliography, see DiTommaso, "Apocalypses and Apocalypticism in Antiquity (Part I)" and "Apocalypses and Apocalypticism in Antiquity (Part II)." On early medieval views of apocalypse, see esp. Palmer, *The Apocalypse in the Early Middle Ages*. On Anglo-Saxon eschatology, see esp. Gatch, *Preaching and Theology in Anglo-Saxon England*; Kabir, *Paradise, Death and Doomsday in Anglo-Saxon Literature*; and Forbes, *Heaven and Earth in Anglo-Saxon England*, 129–200.

useful group of texts for preaching, since they highlight divine judgment for each human individually at death and for humanity collectively at the Last Judgment.

Even apart from associations with the *Apocalypse of Thomas*, the *Apocalypse of Paul* and *Three Utterances* share close ties in their circulation and use. The only surviving Old English translation of the *Apocalypse of Paul* appears along with one version of the *Three Utterances* in Oxford, Bodleian Library, Junius 85 and 86 (s.xi[med.], SE England), as part of a collection of charms and sermons (items 4 and 6).[123] Three other Old English versions of the *Three Utterances* survive: two closely related texts in Cambridge, Corpus Christi College 302 (s. xi/xii, SE England?) and London, British Library, Cotton Faustina A.ix (s. xii[1]), as well as another in Oxford, Bodleian Library, Hatton 114 (1064x83, Worcester) – all three vernacular sermon collections containing anonymous and Ælfrician texts (with Wulfstanian materials in CCCC 302 and Hatton 114).[124] As Rudolf Willard has argued, both the *Apocalypse of Paul* and *Three Utterances* play a role in an anonymous Old English sermon titled *Larspell* that appears in CCCC 419, as well as in two other sermon collections in Oxford, Bodleian Library, Bodley 343 (s. xii[2], West Midlands) and Junius 121 (s. xi[3/4], Worcester).[125] Correspondences between these apocrypha in the Palatine Collection, Junius 85 and 86, and the *Larspell* sermon therefore demonstrate how closely related these texts were for medieval compilers and authors. None of this is to suggest a direct source relationship between the Palatine Collection and Old English translations, but to acknowledge the many ways in which considering these types of collections together provides a broad picture of the transmissions of apocrypha and preaching in early medieval Western Europe.

Tracing the connections and range of contexts in which Old English apocryphal sermons circulated leads us to examine in further detail two manuscripts mentioned previously, CCCC 41 and Tiberius A.iii. Both manuscripts present a wide assortment of contexts for situating vernacular apocryphal sermons within the wider apparatus of Anglo-Saxon Christianity. They exhibit the use of apocrypha within not only preaching contexts specifically but also the general intellectual culture of biblical

---

123 NRK, 336; and *ASM*, 642.
124 NRK, 56, 153, and 331; and *ASM*, 86 and 638.
125 NRK, 310 and 338; and *ASM*, 644. See Willard, *Two Apocrypha in Old English Homilies*, 74–6.

study and worship that fed into Anglo-Saxon belief and practice. By examining these intersections, we are reminded that, for medieval authors
and audiences, apocryphal narratives were not distant from the canonical
Bible, but part of understanding it and filling in the pieces of what the
New Testament does not relate. In this, the preaching of Christian apocrypha fitted in seamlessly among knowledge about biblical subjects that
were presented to Anglo-Saxons through an abundance of media.

CCCC 41 is an anomaly among the manuscripts examined in depth in
this chapter, since it does not properly represent a collection of sermons.
The main text is an Old English translation of Bede's *Historia ecclesiastica
gentis Anglorum* copied by two scribes, but many other texts in both Latin
and Old English line the margins, added by a third scribe working slightly later (before the middle of the eleventh century).[126] As Sarah Larratt
Keefer and Thomas A. Bredehoft demonstrate, the additions appear in
blocks of related texts, indicating that the third scribe copied them over
time, as different exemplars were available.[127] The result is that the margins
provide a discrete "archive" of a variety of Anglo-Saxon texts perhaps in
a process, as Keefer suggests, "brought together on whatever vellum was
best available, and awaiting the next stage of reorganization and recopying
into a[nother] volume."[128] Thus, we might consider this archive of marginalia as a self-contained network of interrelated media in its own right.

Among these accumulations are several relevant texts, foremost of which
are six anonymous vernacular sermons added throughout the manuscript.
A group of four of these sermons (pp. 254–301) includes translations of
an abbreviated version of the *Transitus Mariae* (pp. 280–7), *Apocalypse
of Thomas* (pp. 287–95), and *Gospel of Nicodemus* (pp. 295–301).[129] Since
this block of sermons constitutes a series copied together on consecu-
tive pages – the four make up "the longest continuous stretch of marginal
entries"[130] – they are particularly intriguing together. At another place in
the manuscript, the marginal scribe also copied a sermon in praise of
Saint Michael the Archangel (pp. 402–17) composed from an assortment

---

126 See Scragg, *A Conspectus of Scribal Hands Writing English, 960–1100*, 31.
127 Keefer, "Margin as Archive"; and Bredehoft, "Filling the Margins of CCCC 41."
128 Keefer, "Margin as Archive," 151.
129 Some of these are printed in Grant, ed., *Three Homilies from Cambridge, Corpus Christi
     College 41*. For the *Gospel of Nicodemus*, see *CANT*, 62.
130 Bredehoft, "Filling the Margins of CCCC 41," 723.

of apocryphal traditions.[131] As Bredehoft has demonstrated, the scribe's ruling, sequencing of texts, and procedures for copying in stages indicate some amount of planning for these additions;[132] furthermore, according to his proposed stages for the marginal scribe's work, the block of sermons as well as the one for Saint Michael were likely copied into CCCC 41 at the same time. All of this suggests that the scribe copied these sermons (at least the block of sermons) from a single exemplar, and since no extant manuscript contains all of them together, this group survives perhaps as witness to part of a lost vernacular sermon collection combining apocrypha with other materials.[133]

The version of the *Transitus Mariae* in CCCC 41 raises a number of connections to other sermons because of common sources, forming part of a small network surrounding Anglo-Saxon interests in Marian apocrypha.[134] For example, because they relate to common traditions and key sources, connections may be found to Latin preaching texts already discussed, such as sermons based on the *Gospel of Pseudo-Matthew* in Nero E.i; the *Protevangelium of James*, *Gospel of Pseudo-Matthew*, and *Transitus Mariae* in Pembroke 25; the *Trinubium Annae* in St John's College 35; and *De natiuitate Mariae* in Salisbury 179 and Durham A.III.29. In addition, connections exist with another Old English translation of the *Transitus Mariae* in the Blickling Book (Blickling 13) and also in Cambridge, Corpus Christi College 198 (s. xi¹, Worcester?), a large collection of anonymous and Ælfrician vernacular preaching texts – including a translation of the *Acts of Andrew and Matthias* parallel to Blickling 18.[135] Furthermore, within this network, interest in the life of Mary is also substantially connected to a translation of the first part of the *Gospel of Pseudo-Matthew* in Bodley 343, Hatton 114, and Cambridge, Corpus Christi College 367,

---

131 On this sermon, with discussion of apocryphal analogues, see Grant, ed., *Three Homilies from Cambridge, Corpus Christi College 41*, 42–77; Richard F. Johnson, "Archangel in the Margins," 85–90.

132 Bredehoft, "Filling the Margins of CCCC 41"; cf. NRK, 32; and Keefer, "Margin as Archive."

133 According to Bredehoft's proposed stages, it seems that the marginal scribe copied another sermon on pp. 484–8 in the final stage (stage 4), rather than along with the other sermons – although it is difficult to substantiate relationships or to determine the time between stages of copying; see "Filling the Margins of CCCC 41," esp. 729–31, and suggestions for further study at 732.

134 See Clayton, *The Apocryphal Gospels of Mary in Anglo-Saxon England*.

135 NRK, 48; and *ASM*, 64.

Part II (s. xi[med.], prob. Worcester), a collection of anonymous and Ælfrician vernacular sermons.[136]

Also relevant to the contexts of apocryphal sermons in CCCC 41 are liturgical additions in this manuscript. Raymond J.S. Grant, Keefer, and Jesse D. Billett have traced relationships between the marginal liturgical materials and various interrelated manuscripts.[137] Billett suggests that the liturgical additions in CCCC 41 likely provide early evidence for an antiphoner in late Anglo-Saxon England.[138] Thus, these chants would have been appropriate for the secular office for priests and clerks – the same group who would find the vernacular sermons beneficial for preaching to laity. This suggestion does not preclude the use of these sermons in other contexts like the monastic Office or at meal times, or even for private devotion; but it does allow us to consider contexts for the preaching of Old English apocrypha like the *Transitus Mariae*, *Apocalypse of Thomas*, and *Gospel of Nicodemus* in a range of settings inside and outside of the monastery, for monks, clergy, and laity.

Finally, Tiberius A.iii presents a fascinating case for considering Old English apocrypha in manuscript contexts. As previously noted, the most prominent apocryphon in this collection is an Old English version of the *Sunday Letter*, included in a block of anonymous, Ælfrician, and Wulfstanian preaching texts. Taking account of the many other contents also reveals significant connections to apocryphal traditions and their uses for Anglo-Saxons interested in knowledge of biblical subjects. Most notably, Heide Estes has called attention to several Old English passages containing information about biblical topics throughout this and other manuscripts with many of the same and similar materials.[139] In Tiberius A.iii, these passages explicate details about Adam's life, size at creation, and ages at major events, women in the Bible, Noah's descendants, the ages of the world, special fast days, the ages of Mary at major events, and the names of the criminals crucified with Jesus, as well as dimensions for Noah's Ark, Saint Peter's Church, and Solomon's Temple.[140] Variants of some of these passages appear in other manuscripts, but some (the Adam

---

136 For CCCC 367, see NRK, 63; and *ASM*, 100.
137 Grant, *Cambridge, Corpus Christi College 41*; Keefer, "Margin as Archive"; and Billett, *The Divine Office in Anglo-Saxon England, 597–c. 1000*, 220–51.
138 Ibid., 226.
139 Estes, "Anglo-Saxon Biblical Lore."
140 Edited ibid., 643–7.

riddle and details about his size, the list of biblical women, and information for fast days) are unique to Tiberius A.iii.[141]

Although Estes calls these extracts "biblical lore," they might more properly be called "para-biblical lore," as they demonstrate how biblical, apocryphal, and patristic writings fuse into accretive traditions suitable for medieval learning. Moreover, passages in Tiberius A.iii represent only a portion of related lore found in a variety of Old English, Anglo-Latin, and Hiberno-Latin texts.[142] Apocryphal traditions like these were simply part of early medieval study of the Bible. It is in this setting – among other apocryphal media used to understand the Bible – that we find sermons like the version of the *Sunday Letter* in Tiberius A.iii.

Other items in Tberius A.iii allow for further situating the apocryphal contents within wider contexts of Anglo-Saxon culture, even indicating the type of textual community in which these para-biblical materials were deemed useful. In describing this manuscript, N.R. Ker notes that "This is certainly a manuscript described in the medieval catalogue of Christ Church, Canterbury" – a booklist composed by Henry Eastry, prior from 1284 to 1331.[143] During the middle and second half of the eleventh century, eight scribes working at the Christ Church monastery compiled, corrected, and annotated Tiberius A.iii, made up of three separate sections bound together by the early twelfth century.[144] In addition to the selection of vernacular sermons, the general contents of the manuscript confirm the appropriateness of the miscellany for monastic use: for example, the *Regula Benedicti* and *Regularis Concordia* (both with Old English glosses), as well as excerpts from scientific texts (prognostica and computistica), handbooks for confessors, penitentials, prayers, charms, Ælfric's *Colloquy*, a translation of Bede's *De temporibus*, Fulgentius's *Injunction*, and Benedict of Aniane's *Memoriale*. Many of these are translated into or glossed with Old English, demonstrating both the bilingualism of the monastic life and direct interaction with this manuscript as a used book. Situated among these contents, it seems likely that the vernacular sermons,

---

141 See notes to Estes's edition, as well as parallels, in ibid., 633.

142 On sources and analogues, see ibid., 634.

143 NRK, 186; for the catalogue, see James, *The Ancient Libraries of Canterbury and Dover*, 13–142, with Tiberius A.iii (no. 296) at 50 and identified at 508.

144 In addition to NRK, see description in Estes, "Anglo-Saxon Biblical Lore," 630–1; and extended description in Robertson and Da Rold, "London, British Library, Cotton Tiberius A. iii." Scragg identifies eight distinct scribes in *A Conspectus of Scribal Hands Writing English, 960–1100*, 540–6.

including the *Sunday Letter*, were considered useful for reading or preaching individually or communally. In addition, the para-biblical texts were likely viewed as part of a sort of collection *de natura rerum*, made up of notes on prognostic, computistic, scientific, and biblical knowledge characteristic of monastic learning.

Conclusions

From the evidence of the collections discussed in this chapter, there is no reason to believe that Anglo-Saxon compilers viewed apocrypha in any way distinct from other types of preaching texts. Sources used for preaching in both Latin homiliaries and Old English collections reveal not modern categorical boundaries but texts viewed as useful for teaching. Sermons based on apocrypha share the same pages and bindings as sermons based on the writings of revered patristic and early medieval exegetes. Furthermore, the collections containing apocryphal sermons demonstrate a range of contexts, purposes, and uses for diverse groups of society, many of which overlap (e.g., male and female, monastic and lay). In some of these contexts we find connections to the liturgy, for the common mass as well as monastic Offices, further cutting across classes of society and types of worship. Apocryphal sermons were not esoteric texts to be kept from the people, solely for the study of those who could read and understand well, but were intended for many different occasions and situations for teaching Christian belief and practice.

Returning to network theory, all of the media discussed in this chapter finally provide a sense of a complex overall picture. The results of depicting the connections between Latin and Old English preaching collections and apocrypha as a graph are displayed in figure 3.

The visual graph of this media network depicts two sets of nodes: those representing manuscripts and those representing apocrypha in these collections. Between nodes, lines connect apocrypha and manuscripts to each other to represent relationships. In addition, nodes are represented by size dependent on demonstrative numbers: the size of an apocryphon node is determined by the number of versions of that text within the corpus discussed, and the size of a manuscript node is determined by the number of apocryphal texts included in that collection.

While not meant to be comprehensive, this visualization presents a robust illustration for conceptualizing the existence of apocrypha in preaching media as they would have been accessible for Anglo-Saxons. None of the connective lines within this network visualization are meant to

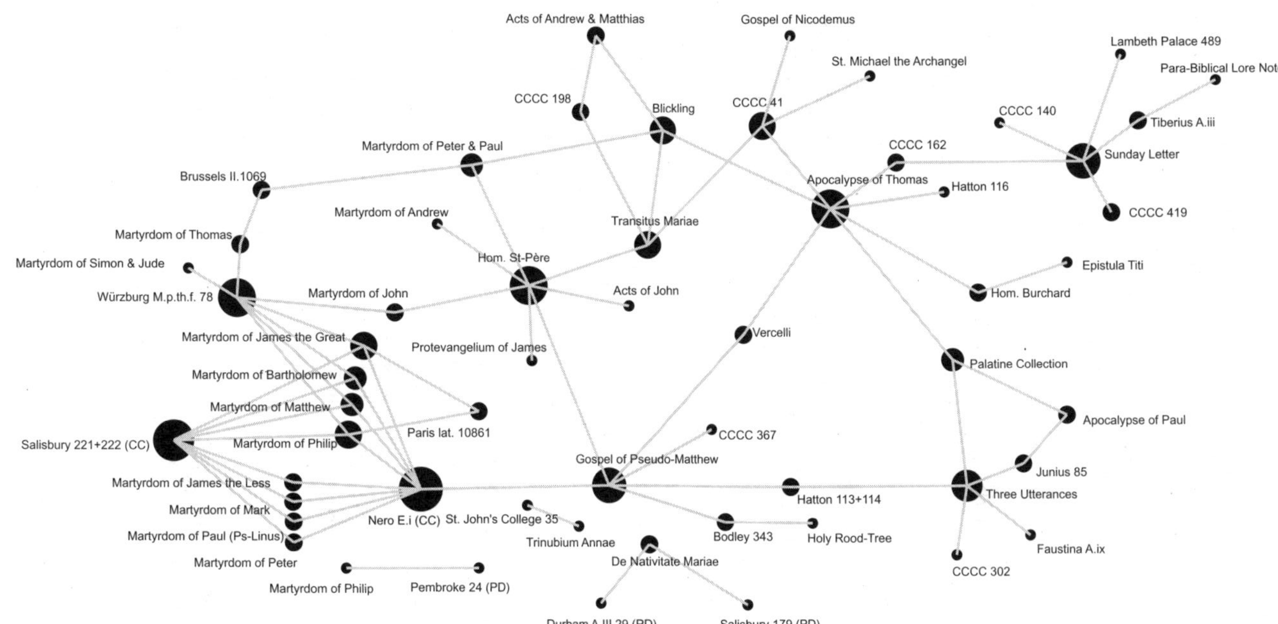

Figure 3 Network visualization of apocrypha in Latin and Old English preaching collections with Anglo-Saxon associations.

suggest direct sources, but to depict the ways in which each version of an apocryphon relates intertextually, in reference to other iterations and manuscripts. As Albert-László Barabási claims, "The construction and structure of graphs or networks is the key to understanding the complex world around us. Small changes in the topology, affecting only a few of the nodes or links, can open up hidden doors, allowing new possibilities to emerge."[145] This claim is certainly true of apocrypha in preaching collections: viewing the network with only Latin or only Old English texts does present a complex system, but neither reveals all of the connections. This visualization usefully exhibits the necessity of simultaneously considering vernacular and Latin sermons together: the whole picture of interconnectedness is incomprehensible without viewing these associations concurrently. Moreover, this is only a portion of the whole network. Since specific, immediate textual sources often remain elusive, and the number of lost manuscripts is indeterminate, it is safe to assume that Anglo-Saxons had access to, read, and relied on other versions of these apocrypha that have not survived. In the chapters to follow, I examine several select sermons within this network, but this is a useful reminder that these are only a few demonstrative examples from a much wider network of preaching apocrypha in Anglo-Saxon England.

---

145 Barabási, *Linked*, 12.

Chapter Two

Apostles, Trinity, and Reform in Blickling 15

Of the apocryphal narratives addressed in this study, extra-biblical acts of apostles held the most direct and lasting influence on Christian worship, since they were extensively used in hagiographical collections, liturgical readings, and preaching texts.[1] Tellingly, apocryphal acts became intertwined in Christian traditions that transmitted the role of institutionalized, apostolic authority. Beyond the liturgical cycle itself, preaching these saints' lives most expressly communicates the apostles as key to the life of the church; naturally, elements of apostolic narratives became integrally linked to the tradition of *imitatio Christi*, since the apostles themselves were the first to adhere to the faith. By relying on apocryphal acts, Anglo-Saxon preachers became conduits for apostolic lessons; yet preachers also shaped these lessons through adaptive translations. In the present chapter, I examine this type of translation with the case of Blickling 15, an adaptation of the *Martyrdom of Peter and Paul* representing intersections of the veneration of the apostles and the teaching of Trinitarian doctrine as a manifestation of ecclesiastical reform agendas in late tenth-century England.[2]

---

1 On widespread influences of apostolic apocrypha in medieval Europe, see esp. Rose, *Ritual Memory*.

2 The only other extended adaptation of an apostolic apocryphon in the Vercelli and Blickling collections appears in Blickling 18 (19 in *BH* because of renumbering since Morris's edition; see NRK, 382), about Andrew and Matthias in the land of cannibalistic Mermedonians. This sermon has received much scholarly attention: recently, for example, see DeGregorio, "*Þegenlic* or *flæsclic*"; Friesen, "The Sources and Analogues of the Old English *Andreas*" and "Legends and Liturgy in the Old English Prose Andreas." For overviews and bibliography on Andrew in Anglo-Saxon England, see Faerber, "Les *Acta apocrypha apostolorum* dans le corpus littéraire vieil-anglais"; bibliography on *Andreas* in Remley, "The Vercelli Book and Its Texts," 328–46; and Cataldi, "St Andrew in the Old English Homiletic Tradition."

While Blickling 15 exemplifies a traditional view of textual translation – and, by extension, transmission – from source to target language, it also typifies how many translators deliberately adapt sources for fresh presentation to new audiences. In terms of media studies, this type of translation represents an intra-medial process of transmission, not crossing boundaries of media but using the same form of communication, despite the language differences.[3] Within any network, the most basic elements are two adjacent nodes connected by associations; in the case of translation, this is representative of source and target texts. The process of translation, then, takes place within the wider media network as a fundamental form of connectivity between two nodes. For the *Martyrdom* and Blickling 15, this link is a direct association, which also facilitates the wider network: as seen in the previous chapter, this link is just one among many that form between related apocryphal media. Examining the particular conceptual link between the two texts focuses in from the big data previously explored, in order to understand the fine points of connection in the process of translation that form the fundamentals of the larger network of transmission.

Central to this argument is the assumption that all translation is ideological, and that adaptation necessarily plays a part in the process. As Lawrence Venuti has demonstrated, the long history of translation that has focused on fidelity has missed the mark, since meaning is more appropriately found in the ideological differences between source and target texts.[4] To ignore adaptations in the work of translation is to render a translator's ideology invisible. Processes of adaptation become both obvious and significant when considering Blickling 15 in relation to the apocryphal *Martyrdom of Peter and Paul*, as this chapter explains the ideological hermeneutics behind their differences. The most important changes that the author of Blickling 15 undertook when translating the Latin *Martyrdom* into Old English are signalled by the fact that narrative plots are cut while speeches by the apostles Peter and Paul are retained – creating moments in which apostolic teaching about the Trinity stands out from the rest of the sermon's content. Beyond preaching Trinitarian doctrine, Blickling 15 also demonstrates how apostolic speech may be used as a didactic medium, since the author's appropriation of apostolic voices lends significant authority to the lesson. Preaching texts like Blickling 15 remediate the authority of the apostles by emphasizing their voices. Moreover,

---

3 See McLuhan on "Media as Translators" in *Understanding Media*, chapter 6.
4 Venuti, *The Translator's Invisibility*.

I suggest that setting moments of Trinitarian devotion in Blickling 15 in relation to tenth-century upsurges of apostolic veneration and Trinitarian thought indicates the cultural significance of this sermon within the milieu of reform during the period. By revealing the task of the translator as a visible process of adaptation, I demonstrate the ideological relationships between this sermon and the cultural currents of the tenth century.

In discussions of the Trinity in Anglo-Saxon England, the anonymous sermons of the Vercelli and Blickling collections have remained underappreciated, as has the role of the anonymous sermons in relation to early medieval theology. In her study of Ælfric's theology, Lynne Grundy claims that "The doctrine [of the Trinity] is virtually absent from the Blickling collection, in which even trinitarian doxology is rare (occurring only at the end of XV and XIX)."[5] Similarly, Barbara C. Raw's *Trinity and Incarnation in Anglo-Saxon Art and Thought* focuses mainly on the works of Ælfric and Wulfstan, with only brief gestures towards anonymous sermons.[6] Yet widespread evocations of Trinitarian doctrine in the Vercelli and Blickling sermons necessitate a reconsideration of this issue.[7] For Blickling 15, this neglect also bears on the need to reassess scholarly attitudes towards apocryphal materials and Christian orthodoxy. Far from heterodox, in fact, the *Martyrdom of Peter and Paul* is just the type of text that challenges modern assumptions. Contrary to scholarly biases towards apocrypha as unorthodox – even heterodox – I argue that the *Martyrdom* and, subsequently, Blickling 15 contain elements in direct correlation with orthodox theology that ecclesiastical reformers hoped to promote. For the author of Blickling 15, the *Martyrdom* was a useful work for expounding necessary doctrine; because it facilitated teaching Trinitarian orthodoxy through the words of venerated apostles, the *Martyrdom* found an appropriate place in the corpus of vernacular preaching in an era focused on reformation.

Before turning to an examination of Blickling 15, the following sections establish some critical background. First, I provide an overview of

---

5 Grundy, *Books and Grace*, 26.

6 Raw, *Trinity and Incarnation in Anglo-Saxon Art and Thought*. Raw briefly cites passages from Vercelli 3 and 16, as well as Blickling 1–3, 5–7, 9–12, and 15, but rarely with analysis; see 52–3 for her most extended discussion of Trinitarian themes in the Blickling sermons.

7 In contrast to previous scholarship, Forbes offers an exemplary consideration of anonymous vernacular sermons among other sources in *Heaven and Earth in Anglo-Saxon England.*

scholarship about the genre of apostolic acts in order to set up the significance of speech as an aspect of both the *Martyrdom* and the Old English translation. Second, I establish the contexts of apostolic veneration and apostolic apocrypha in Anglo-Saxon England, particularly significant for understanding the cultural currents surrounding Blickling 15. The contexts I discuss in these first two sections address traditions about apostles relevant for both this chapter and the next, since Ælfric also engaged with these acts in his sermons. Third, I discuss the transmission of the apocryphal *Martyrdom of Peter and Paul* in Anglo-Saxon England generally, as well as specifically for the Anglo-Saxon author of Blickling 15 – including my assumptions about the text available to the author of the sermon and the general adaptations that the author undertook when translating. Following discussion of these backgrounds, I provide detailed formal analyses of those passages most central for my claims about Trinitarian content and the central doctrinal emphasis of Blickling 15. Finally, in the last section of this chapter, I situate the central Trinitarian elements of Blickling 15 within the contexts of late tenth-century reform agendas, in order to argue for the relevance of such a Trinitarian sermon in that milieu.

Genre and Speeches in Apocryphal Acts

When considering apocryphal acts, it is necessary to address major methodological concerns that have dominated modern scholarship, especially concerning the origins and definitions of the genre.[8] In this regard, scholarly attention has focused particularly on associations with ancient historical fictions.[9] Biblical and apocryphal acts – like gospels – are part of a widespread literary phenomenon that proliferated in Mediterranean literature for several centuries before the advent of early Christianity. This literature, including Greco-Roman and Jewish works, may be characterized by combinations of history and fiction, and, often for ideological reasons, included "a particular attitude toward the uses of the past in service

---

8 For summaries of scholarship, see esp. *NTA*, 1:50–61 and 2:75–100; Jan N. Bremmer, "The Five Major Apocryphal Acts"; Gounelle, "Actes Apocryphes des Apôtres et *Actes des Apôtres* canoniques: État de la recherche et perspectives nouvelles (I)" and "Actes Apocryphes des Apôtres et *Actes des Apôtres* canoniques: État de la recherche et perspectives nouvelles (II)"; and Rose, *Ritual Memory*, 23–78.

9 I prefer the term "historical fiction" to others (e.g., "novel" or "romance"), following Sara Raup Johnson, *Historical Fictions and Hellenistic Jewish Identity*. See also Brant, Hedrick, and Shea, eds., *Ancient Fiction*.

of the needs of the present" – especially related to the construction of communal identities.[10] As stories revolving around the historical heroes of early Christian communities, acts of apostles constitute a specific genre related to the larger category of ancient fictions. To be sure, these acts share some formal and generic characteristics with Greco-Roman parallels, and these issues have preoccupied scholars seeking to trace evolutionary lines between the two literary types. Nonetheless, no clear evidence for specific connections has emerged.[11]

Considering apocryphal acts in medieval cultures also necessitates accounting for scholarly distinctions between acts and hagiography. Much discussion has to do with chronological delimitations in definitions of apocrypha, and the issue is largely connected to the rise of cults of the saints and the transition from early Christian narratives of the apostles to more widespread veneration of saints in the late antique and early medieval periods.[12] This problem is most directly cut through by a return to the definition of apocrypha set forth in the introduction to this study, particularly the essential element that apocrypha are related to the events and characters of the canonical Bible. Stories about the apostles clearly fit this definition, regardless of genres and chronologies. As Els Rose contends, for medieval readers, "Apocryphal Acts of the apostles are by definition additions to or prolongations of the biblical canon: they continue where the biblical story ends."[13] Just as these stories were not composed as categorically "apocryphal," they also were not necessarily perceived this way by medieval authors. This approach, then, shifts the focus of modern scholarly debates in order to centralize apostolic narratives as one genre within the broader corpus of apocryphal literature received and adapted in the Christian tradition.

10 Johnson, *Historical Fictions and Hellenistic Jewish Identity*, xiv. Cf. Thomas, *The Acts of Peter, Gospel Literature, and the Ancient Novel*.

11 Scholars have singled out broad characteristics across a variety of comparable texts, but arguments often fall apart when the focus is shifted to particulars; see Johnson, *Historical Fictions and Hellenistic Jewish Identity*, 1–7; and Thomas, *The Acts of Peter, Gospel Literature, and the Ancient Novel*, 3–13.

12 The classic study of the rise of saints' cults remains Peter Brown, *The Cult of the Saints*; for summaries of scholarship, see esp. Stephen Wilson, "Annotated Bibliography"; and, more specifically relevant for this chapter, Eastman, *Paul the Martyr*, passim; and idem, *The Ancient Martyrdom Accounts of Peter and Paul*.

13 Rose, *Ritual Memory*, 41.

Setting aside debates about origins and definitions of apocryphal acts, what matters most for the present study, above all, is the reception of apocryphal acts by Anglo-Saxon sermon authors.[14] With this starting point in mind, what becomes obvious is that medieval sermon authors viewed *content* as the most important element for translations.[15] François Bovon has recently offered a detailed comparison of the acts of apostles, examining both biblical and apocryphal texts together for tropological similarities and differences. He points out that major characteristics include the episodic nature of the narratives and special attention to geography, as well as emphasis on the ministry of the apostles, especially through signs and miracles, speeches, and passions.[16] These last three elements, as will be seen, are particularly appealing for preachers, since they present models for moral living as well as opportunities to proclaim the words of the saints.

Scholars of early Christianity have singled out speeches as one of the predominant features of apostolic acts, and an important one within the development of Christian literature more broadly. Averil Cameron, for example, has discussed this element of rhetoric and observed, "One feature of the apocryphal Acts that is particularly striking ... is the degree of self-consciousness they too display toward speech, preaching, and indeed language."[17] Because Cameron's main interest is in the literary narratives of these stories, she emphasizes speeches in the acts as central moments of rhetoric for both authors and audiences. Recently, Richard I. Pervo has also singled out speeches as a chief rhetorical element in apocryphal acts, and Bovon has discussed how speeches are fundamental to depictions of apostolic ministry in both canonical and apocryphal acts.[18] Such scholarship demonstrates that apostolic speeches address not only the original audiences of the stories but also the later readers and hearers of the narratives.

---

14 On the importance of receptions of apocryphal acts, see Bovon and Junod, "Reading the Apocryphal Acts," 169–70; and Rose, *Ritual Memory*.

15 Cf. an emphasis on narrative in Cameron, *Christianity and the Rhetoric of Empire*, 89–119.

16 Bovon, "Canonical and Apocryphal Acts of Apostles."

17 Cameron, *Christianity and the Rhetoric of Empire*, 94.

18 Pervo, "Rhetoric in the Christian Apocrypha"; and Bovon, "Canonical and Apocryphal Acts of Apostles," esp. 203. For sustained studies of speech in the biblical book of Acts, see Pervo, "Direct Speech in Acts and the Question of Genre"; and Witherington, *New Testament Rhetoric*, 44–93.

Speeches are also central to the adaptation of apocryphal acts in Old English sermons, as Anglo-Saxon preachers used these discourses to exhort contemporary audiences. The apostolic primacy of speech in the Christian tradition is evident even in Jesus' Great Commission to the apostles, as related in Mathew, Mark, and Luke,[19] and preaching is inherently linked to apostolic succession for early Christian and medieval views of the clergy. The significance of teaching is especially pronounced in the cases of Peter and Paul, viewed as direct successors of Christ in Christian tradition.[20] These two figures hold special apostolic legitimacy, which was institutionalized in the early church along with stories about them in apocryphal acts. In this characteristic, acts of apostles present a special genre of apocrypha that is particularly embedded and authorized in Christian traditions from an early era through the medieval period. As Jesus taught, so the apostles continued this ministry in the world, exemplified in the apostolic acts, and Anglo-Saxon preachers extended this duty to their own people. For the author of Blickling 15, this duty consisted of addressing fundamental Christian doctrines remediated through the authoritative words of Peter and Paul.

Apostles in Anglo-Saxon England

The preeminence of apostles for Anglo-Saxon religious teaching should also be understood in light of the historical development of saints' cults in early England.[21] Not surprisingly, veneration of apostles was predominant and widespread throughout the whole of the Anglo-Saxon period.[22] Apostolic saints' cults form their own network of associations that prove to be far flung and deeply influential in all manner of media. In fact, as Alan Thacker (echoing Wilhelm Levinson) observes, the earliest commemorations of saints in Anglo-Saxon England were mainly related

---

19 Matthew 10:7 and 28:19, Mark 16:15, and Luke 24:47.
20 See, for example, Cubitt, "Images of St Peter."
21 On saints' cults in Anglo-Saxon England, see esp. Rollason, *Saints and Relics in Anglo-Saxon England*; Lapidge, "The Saintly Life in Anglo-Saxon England"; and Hayward, "Saints and Cults."
22 While there is not yet a comprehensive examination of apostles in Anglo-Saxon England, see esp. Thacker, "In Search of Saints"; and O'Leary, "Apostolic *Passiones* in Early Anglo-Saxon England."

to the apostles: "apart from Martin and Gregory himself, almost all of the recorded dedications in England in the seventh and eighth centuries are to the apostles – Peter, Paul, Andrew, Matthew and Bartholomew, to the Blessed Virgin, or to early Roman martyrs – Laurence, Pancras, and the Quattuor Coronati."[23] This trend continued until the late eighth century, when local saints' cults began to emerge in the English landscape. Significantly, Peter, Paul, Andrew, Bartholomew, John, and Thomas were especially prominent figures throughout these early centuries of Anglo-Saxon Christianity, as various English figures, both lay and ecclesiastical, made pilgrimages to Rome to venerate them, dedicated new ecclesiastical sites to them, received relics associated with them, adopted them as special patrons, assembled collections of their *passiones*, and composed dedicatory poems in their honour.[24] All of these commemorations signal what Peter Brown has observed as the Christian recognition of the *praesentia* and *potentia* of saints.[25]

Sustained interest in the apostles in early England is especially evident in a variety of media from the eighth through the eleventh centuries, including collections of *passiones* and martyrologies.[26] In particular, apocryphal traditions about the apostles largely derive from acts composed from the second century onward, relating the deeds and martyrdoms of the earliest saints. Especially important for the transmission of apocryphal acts is the collection known as the *Virtutes apostolorum*, which circulated widely throughout the early medieval period.[27] Representative of Old English poetry concerned with apostles are *Andreas* and Cynewulf's *Fates of the Apostles*, both contained alongside the sermons of the Vercelli Book.[28] In

---

23 Thacker, "In Search of Saints," 258; cf. Levison, *England and the Continent in the Eighth Century*, 259–65.

24 See Thacker, "In Search of Saints," 259–64 and 269–76; and O'Leary, "Apostolic *Passiones* in Early Anglo-Saxon England."

25 See Brown, *The Cult of the Saints*, esp. 86–127.

26 See O'Leary, "Apostolic *Passiones* in Early Anglo-Saxon England"; and entries in *SASLC Apocrypha*, 37–56. See also an important representative text in Rauer, ed. and trans., *The Old English Martyrology*, with further historical context in the introduction.

27 *CANT*, 256. No critical edition exists, although a team led by Els Rose is currently preparing one. See discussion and references in chapter 1. My thanks to Els Rose for sharing and discussing her work with me.

28 Both edited in Brooks, *Andreas and the Fates of the Apostles*.

the visual arts, representations of the apostles remained a staple through-out the entire period.[29] All of these media speak to the associations that help to contextualize sermons and the various types of knowledge that Anglo-Saxons would have had access to concerning the apostles.

In the late tenth century and into the eleventh, a recognizable increase in the veneration of saints and their cults occurred – especially associated with local saints. Concepts of sanctity at the time were, as David Rollason has shown, associated with ecclesiastical reforms, which will be further explored in relation to Blickling 15 towards the end of this chapter.[30] What was most emphasized by reformers of the period was reorganization of ecclesiastical structures, revival of monastic life, standardization of the lit-urgy, and improvements to doctrinal education through preaching. For the latter, literary output particularly reflects these developments, and the evidence of hagiographic accounts in Old English sermon collections is es-pecially significant.[31] While the increase of literary evidence from this pe-riod may merely reflect a loss of earlier materials or a lack of Old English prose in earlier eras, it just as likely indicates the significant increase in saints' cults and attention to literary sources revolving around the saints in general and the apostles in particular.

Blickling 15 and Its Source

As already mentioned, the author of Blickling 15 relied for his work on the Latin *Martyrdom of Peter and Paul*, attributed to Marcellus in some

---

29 See esp. Higgitt, "The Iconography of St. Peter in Anglo-Saxon England, and St. Cuthbert's Coffin"; Lang, "The Apostles in Anglo-Saxon Sculpture in the Age of Alcuin"; Henderson, "The Representations of the Apostles in Insular Art, with Special Reference to the New Apostles Frieze at Tarbat, Ross-shire"; and Biggs, "A Picture of Paul in a Parker Manuscript."

30 Rollason, *Saints and Relics in Anglo-Saxon England*, esp. 164–95.

31 For literary evidence, see esp. Whatley, "An Introduction to the Study of Old English Prose Hagiography"; Scragg, "The Corpus of Anonymous Lives and Their Manuscript Context"; Lapidge and Love, "The Latin Hagiography of England and Wales (600–1550)," 216–23; Whatley, "Acta Sanctorum," *SASLC 1*, 22–486; and Hall, "Latin Sermons for Saints in Early English Homiliaries and Legendaries." See also sermons under the headings of relevant names in DiNapoli, *An Index of Theme and Image to the Homilies of the Anglo-Saxon Church*.

manuscripts.[32] This text (like related recensions in Greek)[33] relates the story of a confrontation between the apostles Peter and Paul and the magician Simon Magus, who gained the support of Emperor Nero in Rome. It features a duel of wits, magic, miracles, and prayer between the key figures of the narrative, as both sides attempt to win over Nero while death is on the line. The story ends with Simon Magus's death, the fury of Nero, and the emperor's execution of the two apostles. This narrative was popular throughout the late antique, medieval, and early modern periods, and Simon Magus was a staple figure for authors seeking a type to associate with heresy.[34] Influencing Old English compositions, the *Martyrdom* was used as a source for not only Blickling 15 but also Ælfric's *Passio apostolorum Petri et Pauli* (*CH* I.26) and *De auguriis*, Wulfstan's *De temporibus Antichristi*, and the prose *Solomon and Saturn*. It is also the source of a Latin prayer excerpted in the *Book of Cerne*.[35] All of these media amount to substantial evidence for the popularity and use of the story in Anglo-Saxon England, as well as to other artefacts related to Blickling 15 through intermedial relationships.

The possibilities for the circulation of the Latin *Martyrdom* in Anglo-Saxon England are myriad. Unfortunately, despite the abundant evidence for its transmission in Anglo-Saxon media, no manuscript containing the *Martyrdom* survives from early England. But the apocryphon was included

---

32 *BHL*, 6659; and *CANT*, 193. References by chapter numbers are to the Latin edition in Lipsius and Bonnet, eds., *Acta Apostolorum Apocrypha*, 1:118–77. See also *NTA*, 2:440–2; Thomas, *The Acts of Peter, Gospel Literature, and the Ancient Novel*; Baldwin, *Whose Acts of Peter?*; D'Anna, "The Relationship between the Greek and Latin Recensions of the *Acta Petri et Pauli*"; and, most recently, introduction, text (reprinted from Lipsius and Bonnet, eds., *Acta Apostolorum*), and translation in Eastman, *The Ancient Martyrdom Accounts of Peter and Paul*, 221–70.

33 For Greek texts (printed opposite the Latin on facing pages), see Lipsius and Bonnet, eds., *Acta Apostolorum Apocrypha*, ed. 1:118–77; cf. text (reprinted from ibid.) and translation of Greek B in Eastman, *The Ancient Martyrdom Accounts of Peter and Paul*, 271–316. See introductory material in Lipsius and Bonnet, eds., *Acta Apostolorum Apocrypha*; Lipsius, *Die Quellen der römischen Petrus-Saga* and *Die apokryphen Apostelgeschichten und Apostellegenden*.

34 On Simon Magus, see Ferreiro, *Simon Magus in Patristic, Medieval, and Early Modern Traditions*, with brief references to Blickling 15 throughout.

35 See "Pseudo-Marcellus Martyrdom of Peter and Paul," *SASLC Apocrypha*; and Lionarons, *The Homiletic Writings of Archbishop Wulfstan*, 63–7, which includes brief discussions of Blickling 15 and Ælfric's *Passio apostolorum Petri et Pauli*, and a more extensive examination of Wulfstan's *De temporibus Antichristi*.

in certain Continental manuscripts of the *Virtutes apostolorum* known to the Anglo-Saxons: for example, the palimpsest Brussels, Bibliothèque Royale, II. 1069, fols. 59–97, written in an eighth-century Anglo-Saxon hand.[36] Given the transmission of the various acts of apostles from this collection more generally, there is good evidence that it was surely known in England. In addition, the *Martyrdom* also circulated independently in many early Continental manuscripts (see appendix 1).[37]

As with many cases of apocryphal sources, we are left with a slight complication about the textual witness that the Anglo-Saxon translator would have encountered and how to approach a comparison of differences. As Biggs and Hall comment, "Without the Latin manuscript from which the [Blickling 15] translation was made, it is impossible to know if the translator was responsible for the change[s]."[38] Two factors help to mitigate this uncertainty in a comparison of the texts. First, when Blickling 15 does correspond to the *Martyrdom*, it is a close rendering of the text as represented by majority readings from manuscripts, suggesting the probability that the Anglo-Saxon author relied on a copy conforming to known witnesses.[39] Second, what emerges from close textual comparisons of Blickling 15 and the Latin *Martyrdom* is a pattern in the sermon author's handling of speeches that is difficult to dismiss as accidental or coincidental. Instead, these differences may be taken as adaptations reflecting the ideological purposes of the translator.

My methodological assumption, therefore, is that when the Old English text diverges from its source with substantial narrative changes, it may be understood as deliberate adaptation on the part of the Anglo-Saxon translator. As comparisons that strengthen this point, adaptations of the Latin *Martyrdom* into Old English sermons by Ælfric and Wulfstan portray

---

36 *CLA*, 10.1551. See *ASL*, 164, no. 91; and discussion in chapter 1.

37 See lists of known manuscripts of Greek and Latin versions in Lipsius and Bonnet, eds., *Acta Apostolorum Apocrypha*, lxii–lxvii and lxxv–lxxxiii; Alberto D'Anna is currently preparing a new conspectus of manuscripts.

38 Biggs and Hall, "Traditions Concerning Jamnes and Mambres in Anglo-Saxon England," 83.

39 I take as majority readings those in Lipsius and Bonnet, eds., *Acta Apostolorum Apocrypha*. This issue has to do with both manuscript collation, which deals with variants at the level of words and phrases, as well as textual versions at the level of structure and narrative (as with Greek A and B). The critical edition in ibid. considers both aspects of the *Martyrdom* (in Greek and Latin), but I consider only the latter, in relation to the Latin and Old English adaptation.

wholly different changes and consequently different theological empha-ses.[40] Such comparisons, in fact, bolster my argument that every translation is an adaptation, and that Anglo-Saxon sermon authors handled apocryphal sources in ways that reflect specific, local, pedagogical needs. In Blickling 15, certain adaptations stand out more than others – especially omissions that condense the narrative plot in favour of retaining apostolic speeches. When taken together, these adaptations indicate a conscious manipulation of the *Martyrdom* in composing Blickling 15.

I discuss important extended examples in the following examination, but some general, structural instances of adaptation portray the sermon author's conscious choices in favouring parts of the *Martyrdom* over oth-ers. The first section of the Latin *Martyrdom* (1–18) deals mainly with ex-position, establishing Peter's mission in Rome, Simon Magus's plot to stir up the Jews in Rome against the apostles, Paul's arrival in Rome, and the dramatic conflict that pervades the rest of the narrative. The Old English translation includes a condensed, paraphrased version of this exposition, relating the general plot about Paul arriving in Rome to meet Peter and the ensuing conflict with Simon Magus, and wholly omitting the story about the magician's dealings with the Jews. For whatever reason, the Blickling author found these scenes revolving around the Jews to be less useful than the apostles' later confrontations with Simon Magus. The solution, then, was to omit the details in favour of moving the narrative forward.

Another telling adaptation is how the author of Blickling 15 condenses the plot of the narrative from chapters 40–7 in the Latin text.[41] The main content of these chapters consists of dialogue between the apostles, Simon, and Nero concerning circumcision – reflecting the author's interaction with early Christian debates.[42] Yet none of this dialogue contains much substance significant to medieval Christian doctrine in the tenth century.

---

40 See Faerber, "Les *Acta Apocrypha apostolorum* dans le corpus homilétique vieil-anglais (x^e–xie s.), Ælfric"; Ogawa, "Hagiography in Homily"; Lionarons, *The Homiletic Writings of Archbishop Wulfstan*, 63–7; and further discussion in chapter 5.

41 Biggs and Hall, "Traditions Concerning Jamnes and Mambres in Anglo-Saxon England," 83 n. 52, also briefly note this omission.

42 Although major discussions about the circumcision of Jews and Gentiles were not current at the time of the composition of the *Martyrdom* (fourth or fifth century), this section likely reflects a desire to situate the narrative in the contexts of the earlier apostolic period (cf. Paul's epistles). This passage probably indicates an authenticating gesture on the part of the author looking toward the past. On discussions of circumci-sion in Anglo-Saxon England, see Zacher, "Circumscribing the Text."

The Anglo-Saxon author, recognizing the subject's lack of appropriateness for the new audience, excludes it, instead glossing over the whole episode with one brief sentence: "Æfter þyssum wæron manegu geflitu" (187.6–7: "After this there were many disputes").

Despite the Blickling 15 author's reliance on speeches over plot, some strategic changes also occur in the speeches. The longest and most complex speech incorporated into the sermon is Paul's, in which he refutes Simon Magus and recounts his own teachings (183.31–185.35; Latin 33–8). In translating this speech for the Anglo-Saxon audience, the sermon author carefully adapts it through a series of omissions and paraphrases, retaining and emphasizing only the elements most useful for doctrinal instruction. For example, as Biggs and Hall have demonstrated, the extended comparison between Simon and the magicians Jamnes and Mambres from chapter 34 is omitted.[43] The adaptations in Blickling 15 are strategic, and the results create a speech that emphasizes the contrast between the devil and God as the respective teachers of Simon and Paul, as well as the orthodox teachings of Paul as mediator of God's doctrines. With these structural differences in mind, I now turn to other adaptations by the sermon author that support my general argument about the use of apostolic speech for authority and Trinitarian doctrine.

Apostolic Authority

The *Martyrdom* consistently emphasizes Peter's status as apostolic leader and Paul's status as teacher, establishing the preeminence of these apostles for church history and doctrine. The first indication of the authority of the apostles in Blickling 15 is the frame added as an introduction to the sermon. The sermon begins, "Men þa leofestan, weorðian we on þissum andweardan dæge Sancte Petres Cristes apostola ealdormannes þrowungtide" (171.2–4: "Dearest beloved, on this present day we venerate the passion of Saint Peter the prince of the apostles of Christ"). While the next line is cut off, due to a binder's trimming the top of the manuscript page, the sermon presumably also addresses Paul's status here. Following this opening are further declarations about Peter and Paul: "se is oþer cyricean hyrde to Cristes handa, oþer is hire lareow. Oþer is, ic cweþe, se æresta apostol,

---

43 See Biggs and Hall, "Traditions Concerning Jamnes and Mambres in Anglo-Saxon England," 83. Comparatively, Ælfric appropriates this image from the *Martyrdom* while condemning magic in his sermon *De auguriis* (*LS* 17, lines 114–21).

oþer is se nehsta: Petrus ær Cristes þrowunga, & Paulus æfter his upas-tignesse" (171.5–8: "the one is the shepherd of the church at the hand of Christ, the other is her teacher. One is, I say, the first apostle, the other is the last: Peter before the Passion of Christ, and Paul after his Ascension"). At the same time as these claims venerate the two apostles, they also lend authority to their words and deeds related in the following narrative.

Implied in this introduction is the belief that Peter and Paul are the two exemplary models of faith next to Christ himself – as his direct disciples, they present logical extensions of Jesus' teachings. The notions of Peter as the "first apostle" and Paul as the "last apostle" derive from Paul's own discussion of the revelation of the gospel in 1 Corinthians 15:8. In this epistle, Paul writes about his revelatory encounter with the resurrected Christ – "novissime autem omnium tamquam abortivo visus est et mihi" ("And last of all, he was seen also by me, as by one born out of due time") – because he needed to justify his role as an apostle in distinction from those who encountered Jesus during his life. Paul was the last apostle called, and the last to witness Jesus after his Resurrection and Ascension, through special divine revelation. This was the widespread view of the medieval church, linked with the notion that Paul was the last teacher, on which his authority was based for succeeding generations. Indeed, this trend is apparent throughout the rest of the sermon: Paul is the main spokesman for doctrinal teachings, while Peter is the rock that affirms the legitimacy of Paul's authority.

Affirmations of the preeminence of Peter and Paul for Christians are abundant in early Christian and medieval texts. One related instance is found at the end of the anonymous preface to the *Virtutes apostolorum*, known as *Licet plurima*.[44] After giving a justification for the collection, the author relates how the collection will begin: "Ergo nos in huius Iesu Christi filii omnipotentis nomine cum adiutorio spiritus sancti ab ipso principum principe Petro sumamus exordium" ("Therefore, in the name of this Jesus Christ, the Son of the Almighty God, with the help of the Holy Spirit, let us start with the prince of princes: Peter").[45] This

---

44 *BHL*, 6663.

45 I quote from Wolfenbüttel, Herzog August Bibliothek, Weissenburg 48 (s. ix²/³), fols. 10r–10v, based on the digital facsimile at *Wolfenbütteler Digitale Bibliothek*, http://diglib.hab.de/mss/48-weiss/start.htm. Cf. Junod and Kaestli, eds., *Acta Iohannis*, 1:753 n. 1. For a discussion of this prologue related to the *Virtutes apostolorum*, see Rose, "*Abdias Scriptor Vitarum Sanctorum Apostolorum?*"

prologue is particularly fascinating in relation to Blickling 15 because of its connections to the *Virtutes apostolorum* and, in turn, the connections of the Pseudo-Marcellus *Martyrdom* with the collection – however complex the versions and transmissions of Petrine and Pauline apocrypha are in this tradition.

A similar attitude of veneration also appears in Cynewulf's *Fates of the Apostles*, in which the poet places Peter and Paul as the first of the apostles enumerated.[46] After a brief introduction, Cynewulf recalls the following:

> Sume on Romebyrig,
> frame, fyrdhwate,   feor ofgefon
> þurg Nerones   nearwe searwe,
> Petrus ond Paulus;   is se apostolhad
> wide geweorðod   ofer werþeoda.

> (11b–15: Some in the city of Rome, vigorous, warlike, gave up life through the narrow deceit of Nero: Peter and Paul; that apostolic dignity [or apostolic office] is esteemed widely throughout the nations.)

Robert Boenig has pointed out the hierarchy implied in the ordering: Peter and Paul remain the archetypal apostles of Rome, as they are traditionally associated with the city.[47] This traditional association is both present within and bolstered by the *Martyrdom* and its narrative of the two apostles' passions. A further connection between Cynewulf's poem and apocrypha about Peter and Paul is the centrality of Nero as the main antagonist – though, curiously, there is no mention of Simon Magus in the poem. Most central here is the honour afforded the apostles ("geweorðod"), who are still renowned throughout the Christian world in the poet's time ("wide … ofer werþeoda"). Throughout the rest of the poem, many of the accounts are straightforward, factual retellings of the death of each apostle; yet with Peter and Paul, Cynewulf is sure to highlight their *apostolhad* from the start.

In terms of apostolic authority manifested through instruction, the most significant speeches in Blickling 15 occur after Simon Magus declares

---

46 References by line numbers are to Brooks, ed., *Andreas and the Fates of the Apostles*, 56–60.

47 Boenig, trans., *The Acts of Andrew in the Country of the Cannibals*, v–vi.

himself the Son of God and explicitly sets himself in opposition to Peter and Paul before Nero. One such moment of instruction occurs when Nero begins to question the magician and apostles about their beliefs. In the question and answer format of this section, the dialogue is reminiscent of colloquies and catechisms used to teach the basics of Christian education. As in the Latin (16: "Quid est Nazareus?"), Nero first asks, "Hwæt bið se Nazarenisca?" (175.18–19: "What is the Nazarene?"), and receives a standard response about Jesus' origin in the city of Nazareth in Judea. Nero also asks the magician why he persecutes the apostles, noting the Christian tenet, "God manaþ ælcne man & lufaþ" (175.21: "God instructs and loves each man"; Latin 17: "Deus omnem hominem monet et diliget"). The instructional content here is obvious, as even the stylized adversarial figure of Nero understands the basic commands of Christ. Also clear is the notion that Peter and Paul hold the authoritative answers to these cat-echetical questions, while Simon's answers are blasphemous distortions of the truth of the gospels.

The tension between Simon's spurious teachings and the authority of the apostles is underscored in the retention of one detail at the end of chapter 34. Here Paul says of Simon, "Þis is manna se wyrresta þe þurh de-ofles wisdom manige unware men beswiceþ mid his costungum" (185.1–3: "This is the worst of men, who through the wisdom of the devil deceives many unwary men with his temptations"). This sentence translates the Latin, "per patris sui diaboli peritiam hominibus persuadet et multa mala facit ... et sic multos incautos seducit ad temptationem" ("through the skill of his father the devil he persuades men to do many evils ... and thus seduces many incautious men to temptation"). Problems of magic in the Latin are displaced in the Old English in order to establish a clearer point about Simon's character. While not distracting the audience with the eccentric details about the problems of magic surrounding Jamnes and Mambres, the Old English still communicates Simon's diabolical char-acteristics.[48] What is more, the Latin term *peritiam* specifically signifies the sense of "knowledge gained by experience"[49] – in this case, skill that implies a type of apprenticeship with the devil. The Old English also retains this experiential quality in the term *wisdom*, an ironic rendering

---

48 See Biggs and Hall, "Traditions Concerning Jamnes and Mambres in Anglo-Saxon England," 83.

49 Lewis and Short, eds., *A Latin Dictionary*, s.v. *peritia*.

that turns the common meaning of the word (often as a gloss for *sapientia*) upon its head.[50]

The most exemplary and extended instance of the sermon author's use of apostolic authority and teaching is Paul's main speech adapted from chapter 36 of the Latin *Martyrdom*. This speech especially stands in stark contrast to the diabolic teachings of Simon that Paul condemns only moments earlier. Not surprisingly, Paul juxtaposes Simon Magus's anti-apostolic teaching with his own, which he claims is the "lare mines lareowes" (185.8: "lore of my teacher"). In rendering the language of the Latin, which relates the "doctrina" of Paul's "magistri," the author of the Old English sermon also offers a rhetorical flourish in the translation, using the paronomastic pair "lare" and "lareowes" (185.8). Adapting the source to emphasize Simon Magus's false teaching, the sermon author makes it clear that Christians must be wary of those who are aligned with the devil in their preaching. Comparably, the sermon author also makes it equally clear that Paul's own instruction is exactly the opposite of that of Simon Magus: his is authorized by the highest authority. By emphasizing the devil as Simon's master and God as Paul's master, and the two types of instruction inherent in the dichotomy, this juxtaposition establishes the basis of the following speech, which revolves around tenets from the New Testament letters.

References in Paul's main speech point to various teachings throughout his epistolary corpus, calling attention to the early formulations of Christian doctrine that pervade later traditions. This speech recalls Romans 12:10, 1 Timothy 6:17 and 6:8, 2 Corinthians 6:10 and James 1:9, Ephesians 6:1–4, Colossians 3:18–22 and Ephesians 6:1, and Romans 13:6–7, Colossians 3:18–19 and Ephesians 5:22–8, Colossians 4:1 and Ephesians 6:9, Colossians 3:22–4 and Ephesians 6:5–6, Colossians 1:15 and 1 Timothy 1:17, as well as Galatians 1:1 and 11–12 – weaving together various theological threads from the New Testament.[51] In its allusiveness, the speech is similar to the *Epistle of Paul to the Laodiceans*, a composite Latin apocryphon drawn from the letters of Paul that was often included in medieval bibles.[52] The

---

50　Toller, ed., *An Anglo-Saxon Dictionary, Based on the Manuscript Collections of the Late Joseph Bosworth*, s.v. *wisdom*.

51　See notes in Lipsius and Bonnet, eds., *Acta Apostolorum Apocrypha*, 151–3; and Eastman, *The Ancient Martyrdom Accounts of Peter and Paul*, 249–51.

52　*CANT*, 305. See *NTA*, 2:42–6; Hall, "Ælfric and the Epistle to the Laodicians"; "Epistle of Paul to the Laodiceans," *SASLC Apocrypha*, 58; and extended analysis in Tite, *The Apocryphal Epistle to the Laodiceans*, with further references there.

speech in the *Martyrdom* and Blickling 15, therefore, draws attention to, highlights, and carries weight because of its constant reliance on Paul and his authority as one of the apostles; through this speech, both texts act as direct receivers of Paul's revelation from the Resurrected Christ. The recurring Old English *ic lærde* for Latin *docui* emphasizes Paul's role as teacher, simultaneously urging the audience to reflect upon the learning they received from Paul's epistles. Beyond the emphasis on Paul's role as teacher, these allusions lend biblical authority to the speeches of the apocryphon. The *Martyrdom* is, in this respect, composed upon the orthodox tenets of the New Testament, and the author of Blickling 15 is able to retain this same foundation for his own preaching through the words of the apostles.

Paul's main doctrinal speech finally culminates in renewed emphasis on the force of divine authority behind his preaching. His last words focus on his mission as a preacher: "& þeos lar me wæs seald næs na for mannum ac þurh God sylfne. Hælende Crist & wuldres Fæder he me to bodunga sende & þus cwæþ, 'Gong þu, ic beo lifes gast on þe & on eallum rihtgely-fendum on me & on Hælendne Crist; & eall ic gerihtwisige þæt þu cwist'" (185.31–5: "And this teaching was given to me not from men but by God Himself. Christ the Saviour and the Father of Glory sent me to preach and thus said, 'Go, I shall be the Spirit of Life in you and in all righteous believers in me and in Christ the Saviour; and I will make righteous all that you say'"). This is a close translation of the Latin of chapter 38, but here we encounter a textual crux in the *Martyrdom*.[53] The Latin reads, "Vade et ego ero in te spiritus uitae omnibus credentibus in me; et omnia quaecumque dixeris aut feceris ego iustificabo," but as both Alberto D'Anna and David L. Eastman observe, there is no discernible source for the quotation in the canonical gospels or otherwise.[54] The saying does, in some ways, echo Jesus' Great Commission in Matthew 10:7 and 28:19, Mark 16:15, and Luke 24:47, and Eastman draws attention to Acts 22:21;[55] but none of these passages offers a close source. This quotation, then, is part of the larger tradition of *agrapha*, sayings of Jesus not included in the canonical gospels.[56] While most scholars tend to focus on materials from the first few centuries of Christianity for the identification of agrapha,

---

53 See D'Anna, "The Relationship between the Greek and Latin Recensions of the *Acta Petri Et Pauli*," 336–7.

54 Ibid., 337; and Eastman, *The Ancient Martyrdom Accounts of Peter and Paul*, 251 n. 55.

55 Ibid.

56 On *agrapha*, see *NTA*, 1:88–91; and Stroker, *Extracanonical Sayings of Jesus*. For summary of scholarship, see esp. Jeremias, *Unknown Sayings of Jesus*, 1–43.

this saying represents a later example. The Latin *Martyrdom* is, in fact, the only version to preserve this spurious quotation in full, although the most closely related Greek A text contains a reading which adapts the saying to conform with Acts 18:10.[57]

Two important points about Blickling 15 arise from the use of this final assertion. First, the sermon author more than takes over this quotation by adapting it. While the final phrase of the quotation in the Latin indicates God's justification of both words and deeds ("dixeris aut feceris"), the Old English adaptation simplifies to only speech ("cwist"). This adaptational technique foregrounds preaching – especially its apostolic authority, given from the divine. Second, the Anglo-Saxon sermon author saw fit to incorporate the words into Blickling 15 to the effect of an envelope pattern for the speech. The apostolic instruction begins with Paul's reliance on God as the greatest teacher, in contrast to the devil as Simon's teacher, and again at the conclusion reifies such reliance with the authoritative words of God himself. Simultaneously, this adaptation also affords the same inherited authority to the Anglo-Saxon preacher, who remediates the apostolic speech, aligning the new text with both Paul and God's inspiration.

At least three layers of voices exist in the use of Paul's main speech in the sermon: the voice of God who taught these doctrines to Paul, the voice of Paul as apostle who mediates these doctrines, and the voice of the preacher who transmits these doctrines to the Anglo-Saxon audience. By using this speech in the sermon, the author effectively calls the audience to hold to the preacher's own remediation of these teachings by invoking the highest authorities, previously given from God and mediated through his apostle. Even more than Paul's emphasis on God's instruction is the invocation of the Trinity in his conclusion. Paul thus recalls that these words came from "God himself" ("God sylfne"), and follows this up by mentioning all

---

57 D'Anna, "The Relationship between the Greek and Latin Recensions of the *Acta Petri Et Pauli*," 337. Acts 18:10 in the Vulgate reads: "propter quod ego sum tecum et nemo adponetur tibi ut noceat te quoniam populus est mihi multus in hac civitate" ("Because I am with thee and no man shall set upon thee, to hurt thee. For I have much people in this city"). The fact that this quotation is fully incorporated (unmodified) only in the Latin *Martyrdom* is one point that D'Anna uses to support the primacy of the Latin text, since the Greek versions of the *Martyrdom* appear to independently modify the quotation to provide solutions for the problems it presents ("The Relationship between the Greek and Latin Recensions of the *Acta Petri Et Pauli*," 336–7). Eastman also claims the primacy of the Latin text in *The Ancient Martyrdom Accounts of Peter and Paul*, 221–7.

three persons of the Godhead: the Son ("Hælende Crist," used twice), the Father ("wuldres Fæder"), and the Holy Spirit ("lifes gast") – all invoked together, even conflated, in this doxological conclusion to the speech. It is no wonder that the sermon author retained this detail of the speech for its essential instructional value.

Directly following Paul's main speech is further confirmation of the apostle's authority on doctrinal matters. Nero asks Peter, "Hwæt cwist þu, Petrus?" (187.1: "What do you say, Peter?"), and Peter responds, "Ealle þa word sint soþe þe Paulus sægþ. Manige gear syndon agan nu seoþþan ure bisceopas geond eal Romana rice an to me gewreoto sende, & me be his clænnesse cyþde & be his lare. Wæs he ær ehtere Cristes æ; þa gecegde hine stefn of heofenum & hine soþfastnesse lærde" (187.2–6: "All the words that Paul says are true. Many years have now gone by since our bishops throughout all of the Roman Empire sent letters to me, and told me about his purity and about his teaching. He was before a persecutor of Christ's law; then a voice from heaven saved him and taught him faithfulness"). Significantly, the detail about the bishops' letters is present only in four Greek manuscripts of the *Martyrdom*, while it is a standard feature in the Latin text,[58] and the Anglo-Saxon author retains it while also omitting the rest of the speech given in chapter 40 of the Latin *Martyrdom*. Peter's speech in the sermon thus emphasizes three things about Paul: his reputation among other Christian holy men, his famous conversion on the road to Damascus, and (recalling Paul's own assertions) his learning derived directly from a revelation from Christ. All of these aspects of the short speech lend credibility to the person of Paul as well as authority to the teachings expounded moments earlier.

Affirming the Trinity

With the authority of apostolic teaching firmly established in Blickling 15, the Trinitarian doctrinal elements of the speeches stand out all the more clearly. The high merit of apostolic authority and evocations of the Trinity

---

58 See the apparatus to Greek and Latin versions of chapter 39 in Lipsius and Bonnet, eds., *Acta Apostolorum Apocrypha*, 1:152–5; and Walker, *Apocryphal Gospels, Acts, and Revelations*, 269 n. 9. This feature presumably supports the claim that the Latin text is prior to the Greek verstions; see D'Anna, "The Relationship between the Greek and Latin Recensions of the *Acta Petri Et Pauli*"; and Eastman, *The Ancient Martyrdom Accounts of Peter and Paul*, 221–7.

work together to strengthen the fundamentally didactic nature of the sermon. Such didacticism is, of course, expected in sermons, but Blickling 15 depicts trends otherwise neglected in scholarship. Apostolic authority, didactic orthodoxy, and Trinitarian teaching all manifest themselves in this sermon, placing it firmly within late Anglo-Saxon devotional traditions in ways previously unacknowledged for anonymous Old English sermons.

A direct creedal confession of Trinitarian belief occurs in a speech adapted from the Latin chapter 48. This passage follows the omission in the Old English of an extended focus on circumcision in the source; important here is that the sermon author consciously excludes the section on circumcision, but resumes the translation just as a central doctrinal tenet becomes apparent in the speech. Peter professes his faith in "An God Ælmihtig, God Fæder, on Hælendum Criste, mid þon Halgan Gaste, Scyppend ealra gesceafta, þone ic bodige, þe geworhte heofen & eorðan & sæ, & ealle þa þing þe on þæm þrim syndon, se is soþ Cyning & his rices nis nænig ende" (187.7–11: "One God Almighty, God the Father, in Christ the Saviour, with the Holy Spirit, Creator of all creatures, whom I preach, who made heaven and earth and sea, and all things which are therein, who is the true King, and of his kingdom is no end"). The Old English renders a close translation of the Latin, but it is useful to quote here: "Ego unum esse deum patrem in Christo saluatore cum sancto spiritu creatorem omnium rerum praedico, qui fecit caelum et terram, mare et omnia quae in eis sunt, qui uerus rex est, et regni eius non erit finis" ("I preach the one God the Father in Christ the Saviour, with the Holy Spirit, Creator of all things, who made heaven and earth, sea and all that is therein, who is the true King, and of whose kingdom shall be no end"). Because of the significance of this passage for the Trinitarian features of the sermon, an extended examination is warranted.

Comparing this proclamation of faith in the *Martyrdom* with the fourth-century Niceno-Constantinopolitan Creed further illuminates the passage and its historical contexts.[59] What such comparison reveals is that

---

59 References are to Pelikan and Hotchkiss, eds., *Creeds and Confessions of Faith in the Christian Tradition, Volume I*, 162 (Greek) and 672 (Latin). This creed is now more precisely recognized as the *Niceno-Constantinopolitan Creed*, but it was identified as the *Nicene Creed* through the medieval period and well into the modern era; indeed, it is still most often referred to by this title. See esp. Kelly, *Early Christian Creeds*; and Miranda Wilcox, "Creeds and Confessions of Faith"; my thanks to Miranda Wilcox for allowing me to read an unpublished version of her work.

most of this passage is reliant upon the Creed.[60] The parallels may be outlined as follows:

Martyrdom	Creed
Ego **unum** esse **deum patrem**	Credo in **unum deum patrem**
in Christo saluatore	Et **in** unum Dominum Iesum **Christum**
cum **sancto spiritu**	Et in **spiritum sanctum**
qui **fecit**	**factorum**
caelum et terram	**caelum et terram**
mare et **omnia** quae in eis **sunt**	per quem **omnia** facta **sunt**
qui **uerus** rex est	deum **verum** de deo **vero**
et **regni** eius **non erit finis**	cuius **regni non erit finis**

There are, of course, biblical precedents for some of these formulas. For example, "fecit caelum et terram [et] mare" occurs in 2 Chronicles 2:12, Psalm 123:8, Acts 14:14, and Apocalypse 14:7; the New Testament passages also include the following phrase – "et mare" – and Luke's Acts further includes "et omnia quae in eis sunt." In addition, "et regni eius non erit finis" ultimately derives from Luke 1:33. Significant is the intertextual layering across these texts, since these biblical phrases are present in Luke's Gospel and Acts of the Apostles, which were drawn on for the apocryphal acts. Yet the striking feature for the present argument is the arrangement of these formulas together in both the Creed and the *Martyrdom*, framed in both cases by Trinitarian declarations.

The preceding comparison reveals that this speech points towards a particular emphasis on the Trinity through creedal affirmation in the Latin *Martyrdom* and adopted into Blickling 15. As Bovon notes, "Speeches are both an effective place to insert the creed that the author seeks to defend and a strategic opportunity to give meaning to the present situation."[61] Just as creedal formulations were relevant in relation to ecclesiastical controversies in the fourth and fifth centuries, they were relevant in relation to Christian teaching in the tenth century. Speaking through Peter's words,

---

60 Eastman also notes parallels between the *Martyrdom* and the *Creed*, although he does not demonstrate parallels or discuss implications; see *The Ancient Martyrdom Accounts of Peter and Paul*, 257 n. 64 (on the Latin text) and 299 n. 152 (on Greek B); for other references to creedal parallels in the apocryphal acts that Eastman translates, see also 28, 55 n. 42, and 368.

61 Bovon, "Canonical and Apocryphal Acts of Apostles," 203.

the sermon author embraces a didactic moment in order to impart the principles of Trinitarian faith to his audience. Indeed, this creedal speech stands as a key moment in Blickling 15, representative of the ideological assimilations of apostolic speech undertaken by the voice of the preacher.

Recognition of the creedal and, more importantly, Trinitarian characteristics at the heart of Blickling 15 also forms a lens with which to read the importance of other Trinitarian affirmations held over from the *Martyrdom* in the Old English sermon. For example, the centrality of basic Trinitarian doctrine appears in the last words of Paul's main speech, in which the apostle reminisces that he taught "ealle men þæt hie beeodan anne Ælmihtigne God unbegripendlicne & ungesynelicne God" (185.30–1: "all men that they ought to serve one God Almighty, God incomprehensible and invisible"). With this exhortation, Paul's speech again moves outward from human relations to indicate the focus on God with which he started (185.10: "sibbe & Godes lufan"). The envelope structure to this speech echoes Jesus' own command from Matthew 22:37, "diliges Dominum Deum tuum ex toto corde tuo et in tota anima tua et in tota mente tua" ("Thou shalt love the Lord thy God with thy whole heart and with thy whole soul and with thy whole mind"), followed by his assertion that "hoc est maximum et primum mandatum" (Matthew 22:38: "This is the greatest and the first commandment"). For Paul (as preacher in this apocryphon), who follows this command with his own exhortations to love based in one God (1 Corinthians 13), the beginning of doctrine is God's love, towards the end of the service of the divine. Moreover, the terms "Ælmihtigne," "unbegripendlicne," and "ungesynelicne" indicate typical conceptions associated with the mystery of the Trinitarian Godhead, omnipotent, singular, but three persons.

Another example worth extended examination appears in the section of the narrative comprising Nero's catechetical questions and the apostles' answers. At the end of this question and response section, Nero also asks, "Hwæt is se Crist?" (175.30: "What is the Christ?"; Latin 18: "Quid est Christus"). In his response, Peter both denounces Simon Magus and suggests to Nero, "Þu þonne, dugoþa cyning, gif þu witan wille hwæt be Criste gedon wæs on Iudea lande, hat þe niman Pilatus ærendgewrit þe he sende to Claudio þæm casere ymb Cristes þrowunga" (177.1–4: "Then you, noble king, if you desire to know what was done concerning Christ in the land of Judea, command to be brought to you the letter of Pilate, which he sent to the Emperor Claudius, about the Passion of Christ"). The author closely translates the Latin (18: "Si autem uis scire, bone imperator quae gesta sunt in Iudaea de Christo, accipe litteras Pontii Pilati

missas ad Claudium") – but emphasizes the Passion ("Cristes þrowunga").[62] Embedded in this section of the sermon is yet another apocryphal
tradition known as the *Letter of Pilate to Claudius*.[63] This *Letter* appears in
chapters 19–21 of the Latin *Martyrdom*, and is rendered into Old English
in full, closely following the Latin, in Blickling 15 (177.5–35). Although
not a speech in its most basic form – it is primarily a documentary source
– the *Letter* presents a foundational moment in the narrative pointing to
notions of Christological doctrine.

Comprising a testimony about the gospels pseudonymously attributed
to Pilate,[64] versions of this document circulated from at least the second
century onward, and the *Letter* is associated with a range of Christian
apocrypha. Most notably, it is included in the Greek *Acts of Peter and
Paul* as well as the Greek and Latin *Martyrdom of Peter and Paul*, and it is
often appended to the end of the Latin *Gospel of Nicodemus*.[65] Related to
the latter tradition, the *Letter* exists in two eleventh-century Old English
versions of the *Gospel of Nicodemus* translated from a Latin version of
the apocryphon.[66] The contents of the *Letter* relate a condensed story of
the gospels, written from the perspective of Pilate, containing references
to the key features of the story of Jesus: the virgin birth, his teaching and
healing ministry, acknowledgment of his status as Christ, his Crucifixion,
and the Resurrection. The narrator also explains the farcical plot to cover
up the Resurrection, the ultimate failure of this conspiracy, and Pilate's
own recognition of Jesus as Christ.

---

62 Christine E. Fell has observed, "By far the commonest translation for both words [Latin
litterae and *epistola*] is Old English *ærendgewrit*," since we find this rendering of the
Latin "litteras Pontii Pilati" as Old English "Pilatus ærendgewrit"; see "Introduction
to Anglo-Saxon Letters and Letter-Writers," 282.

63 See von Tischendorf, ed., *Evangelia Apocrypha*, 413–16; Speyer, "Neue Pilatus-
Apokryphen"; *NTA*, 1:526–7; Izydorczyk, "The *Evangelium Nicodemi* in the Latin
Middle Ages," 55–7; for further scholarship, see Gounelle and Izydorczyk, "Thematic
Bibliography of the *Acts of Pilate*" and "Thematic Bibliography of the *Acts of Pilate*:
Addenda and Corrigenda." There is no separate entry for the *Letter of Pilate to Claudius*
in *SASLC Apocrypha*, but it is briefly discussed in Biggs and Morey, "Gospel of
Nicodemus," in ibid., 29–31, at 30.

64 On the historical Pilate, see esp. Grüll, "The Legendary Fate of Pontius Pilate,"
with further references there.

65 For the complicated history of this *Letter* and other apocrypha, see Hall, "The *Euangelium Nichodemi* and *Vindicta saluatoris* in Anglo-Saxon England," esp. 64–6.

66 Both the Old English translations and their ultimate Latin source are edited in Cross,
ed., *Two Old English Apocrypha*, 242–7.

It is especially appropriate to account for this portion of the apocryphon as a documentary source and, in this respect, as part of the culture of medieval epistles.[67] As pseudonymous apocryphon, the *Letter* is best understood as part of the category of "fictional" letters, transmitted with spurious attributions but often taken as authentic in their later reception.[68] Most important for these types of letters is their "representative function," polemically linked to the ideology of the letter writer.[69] In the case of the *Letter of Pilate to Claudius*, the polemical intent is to corroborate the gospel narratives of the Passion with yet another account not only by an eyewitness but also by a Roman official. Lending legitimate, historical credence to the gospel narrative is a prime goal for the author of the *Letter*. It is this historicity that provides the lasting endurance of the document for later readers and authors. In the contexts of Anglo-Saxon letters, these types of documents are abundantly alluded to in sermon literature, most often in saints' lives.[70] Indeed, Christine E. Fell singles out biblical epistles, and also notes the importance of certain texts as links between the divine and humanity – even if remediated through another voice, as in the case of Pilate's witness to the Passion.[71]

Such a narrative is an important addition for both the story of the apostles and a text preached at mass, since the gospel Passion (however distilled through the supposed words of Pilate) is a necessary precursor for the deeds and words of the apostles.[72] Furthermore, the narrative conceit of the included *Letter* establishes many of the basic aspects of Christological doctrine. Solidifying the testimony of this document, after it is read, Nero asks, "Saga me, Petrus, wæs hit eal swa swa þæt gewrit sæg þurh hine geworden?" (179.1–2: "Tell me, Peter, was it all just as that letter says through

---

67 On letter writing in the ancient and medieval periods generally, see esp. Constable, *Letters and Letter Collections*; Camargo, *Ars Dictaminis/Ars Dictandi*; and Poster and Mitchell, eds., *Letter-Writing Manuals and Instruction from Antiquity to the Present*, and bibliographies there – though (as represented by these studies) attention to letter writing in the medieval period tends to focus on the later Middle Ages.

68 Constable, *Letters and Letter Collections*, 12–13 and 49–50.

69 Ibid., 13.

70 Fell, "Introduction to Anglo-Saxon Letters and Letter-Writers," 284–5.

71 Ibid., 285.

72 Hall makes a similar point: "because it contains an account of Christ's Passion told from Pilate's point of view, it satisfactorily complements the [gospels'] Passion narrative"; "The *Euangelium Nichodemi* and *Vindicta Saluatoris* in Anglo-Saxon England," 65.

that story?"), and Peter affirms the *Letter* as true. Here we find the gospel distilled into a source claiming historical authenticity, given further authority through the legitimization of the apostle Peter, and translated into an Old English sermon primarily intended for preaching based on the authority of Christian predecessors. Layers of authority and authenticity begin to pile up in Blickling 15.

The Christology of this section is also significant for reading this sermon with orthodox doctrine in mind. Indeed, Pilate's *Letter* contains a variety of epithets that witness to Christ's role in the Trinity: he is related to the Father through the titles "halgan Sunu" (177.10: "holy Son") and "Godes Sunu" (177.18: "Son of God"), incarnated miraculously "þurh clæne fæmne" (177.11–2: "through a pure virgin"), a redeeming "cyning" of the Jews (177.11: "king"), and living God since he "of deaðe aras" (177.25–6: "arose from the dead"). Peter's affirmation following the reading of the *Letter* further confirms these attributes of incarnation, when he tells how Christ achieved victory (179.6, "þurhtogen") "þurh þone man þe he on hine sylfne onfeng, þæt is se myccla mægenþrym & se unbegripendlica, se þurh þone man gemedemod wæs mannum to helpe" (179.6–9: "through the manhood which he took on himself, which is the great and incomprehensible mystery, which through manhood was humbled"). This passage translates the theological point from chapter 22 of the Latin *Martyrdom*, which tells that Christ "adsumpsit illa maiestas inconprehensibilis, quae per hominem hominibus dignata est subuenire" ("assumed incomprehensible majesty, which deigned to come to humanity through a man"). Thus, these passages emphasize the importance of expressing orthodox incarnational theology, and subsequently point towards the deeper mysteries of the Christian faith.[73]

Most notable of the speeches in the latter section of Blickling 15 is the depiction of the verbal power of apostolic prayer, again with the inclusion of creedal formulas. The most prominent moment occurs when Simon Magus attempts to trick Nero and the Roman people into believing he can fly by conjuring demons to hold him in the air. When Nero sees this and believes Simon's trick, he confronts Peter and Paul. In response, Peter utters the following (a rendering of the Latin 56):

---

73 Cf. Raw, *Trinity and Incarnation in Anglo-Saxon Art and Thought*, 52–3.

Ic eow halsige scucna englas, ge þe hine on þære lyfte beraþ to beswicenne
ungeleaffulra manna heortan, þurh God Ælmihtigne ealra Scyppend & þurh
Hælende Crist, se þe on ðone þriddan dæg fram deaþe aras, ic bebeode þæt
ge hine of þisse tide leng ne beran, ac hine anforlætan.

(189.7–12: I adjure you angels of the devil, you who bear him in the air to
deceive the hearts of unbelieving men, through God Almighty Creator of
all and through Christ the Saviour, who on the third day arose from death,
I command that from this time forth you no longer bear him, but abandon
him.)

The result is the demons' abandonment of Simon Magus and his subsequent fall to death. The power of speech, spoken with the authority of an
apostle calling upon God and Christ, is victorious. This shifts the use of
speech in this sermon from didactic, instructional address to portray the
power of prayer in the spiritual realm. Yet this adjuration does not wholly shift speech away from previous uses, as it is still heavily indebted to
Trinitarian conceptions of the divine (albeit not directly mentioning the
Holy Spirit). While the sermon author's use of this speech by Peter verifies
the spiritual power given by God, it also continues to use speech as an instructional moment, echoing common Trinitatian affirmations about "God
Ælmihtigne," "Scyppend," and "Hælende Crist."
   Beyond the evocations of the Trinity in the speeches of Blickling 15,
another nuanced aspect of the narrative also supports a Trinitarian reading
of this sermon: the portrayal of Simon Magus as a figure of the Antichrist.
In her examination of the Trinity in Anglo-Saxon England, Raw demonstrates close associations (or oppositions) between Trinitarian doctrine and
ideas about Antichrist in the early medieval period.[74] Surveying medieval
theologians' interests in the Trinity, Raw finds a rationale for these connections in the early medieval conception that "Antichrist ... promotes
heresy and, in particular, heretical beliefs about the Trinity."[75] To coun-
ter these heresies, medieval theologians also came to the logical conclusion "that people need a firm belief in the Trinity if they are to resist

---

74 Ibid., 21–8; see also, more generally, Emmerson, *Antichrist in the Middle Ages*; McGinn,
    Antichrist; Hughes, *Constructing Antichrist*; and Palmer, *The Apocalypse in the Early
    Middle Ages*, passim.
75 Raw, *Trinity and Incarnation in Anglo-Saxon Art and Thought*, 23.

the attacks of Antichrist."[76] This appears to be the precise situation for Peter and Paul in confronting Simon Magus, who both teaches heresy and figures as a type of Antichrist. It is obvious from the outset that Simon is a wicked character, but the details suggest even darker implications. Joyce Tally Lionarons has noted the association between Simon and the Antichrist while discussing the three Old English sermons adapted from the *Martyrdom* – Blickling 15, Ælfric's *Passio apostolorum Petri et Pauli* (*CH* I.26), and Wulfstan's *De temporibus Antichristi*: "Simon Magus is depicted throughout [Blickling 15] as a type of Antichrist who pretends to Christ's power and tries to persuade the Emperor to worship him as God."[77] Although Lionarons does not elaborate with details, this is apparent throughout Blickling 15, as it is in Wulfstan's adaptation of the *Martyrdom* for his sermon *De temporibus Antichristi*.

One central example suffices to demonstrate the correlation between Simon and the Antichrist in Blickling 15. Towards the beginning of the narrative, Simon Magus performs several feats through sorcery, and it is related that "Þa Neron þa þæt geseah þa wende he þæt hit Godes Sunu wære" (175.4–5: "Then when Nero saw that, he thought that he [Simon] was the Son of God"). To further confirm this false belief, Simon announces to Nero, "Gehyr me dugoþa casere: ic eom Godes Sunu þe of heofonum astag" (175.10–11: "Hear me, noble Caesar: I am the Son of God who descended from heaven"). The direct contradiction to proper belief in Christ as the Son of God, which the apostles preach, is obvious. Yet Peter vehemently denounces this claim, saying that Simon is so deceived ("beswicen") and overcome ("ofercumen") "þæt he weneþ furþon þæt he man ne sy, ac weneþ þæt he sy þæt God is" (179.4–5: "that he therefore believes that he is not man, but believes that he is God"). Peter continues this reasoning with his explanation about Christ's incarnation, and the following dialogue is concerned with Nero inquiring of the apostles how they refute Simon's claims to divinity.

In the unfolding dialogue, the sorcerer continues to claim his divinity, while the apostles insist on belief only in the true God. As the mediator of this scene, Nero asks, "Ne ondrædest þu þe Simon, Petrus, se þe his godcundnesse mid soþum wisum gerymeþ?" (179.20–3: "Do you not fear Simon, Peter, who in true ways reveals his divinity?"), to which Peter

---

76 Ibid., 24.
77 Lionarons, *The Homiletic Writings of Archbishop Wulfstan*, 64.

replies, "On þam is godcundnesse wen þe manna ingehygd wat & can, & heora heortena deagol ealle smeaþ & rimeþ" (179.24–6: "The idea of divinity is in him who understands and knows the intentions of men, and examines and reckons all the secrets of their hearts"), indicating that only the true God is capable of this. He also quickly proves that Simon does not have this ability, through another test between them, further emphasizing the truths abundant in Blickling 15: the authority of apostolic teachings, as well as the doctrine of the Trinity as a central affirmation for belief.

Finally, the sermon ends on a note that brings Trinitarian concerns into sharp focus. Whereas the Latin *Martyrdom* ends by relating the translations of the apostles to their respective resting places (66), the Old English offers an alternative conclusion: "þonne onfoþ hie forgifnesse ealra heora gylta æt urum Drihtne on þæm ecan wuldre se leofað mid Fæder & mid Suna & mid þæm Halgan Gaste in ealra worlda world abuton ende on ecnesse. Amen" (193.24–6: "then they received forgiveness of all of their sins from our Lord, [they] who live in eternal glory with the Father and with the Son and with the Holy Spirit, eternally, world without end into eternity. Amen"). Although one might assume that this is a typical formula to end the sermon, other anonymous sermons do not commonly conclude in this manner; the earlier portions of Blickling 15 examined already indicate more explicit intentions at work here. This final assertion signals the doctrinal instruction at the heart of the sermon with a reminder of Trinitarian elements in the previous speeches of Peter and Paul. While the sermon is a celebration of the two preeminent apostles, it is also a celebration of Christian doctrine, and thus leaves audiences with a meditation on the resounding eternal importance of the Trinitarian Godhead.

Conclusions

The implications of my argument for a Trinitarian reading of Blickling 15 point towards the role this sermon played in contemporary currents of reform in tenth-century England. Such a reading necessitates situating this sermon first in relation to specific doctrinal currents of the tenth century, and, second, in relation to some of the roots of these trends. Doing so means moving beyond the connections between only the *Martyrdom* and Blickling 15, in order to look at related media. In looking outward from the one-to-one relationship between these texts, it becomes apparent that the apocryphal narrative of Peter and Paul is only one part of the larger media ecology of Anglo-Saxon religious culture. Following these threads, we start to see various connections that lead to understanding the apocryphal content of Blickling 15 as part of the much larger network of concerns circulating in mainstream Anglo-Saxon Christianity at the time.

First, it is important to emphasize the upsurge of evidence for increased attention to the Trinity in England during the late tenth and early eleventh centuries. Trinitarian affirmations in Blickling 15 especially fit alongside the wide range of formulations of the Niceno-Constantinopolitan Creed.[78] In large part, the Creed was prevalent in this period because of its inclusion in the liturgy. The Niceno-Constantinopolitan Creed in particular was a standard part of the Roman tradition, and was the primary liturgical creed in Anglo-Saxon England. Thirteen extant manuscripts known to the Anglo-Saxons include the Latin Niceno-Constantinopolitan Creed (another six include the earlier Nicene Creed from 325), while quotations, citations, and references range in the dozens.[79] Two Old English translations also exist: one by Ælfric, known as the *Mæsse Creda*;[80] and a twelfth-century version by the Tremulous Hand of Worcester, in Oxford, Bodleian Library, Junius 121 (s. xi$^{3/4}$, additions s. xi^2 and x. xi$^{ex.}$, Worcester), fol. VIr.[81] Blickling 15, then, is yet another witness to contemporary growing concerns for creedal affirmations of the Trinity.

Second, more broadly, Blickling 15 reflects ecclesiastical endeavours to standardize the liturgy and to teach the laity during the tenth and eleventh centuries, particularly due to reforms under Benedictine leaders.[82] These currents are often invoked in relation to late tenth- and eleventh-century religious concerns as major factors to consider – whether the reforms were

---

78 The following is largely reliant on Miranda Wilcox, "Creeds and Confessions of Faith."

79 For manuscripts containing the Niceno-Constantinopolitan Creed, see NRK, appendix 19; and *ASM*, 12, 76, 111, 306, 500, 629, 790, 836, and 923. For manuscripts containing the earlier Nicene Creed, see NRK, appendix 6; and *ASM*, 137, 552, 629, 836, and 923 (significantly, these last three manuscripts include both creeds). A full list of manuscripts (including some not listed in *ASM*), quotations, citations, and references is provided in Miranda Wilcox, "Creeds and Confessions of Faith."

80 Thorpe, ed., *The Homilies of the Anglo-Saxon Church*, 2:596–9. This text is extant in two manuscripts: Cambridge, University Library, Gg.3.28 (s. x/xi), fols. 261v–262r; and Oxford, Bodleian Library, Hatton 114 (1064x83), fols. 247r–247v; see NRK, 15 and 331; and *ASM*, 11 and 638.

81 NRK, 338; and *ASM*, 644. Edited in Crawford, "The Worcester Marks and Glosses of the Old English Manuscripts in the Bodleian, Together with the Worcester Version of the Nicene Creed," 5.

82 For summaries of scholarship, see esp. Cubitt, "Review Article"; and Nicola Robertson, "Review."

focused locally or generally throughout England.[83] Increased evidence of the Creed in the tenth and eleventh centuries represents one outcome of reform agendas (whether directly or indirectly caused by the principal players). For example, the provenances of seven of the nine extant manuscripts including the Niceno-Constantinopolitan Creed (two of these manuscripts also include the earlier Nicene Creed) have been indicated as the reform centres of Canterbury, Sherborne, and Winchester.[84] Ælfric certainly belonged to this reform tradition, as his mentor was Bishop Æthelwold, who in turn followed the reformer Saint Dunstan. No doubt the continuation of liturgical and educational trends from these reforms also explains the proximity of the twelfth-century version of the Creed to the so-called *Old English Benedictine Office* in Junius 121 (fols. 42a–53b).[85]

Along with these reforms, the late tenth century saw a major increase in attention to the cult of saints.[86] As Rollason claims, "the fact that the increase in [hagiographic] writing occurred at the same time as the reforming movement indicates a connection between the efforts of the hagiographers and the general ambience created by the reformers."[87] Some of these developments brought about several new cults (e.g., for the great reformers Dunstan, Æthelwold, and Oswald), but there was also a parallel increase in the veneration of universal saints like Mary and the apostles. Legislation from the period reflects ecclesiastical desires to integrate the veneration of the apostles into the lives of the laity.[88] The most relevant examples appear in the law codes known as Æthelred V and VI, composed in 1008.[89] In these codes, festivities for various feast days are made mandatory, among

---

83 For a recent, circumspect assessment, see Blair, *The Church in Anglo-Saxon Christianity*, esp. 341–67.

84 At Canterbury, *ASM*, 12, 76, and 306; at Sherborne, *ASM*, 111 (though this is only a probable provenance); at Winchester, *ASM*, 500 and 923; and *ASM*, 629, present at both Canterbury and Worcester around the turn of the eleventh century. On the importance of these centres, see esp. Cubitt, "Review Article"; Nicola Robertson, "Review"; and Farmer, "The Monastic Reform of the Tenth Century and Sherborne."

85 See discussion in *ASPR*, 6:lxxiv–lxxviii; and NRK, 338.

86 See Rollason, *Saints and Relics in Anglo-Saxon England*, 164–95.

87 Ibid., 176.

88 References to legal documents by title and chapter nos. are to *Early English Laws*. I have also consulted Liebermann, *Die Gesetze der Angelsachsen*. Some of these laws are mentioned in Rollason, *Saints and Relics in Anglo-Saxon England*, 188–92. On Anglo-Saxon laws generally, see Patrick Wormald, *The Making of English Law*.

89 For dates of Anglo-Saxon laws, see ibid., esp. 112–17, table 3.1.

which is commanded that "to æghwylces apostoles heahtide fæste man georne ꝺ freolsige" (Æthelred V, 14.1: "for the feast day of each apostle men shall eagerly fast and celebrate"; cf. Æthelred VI, 22.3).[90] The same clause was included again in the laws of King Cnut (composed c. 1020–35), for example, in Cnut 1018 (14.3) and Cnut I–II (16a); the latter is outstanding since it is composed largely from previous English laws.[91] These laws most explicitly spell out such obligatory observations, but various legal codes and ecclesiastical calendars of the period also emphasize the sanctity of feast days.[92]

More specifically, compulsory observance of the feast day of Peter and Paul (29 June) was highlighted in law codes. A pertinent example appears in the late ninth-century laws of King Alfred (composed c. 895), which Anglo-Saxon leaders reaffirmed throughout the tenth century. Among the list of feast days that freemen should observe, singled out for special comment is "an dæg to sancte Petres tide ꝺ sancte Paules" (43: "one day for the feast of Saint Peter and Saint Paul"). References to this feast day continue to appear in twelfth-century collections, which likely reflect earlier legislation. A Latin translation of Alfred's laws known as the *Quadripartitus* (c. 1108) contains a rendering of the same clause: "unus dies in festo beatorum apostolorum Petri et Pauli" (43: "one day for the feast of the blessed apostles Peter and Paul").[93] The *Leges Edwardi Confessoris*, compiled in the 1130s, refers to livestock taxes due specially "in festis sanctorum apostolorum Petri et Pauli" (10: "on the feast of the holy apostles Peter and Paul"). While these legal documents represent prescriptive elements of Anglo-Saxon culture, they also reveal sustained concern about the apostles throughout the period – particularly for ecclesiastical leaders like Wulfstan who played their parts in drafting these legal codes. Similar attention to the feast day of these two apostles is found in English calendars through the tenth and eleventh centuries: of twenty-seven extant calendars – only four of which are dated before the tenth century – twenty-one

---

90 The verb *freolsian* especially denotes keeping a holy day; see Momma, ed., *The Dictionary of Old English*, s.v. *freolsian*.

91 On the sources of Cnut I–II, see Wormald, *The Making of English Law*, 356–60. See also the headnote for Cnut I–II at *Early English Laws*.

92 See Francis Wormald, ed., *English Kalendars before A.D. 1100*; and Rushforth, *Saints in English Kalendars before A.D. 1100*.

93 On the date, see esp. Sharpe, "The Dating of *Quadripartitus* Again."

observe the feast for Peter and Paul on 29 June, while all others mention at least Peter.[94]

Given connections between these cultural currents and Blickling 15, it is possible to suggest that this sermon also fits into tenth-century reform programs and associated determinations to teach orthodox declarations of faith to the people though preaching. Significant for the adoption of Trinitarian declarations by the author of Blickling 15 is the extent to which the *Martyrdom* itself is aligned with orthodox theologies. Evidence of this characteristic most significant for the present argument is the abundance of creedal and Trinitarian language throughout the apocryphon, but other theological points discussed in this chapter also attest to these qualities. As already indicated, at the time of composition of the *Martyrdom*, such elements helped to uphold anti-heretical orthodoxies as promulgated by church councils of the period. With the resurgence of similar concerns for orthodox ideologies in the late tenth century, Blickling 15 fits well within "the church's seeking further to increase the influence of the cult of saints as a means of integrating the lives of the laity into the machinery of the church."[95] Towards this end – perhaps even for the very concerns held by important ecclesiasts of the period – the author of Blickling 15 found special interest in the speeches of the *Martyrdom*, and ably translated them for a Trinitarian lesson through the words of the two greatest apostles.

---

94 Two calendars are fragmentary, with sections for this feast day missing. See Rushforth, *Saints in English Kalendars*, "Table VI: June"; for editions, see Wormald, ed., *English Kalendars before A.D. 1100*.

95 Rollason, *Saints and Relics in Anglo-Saxon England*, 188.

Chapter Three

Ælfric and Correct Doctrine

With Ælfric of Eynsham, the history of English preaching encounters a great shift – at least according to previous scholarship.[1] With Ælfric, we have a known, named preacher, a persona to connect to specific, identifiable texts, as well as a breadth of writing and textual circulation unequalled in the corpus of Old English literature.[2] His own corpus of Latin and Old English literature includes an English *Grammar*, a Latin–Old English *Glossary*, a *Colloquy*, a *Hexameron*, treatises on a variety of religious and scientific subjects, and a vernacular translation of Genesis, as well as various letters in Latin and Old English.[3] Foremost of his literary output, however, are his two series of *Catholic Homilies*, the *Lives of Saints*, and a number of other sermons for specific occasions, amounting to a mass of preaching texts that has been heralded as a major innovation in the tradition of English preaching. Yet, for all of the differences established by scholarship regarding Ælfrician and anonymous sermons, recent work has questioned the fissure, partly regarding the prevalence of apocrypha

---

1 See a classic formulation by Gatch, *Preaching and Theology in Anglo-Saxon England*: "The monastic revival of the tenth century is, I believe, the theological watershed which lies between the work of the earlier anonymous Old English homilists and that of Ælfric and Wulfstan" (8); and his claims that these two authors "were far more sophisticated, theologically and rhetorically, than the earlier homilists" (11).

2 For overviews and summaries of scholarship, see esp. Kleist, "An Annotated Bibliography of Ælfrician Studies"; and Magennis and Swan, eds., *A Companion to Ælfric*.

3 On the corpus of Ælfric's works, see Clemoes, "The Chronology of Ælfric's Works"; Kleist, "Ælfric's Corpus"; and Joyce Hill, "Ælfric: His Life and Works."

in Anglo-Saxon preaching.[4] It is, therefore, valuable to set Ælfric's translations of apocrypha in his sermons in closer relation to similar ways of preaching found in contemporary, anonymous sermons.

My starting point rests on the assumption that scholars have too often read Ælfric's few explicit statements about apocrypha as normative, and have subsequently constructed an exaggerated view of his condemnations. In other words, in generalizing Ælfric's specific comments, scholarship has stressed what he openly excludes. What I find more revealing, however, is what and how he chooses to include materials from apocryphal sources, especially acts of apostles like those found in the *Virtutes apostolorum*. Aideen O'Leary has most directly examined Ælfric's use of apocryphal acts, concluding, "Enthusiasm, therefore, not criticism, characterised his adoption of apocryphal *acta*."[5] Indeed, there is more to consider regarding Ælfric's attitudes and how he adopts and adapts these apocrypha in his sermons. A sensitive reading of Ælfric's treatment of apostolic acts reveals that he held nuanced attitudes towards apocryphal sources that depend on his own veneration of the apostles, especially based on their authority and their examples as model believers. I present a variety of examples for how Ælfric deals with apostles in his sermons in order to elucidate his general views, rather than focusing only on select statements. While Ælfric rarely assesses apocryphal acts openly, his sermons show particular strategies for inclusion, largely though the combination of materials in order to create a whole picture of each apostle as a model for the needs of his audience.

I address two aspects of Ælfric's corpus: his use of apocryphal acts, with special attention to the *Catholic Homilies*, and the transmission of some of his works in conjunction with other Old English sermons containing apocryphal content. In both cases, the adaptive techniques involved are appropriative, as Ælfric and other authors combine previous sources for new creations relevant to their immediate contexts. The combinative, adaptive translations undertaken for Ælfrician sermons create conjunctions that place apocrypha alongside other authoritative Christian materials. For example, the range of sources appropriated include apocrypha as

---

4 See esp. references in my Introduction as well as Clayton, "Ælfric and the Nativity of the Blessed Virgin Mary"; Joyce Hill, "Reform and Resistance," 15–46; and essays by Biggs: "Ælfric's Andrew and the Apocrypha," "Ælfric's Comments about the *Passio Thomae*," "'Righteous People According to the Old Law,'" and "Ælfric's Mark, Other Things, and Apostolic Authority."

5 O'Leary, "An Orthodox Old English Homiliary?," 22.

well as biblical, patristic, and early medieval texts; furthermore, in most cases, there is no distinction between them mentioned in the sermons, as they are all acceptable for teaching. To Ælfric, these materials are all orthodox, even if modern scholars have relegated some to heterodoxy, and represent manifestations of diverse traditions in Anglo-Saxon Christianity. This is important to recognize in light of what Joyce Hill has observed as "the complexities of the intertextual tradition" in Christian learning and the "complex textual community" of which Ælfric was a part.[6] Apocryphal narratives in Ælfric's sermons are best understood as one part of the range of traditions that Anglo-Saxon authors received as filtered through Christian learning.

This chapter focuses on a smaller, self-contained set of interrelations constituting part of the whole, larger media network of apocrypha in Anglo-Saxon England. In the first part of the chapter, I focus on a network comprised of a group of Ælfric's sermons related by their common sources in apostolic apocrypha. As narratives about the earliest disciples, and part of a distinct genre (as discussed in the previous chapter), apocryphal acts and Ælfric's translations of them make up a coherent network on their own. In the second part of the chapter, this network is expanded, to include later works demonstrating how Ælfric's sermons based on apocryphal acts are grouped with other apocryphal sermons in Anglo-Saxon manuscripts. By examining the relationships that scribes formed by adapting and copying Ælfrician sermons in books with other apocrypha, I show how Ælfric's works become bound up with the wider network explored in chapter 1. For Anglo-Saxon compilers of preaching collections, anonymous and Ælfrician works were not distinct, but part of the same media ecology, the same media network.

Ælfric's Attitudes: Rejection, Acceptance, and Authority

It must be acknowledged at the outset that Ælfric does explicitly condemn certain apocrypha in some of his works. The condemnation most often invoked in discussions of Ælfric's attitude towards apocrypha appears in his Old English Preface to the *Catholic Homilies*: "ic geseah ꝺ gehyrde mycel gedwyld on manegum engliscum bocum" (50–1: "I have seen and heard of much error in many English books"). More specifically,

---

6 Joyce Hill, "Ælfric's Authorities," 58 and 65.

throughout the *Catholic Homilies*, Ælfric rejects certain Marian apocrypha (I.30, II.29, and II.31) and the *Apocalypse of Paul* (II.20), and cautions his audience about historical error in the *Martyrdom of Thomas* (II.34, cf. *LS* 36). He also directly addresses the orthodox authority of the four accepted gospels, as opposed to the dubiousness of other works circulating as gospels, in his sermon on Mark the Evangelist in the *Lives of Saints* (*LS* 15). Like his patristic predecessors, Ælfric portrays caution above all else.[7] Curiously, even when Ælfric explicitly levels negative charges against apocrypha, the references indicate that he was familiar enough with their contents to discuss them. These facts reveal that he may have viewed such works as dangerous for some readers, but that had not stopped Ælfric from familiarizing himself with them.

On the other hand, it is misleading to use such specific claims in order to generalize about Ælfric avoiding or condemning all apocrypha, since some of his sermons clearly derive from materials (though, notably, sometimes through intermediate sources) that modern scholars categorize as apocryphal.[8] Much of this reliance is on apostolic acts, though other apocrypha also influenced his works in various ways. In his *Catholic Homilies* and *Lives of Saints*, ten of the sermons derive from apocryphal acts (see appendix 2).[9] Strikingly, in the case of the *Passio Sancti Thome Apostoli* (*LS* 36), Ælfric uses the *Martyrdom of Thomas* regardless of his previous reluctance to translate the text in his *Catholic Homilies* (*CH* II.34).[10] Beyond Ælfric's uses of apostolic apocrypha in his preaching corpus, other texts also point to his knowledge of, and sometimes reliance on, apocrypha. A few examples suffice. Most notably, his *Letter to Sigeweard* includes the *Epistle of Paul to the Laodiceans* in the list of canonical biblical books; given his approach to authority, this is not altogether surprising, although it does complicate the imposition of modern conceptions onto medieval documents.[11] Ælfric also relies on material ultimately derived from an apocryphal epistle (mediated through Rufinus of Aquileia's Latin

---

7 For an overview of these attitudes, see esp. Biggs, "An Introduction and Overview of Recent Work."

8 The following data relies on McCoy, "The Use of the Writings of English Authors in Old English Homiletic Literature"; *CH Introduction*; entries in *Fontes*; *ASL*, esp. 250–66; and *SASLC Apocrypha*.

9 For comparative lists of Ælfric's saints' lives (in *CH*, *LS*, and others), see tables 1–2 in Joyce Hill, "The Context of Ælfric's Saints' Lives," 23–7.

10 See Biggs, "Ælfric's Comments about the *Passio Thomae*."

11 See Hall, "Epistle of Paul to the Laodiceans," *SASLC Apocrypha*, 58.

translation of Eusebius of Caesarea's *Historia ecclesiastica*) for his sermon on *Natalis Sanctorum Abdon et Sennes* (*LS* 24). In terms of content, these appropriations of apocrypha are similar to anonymous hagiographical sermons, especially those in the Vercelli and Blickling collections.[12]

What should scholars make of these explicit and implicit discussions and uses of apocrypha throughout Ælfric's corpus? Surely the summary I have given so far must point towards a less than clear picture of Ælfric's biases. Taken together, these observations indicate the need to view Ælfric's attitudes towards and uses of apocrypha with a certain amount of nuance. This is not a simple matter. Frederick M. Biggs has observed "that Ælfric's task of identifying apocryphal traditions was very different from our own, aided as we are by modern critical editions and studies that seek to determine when and why a text was written and what sources it used."[13] Especially significant in this regard is the need to remember that "our judgments may assume knowledge that Ælfric did not have"[14] – and, conversely, our judgments may lack contexts that Ælfric did have, of which we may be unaware.[15]

Many of Ælfric's attitudes and judgments are directly related to the works of authorities that he had inherited and grown to respect. Ælfric's continual recourse to inherited authorities is, therefore, a major aspect of how he interacted with the complex tradition of sources handed down to him. Ælfric's Old English *Letter to Sigeweard* (also known by the Latin title *Libellus de Veteris Testamento et Novo*) provides what is perhaps his most important discussion of the biblical canon and its relation to authority, since it includes an extensive and detailed exposition.[16] Much of Ælfric's discussion in this epistle contains an introduction to and summary of the Bible, addressing the relationship between the two sections of the so-called Old and New Testaments (816: "þa twa gecyðnyssa"). Ælfric's concerns are especially pronounced in his typological approach,

---

12 See Vercelli 18 and 23 and Blickling 15–18; esp. noteworthy are apostolic apocrypha in Blickling 15 (Peter and Paul) and 18 (Andrew and Matthias).

13 Biggs, "'Righteous People According to the Old Law,'" 153.

14 Ibid.

15 One relevant example of such differences is the relationship between apocrypha and hagiography; see Biggs, "Ælfric's Andrew and the Apocrypha," as well as discussion in chapter 2.

16 References by line no. are to Marsden, ed., *The Old English Heptateuch and Ælfric's Libellus de Veteri Testamento et Novo, Volume 1*, 201–30.

through which he continually explains the Old Law of the Jews prefiguring the New Law of Christians (815–16: "on þære ealdan æ and eac on þare niwe"). Written towards the end of his life (c. 1005–6), this treatise offers a conspectus of Ælfric's attitudes about the Bible as he looked back across his learning and works.

One particular passage in the *Letter* reveals a striking instance of how Ælfric viewed materials inherited from the past. He cites Jesus' teachings (832, "swa swa Crist eft sylf cwæð") when he quotes and translates Matthew 13:52: "'Omnis scriba doctus in regno celorum similis est homini patri familias qui profert de thesauro suo noua & uetera.' 'Ælc gelæred bocere on Godes gelaðunge ys gelic þam hlaforde þe forlæt simble of his agenum goldhorde ealde þing & niwe'" (832–6: "'Every scribe instructed in the kingdom of heaven is like to a man that is a householder, who bringeth forth out of his treasure new things and old.' 'Every learned scribe in the kingdom of God is like the lord who continually brings out of his own gold-hoard old things and new'").[17] Drawing on a moment of Jesus' own teaching, this passage reflects Ælfric's practices of composition, as seen in his reliance on authoritative sources throughout his corpus.[18]

Following the quotation and translation of Jesus' words, Ælfric further explains the whole structure of the Bible and alludes to the role of other authoritative texts. He remarks, "Twa and hundseofontig boca sind on bibliothecan" (836–7: "Seventy-two books are in the Bible"). Yet he is not concerned only with the biblical books, since he also indicates that "Syndon swa þeah gesette oðre bec ðurh halige lareowas þa man hæfð wide gehwær on cristendome, Crist to lofe" (844–5: "Though there are also written other books by holy teachers which men have everywhere wide throughout Christendom, to the praise of Christ"). For Ælfric, then, the "eald" and "niwe" refer to Christian tradition extended from antiquity to his own time. This passage is a clear instance of how Ælfric indicates

---

17 Two other renderings of this biblical verse stand out in Old English. The first is Matthew 13:52 in the Old English Gospels: "Þa sæde he him. Forþam is ælc gelæred bocere on heofenan rice gelic þam hiredes ealdre þe forð bringð of his goldhorde niwe þing & ealde"; see Liuzza, ed., *The Old English Version of the Gospels*, cited by chapter and verse nos. The second is in the Old English gloss to Defensor's *Liber scintillarum*: "ælc bocere gelæred on rice heofena gelic he ys menn hiredes ealdre se forþbringð of goldhorde his niwe & ealde"; see Gerry, "An Edition with Commentary of the Latin/ Anglo-Saxon *Liber scintillarum*," chapter 32, sentence 3.

18 See, for example, sources listed in entries for Ælfric's works in *Fontes*; and, more specifically, *CH Introduction*.

his own strategies of inclusion and adaptation in his writing, as he seeks to bring together the writings of learned authors from the past to bear upon his own present concerns.

Ælfric signals the most prominent figures of his intellectual inheritance in the Latin Preface to his First Series of *Catholic Homilies*. He acknowledges these authors when he writes, "Hos namque auctores in hac explanatio sumus secuti. uidelicet Augustinum. ypponiensem. Hieronimum. Bedam. Gregoriam. Smaragdum, et aliquando Hægmonem" (14–16: "For we have followed these authors in this exposition, of course Augustine of Hippo, Jerome, Bede, Gregory, Smaragdus, and sometimes Haymo").[19] Throughout his corpus, Ælfric often cites these names, and it is clear that he consulted their works with reverence. Such authorities underlie several of his comments on apocrypha already noted in this chapter. Notably, further examination of his discussion of error ("gedwyld") in the Preface to the *Catholic Homilies* has revealed that it corresponds to reasons given by Paul the Deacon for compiling his Homiliary, used as a literary trope associated with notions of promoting Christian orthodoxy in reform.[20] Ælfric's scepticism about the *Martyrdom of Thomas* derives from criticism by Augustine,[21] and his comments about the authority of the four gospels above all others derive from Jerome's works.[22] Ælfric not only explicitly cites his authorities but also implicitly mimics them in his style and attitudes.

Ælfric's notion of authority also extended beyond his attitudes towards his forbears, as he sought to construct his own persona of authority.[23] Throughout his writings are constant reminders about the need to follow correct doctrine and avoid error. In each of these statements, Hill claims, Ælfric "expresses the need for the preservation of orthodoxy as Ælfric saw it. It was a form of self-definition that set Ælfric apart and established his

---

19 See Godden's discussion of authorities in *CH Introduction*, xxxviii–xliv, with more detailed specifics throughout.

20 *CH Introduction*, 3; see also Lionarons, *The Homiletic Writings of Archbishop Wulfstan*, 59. On homiliaries and Ælfric's reliance on them, see references in chapter 1.

21 See Godden, "Ælfric's Saints' Lives and the Problem of Miracles"; and "Martyrdom of Thomas," *SASLC Apocrypha*, 55–6.

22 See Biggs, "Ælfric's Andrew and the Apocrypha," 478–82, and "Ælfric's Mark, Other Things, and Apostolic Authority."

23 On studies concerned with Ælfric's construction of identity and authority, see esp. Jonathan Wilcox, *Ælfric's Prefaces*; Swan, "Identity and Ideology in Ælfric's Prefaces"; and Stephenson, *The Politics of Language*.

polemical stance."[24] Anonymous sermons do not have this type of voice, largely because we do not have identified authors who wove clear, identifiable personas across their compositions. Using this type of self-fashioning rhetoric, Ælfric is simultaneously able to establish his voice as an authoritative teacher and to set himself apart from contemporary voices. This difference, of course, was rhetorically meaningful for the Benedictine reformers, as they sought to separate themselves from the past, to establish the significance of their work. Ælfric's outspoken attitudes manifest as a way for him to synthesize his own authority and persona in relation to his forbears and his own reform agenda.

The passages already discussed serve as cogent illustrations, but they are not the only instances, as Ælfric expresses anxieties and warnings about correctness in a number of his writings. He exhorts scribes to accurately copy his writings in the Old English Preface to the first series of the *Catholic Homilies*, saying:

> Nu bydde ic ⁊ halsige on godes naman gif hwa þas boc awritan wylla þæt he hi geornlice gerihte be ðære bysene. þy læs ðe we ðurh gymeleas writeras geleahtrode beon; Mycel yfel deð se ðe leas writ. buton he hit gerihte. swylce he gebrine þa soðan lare to leasum gedwylde.

> (128–32: "Now I ask and entreat, in the name of God, if anyone desires to copy this book, that he eagerly correct it by the exemplar, lest we might be rebuked through careless writers. He does much evil who writes lies, unless he corrects it, just as he turns true learning to false error.")

At the same time as he admonishes scribes to copy texts correctly, he also links bad practice with "false error" ("leasum gedwylde"). Those scribes who uphold Ælfric's entreaty, then, are aligned with correctness and his ideals of establishing right teaching. Ælfric makes similar statements (offering verbatim parallels in some instances) about scribes and the transmission of his correct doctrine at the ends of the Preface to his translation of Genesis (118–22) and his *Letter to Sigeweard* (934–6).[25]

In other examples, Ælfric similarly expresses anxieties about scribes incorrectly copying his work alongside other materials. In his *Oratio* at the

---

24 Joyce Hill, "Ælfric: His Life and Works," 54.

25 Marsden, ed., *Old English Heptateuch and Ælfric's Libellus de Veteri Testamento et Novo, Volume 1*, 7 and 230.

end of the second series of the *Catholic Homilies*, he both disavows further translation of the gospels and asks scribes not to add their own work to his collection:

> Ic cweðe nu þæt ic næfre heononforð ne awende godspel. oþþe gospeltrahtas of ledene on englisc; Gif hwa man awendan wille. ðonne bidde ic hine for godes lufon þæt he gesette his boc onsundron. fram ðam twam bocum ðe we awend habbað we truwiað þurh godes diht.

> (5–9: "Now I say that henceforth I will never translate the gospel, or gospel lections, from Latin into English. If any man desires to translate them, then I ask, for the love of God, that he sets his book separate from the two books that we have translated, we trust according to the word of God.")

In this statement, Ælfric closely links the issues of biblical knowledge and translation with scribal practice, especially noting his own desires to only transmit the *Catholic Homilies* as he composed them. Again, his notion of correct doctrine in this collection is linked with both the authority of his sources and his own learning.

In addition to modern biases towards apocrypha, this construction of authority also plays a part in modern scholars' acceptance of Ælfric's condemnations as normative. His focus on reform infuses his texts with an ideology in which he must adhere to and demonstrate orthodoxy, as much as he must distinguish himself from others who do not follow the same perspective. Discussing Ælfric's construction of identity and the ideology behind it in his prefaces, Mary Swan concludes:

> In order to model and to perform the primacy of Winchester-affiliated reformed monasticism, Ælfric must position himself so that he embodies it, must establish positions for his addressees which either identify them as fellow-members or allow them the possibility of joining this circle by means of correct belief and practice, and must remind his addressees of those unlearned, erroneous others whose position outside the circle gives the circle its identity.[26]

---

26 Swan, "Identity and Ideology in Ælfric's Prefaces," 269.

Anglo-Saxons apparently accepted this authority, as is apparent in their continued and proliferate copying of his works into the twelfth century. Despite some scribes who clearly went against Ælfric's wishes to preserve his works as he composed them and without modification (as I address later in this chapter), he crafts his voice as an authority that dominates the late Anglo-Saxon textual record of preaching. It is likely that those reading and copying his work welcomed a clear authority to follow. It is not difficult to see how and why modern scholars so willingly accept Ælfric's attitudes as normative. Yet there is also more to see in Ælfric's own practices to nuance our understanding of his use of apocryphal media for preaching.

Framing Apocrypha

Ælfric's notion of authority in relation to apostles as exempla allows for considering several cases of his adaptations that are particularly telling for elucidating his uses of apocrypha. The practice of reading apostolic lives – and saints' lives in general – is, of course, common to liturgical practices, but this does not specifically explain Ælfric's uses of them in his sermons. The essential collections of sources that Ælfric regularly consulted (the homiliaries of Paul the Deacon, Smaragdus, and Haymo of Auxerre) also offered alternative, authoritative readings for these days from authors such as Augustine and Bede;[27] yet Ælfric chose to incorporate apocryphal narratives instead of or appended to such standard readings. Malcolm Godden makes this clear in his commentary on several of the *Catholic Homilies* composed for apostles' feast days, as for John (I.4), Peter and Paul (I.26), Bartholomew (I.31), Philip and James the Less (II.17), James the Great (II.27), Matthew (II.32), and Simon and Jude (II.33).[28] As is evident, some of these apostolic sermons in the *Catholic Homilies* portray Ælfric's technique of blending together authoritative exegesis with apocryphal narratives. His goal was not only to follow the estimation of the apostles inherited from his predecessors but also to relate the stories of the apostles as specific models for his audience.

Structurally, several sermons with apostolic apocrypha embedded in them include substantial translations of biblical passages or commentary at the beginning or end, appended to the narratives like prefaces or epilogues.

27 See references in chapter 1, n. 1.
28 See esp. entries in *Fontes*; and *CH Introduction*.

For John (I.4), Ælfric introduces the occasion with a passage from Bede's *Homilia in euangelia* I.9; for Peter and Paul (I.26), he provides a two-part sermon, with the first part drawn from statements about the apostles in the gospels and Bede's *Homilia in euangelia* I.20; for Bartholomew (I.31), he ends the sermon with a series of exhortations echoing Augustine and Gregory, alongside relevant biblical passages; for Andrew (I.38), he provides another two-part sermon, with the first part drawn from the gospels and exegesis from Gregory's *Homilia v in euangelia* for his exposition, with details from Haymo of Auxerre's *Homilia de Sanctis* I and Heiric of Auxerre's *Homilia in Circulum Anni* II.46; for Philip and James the Less (II.17), as already discussed, he incorporates the Eusebius-Rufinus *Historia ecclesiastica* as a historical source for James's martyrdom; and for Matthew (II.32), he introduces the occasion with the biblical gospels and passages from Bede's *Homilia in euangelia* I.21.[29] Comparably, similar uses of biblical and patristic authorities alongside apocryphal narratives are also found in the *Lives of Saints* for Mark (*LS* 15) and Thomas (*LS* 36).[30] Many of these instances are explainable by comparing Ælfric's sermons to the homiliaries on which he continually relied; but these collections do not explain his recourse to apocrypha.

In the following, I consider Ælfric's adaptive combinations in his *Catholic Homilies* for Bartholomew (I.31) and Matthew (II.32), since these both present extensive cases that have been relatively unexamined.[31] While scholarship has not paid as much attention to these narratives, they present useful cases for understanding Ælfric's techniques of translating apocrypha while also adapting and combining these narratives with doctrinal statements from previous authorities for pedagogical purposes. They demonstrate how and why Ælfric incorporated apocrypha as useful narratives for teaching specific – and potentially complex – doctrinal points. In the previous chapter, I highlighted the ways in which the author of Blickling 15 translated the source text as a redacted form, though this is generally not

---

29 See esp. details in *Fontes*; *CH Introduction*; and *SALSC Apocrypha*.

30 See Godden, "Ælfric's Saints' Lives and the Problem of Miracles," 88–90; and Biggs, "Ælfric's Mark, Other Things, and Apostolic Authority."

31 On John, see Starr, "Raising John's Body"; on Peter and Paul, see Faerber, "*Acta Apocrypha apostolorum* dans le corpus homilétique vieil-anglais"; Ogawa, "Hagiography in Homily"; and Lionarons, *The Homiletic Writings of Archbishop Wulfstan*, 63–7; on Andrew, see references in chapter 2, n. 2; and Biggs, "Ælfric's Andrew and the Apocrypha."

the case with Ælfric's translations. Based on comparisons with apostolic acts, O'Leary has observed, "Ælfric's translations are, for the most part, faithful to the original accounts ... Ælfric did not feel a need to transpose or rework the originals in any significant way."[32] A few exceptions exist, but this close adherence to a source is certainly the case with Ælfric's sermons on Bartholomew and Matthew.[33] In studying Ælfric's translations of these narratives, I am less concerned with specific renderings into English than I am with how he combines these narratives with other materials for specific, ideological teaching purposes. By revealing the translator's processes as visibly adaptive, rather than eliding the translator as invisible (to evoke Venuti's formulation),[34] this investigation reveals the very reasons for Ælfric's reliance on apocrypha as helpful for his reform-based desires to teach doctrine.

Bartholomew as Prelude to Theodicy

In his *Passio Sancti Bartholomaei Apostoli* (*CH* I.31), Ælfric reserves his expansion on the apostolic narrative for the exhortations at the end of the lesson. In this way, the didactic afterword to the narrative serves to reinforce the apocryphon as more than a fanciful story, since it works as an example for the audience to follow. These additions explicitly turn from exemplum towards homiletic teaching, as Ælfric highlights practical lessons that his audience should glean from the story – lessons directly applicable to the author's cultural concerns. Furthermore, he does so with appeal to authoritative doctrine, supported by materials from the Bible and Augustine. Ælfric's use of the apostolic narrative enables him to teach to his Anglo-Saxon audience points of pragmatic doctrine about righteousness, sin, and suffering. The apocryphon's narrative, therefore, creates a useful springboard for Ælfric's own teaching on the difficult theological subject of theodicy.

---

32 O'Leary, "An Orthodox English Homiliary?," 22.

33 O'Leary mentions that Ælfric's "Passion of Andrew is the only possible exception" (ibid., 22), though another is Ælfric's *Passio Apostolorum Petri et Pauli* (*CH* I.26), for which he redacted a version of the Pseudo-Marcellus *Martyrdom of Peter and Paul* – explainable by his comments about relating only a short narrative in that sermon; see Godden, "The Sources of Catholic Homilies 1.26 (Cameron B.1.1.28)," *Fontes*; *CH Introduction*, 209–21; and references above, n. 31.

34 Venuti, *The Translator's Invisibility*; see further discussion in chapter 2.

The heart of this sermon (1–243) is a translation of the Latin *Martyrdom of Bartholomew*,[35] which relates Bartholomew's mission to India in order to free the people from a demon named Astaroth who deceives them into worshipping him. Astaroth torments the people with illness, causing them to make sacrifices for cures; in turn, the demon pretends to cure them, but only for a limited time, creating a cycle of illness and idolatry that poisons India. In the course of the narrative, Bartholomew confronts Astaroth, achieving victory over both him and another neighbouring demon, in the process freeing the people from illness and idolatry as well as converting them to Christianity. Despite Bartholomew's victory over the demons, one of the local kings becomes upset about the religious change and kills Bartholomew in vengeance – a type of martyr's victory that has resounding implications as he is venerated as an example of Christian virtue.

In his sermon, Ælfric moves from the apostolic narrative to more doctrinal considerations with a direct statement about following Bartholomew as an exemplum: "We magon niman bysne be ðære apostolican lare. þæt nan christen man ne sceal his hæle gefeccan buton æt þam ælmihtigum scyppende" (244–6: "We may take example from that apostolic teaching, that no Christian man shall gain his health except from the Almighty Creator"). Following this transition, the rest of this sermon contains a discussion of health and condemnations of seeking relief through seemingly pagan practices. Ælfric emphasizes that "God is se soða læce þe ðurh mislicum swincgelum his folces synna gehælð" (266–7: "God is the true doctor, who through various afflictions heals the sins of his people"). The underlying point is that the Indians – who turned to a pagan demon in their afflictions – serve as a negative example of proper behaviour. Instead, the audience should look to Bartholomew as a model for facing affliction in the proper manner, by turning to Christ for salvation even in the midst of suffering.

Continuing this theme, Ælfric uses a number of biblical examples of affliction and healing: Herod as a model of the destruction of the sinful by God's vengeance (255–9); Job as a model of patience under trial (279–87); the blind man whom Christ healed as a model of God's miracles (288–95); Paul as a model of humility (295–302); and King Hezekiah as

---

35 *BHL*, 1002; and *CANT*, 259. See *NTA*, 1:452–3; Godden, "The Sources of Catholic Homilies 1.31 (Cameron B.1.1.33)," *Fontes*; *CH Introduction*, 256–66; and "Martyrdom of Bartholomew," *SASLC Apocrypha*, 43.

a model for properly seeking a doctor's aid (315–18). In these exempla, Ælfric draws on biblical materials from Matthew 2, Job (and Gregory's *Moralia in Iob*), John 9, 2 Corinthians 12:7–9, and Isaiah 38. All of this leads to Ælfric's connection with the apocryphal narrative, that true health is not to be sought "æt unalyfedum tilungum oððe æt awyrigedum galdrum oððe æt ænigum wiccecræfte" (304–5: "from unpermitted activity or from cursed charms or from any witchcrafts"), nor from any idol (306, "deofolgylde").

Besides biblical examples, Ælfric's reliance on authority is clear when he turns to Augustine, even citing him by name (319: "Se wisa agustinus cwæð"). He quotes Augustine as saying, "þæt unpleolic sy þeah hwa læcewyrte þicge; ac þæt he tælð to unalyfedlicere wigelunge. gif hwa þa wyrt on him becnytte buton he hi to þam dolge gelecge" (319–21: "it is not dangerous if anyone eats a medicinal herb; but he will reproach it as unlawful witchcraft, if anyone ties that herb on himself, unless he lays them on a wound"). Medicinal help is laudable, but superstitious charms are unlawful. As Godden has observed, this reference most closely corresponds to Augustine's views on the issue of herbs as medicine and charms in *De doctrina Christiana* II.xxix:[36] "Aliud est enim dicere 'tritam istam herbam si biberis, uenter non dolebit', et aliud est dicere 'istam herbam collo si suspenderis, uenter non dolebit'. Ibi enim probatur contemperatio salubris, hic significatio superstitiosa damnatur" ("For it is one thing to say, 'If you drink the juice of this herb, your stomach will not hurt,' and quite another to say, 'If you hang this herb around your neck, your stomach will not hurt.' The first course is recommended as a healthful remedy; the second is to be condemned as a superstitious sign").[37] The lesson to be learned about illness and seeking cures through God's help as opposed to pagan practices – as in Bartholomew's narrative – is further solidified by this specific discussion and Ælfric's adherence to a revered patristic authority.

Ælfric's emphasis on apostles as exempla is again brought out in the final exhortations. He discusses the hardships (325, "earfoðnyssum") of the "apostoli. ꝉ þa halgan martyras" (327: "apostles, and the holy martyrs"), using this as the basis to ask a rhetorical question on which his audience

---

36 Godden, "The Sources of Catholic Homilies 1.31"; and *CH Introduction*, 266.
37 Martin and Daur, eds., *Sancti Aurelii Augustini*, 64, lines 9–13; translation from D.W. Robertson, trans., *Saint Augustine: On Christian Doctrine*, 65.

should meditate for the lesson: "Hwæt wylle we endemen þyssere wor-ulde gif we for urum synnum gebrocode beoð buton herian urne drihten ꞇ eadmodlice biddan þæt he us þurh þa hwilwendlican swingela. to þam ecum gefean gelæde?" (331–4: "What do we men of this world desire, if we are afflicted for our sins, but to praise our Lord and humbly ask that he lead us, through transitory afflictions, to eternal joys?"). The implicit answer, of course, is that Ælfric's audience should follow the models of the apostles, especially the example of Bartholomew, who dealt with the illness of a whole people through his devotion to God. The latter part of Ælfric's homily for Bartholomew thus moves from narrative to prag-matic exegesis, expounding on the notions of illness and suffering from the hagiographic account in order to address concerns about charms in late Anglo-Saxon England.[38]

Ælfric's theme is not only about health and superstition, however, since the positive exempla used in the sermon (notably, Bartholomew, Job, Paul, and Hezekiah) also point towards issues of theodicy. At the heart of this sermon is a sophisticated doctrinal issue surrounding the nature of sin and suffering. Although the members of Ælfric's audience were not likely to encounter martyrdom for their faith at the hands of pagan kings, the fre-quency of Viking raids throughout the ninth, tenth, and early eleventh centuries did make them familiar with the idea of affliction. So too did ill-ness, famine, and other common reasons for suffering. Within this frame-work, Ælfric validates his use of the apocryphal narrative as a precursor to the lesson, and uses it as an appeal to what he saw as a contemporary problem with superstition. His purpose, then, is to move back and forth between biblical and apocryphal narrative exempla, doctrines about the problem of pain, and local pragmatic solutions that may need to be curbed.

Matthew as *Imitatio Christi*

Ælfric's *Natali Sancti Mathei Apostoli et Evangelistae* (*CH* II.32) pres-ents a similar case, though his additions to the narrative occur at the start of the lesson, like a prefatory, thematic introduction to the story. While the majority of this sermon (80–225) consists of a translation of the Latin

---

38 On charms, see esp. Jolly, *Popular Religion in Late Saxon England*, esp. on this passage at 92–3.

Martyrdom of Matthew,[39] the first part of the sermon focuses on the story of Matthew's calling to be an apostle.[40] Much of this comes from the parallel gospel accounts in Matthew 9:9–13 and Luke 5:27–32, which Ælfric acknowledges directly (19–20, "þises godspelles ægðer ge of mathees gesetnysse ge of lucas"), followed by allegorical exegesis derived from Bede's *Homilia in euangelia* I.21. Ælfric's reliance on Bede is typical, since Bede's gospel sermons are found throughout Paul the Deacon's Homiliary, and I.21 is specifically assigned for Matthew's feast day.[41]

This reliance on Bede is not wholly without adaptations, and it is through Ælfric's changes that he is able to address his audience and offer connections between the gospel and the apocryphon as an exemplum. As Godden points out, in comparison to Bede's emphasis on Matthew's sin because he was a tax collector, Ælfric "omits all Bede's references to Matthew as a publican" and, subsequently, "Matthew's sins are those of 'all mankind.'"[42] What Godden does not observe, however, is how this adaptation creates an appeal to the audience, as they are also part of the universalizing problem of sin and must follow Christian examples in their faith. Matthew is just such an example – as is the case with all of the apostles – since he is an archetype for the practice of *imitatio Christi*. For Christians following the example of an apostle, they also follow Christ himself.

Ælfric finds foundation for the notion of holy imitation in Bede's use of biblical doctrine, based on 1 John 2:6. Bede explains Jesus' words to Matthew about following him: "Sequere me. Sequere autem dixit imitare; sequere dixit non tam incessu pedum quam exsecutione morum. Qui enim dicit se in Christo manere debet sicut ille ambulauit et ipse ambulare" ("'Follow me'. By 'follow' he meant imitate; by 'follow' he meant not so much the movement of feet as the carrying out of a way of life. For one who says that he abides in Christ ought himself to walk just as he walked").[43] Ælfric incorporates this same concept into his sermon, but places the words into the mouth of Jesus himself: "and [Jesus] cwæð. folga

---

39 *BHL*, 5690; and *CANT*, 270. See also *NTA*, 2:460; and "Martyrdom of Matthew," *SASLC Apocrypha*, 49–50.

40 See Godden, "The Sources of Catholic Homilies 2.32 (Cameron B.1.2.40)," *Fontes*; and *CH Introduction*, 605–13.

41 See the reconstruction of this homiliary's contents in Grégoire, *Homéliaires liturgiques médiévaux*, no. 99, "In Sancti Mathaei apostoli."

42 *CH Introduction*, 606.

43 Hurst and Fraipont, eds., *Bedae Venerabilis opera, pars III*, 149–50, lines 56–9; translation is from Martin and Hurst, *Bede the Venerable*, 206.

me; Folga me na þætan on fotlicum gange. ac eac swilce on goddra ðeawa geefenlæcunge. swa swa se apostol cwæð. Se ðe cweð þæt he on criste wunige. he sceal faran swa swa crist ferde" (27–30: "and [Jesus] said, 'Follow me.' 'Follow me not only going on feet, but also in imitation of good practices,' just as the apostle said, 'He who says that he dwells in Christ shall go just as Christ went'"). Just as this verse by John serves to explicate Matthew's situation, it also further implies that the audience should imitate Christ through Matthew's example.

Ælfric's adaptation of Bede's exegesis also highlights his own practices – he not only uses Bede's commentary but also emphasizes the original basis of these words as coming from Jesus and his apostle John ("swa swa se apostol cwæð"). Perhaps most surprising is that the call to imitation attributed to Jesus ("Folga me na þætan on fotlicum gange. ac eac swilce on goddra ðeawa geefenlæcunge") has no equivalent in either the Bible or Bede's work, nor does Godden attribute this saying to any source.[44] Ælfric takes the concept from Bede's homily, but situates the precise words within his own sermon as if spoken by Jesus himself. In this, Ælfric seemingly creates his own apocryphal saying not unlike the *agrapha* of early Christian writings, similar to the instance of an *agraphon* incorporated into Blickling 15 through the *Martyrdom of Peter and Paul*.[45] For Ælfric, placing these extracanonical words in the mouth of Christ is acceptable practice in the service of spurring his audience towards holiness. It is the sense of Jesus' teaching that is to be understood here.

Ælfric again presents the same notion of Matthew's holiness and the implicit exhortation to imitate him at the end of the first part of his sermon, just before relating the translation of the *Martyrdom of Matthew*. As a final veneration of the apostle, Ælfric includes the following:

Eal mennisc wæs synfull. ac dryhten gerihtwisode buton geearnungum ðurh his gife ða ða he geceas. swa swa he did þysne godspellere. matheum. ðe we nu todæg wurðiað; He wæs bedofen on deoppre nytennysse woruldlicra gewilnunga. ac dryhten hine ætbræd of ðam fenlicum adelan. to heofonlicum geðincðum. and hine gesette eallum ðeodum to godspellere;

---

44 Godden makes no direct comment on this saying in either "The Sources of Catholic Homilies 2.32" or *CH Introduction*, 607. Cf. Jesus' various utterances of "Sequere me" (mostly to disciples) in the gospels, none of which correspond to this passage: Matthew 8:22, 9:9, 19:21; Mark 2:14, 10:21; Luke 5:27, 9:59, 18:22; and John 1:43 and 21:19.

45 See my discussion in chapter 2, with further references there.

(72–8: All humankind was sinful, but the Lord justified without merits, through his grace, those whom he chose, just as he did with this evangelist, Matthew, whom we now honour today. He was drowned in deep ignorance of worldly desires, but the Lord rescued him from the fen-like filth, to heavenly honours, and set him as an evangelist to all peoples.)

This final note follows Bede's reasoning about righteousness and justification, which Ælfric follows for the previous lines,[46] but he also applies Bede's general words to an understanding of Matthew, original to the Old English sermon. Ælfric's own reading of Bede's homily allows him to move from the Gospel of Matthew and commentary directly into a consideration of the apostle's *Martyrdom* as a direct example of his application of Jesus' call. Similarly, this exegetical move allows Ælfric to make statements about Matthew's calling and salvation in terms that are equally applicable to his audience, for they also are part of "those whom [Christ] chose" ("ða ða he geceas"), those who should follow the apostle's exemplum in their own devotion.

The foregoing analyses of specific *Catholic Homilies* reveal that Ælfric's distance from apocryphal content is not so much as previous scholars have stressed. Similarly, the distance of these preaching texts is not so far from collections with anonymous sermons as previous scholarship sometimes indicates. We must acknowledge, of course, that there is surely a difference between different apocrypha (generically and with individual texts), since Ælfric does avoid certain texts. He relies on no expansive stories about Christ or Mary such as those found in apocryphal gospels (see chapter 4), nor speculative imaginings of eschatology such as those found in apocryphal apocalyptica. As some of his specific condemnations attest, Ælfric is indeed circumspect. Yet this attitude does not wholly set him apart, since he does use the same types of narratives about the apostles as those found in Blickling 15 (on Peter and Paul) and 18 (on Andrew and Matthias), and a host of other anonymous sermons for saints' feast days. It seems that scribes copying Ælfric's sermons were also aware of this overlap, and viewed them within the same traditions as anonymous Old English sermons as they copied them together. It is towards this aspect of the transmission of Ælfric's sermons that I now turn.

---

46 Cf. Hurst and Fraipoint, eds., *Bedae Venerabilis opera, pars III*, 153, lines 204–10; and *CH* I, 32, lines 68–72.

Ælfrician Receptions

Another way to examine associations between Ælfrician and apocryphal materials within broader Anglo-Saxon contexts is through the transmission of the *Catholic Homilies* in manuscripts from the eleventh and twelfth centuries. Just as I argue that Anglo-Saxons did not strictly demarcate between biblical and apocryphal narratives, neither did they hold to firm boundaries between what we now consider anonymous sermons and those of named authors. For this reason, extant manuscripts containing texts of the *Catholic Homilies* also include a range of preaching texts from the corpus of anonymous vernacular sermons.[47] Nancy M. Thompson provides one case study of this issue in Cambridge, Corpus Christi College 41 (s. xi[1]),[48] and in the following I use her examination as a starting point for my own claims about manuscript compilations.[49] Thompson challenges modern assumptions about the pairing between "orthodox" and "heterodox" materials, instead offering a cogent analysis of the manuscript as participating in mainstream religious belief. As seen in chapter 1, CCCC 41 has many links to the wider media network of sermons and apocrypha as they circulated and were used in late Anglo-Saxon England. Certainly the same is true of the collective coherence that we find between anonymous and Ælfrician texts in other eleventh- and twelfth-century manuscripts within the larger media network.

Three manuscripts especially stand out in this regard: Cambridge, Corpus Christi College 162 (s. xi[in.], SE England);[50] London, British Library, Cotton Vespasian D.xiv (s. xii[med.], Christ Church Canterbury or Rochester);[51] and Oxford, Bodleian Library, Bodley 343 (s. xii[2], West Midlands).[52] These manuscripts tellingly range across the temporal range of the transmission of Ælfric's works. The earliest is dated to within Ælfric's own lifetime – possibly only a few years after his completion of the *Catholic*

---

47 For overviews, see Scragg, "The Corpus of Vernacular Homilies and Prose Saints' Lives before Ælfric"; and discussions of manuscripts in *CH* I, xix–lxxviii; and *CH* II, 1–168. A number of examples may also be gleaned from the general discussion in chapter 1.

48 NRK, 32; and *ASM*, 39.

49 Thompson, "Anglo-Saxon Orthodoxy."

50 NRK, 38; and *ASM*, 50. See also Scragg, "Cambridge, Corpus Christi College 162," and Treharne, "Making Their Presence Felt."

51 NRK, 209. See esp. Treharne, "London, British Library, Cotton Vespasian D. xiv."

52 NRK, 310. See Conti and Da Rold, "Oxford Bodleian Library, Bodley 343"; and further discussion in chapter 5.

Homilies – while the latest was collected beyond the period traditionally known for the flourishing of Anglo-Saxon sermon production.[53] In what follows, I examine specific cases in these collections as representative of the ways in which readers and copiers of Ælfric's texts paired them with anonymous sermons, and the ways in which they recognized associations with apocryphal materials. In other words, I highlight how anonymous and Ælfrician sermons are similar in kind, and how Anglo-Saxons found them useful for placing together in preaching collections.

At the outset, it should be acknowledged that each case that I discuss here is part of much more general practices of later scribes appropriating Ælfric's works. These are also practices that Ælfric himself would have opposed. As already seen earlier in this chapter, he posed rather stern warnings against scribes mishandling his works, part of his establishing a persona of authority and seeking to promote his own notions of correctness. Again, Hill's remarks are cogent:

> He clearly felt strongly that there were standards to be set and that his own homily collection provided a unique exemplar; yet his injunctions express the sense that the conditions for the preservation and dissemination of such standards might not be wholly favourable. Indeed they were not, since there is ample evidence that Ælfric's homilies were subsequently mingled with others not within his chosen traditions of exegesis and authority, and that composite homilies were produced, even at Winchester, which in effect dismembered individual Ælfrician items.[54]

This presents us with a paradox in the transmission of Ælfrician sermons. On the one hand, later scribes clearly saw the authority of Ælfric's works, as they were dominant in eleventh- and twelfth-century collections. But, on the other hand, it is clear that scribes also did not share Ælfric's attitudes, and even defied his wishes if they knew about them. In all of these cases, then, we see the fluidity of traditions of authority: even Ælfric's constructed personal authority is subverted as later scribes

---

53 The classic study is Ker, *English Manuscripts in the Century after the Norman Conquest*. More recently, see esp. Gameson, *The Manuscripts of Early Norman England*; Swan and Treharne, eds., *Rewriting Old English*; Treharne, *Living through Conquest*; and Treharne, Da Rold, and Swan, eds., *Producing and Using English Manuscripts*.
54 Joyce Hill, "Ælfric: His Life and Works," 54.

reconstructed their own notions of authority by combining Ælfrician materials with apocrypha.

One telling example is a unique eschatological sermon titled *In die Sancto Pasce* in CCCC 162, pages 382–91.[55] As Clare A. Lees has pointed out, the five main themes are "the Earthly Paradise, the Evils of the Sixth Day, the Sunday List, the Harrowing of Hell, and the Last Judgment," all compiled from extra-biblical sources.[56] Embedded among these narratives are selections from Ælfric's *Sermo de sacrificio in die Pascae* (*CH* II.15). The technique used here, therefore, constitutes an appropriative adaptation, since the author of *In die Sancto Pasce* took the Ælfrician passage wholesale from a vernacular text in order to create a new text altogether – what is often called a "composite" or "scissors and paste" sermon.[57] The author saw fit to use Ælfric's Easter sermon, but also understood the value of combining it with thematically relevant material from elsewhere. This portrays the work of a homilist comfortable with a range of long-standing traditions of belief in the eternal consequences of earthly deeds. For the author of *In die Sancto Pasce*, such traditions need not be rooted in clearly traceable biblical ideas, but in sources useful for reforming the souls of the preacher's audience.

While extended analyses of the content of the composite *In die Sancto Pasce* appear elsewhere, I will focus on a comment left by an eleventh-century reader in the margins of the manuscript. Particularly striking about this sermon is that it provides evidence of one near-contemporary reader's reception. On page 382 beside the title of this sermon, an eleventh-century glossator has noted *apocrifum* in the margin.[58]

---

55 Schaefer, "An Edition of Five Old English Homilies for Palm Sunday, Holy Saturday, and Easter Sunday," 245–59; and Lees, "Theme and Echo in an Anonymous Old English Homily for Easter." A stylistic analysis is provided by Ogawa, *Language and Style in Old English Composite Homilies*, 139–72, esp. 141–54, though his concerns are different from my own. References by line numbers are to Lees, "Theme and Echo in an Anonymous Old English Homily for Easter."

56 Ibid., 125.

57 See esp. Scragg, *Dating and Style in Old English Composite Homilies*; Thompson, "'Hit segð on halgum bocum'"; Szarmach, "Vercelli Prose and Anglo-Saxon Literary History," 32–7; and Ogawa, *Language and Style in Old English Composite Homilies*.

58 To my knowledge, this marginal annotation has been noted only in the edition by Lees, "Theme and Echo in an Anonymous Old English Homily for Easter"; my thanks to Kathryn Lowe for bringing this annotation to my attention.

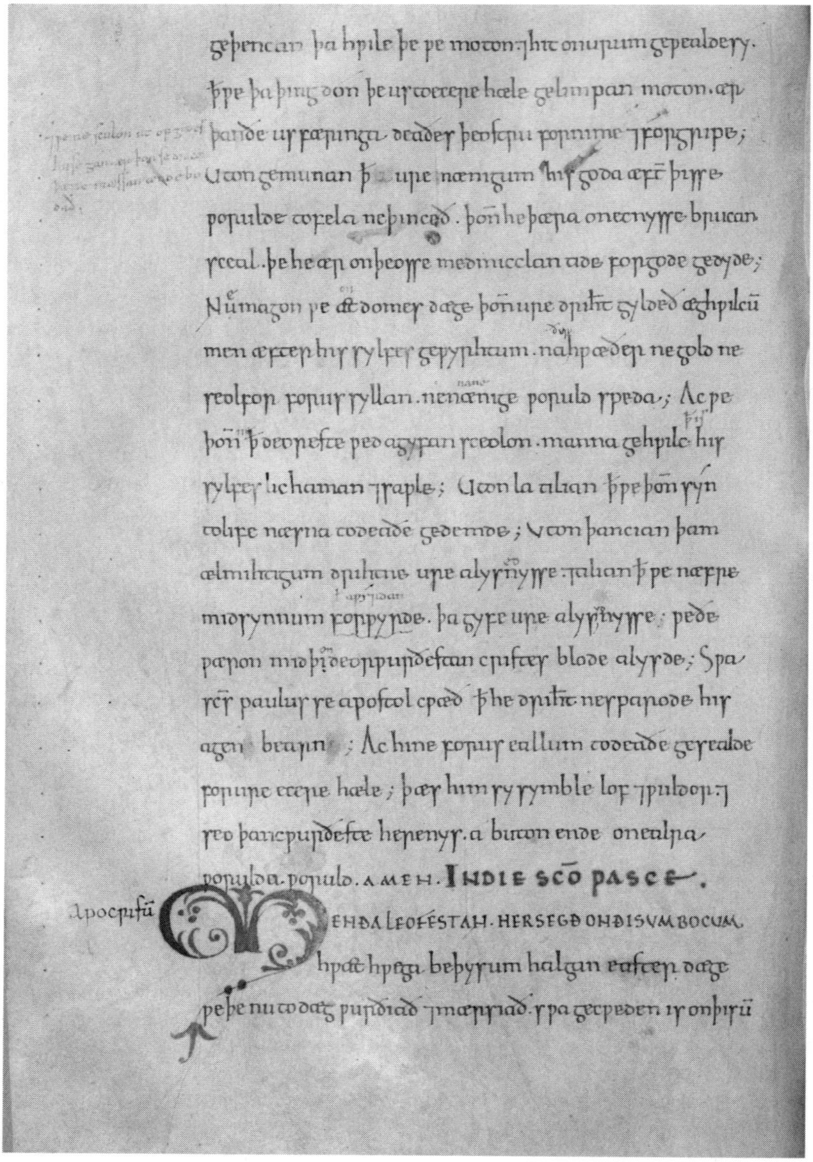

Figure 4 Cambridge, Corpus Christi College 162, page 382. By permission of the Master and Fellows of Corpus Christi College, Cambridge.

The placement of this note is, in itself, curious. After the rubric, the sermon begins with a standard admonition to the audience: "Men ða leofestan her segð on ðisum bocum hwæt hwega be þysum halgan Easter dæge we þe nu todæg wurðiað and mærsiað, swa gecweden is on þisum ..." (1–3: "Dearest men, here in these books it tells something about this holy Easter day, which now today we honour and celebrate, as it was said in these ..."). After this opening clause, a page is missing from the manuscript, but the sermon presumably continued onto the next page.[59] At the outset, there is nothing identifiably apocryphal about this opening – many texts, biblical, patristic, and medieval, address the subject of Easter, concerning Jesus' Crucifixion and Resurrection. The marginal gloss raises a number of questions. What does the annotation refer to, and why is it placed at the head of this text? Does the gloss refer to the books ("bocum") used by the sermon's author as sources, or is it meant to signal the content of the sermon for future readers? Did the annotator mean this as a warning, or simply as a note – for oneself or for others?

This gloss is one of many concerning apocrypha in Anglo-Saxon materials.[60] Among these, the meanings range across etymological descriptions, ambivalence, and outright negative assessments, including "Apocriphon .i. secretum" ("apocryphon, which is secret");[61] "Apocrifa dyrngewrita" ("apocrypha, secret writings");[62] "Apocrifa occulta" ("apocrypha, occult");[63] "Apocrifarum tweoniendlicra gewrita" or "Apocriforum tweogendlicra gewrita" ("apocrypha, doubtful writings");[64] and, in one especially condemning set of glosses, "apocrifarum, .i. falsorum scriptorum wiþersacana" ("apocrypha, which is, false scriptures, apostasy").[65] Yet the gloss in CCCC 162 has no further definition or judgment – it is just one word, a marker. A further mystery is the fact that we cannot tell if this is meant as a warning, a noticeable bookmark to facilitate finding the text with ease, or

---

59 See Lees, "Theme and Echo in an Anonymous Old English Homily for Easter."

60 Biggs discusses Old English glosses in "An Introduction and Overview of Recent Work," 18–19. Here I discuss only examples from glossaries, as found in the *Web Corpus* of Momma, ed., *The Dictionary of Old English*, by searching for *apocrif** and *apocriph**.

61 Oliphant, *The Harley Latin–Old English Glossary*, no. A43.

62 Stryker, "The Latin–Old English Glossary in MS. Cotton Cleopatra A.III," no. 304.

63 Hessels, *An Eighth-Century Latin-Anglo-Saxon Glossary*, section 1, line 689.

64 Napier, ed., *Old English Glosses, Chiefly Unpublished*, no. 5103.

65 Ibid., no. 1960.

something of both. Either way, the marginal comment acts as a distinctive sign of identification: it is clear that the scribe who wrote this gloss recognized the apocryphal material of this sermon. While this identification should not surprise us, what is striking is that contemporary scribes were not only combining apocrypha with Ælfric's sermons so soon after their composition but also recognizing these extra-biblical texts when they encountered them. Clearly Anglo-Saxon authors and scribes were reading apocrypha, despite (or maybe in spite of) whatever cautions or condemnations they might find elsewhere.

Another example of a scribe extracting and transmitting Ælfric's works alongside apocryphal material is found in the twelfth-century sermon collection Vespasian D.xiv.[66] In this manuscript we find a wide swathe of Old English preaching texts, many of them from Ælfric's *Catholic Homilies* – though a number also represent anonymous preaching. Many of the Ælfrician texts – like many of the texts of the collection generally – are for apostolic feast days, such as sermons for John the Baptist (*CH* I.25, item 11), Peter and Paul (*CH* II.24, item 15), the Assumption of the Virgin (*CH* I.30 and II.29, items 18–20),[67] the Decollation of John the Baptist (*CH* I.32, item 21), Matthew (*CH* II.32, item 23), All Saints (*CH* I.36, item 31), and Paul (*CH* I.27, item 42). Indeed, some of these draw on apocryphal acts, as discussed in the first part of this chapter. Other apocryphal texts in the collection include anonymous Old English sermons for James the Greater (item 13), the *Gospel of Nicodemus* (item 33), the *Vindicta Salvatoris* (item 34), and the *Fifteen Signs before Judgment* (item 35).[68]

Particularly interesting for the use of Ælfrician material and the transmission of apocrypha is the relationship between items 13 and 14: the first titled *Of Iacobe Iohannes broðer* (unique to this manuscript), the second extracted from Ælfric's sermon on James the Great and the Seven Sleepers (*CH* II.27). Particularly significant for considering the adaptation

---

66 References by page and line numbers are to Warner, ed., *Early English Homilies from the Twelfth Century MS. Vesp. D. XIV*. For item numbers, I follow Treharne, "London, British Library, Cotton Vespasian D. xiv," reflecting reevaluation of these texts since Warner's edition.

67 These sermons are, curiously, adapted into three individual items from two texts: the first part of *CH* I.30 (fols. 48v–54v), followed by *CH* II.29 (fols. 54v–57v), then the second part of *CH* I.30 (fols. 58r–60r).

68 On all of these, see *SASLC Apocrypha*; for the Fifteen Signs before Judgment, see also "De quindecim signis ante diem iudicii," in Hawk, "Pseudo-Bede" and "The *Fifteen Signs before Judgment* in Anglo-Saxon England."

of Ælfrician materials is the use of an anonymous sermon for James in this collection. In the *Catholic Homilies*, Ælfric includes his own narrative about this apostle, followed directly by the account of the Seven Sleepers – but the compiler of Vespasian D.xiv omitted the Jamesian beginning and used the anonymous sermon in its place while retaining Ælfric's section on the Seven Sleepers. Like Ælfric's piece in the *Catholic Homilies*, this anonymous sermon for James in Vespasian D.xiv is a translation of the Latin *Martyrdom of James the Great*;[69] as Joana Proud observes about this later adaptation, "The extant text is dependent on the same version of the James legend as Aelfric's [*sic*] ... but selects a different portion of the legend for translation, with some overlap."[70]

The Vespasian sermon begins with the imprisonment of James, which is towards the end of the narrative as given in Ælfric's sermon. While Ælfric focuses on James's confrontation with the sorcerer Hermogenes and the apostle's martyrdom, the author of the Vespasian sermon focuses on the speeches that James gives in order to legitimate Jesus' status as Christ according to the Hebrew Scriptures. Thus, in the Vespasian sermon, "Jacobus soðlice wæs afylled mid þan Halgen Gaste" (21.10: "James truly was filled with the Holy Spirit"), giving a summary of biblical history starting with Abraham, discussing the Israelite prophets, ranging through the Davidic monarchy, and highlighting the significance of the narrative and key players for Jesus as Christ and the Christian faith. All of this is omitted from Ælfric's sermon. In this way, the Vespasian sermon uses a similar adaptive technique as Blickling 15 (as discussed in chapter 2), omitting narrative action in favour of speeches. Presumably, it was this characteristic of the anonymous sermon that appealed to the compiler of Vespasian D.xiv, instead of Ælfric's own pairing of Jamesian materials with the Seven Sleepers. Whatever the reason, this particular collection demonstrates how selection affects the processes of scribes, at the same time that it complicates modern assumptions. From the standpoint of modern scholarship, it is easy to favour Ælfric because he is a named, known author and because he has been held up as a figure of authority for late Anglo-Saxon England. Yet, for the compiler of Vespasian D.xiv, the preference was for an anonymous translation that retained a different aspect of the apocryphal narrative.

---

69 See "Martyrdom of James the Great," *SASLC Apocrypha*, 45–6.
70 Proud, "The Sources of the ANON (OE) St James the Greater (Cameron B.3.3.11)," *Fontes*.

The last case is found in Bodley 343, a rich witness to the transmission of Ælfric's sermons and apocrypha together. While I discuss this collection in more detail in chapter 5 (with further references to Ælfric's works there), in the following I focus on a specific case of associations between Ælfrician sermons and the anonymous Old English *History of the Holy Rood Tree*.[71] The only complete version of this apocryphon in Old English survives in Bodley 343, on folios 14v–20v, though two earlier manuscript fragments (originally part of the same manuscript) with corresponding text have also been recovered: Cambridge, Corpus Christi College 557 and Lawrence, University of Kansas, Kenneth Spencer Research Library, Pryce C2.1 (s. xi^med., Worcester).[72] These fragments substantiate Arthur S. Napier's earlier claims that this Old English text was composed and circulated at least by the middle of the eleventh century (if not earlier).[73] This text has been largely neglected, as Thomas D. Hill has offered the only sustained analysis, examining one episode that relates the conversion of the Sibilla.[74] Yet the *Holy Rood Tree* reveals much more about apocrypha, relationships within the wider network of Anglo-Saxon preaching, and the significance of selection surrounding the transmission of Ælfrician and anonymous sermons.

The *Holy Rood Tree* shares a number of intertextual associations with Ælfric's engagement with legends of the Cross in his own works. For example, Ælfric incorporated legends about the Holy Cross most prominently in his sermons for the *Inventio Sanctae Crucis* (*CH* II.18) and the *Exaltatio Sanctae Crucis* (*LS* 27).[75] All of these texts add to our knowledge of legends about the Holy Cross in Anglo-Saxon England,[76] popular

---

71 References by page and line numbers are to Napier, ed., *History of the Holy Rood-Tree*.

72 NRK, 73; and *ASM*, 117. See also Ker, "An Eleventh-Century Old English Legend of the Cross before Christ"; Colgrave and Hyde, "Two Recently Discovered Leaves from Old English Manuscripts"; and Page, Budny, and Hadgraft, "Two Fragments of an Old English Manuscript in the Library of Corpus Christi College, Cambridge."

73 Towards the conclusion of his study of the manuscript and language of the text, Napier wrote, "I am inclined to think that the existing *Rood-tree* is a copy of an OE. version, written probably in the first half of the eleventh century"; and, again, "I feel driven to the conclusion that the *Rood-tree* is a copy of an eleventh century English original" (*History of the Holy Rood-Tree*, lviii–lix).

74 Thomas D. Hill, "The Conversion of Sibilla in the *History of the Holy Rood Tree*."

75 *CH* II, 174–9; and *LS*, 2.144–58.

76 See Stevens, *The Cross in the Life and Literature of the Anglo-Saxons*; McEntire, "The Devotional Context of the Cross before A.D. 1000"; Gittos and Bedingfield, eds, *The Liturgy of the Late Anglo-Saxon Church*, 143–84; and the volumes produced by the

narratives that influenced many Old English and Anglo-Latin texts, especially those for the Invention and Exaltation of the Cross in the liturgy.[77] Like other traditions discussed throughout this study, associations with the Cross in Anglo-Saxon England form a prevalent, intermedial network, bringing together texts (Latin and Old English, prose and poetry), visual arts (including manuscript illustrations), material culture (stone crosses, inscriptions, and ecclesiastical staves), and lived experiences (such as processional rituals).[78] For the present case, I focus on those aspects of intertextuality that link the transmissions of Holy Cross legends to other Ælfrician preaching texts in Bodley 343. This examination, therefore, demonstrates the ways in which later Anglo-Saxons profitably read Ælfric's works alongside related apocrypha.

The most obvious connections are between Ælfric's *Inventio Sanctae Crucis* and the *Holy Rood Tree*, since both relate the Invention of the Holy Cross by Helen, the mother of the Emperor Constantine. Ælfric's identified source for the *Inventio* is Rufinus's Latin translation of Eusebius's *Historia ecclesiastica* (although Ælfric mistakenly attributes it to Jerome),[79] although the more popular source for the narrative is the Latin *Inventio Sanctae Crucis* (also known as the *Acta Cyriaci*).[80] For instance, the *Inventio Sanctae Crucis* was used as a source for details about the Invention in the ninth-century *Old English Martyrology* (3 May),[81] Cynewulf's Old English poem *Elene* (included in the Vercelli Book),[82] and an anonymous Old English sermon for the Invention in Oxford, Bodleian

---

   Sancta Crux/Halig Rod project: Karkov, Keefer, and Jolly, eds., *The Place of the Cross in Anglo-Saxon England*; Jolly, Karkov, and Keefer, eds., *Cross and Culture in Anglo-Saxon England*; and Keefer, Jolly, and Karkov, eds., *Cross and Cruciform in the Anglo-Saxon World*.

77 See entries for the *Inventio* and *Exaltatio* (esp. under the name Hrabanus Maurus [Hrab.Maur.]) in *Fontes*; Whatley, "Iesus Christus, Exaltatio Sanctae Crucis," *SASLC 1*, 259–63; Biggs and Whatley, "Iesus Christus, Inventio Sanctae Crucis," *SASLC 1*, 264–7.

78 For study with further details, see Hawk, "'Id est, crux Christi.'"

79 References by page and line numbers are to Mommsen, ed., *Historia ecclesiastica in Eusebius Werke*; relevant passages are also printed in *CH Introduction*, 513–16.

80 See Godden, "The Sources of Catholic Homilies 2.19 (Cameron B.1.2.24)," *Fontes*; *CH Introduction*, 513–16; and Biggs and Whatley, "Iesus Christus, Inventio Sanctae Crucis."

81 Rauer, ed. and trans., *The Old English Martyrology*, 94–5 and 257.

82 References by line numbers are to Gradon, ed., *Cynewulf's "Elene."*

Library, Auctarium F.4.32 (s. xi²), folios 10r–18v.[83] Indeed, these texts –
like many about the Holy Cross – open up questions about the relationships between apocrypha, legends, hagiography, and historiography in
Christian traditions. Thus, the Eusebius-Rufinus *Historia ecclesiastica* and
Ælfric's use of this source appeal to historiography, while the *Inventio*
(*Acta Cyriaci*) draws on hagiographic conventions, and the *Holy Rood
Tree* constitutes a legendary narrative spanning Jewish and Christian chronologies from the Hebrew Bible and New Testament. Yet, generically, all
of these texts overlap, since they all deal with the biblical figure of the
Cross. Such issues remind us that medieval authors did not see textual
genres and boundaries according to our modern classifications. After all,
we have already seen that Ælfric accepted and used apocryphal acts (arguably prototypical of the hagiographic genre) as extensions of biblical history, not in contention with the New Testament. The same is true of the
Inventio legends, which take the biblical figure of the Holy Cross as the
starting point for their narratives.

A closer examination of the overlapping narratives and intertextualities between Ælfric's *Inventio Sanctae Crucis* and the *Holy Rood Tree* is
instructive. Ælfric transitions from his discussion of Constantine to Helen
by relating, "His modor wæs cristen. Elena gehaten. swiðe gelyfed mann.
and ðearle eawfæst; Þa ferde heo to hierusalem. mid fullum geleafan. wolde
ða rode findan. ðe crist on ðrowade" (38–40: "His mother was Christian,
named Elena, a very faithful person, and very devout. Then she went to
Jerusalem, with full belief, she wished to find the Rood, on which Christ
had suffered").[84] The parallel account in the *Holy Rood Tree* takes place
almost at the end of this narrative, when "sancta helena to hirusalem com.
ꞇ þa halga rode sæcan ongon" (32.8–9: "Saint Elena came to Jerusalem, and
then began to seek the Holy Rood"). As in other Holy Cross accounts,
Helen finds the Holy Rood hidden away (or buried), with the help of
divine signs, and even discerns the True Cross (as it is often called) by a
miracle, after which she builds a church on the site to honour the figure

---

83 NRK, 297, art. a; and *ASM*, 538.5. Edited in Morris, *Legends of the Holy Rood*. On
source relationships, see esp. Biggs and Whatley, "Iesus Christus, Inventio Sanctae
Crucis."
84 Cf. Mommsen, ed., *Eusebius Werke*, 2:969, lines 11–15: "Per idem tempus Helena
Constantini mater, femina inconparabilis fide religion animi ac magnificentia singulari
… Hierusalem petit atque ibi locum, in quo sacrosanctum corpus Christi patibulo
adfixum pependerat, ab incolis perquirit."

and to establish a reliquary. Ælfric condenses the details of the miracles in the Invention, but the general story remains the same.

In addition to the common narrative of Helen's finding the Cross, however, there are further parallels, with Ælfric bringing his account into closer association with the *Holy Rood Tree* legend through details not altogether clear or explained in the Eusebius-Rufinus narrative. Although the Eusebius-Rufinus account mentions that Helen "found three crosses jumbled together" ("tres confuso ordine repperit cruces") in Jerusalem, it is not clear about the reason for the appearance of more than one cross.[85] Ælfric clarifies: "Heo becom to þære stowe swa hire geswutelode god. þurh heofenlicere gebicnunge. and afunde ðreo roda. an wæs ðæs hælendes. and ða oðre ðæra ðeofa" (40–3: "She came to the place as God had manifested to her, through a heavenly sign, and found three roods; one was the Saviour's, and the others were the thieves'"). The numbers here are echoic of the continued emphasis on three roods (or rods) throughout the *Holy Rood Tree*. For example, the first appearance is when "three rods grew" (2.8–9: "iwæxene ðreo gyrden") beside Moses in his sleep, and emphasis on these three rods runs throughout the legend. After Helen has found the Cross (also through God's providence), the *Holy Rood Tree* relates, "hæfde heo eacswylce ða oðre rode þe ðe sceaþe on ahongen wæs" (32.25–6: "she also had the other cross on which the thief was hanged"). Descriptions by Ælfric and the author of the *Holy Rood Tree* also correspond to the events of Cynewulf's *Elene*, which says of Judas, digging for the Cross, "he ðær þreo mette / ... roda ætsomne" (832b–833b: "there he found three ... roods together"); the poem later explains, "þæt twegen mid him / geþrowedon ⁊ he wæs þridda sylf / on rode treo" (853a–855a: "that two suffered with him [Jesus], and he himself was the third on the Rood Tree"). Ælfric's account, while resting on the Eusebius-Rufinus *Historia ecclesiastica*, demonstrates how clarifying details from other accounts of the Invention of the Cross bleed into his sermon.

Finally, one more point about the *Holy Rood Tree* in Bodley 343 may be noted for its significance in relation to Anglo-Saxon preaching, and for its relationship to the circulation of Ælfric's sermons. In Bodley 343, the *Holy Rood Tree* directly follows Ælfric's *Dominica I in Mense Septembri* (*CH* II.30, fols. 12r–14v) in its proper liturgical order, since the Exaltation of the Cross – which the legend could plausibly commemorate – is celebrated on 14 September. Though not all of the sermons of Bodley 343

---

85 Ibid., lines 21–2.

are organized according to the liturgical cycle, some texts do form distinct sequences meant to circulate together for certain seasons (and possibly copied from exemplars that did arrange texts in their liturgical order). I suggest that the preceding Ælfrician text for September and the *Holy Rood Tree* together form a sequence in their proper liturgical order, in which the apocryphal legend stands in the place of Ælfric's *Exaltatio*. As already seen with Vespasian D.xiv, scribal preference wins out in the process of selection. The apocryphal legend of the *Holy Rood Tree*, therefore, fits into a coherent cycle of preaching in the twelfth-century collection, as a useful text for teaching the significance of the Holy Cross in the vernacular.

Conclusions

In considering my examinations of Ælfric's works in relation to apocrypha, it is useful to recall John Blair's claims about the "virtual monopoly of record" that looms in the Anglo-Saxon written record, particularly in the case of sermons.[86] Ælfric himself often looms, in the record as well as scholarship, in two major aspects: for his authoritative voice, perceived as one of the established ecclesiastical institution, and for his prolific corpus and the widespread circulation of his works that can be attached to a known historical figure. As I have demonstrated in this chapter, there is more to account for than the normative assumptions drawn out of these two issues. Looking beyond Ælfric's loud voice of condemnation leads to a more nuanced understanding of his practices of adapting apocrypha for useful teaching purposes.

From this examination, no single, monolithic reason for the use of apocrypha emerges, but Ælfric's processes taken together speak to pedagogical practicality. By pairing apocryphal acts like those of Bartholomew and Matthew with authoritative sources like Augustine and Bede, Ælfric is able to address such deep doctrinal issues as theodicy and the imitation of Christ. Similarly, looking towards the circulation of Ælfric's sermons in their manuscript contexts reveals how readers often set them in contact with anonymous sermons also usefully adapting apocryphal materials. We find that compilers looked to anonymous materials for their purposes, even when Ælfric's sermons remained as alternatives. In the case of the Easter sermon in CCCC 162, an expanded, adapted form of Ælfric's

---

86 Blair, *The Church in Anglo-Saxon Christianity*, 353.

sermon was used, rather than the original text from the *Catholic Homilies*; and clearly a near-contemporary reader recognized the apocryphal content used. In the cases of both the sermon on James in Vespasian D.xiv and the *Holy Rood Tree* in Bodley 343, scribes chose anonymous, apocryphal materials rather than alternatives from Ælfric's corpus.

These observations about Ælfric should also cause us to entertain questions about whether or not others shared similar attitudes. Perhaps, without further knowledge of the authors and compilers of the many anonymous Old English sermons and the many collections of vernacular preaching texts, this leads only to speculation. But whatever attitudes individuals or groups held towards apocrypha – acceptance, condemnation, or ambivalence towards any single text or any group of texts – attitudes were not universal. If nothing else, acknowledging these complexities should cause us to rein in generalizations imposed by modern biases towards the traditions that circulated in many guises in Anglo-Saxon England.

Chapter Four

Translating Jesus in Text and Image

Narratives about the figure of Jesus are central in the life of the Christian Church for teaching basic beliefs. After all, Christianity revolves around Jesus' birth, life, crucifixion, resurrection, and ascension; for good reason, these were central topics in medieval preaching.[1] Yet the gospels were not self-contained narratives, and medieval authors drew on a combination of sources to tell stories ultimately rooted in the gospels but requiring hermeneutic elaboration. While composing vernacular sermons, Anglo-Saxon authors were not shy about using materials from apocryphal gospels. Two sermons in the Vercelli and Blickling collections stand out as exemplary representatives of apocryphal narratives about Jesus: Vercelli 6 and Blickling 7, both unique within the corpus of Old English sermons.[2] The first is intended for Christmas and focuses on Jesus' infancy, with the main narrative from the *Gospel of Pseudo-Matthew*. Scragg rightly observes the rarity of Old English Christmas sermons, since Vercelli 5 and 6 are the only extant anonymous sermons on the subject[3] – a fact that points

---

1 See, for example, lists of sermons under the headings of relevant themes in DiNapoli, *An Index of Theme and Image to the Homilies of the Anglo-Saxon Church*.

2 Part of Blickling 7 was also adapted into an eleventh-century Old English sermon in Oxford, Bodleian Library, Junius 121 (s. xi³/⁴, Worcester), fols. 148v–154v; NRK, 338, item 33; and *ASM*, 644. For an edition, see Fadda, "'De descensu Christi ad inferos'"; see also Scragg, "A Late Old English Harrowing of Hell Homily from Worcester and Blickling Homily VII."

3 *VH*, 109. Scragg points out that, in the Vercelli Book, sermons 5 and 6 "are not contiguous … as *Andreas* and *The Fates of the Apostles* stand between" (*VH*, 126). Copies of Vercelli 5 are found in Cambridge, Corpus Christi College 198 (s. xi) and Oxford, Bodleian Library, Bodley 340 and 342 (s. xi); see NRK, 48 and 309; *ASM*, 64 and 569; and, for further details, *VH*, 108.

to the significance of Vercelli 6 as characteristic of how Anglo-Saxon authors used apocryphal elements to supplement the story of the Nativity. Blickling 7 is intended for Easter, representing another early preaching text for a major liturgical high point, as well as providing the earliest Old English prose narrative of the Harrowing of Hell.[4]

Even beyond translations undertaken by Old English preachers, however, representations of apocryphal narratives about Jesus' life are evident in Anglo-Saxon visual arts. Scenes of the Nativity often included details related not only to the canonical gospels but also to extra-biblical sources expanding the basic narrative, and the Harrowing of Hell was a popular scene in a range of art despite its ambiguous presence in the New Testament. Both Jessica Brantley and Thomas D. Hill have demonstrated how images can reveal possible sources for texts translating theological ideas, opening up ways of thinking more deeply about relationships between media.[5] One of my central questions seeks to further investigate text-image relationships: how can we theorize intermedial translations between texts and images, as part of a wider multimedia network related to preaching? In this chapter, I specifically address how visual media serve as translations of apocrypha, and, therefore, as cultural parallels to narratives in Anglo-Saxon preaching texts. Exploring this notion reveals analogues in visual media that help to situate the sermons in popular culture across social classes, bringing together varieties of learned and popular discourses in which apocrypha circulated in late Anglo-Saxon England.

Taken together, Anglo-Saxon witnesses across media further demonstrate how apocrypha permeated contexts surrounding sermons. Influences may be found across a variety of porous social boundaries, which are, in actuality, linked by common materials. Apocrypha were communicated in many contexts beyond the verbal medium of preaching. Indeed, connections with the liturgy and mass in which many different audiences could interact are common to the artefacts depicting Jesus' apocryphal deeds to be discussed in this chapter. Just as vernacular sermons containing apocrypha could have been preached to both elites and commoners, these narratives appeared in other media accessible to audiences across a social spectrum. In this way, apocryphal sermons coexisted with material

---

4 On liturgy and the major Christian feasts such as Christmas and Easter, see esp. Bedingfield, *The Dramatic Liturgy of Anglo-Saxon England*.

5 Brantley, "The Iconography of the Utrecht Psalter and the Old English *Descent into Hell*"; and Thomas D. Hill, "The Baby on the Stone."

objects such as ecclesiastical trappings and mass-books (accessible mainly to ecclesiasts and monks), psalters (accessible to ecclesiasts, monks, and elite laity), and stone carvings (accessible to anyone visiting the site where they stood). Cultural artefacts such as these specifically point towards liturgical materials and settings, not unlikely connections for vernacular preaching texts.

Multimedia Translation

Surprisingly, methodological discussions of translation are not commonly addressed in scholarship about text-image relationships.[6] The interplay between texts and images is well-trodden territory in scholarship – though, instead of "translation," scholars tend to employ terms such as "interchange" and "exchange," "transformation," "dynamic interaction," "appropriation," and, perhaps most often, "illustration"; when the word "translation" is used, it is often not accompanied by methodological explanation.[7] Adding to this muddled proliferation of vocabulary without elucidation, one recent critic describes an image as "translated" from text, but places it within inverted commas without comment, as if the word stands as a surrogate for an undefined concept.[8] Comparably, extended discussions of translation rarely acknowledge the possibilities of this practice outside of a verbal medium, and only recently have scholars of translation studies begun to explore relationships across media.[9] These criticisms are not meant to challenge previous contributions to scholarship, but to question the methodological assumptions for a significant subject that could benefit from further exploration.

---

6 The classic studies of text-image relationships are Mitchell, *Iconology* and *Picture Theory*; translation is not addressed in either. A related problem, Brantley observes, is that "Links between the visual and the narrative arts in the Anglo-Saxon period remain largely unexplored" ("The Iconography of the Utrecht Psalter and the *Old English Descent into Hell*," 43 n. 2, where exceptions are cited); references in this chapter point to some further studies. On "image" in relation to media studies, see Mitchell, "Image."

7 For example, see Hoffman, "Pathways of Portability"; Karkov, *Text and Picture in Anglo-Saxon England*; Woodfin, "An Officer and a Gentleman"; Cynthia Robinson, "Arthur in Alhambra?"; Smith, "Chivalric Narratives and Devotional Experience in the Taymouth Hours."

8 Ibid., 35.

9 For recent notable examples of these shifts, see Venuti, "Adaptation, Translation, Critique"; Zanoletti, "Marinetti and Buvoli"; and Wilson and Maher, eds., *Words, Images and Performances in Translation*.

This chapter extends the overall assumption of this book that translation is possible in and across all media. Addressing text-image relationships, Marco Mostert poses the challenge of considering diverse media representations in the following way:

> Writing is a visual system representing speech, and because of its visuality, all writing is also image. This implies that every written text shares some of its aspects with images. Hence the metaphor of reading may be useful to refer to the search for meaning in images as it does for that in texts. This suggests that the historians of the image might try having a look at the questions posed by the historians of reading, so that these may be adapted to the study of images. If images can be regarded as symbols or representations to which different contemporary audiences ascribed different meanings, and if these meanings show a development over time, have a history, then the questions put by historians of reading seem, *mutatis mutandis*, if not identical then at least similar.[10]

Similarly, it is my hope that exploring theories of intermedial translation with the help of work by those who study images will open up new assessments worth pursuing. From this perspective, the uses of apocryphal narratives in Anglo-Saxon England – in both verbal and visual media – should lead to reconsidering notions of intermedial translations represented in a wider network of relationships.

As discussed in my introduction, intermedial relationships are central to my approach, since they remind us that artefacts were not disconnected from each other in culture, but interconnected in significant ways that speak across the boundaries that modern scholars have established. Leslie Webster indicates as much when pairing literature and visual art, commenting that "The Anglo-Saxon imagination was an intensely visual one: images contained stories just as much as words."[11] The boundaries sometimes set up between different types of literary texts – such as Latin and Old English, poetic and prose – and the visual arts, as well as creators and audiences, are no less imaginary than the boundaries often set up between biblical and apocryphal materials.

---

10 Mostert, "Reading Images and Texts," 6.
11 Webster, *Anglo-Saxon Art*, 13; for her extended discussion of relationships between Anglo-Saxon texts and visual arts, see 13–41.

One claim in the following examination is that sermons and visual arts are similar in their adaptive translations of apocryphal gospels. Catherine E. Karkov has pointed out that visual translations (like sermons) refer to influences besides textual sources, such as pictorial resonances.[12] If, as scholars have readily acknowledged, translation is a process contingent on complex contexts and influences, then associations that may not be apparent in a primary written source should be considered seriously. In this manner, it is useful to examine intermedial translations across multimedia related to a common source as analogous to each other. Thus, parallels open up differences as well as commonalities in adaptive translations, which may be understood as keys to cultural associations that resonate in and across media. When multimedia are examined together as comparative projects of translation, it becomes apparent, as Brantley has pointed out, that they "represent related responses in different media."[13] In considering this issue, it is pertinent to remember that every translation is a specific, ideological representation of how the creator(s) perceived and used traditions from which the specific medium was shaped.[14] This reminder is particularly important for the present study, since various Anglo-Saxon media provide an understanding of not only the transmissions but also the receptions of apocrypha in Anglo-Saxon Christianity.

One common feature of representations in sermons and visual media is how they emphasize Jesus' deeds rather than his teachings. In Christian tradition, Jesus' teachings are of course central, but the sermons examined in this chapter do not use them as a basis; instead, they generally focus on narrating his actions. Similarly, artistic representations of Jesus' life depict scenes that emphasize narrative action – not surprisingly, since actions lend themselves to pictures more readily than words do. By highlighting narrative actions in verbal and visual media, Anglo-Saxons acknowledged that Jesus' deeds are as significant as his words for teaching Christian doctrine,

---

12 Karkov, *Text and Picture*, 17.

13 Brantley, "The Iconography of the Utrecht Psalter and the *Old English Descent into Hell*," 62.

14 While much of this examination is related to the concept of "representation," I will not address it directly here; for discussions of this concept, see esp. classic studies such as Auerbach, *Mimesis*; and Mitchell, *Picture Theory*; as well as, more recently, Prendergast, *The Triangle of Representation*; and Webb, *Understanding Representation*, with further references there.

even when certain events are either not present or not related explicitly in the canonical gospels. When set in relationship to other accessories of worship – such as psalters, sacramentaries, croziers, and architectural inscriptions – these sermons may be seen as participating in what M. Bradford Bedingfield has called "the dramatic liturgy of Anglo-Saxon England."[15]

Extended narratives surrounding Jesus' infancy miracles are wholly absent from biblical accounts, and only Matthew 12:40 contains a tangential link to the Harrowing of Hell; the popularity of these traditions largely relies on details from apocryphal narratives. In other words, for medieval authors, apocryphal stories suitably embellish those in the canonical gospels. These deeds are central to understanding Jesus' miraculous and divine nature as well as soteriological doctrines, making them, subsequently, central to Christian teaching. In fact, when considering the incarnational theology surrounding Jesus' life – especially for the Nativity, Crucifixion, and Resurrection – the lines between Jesus' words and actions are blurred, since he is considered the Word of God. Jesus' words and actions are simultaneously representative of his transcendent character, entwined together as signifiers of his divinity. In this sense, messages relayed through his speeches are no different from messages relayed through his actions. Reflection upon translations of *Pseudo-Matthew* and the Harrowing of Hell in both verbal and visual media together reveals this convergence.

Miraculous Infancy

Apocryphal infancy gospels are not generally common in Anglo-Saxon England, but Vercelli 6 stands out as one of a few examples that do survive. This text includes an incipit (the only one in the Vercelli Book, though some items have titles) that states, "Incipit narrare miracula que facta fuerant ante aduentum Saluatoris Domini nostri Iesu Christi" ("We begin to narrate the miracles which had been done before the arrival of our Saviour the Lord Jesus Christ"). Following this headnote, the sermon begins, "Her sagað ymb ðas mæran gewyrd þe to þyssum dæge gewearð, þætte ælmihtig dryhten sylfa þas world gesohte ꝺ þurh unwemme fæmnan on þas world acenned wæs, to þan þæt he eall manna cyn fram hellwara wite

---

15 Bedingfield, *The Dramatic Liturgy of Anglo-Saxon England*, passim.

alysde ꝫ to heofona rices wuldre gefremede" (1–4: "Here we will tell about the famous event which happened on this day, that the Almighty Lord Himself sought this world and through an unspotted virgin he was born to this world, so that he freed all of humankind from the torments of hell and brought them to the glory of the kingdom of heaven"). In both theme and content, Vercelli 6 is intended for Christmas in its aims to centre on the Nativity and the salvific implications for that feast. For the impetus of the narrative, however, the sermon's author looked beyond the canonical gospels to a host of traditional materials suitable for translation. Foremost among these sources is *Pseudo-Matthew*, which is used along with the canonical Gospel of Luke and historiographical traditions.[16] Various versions and translations of *Pseudo-Matthew* survive from Anglo-Saxon England, particularly in relation to preaching.[17] In translating these sources, Vercelli 6 incorporates biblical and apocryphal materials synthetically, fusing together details about the Nativity from a variety of sources rather than relying on a single text. In translating these sources strategically, the author highlights the central theme of this sermon: Jesus' miraculous nature in birth and childhood deeds.

Para-biblical details at the start of Vercelli 6 include a series of miracles purported to have occurred before Jesus' birth, some of which overlap with similar signs in the preceding sermon, Vercelli 5. As a contribution to source studies, J.E. Cross offered the first detailed examination of these portents and linked them to Insular traditions derived from Roman writers such as Livy, Orosius, and Julius Obsequens.[18] Recently, Thomas N. Hall has provided an extensive treatment of the tradition in the early medieval period, and has demonstrated that such portents were widespread in biblical commentaries and homilies – especially those associated with Irish learning.[19] Hall's work thus complicates previous studies seeking to create

---

16 *BHL*, 5334–42; and *CANT*, 51. References are to Gijsel, ed., *Libri de nativitate Mariae*, 277–481 (Forma textus A). Translations are my own, from *The Gospel of Pseudo-Matthew*.

17 See esp. Clayton, *The Cult of the Virgin Mary in Anglo-Saxon England* and *The Apocryphal Gospels of Mary in Anglo-Saxon England*. For summaries of scholarship, see Hall, "Gospel of Pseudo-Matthew," *SASLC Apocrypha*, 23–5; and Clayton, "De Nativitate Mariae," *SASLC Apocrypha*, 25–6.

18 Cross, "Portents and Events at Christ's Birth."

19 Hall, "The Portents at Christ's Birth in Vercelli Homilies V and VI."

clear source links.[20] The portents in the two sermons may be catalogued as follows:[21]

Golden ring(s) around the sun
Roman emperor forgives all the people
Slaves are restored to their masters (not in Vercelli 6)
Peace throughout all the earth, no weapons
Men are obliged to pay tribute to the emperor (not in Vercelli 6)
Sun shines as brightly as in summer for seven nights before Nativity
   (not in Vercelli 5)
Three wells flow with oil (not in Vercelli 5)

The effect that these miracles precipitate for the Christian audience is wonder, especially at the universal recognition of the coming birth of Jesus. These portents, in fact, have certain affinities with ancient oracular literature such as the *Sibylline Oracles* and other apocalyptica of Hellenistic Judaism and early Christianity,[22] particularly since astrological signs to foretell politico-religious changes were taken over by late antique and medieval historiographic writers.[23] Setting the scene for the Nativity in Vercelli 6, these miracles point out the acknowledgment of Jesus' cosmic advent not only by the Roman emperor (forgiveness) and people (loyalty to the emperor) but also by the population of the whole earth (worldwide

---

20 The primary analogue compared by Cross is the *Catechesis Celtica*, a Hiberno-Latin florilegium of exegetical materials compiled sometime before the tenth century, although he notes that closer immediate sources must rest behind the Vercelli sermons ("The Portents at Christ's Birth in Vercelli Homilies V and VI"). In entries for Vercelli 5 and 6 in *Fontes*, Atherton notes the *Catechesis* variously as a direct source, antecedent source, and one possible source of multiple (see "The Sources of Vercelli 5 (Cameron B.3.2.1)," and "The Sources of Vercelli 6 (Cameron B.3.4.10)"); cf. Zacher, *Preaching the Converted*, 20–1, who follows Atherton's entry in *Fontes*. Wright provides a more circumspect assessment in *The Irish Tradition in Old English Literature*, 80–1. Scragg prints the *Catechesis* in the critical apparatus for Vercelli 5, though he cautions, "It is not intended to suggest that the Latin text is a direct source" (*VH*, 109 n. 1).
21 Cf. Hall, "The Portents at Christ's Birth in Vercelli Homilies V and VI," 94–5.
22 See esp. Collins, "Sibylline Oracles" and *The Apocalyptic Imagination*, esp. 116–27.
23 Astrological concerns run through many early Jewish pseudepigrapha; see Charlesworth's remarks in "Introduction for the General Reader," *The Old Testament Pseudepigrapha*, 1:xxxiii–iv. Astrological concerns were also of interest to early medieval authors; see Flint, *The Rise of Magic in Early Medieval Europe*; and, more specifically, Mark Williams, *Fiery Shapes*.

peace), the earth itself (wells springing forth oil), and even celestial bodies (the sun).

After enumerating these portents, the author of Vercelli 6 moves from the classically derived portents to the miraculous Nativity itself. Here the narrative relates, "⁊ þa to þære sylfan niht ær morgensteorra upeode, dryhten wæs geboren on ðysne middangeard, ⁊ hine geborene englas onfengon ⁊ hine gebædon, ⁊ him wundorlico lof sungon ⁊ swa cwædon: 'Wuldor on heannesse Gode, ⁊ on eorðan sib mannum ðæs godan willan'" (55–8: "And then in that same night before the morning-star arose, the Lord was born on this earth, and angels received Him who had been born, and prayed to Him, and sang praise to Him, and so said: 'Glory to God in the highest, and on earth peace to all men of good will'"). The recognizable words of praise are, ultimately, derived from Luke 2:14,[24] but this passage presents a translation from *Pseudo-Matthew* 13:2: "Quae lux non defecit nec in die nec in nocte, quamdiu ibi Maria peperit masculum, quem circumdederunt nascentem angeli, et natum super pedes suos stantem adorauerunt eum dicentes: Gloria in excelsis deo et in terra pax hominibus bonae uoluntatis" ("This light did not withdraw, neither day nor night, until Mary gave birth to a male, whom angels surrounded at birth; and as he was born standing on his feet, they worshipped him saying: 'Glory to God in the highest, and on earth peace to men of good will'").[25] Rather than signalling a break from the canonical gospel and the start of the translation of the apocryphon, the author incorporates a passage that blends the two sources. This is especially notable since the biblical *gloria* easily could have been used, especially considering that this passage from *Pseudo-Matthew* comes from a chapter not otherwise incorporated into the Old English sermon. This transitional passage seems to indicate that, for the author of Vercelli 6, traditions were blurred enough that preferring *Pseudo-Matthew* raised no problems – especially if the author were familiar with the Old Latin variant it preserves, rather than the Vulgate reading. This instance allows a

---

24 The Vulgate for Luke 2:14 reads: "gloria in altissimis Deo et in terra pax in hominibus bonae voluntatis."

25 With "gloria in excelsis Deo," both *Pseudo-Matthew* and Vercelli 6 represent Old Latin readings carried over into the apocryphon and the liturgy; see Sabatier, ed., *Bibliorum sacrorum Latinae versiones antiquae, seu Vetus Italica*, 3:267–8. Cf. Vercelli 5, 167–8: "'*Gloria in excelsis Deo*. Wuldor sie on heannessum Gode ⁊ sibb on eorðan þam mannum þe godne willan habbað."

glimpse into the convergence of canonical and apocryphal narratives for the author's ultimate purpose of narrating miraculous events.

For the most part, the rest of Vercelli 6 translates selections from *Pseudo-Matthew* in order to narrate Herod's plot to kill all infants in the land, the holy family's Flight into Egypt, and Jesus' miracles while there. Unfortunately, the manuscript – the sole witness to this sermon – is defective, and a leaf is missing after line 67. As Scragg notes, the author "presumably followed the source," which relates a number of Jesus' infancy miracles.[26] While not translating the entire source, the sermon's author selectively appropriates passages from *Pseudo-Matthew*; when using this source, however, the author closely follows the Latin for rendering these selections into Old English. The Anglo-Saxon author's strategy, then, is to create an abridged translation, including only certain passages rather than the entire apocryphal story.

The selections from *Pseudo-Matthew* in Vercelli 6 focus on two aspects of the narrative: Jesus' miracles and various scenes of veneration from Creation. Following on the cosmic miracles and veneration already present at Jesus' birth, the narrative relates Jesus subjugating dragons, other beasts, and a fruit tree,[27] as well as his casting down pagan idols in an Egyptian temple (71–3) and veneration by a certain Afradisius in Egypt (74–80). This last episode serves as an example to highlight how Jesus' miracles and his veneration are handled in the text. When Jesus casts down idols in a pagan temple, Afradisius and his troops arrive to survey the scene, with the following response: "He eode to Marian þære fæmman, ⁊ he gebæd hælend þæt cild, ⁊ he spræc to eallum his werode, ⁊ cwæð: 'Þær ðe þis God ne wære, nænige þinga ura goda on hyra onsyne gefeollon. ⁊ for þan us is þearf þæt we don swa ura god, þy læs his yrre ⁊ deaðes frecnes ofer us cume'" (78–80: "He [Afradisius] went to the Virgin Mary, and he prayed to the child Saviour, and he spoke to all of his troop, and said: 'If this were not God, our gods would not for anything fall on their faces.

---

26 *VH*, 132.

27 The text breaks off at line 68 (the end of fol. 55v), with a tantalizing start to the scene with dragons: "Semninga þa uteodon of ðam scrafe manige dracan, þæt mitte ðe …" ("Then suddenly out of the cave went many dragons, so that when …"). The text picks up again (at line 69, the beginning of fol. 56r) just as the holy family enters Egypt: "denum hy locedon on Egypta dune hie wæron swiðe gefeonde" ("from the valley they looked on the hill of Egypt, and they were greatly rejoicing").

And therefore it is necessary for us that we do as our gods, lest his ire and the danger of death overcome us'"). Just as the miracles testify to Jesus' sanctity, so too do the actions and words of Afradisius as a witness. All of this serves to extend the miracles surrounding the birth of the child Jesus, and to further demonstrate to the audience that he is Christ.

That these episodes are meant to demonstrate Jesus' miraculous personage is made most explicit in the final exhortation of the sermon, not drawn from any identified source. The author begins this exhortation, "Hwæt, we nu gehyrdon secgan hwylcnehwegu dæl ymb usses dryhtnes gebyrd, swylce eac ymb þa wundor þe he on his cildhade worhte. Utan we nu eorne tilian þæt we þe selran syn þonne we þylleca bysene usses dryhtnes beforan us reccan ꝼ rædan gehyrað" (86–9: "Lo, now we have heard told some portion about the birth of our Lord, likewise also about the wonders which he worked in his childhood. Let us now eagerly strive so that we are the better when we hear told and hear read such examples of our Lord before us"). About this sermon, Scragg mentions, "its conclusion is a more limited exhortation than is found in any piece [in the Vercelli Book] other than [Vercelli] XXIII."[28] Notably, it is also a specific echo of the incipit at the start. Thus, the sermon is enclosed by a ring structure, drawing the audience in with promise of wonders ("miracula"), as well as the admonition that knowledge of these holy works ("wundor … worhte") should help the audience to be spiritually better ("selran"). Reliance on *Pseudo-Matthew* is not merely an exercise in translation, but a way to help Anglo-Saxon audiences know and meditate on holy miracles for the betterment of their piety.

Visualizing Infancy Miracles

An appreciation for the importance and role of *Pseudo-Matthew* in Vercelli 6 is further highlighted with examination of translations in other media. Previously, textual influences of this apocryphon have gained much attention, especially in relation to Marian devotion.[29] Yet, as with many Christian apocrypha in Anglo-Saxon culture, one aspect of this text's influence

---

28 *VH*, 127.
29 See Clayton, *The Cult of the Virgin Mary in Anglo-Saxon England* and *The Apocryphal Gospels of Mary in Anglo-Saxon England*; and further references in Hall, "Gospel of Pseudo-Matthew."

that remains largely overlooked is in visual arts.[30] As I suggest in the following, the early eleventh-century Sacramentary of Robert of Jumièges (Rouen, Bibliothèque municipale 274 (Y.6)) contains a series of thirteen illuminations, two of which portray iconography ultimately indebted to *Pseudo-Matthew*. Such identifications provide further circulation of these apocryphal traditions as well as expanded contexts for Vercelli 6 and related preaching texts based on this apocryphon.[31] The Sacramentary was compiled in the first quarter of the eleventh century (1014x1023), in the south of England, possibly at Christ Church, Canterbury (the location of its provenance before the mid-eleventh century). The book was later donated to the Abbey of Jumièges by the former abbot Robert Champart while he was bishop of London (1044–51).[32] J.O. Westwood provided the earliest and most extensive formal descriptions of all of the illuminations together,[33] and some images have received subsequent individual attention, though without reference to *Pseudo-Matthew*.[34] Mary Clayton has claimed associations between Marian devotion and the Sacramentary, but she also does not directly link the images to *Pseudo-Matthew*.[35]

I argue that translations of *Pseudo-Matthew* in the Sacramentary are contained in a visual sequence across two illuminated pages (folios 32v and 33r) depicting events from Jesus' Nativity and the Flight into Egypt. In the following examination, I focus on three characteristics of these scenes: the ox and ass by Jesus' crib, a common motif in early medieval art; a midwife attending the Virgin Mary, a less common motif; and Jesus' childhood miracle with a palm tree, an uncommon image in Anglo-Saxon art. For its rarity among other Anglo-Saxon depictions, the last is the most

---

30 No overview or survey of apocrypha depicted in Anglo-Saxon visual arts exists. For a more general survey, see Cartlidge and Elliott, *Art and the Christian Apocrypha*. Cartlidge has also compiled a searchable database of information about Christian art related to apocrypha at *ApocIcon*.

31 Henry A. Wilson, ed., *The Missal of Robert of Jumièges*, with illuminations printed as plates I–XIII. See NRK, 377; *ASM*, 921; and Lucas and Lucas, *Anglo-Saxon Manuscripts in Microfiche Facsimile, Volume 18*, 117–25.

32 For summaries of scholarship, see Pfaff, "Massbooks," esp. 15–19, and *The Liturgy in Medieval England*, 88–91; and Lucas and Lucas, *Anglo-Saxon Manuscripts in Microfiche Facsimile, Volume 18*, 117–25.

33 Westwood, *Facsimiles of the Ornaments of Anglo-Saxon and Irish Manuscripts*, 136–8.

34 See esp. Temple, *Anglo-Saxon Manuscripts, 900–1066*, no. 72; Turner, "Illuminated Manuscripts," no. 50; Karkov, *The Art of Anglo-Saxon England*, 234–5; and Webster, *Anglo-Saxon Art*, 187–8.

35 Clayton, *The Cult of the Virgin Mary in Anglo-Saxon England*, 169–71.

Figure 5 Sacramentary of Robert of Jumièges (Rouen, Bibliothèque municipale 274 (Y.6)), folios 32v–33r. By permission of the *Bibliothèque virtuelle des manuscrits médiévaux*, Institut de recherche et d'histoire des textes, via a Creative Commons license.

notable and most significant for understanding this sequence as a series of episodes translated from *Pseudo-Matthew* into images. Although not identified previously, this sequence in the Sacramentary is dependent (either directly or indirectly) on the apocryphal gospel and should be read as a translation of the narrative into visual art.[36] In this assessment, it is difficult, from an iconographic standpoint, to know whether these connections to *Pseudo-Matthew* were the intentions of the artist or the director who oversaw the book's creation, or were simply derived from models lying behind the imagery. Nonetheless, the Sacramentary represents how the apocryphal *Pseudo-Matthew* became enmeshed in Anglo-Saxon media, even to the extent that its details were translated into visual depictions of gospel events.

The first relevant illumination is a depiction of the Nativity on folio 32v, which includes an angel overseeing the scene (in the upper register), a midwife attending the Virgin Mary (in the middle register), and an ox and ass at the side of the manger next to the child Jesus (in the lower register).[37] Little here is especially unique to contemporary depictions of the Nativity, but it is significant that the midwife and the two animals are not included in any of the canonical gospels, while they all appear in the Nativity narrative of *Pseudo-Matthew*. Regarding the animals, the apocryphon relates the following:

Tertia autem die natiuitatis domini egressa est Maria de spelunca et ingressa est in stabulum et posuit puerum in praesepio, et bos et asinus genua flectentes adorauerunt eum. Tunc adimpletum est quod dictum est per Esaiam prophetam dicentem: Agnouit bos possessorem suum et asinus praesepium domini sui. [Isaiah 1:3] Et ipsa animalia in medio eum habentes incessanter adorabant eum. Tunc adimpletum est quod dictum Abacuc prophetam dicentem: In medio duorum animalium innotesceris. [Habakkuk 3:2][38]

---

36 Issues of "direct" and "indirect" influence echo the similar terms "immediate" and "antecedent" in source study; see esp. Scragg, "Source Study"; and Wright, "Old English Homilies and Latin Sources."

37 All images of the Sacramentary of Robert of Jumièges are used by permission of the *Bibliothèque virtuelle des manuscrits médiévaux*, via a Creative Commons BY NC 3.0 license.

38 Both biblical quotations correspond to the Old Latin; see Sabatier, ed., *Bibliorum sacrorum*, 2:515 and 966. Cf. the Vulgate: "Cognovit bos possessorem suum et asinus praesepe domini sui" ("The ox knoweth his owner, and the ass his master's crib"); and "in medio annorum notum facies" ("In the midst of the years thou shalt make it known").

Figure 6 Sacramentary of Robert of Jumièges (Rouen, Bibliothèque municipale 274 (Y.6)), folio 32v. By permission of the *Bibliothèque virtuelle des manuscrits médiévaux*, Institut de recherche et d'histoire des textes, via a Creative Commons license.

(14:1: Now, on the third day after the birth of the Lord, Mary went out of the cave and went into a stable, and she placed the boy in a manger, and an ox and an ass bent their knees and worshipped him. Then was fulfilled what was spoken by the prophet Isaiah, who said, "The ox knows his owner and the ass the manger of his Lord." And these animals, staying by his side, were constantly worshipping him. Then was fulfilled what was spoken by the prophet Habakkuk, who said, "Between the two animals you will make yourself known.")

It is clear that the purpose of this passage is to establish a typological relationship with the Old Testament prophets, as an authenticating device for both Jesus' birth and the gospel in which it was related. Regarding such associations, David R. Cartlidge and J. Keith Elliott observe, "A connecting of the old and new covenants stands out in virtually every scene of the Marian gospels."[39] As they further discuss, pictorial representations of the Nativity abound in medieval manuscripts, and the iconography consistently evokes these typological tropes for viewers.[40] Furthermore, for viewers familiar with *Pseudo-Matthew*, the inclusion of the ox and ass in the lower register of the Nativity illumination creates a symbolic link with the Marian subject just above the crib in the middle register of the same image.

A second passage from *Pseudo-Matthew* serves as the source for the scene with Mary and her midwife in the middle register of the illumination. The apocryphon relates that after Mary had given birth in a cave, Joseph brings a midwife named Zahel, who inspects the Virgin and child, exclaiming, "Nulla pollutio sanguinis facta est in nascente, nullus dolor in pariente apparuit. Virgo peperit et postquam peperit uirgo esse perdurat" (13:3: "No stain of blood is on the child, and no pain was evident in the birth. A virgin has given birth and after giving birth she has continued to be a virgin"). Following this claim, an unconvinced midwife named Salome is brought to belief by inspecting the Virgin Mary herself – an episode not unlike that of the apostle Thomas in John 20:24–9. As a result of her unbelief, Salome suffers from a withered hand, which is later miraculously healed when she touches the infant Jesus. Consequently, Salome is often portrayed with a visibly disabled hand when she is present at the Nativity.[41]

---

39 Cartlidge and Elliott, *Art and the Christian Apocrypha*, 23.
40 On the influence of *Pseudo-Matthew* on visual representations of the Nativity, see ibid., 88–94.
41 See esp. Deshman, "Servants of the Mother of God in Byzantine and Medieval Art."

In his assessment of the Sacramentary, C.R. Dodwell gestured towards apocryphal traditions for the imagery of Mary and her midwife, linking it to the Greek *Protevangelium of James* and identifying the midwife as Salome.[42] Similarly, Robert Deshman has examined the symbolic importance of the midwife in Byzantine and medieval iconography,[43] citing both the *Protevangelium* and *Pseudo-Matthew* as examples of apocryphal details for the Nativity on folio 15v of the Benedictional of Æthelwold (London, British Library, Additional 49598; 971x984, Winchester).[44] Casting doubt on the *Protevangelium* as source for these images, however, is the lack of substantial evidence for the circulation of this apocryphon in Anglo-Saxon England or generally in Western Europe.[45] No complete Latin manuscript of the *Protevangelium* survives from the medieval period. The sole extant witness from Anglo-Saxon England appears in the Pembroke 25 Homiliary of Saint-Père, in a sermon for the Nativity of Mary (item 51) that adapts chapters 1 to 8:1; yet this account relates only the lives of Anna and Joachim, Mary's birth, and her early life, not any of the episodes concerned with Jesus' birth and childhood.

Proposed correlations with the Greek *Protevangelium*, therefore, are often uncertain or likely mediated through other traditions such as the adaptive expansion in the Latin *Pseudo-Matthew*, since it remained the more popular apocryphon in Western Europe throughout the medieval period. Given the known circulation and associations of *Pseudo-Matthew* with a variety of other Anglo-Saxon media, and on the Continent in the early medieval period, the more probable conclusion is that the iconography of the Sacramentary relies on this apocryphon rather than the *Protevangelium*. The same conclusion may also be applied to the image in the Benedictional of Æthelwold, adding its Nativity illumination to the network of media related to *Pseudo-Matthew* in late Anglo-Saxon England. As for depictions of the midwife in the Sacramentary and Benedictional, both images

---

42 Dodwell, *Anglo-Saxon Gestures and the Roman Stage*, 106–9.

43 Deshman, "Servants of the Mother of God in Byzantine and Medieval Art" and *The Benedictional of Æthelwold*, 18–19.

44 *ASM*, 301. See Prescott, ed., *The Benedictional of St Æthelwold*. See also Thomas D. Hill, "The Baby on the Stone," 73–5, with image at 74. More generally, see Dzon and Kennedy, eds., *The Christ Child in Medieval Culture*; though all focused on late medieval examples, the studies nonetheless demonstrate similar links in various media.

45 For a summary of scholarship, see Hall, "Protevangelium of James," *SASLC Apocrypha*, 21–3. On Latin manuscripts and possible wider circulation, see Beyers, "The Transmission of Marian Apocrypha in the Latin Middle Ages," with further references there.

lack signs of a crippled hand, and she uses both hands to prop up Mary's head with a pillow. Contrary to Dodwell's suggestion, the midwife in these Nativity scenes is more likely the woman named Zahel, not the disabled Salome.[46]

The other image in the Sacramentary related to *Pseudo-Matthew* appears in the bottom register of the illumination on folio 33r, depicting the Flight into Egypt. Westwood offered the following description: "The Virgin, seated on an ass, holds the Child in her lap, who stretches out its hands to Joseph leading the ass, and carrying the Virgin's distaff on his shoulder."[47] But this explanation misses a major point. The Flight into Egypt is, of course, well attested in the canonical Gospel of Matthew 2:13–23, though the inclusion of a tree in the Sacramentary illumination provides an unnoticed detail pointing towards an episode not included in any of the canonical gospels. During the journey into Egypt as narrated in *Pseudo-Matthew*, the holy family stop to rest under a palm tree where Mary desires its fruit, although she cannot reach it. The apocryphon continues:

Tunc infantulus Iesus sedens in sinu matris suae uirginis exclamauit ad palmam et dixit: Flectere, arbor, et de fructibus tuis refice matrem meam. Statim autem ad uocem eius inclinauit palma cacumen suum usque ad plantas Mariae, et colligentes ex ea fructus quos habebat omnes refecti sunt.

(20:2: Then the baby boy Jesus, sitting in the lap of his mother, the virgin, called out to the palm tree and said, "Bend down, tree, and refresh my mother with your fruit." Immediately, then, at his voice, the palm bent its top down to Mary's feet, and gathering the fruit from it, all were refreshed.)

I suggest that in the Sacramentary illustration, the child Jesus gestures not towards Joseph but towards the tree, pointing with his right hand and reaching with his left hand open. The tree, in turn, bends a branch towards Jesus, in comparison with the other more upright stalks in the middle and to the left.

Beyond relying on the same apocryphal gospel for details, both illuminations in the Sacramentary appear on facing folios (32v–33r), depicting the same visual organization and architectural frames – suggesting that

---

46 Cf. Deshman's assessment of the Nativity image in the Benedictional of Æthelwold (*The Benedictional of Æthelwold*, 18–19).

47 Westwood, *Facsimiles of the Ornaments of Anglo-Saxon and Irish Manuscripts*, 136–7.

Figure 7 Sacramentary of Robert of Jumièges (Rouen, Bibliothèque municipale 274 (Y.6)), folio 33r. By permission of the *Bibliothèque virtuelle des manuscrits médiévaux*, Institut de recherche et d'Histoire des textes, via a Creative Commons license.

these images are most significantly understood as a narrative sequence read together. There is a noticeable trend in two earlier Anglo-Saxon depictions of similar narrative sequences: the Benedictional of Æthelwold and the Boulogne Gospels (Boulogne, Bibliothèque municipale 11; s. x/xi, St Bertin).[48] While the Boulogne Gospels were produced in St Bertin, they were decorated by an Anglo-Saxon artist, making both the Benedictional and the Boulogne Gospels witnesses to iconographic trends in England around the same time as (or just before) the production of the Sacramentary. Parallels with the Nativity in the Sacramentary appear in both the Benedictional (fol. 15v) and the Boulogne Gospels (fol. 12r), as all three images contain the extra-biblical midwife and livestock. Unlike the Sacramentary, however, neither the Benedictional of Æthelwold nor the Boulogne Gospels contains a depiction of the Flight into Egypt. Nonetheless, the framing of sequences in all three manuscripts helps to demonstrate that this design was in style for Anglo-Saxon artists at the end of the tenth century and into the beginning of the eleventh.

The framing design for the Nativity and the Flight into Egypt in the Sacramentary also reinforces reading the two illuminations together as a visual narrative sequence: both borders consist of a floriated archway resting on two pillars, with towers at the top right and left corners and stylized falcons perched on the archway beside these towers. Furthermore, these two pages share other formal characteristics such as the same ground-line as well as a tripartite structure to the registers. Framing devices across facing pages elsewhere in the Sacramentary also strengthen the reading of illuminations as sequential in this manuscript. For example, shared framing and formal elements appear for the journey of the Magi and the Adoration (fols. 36v–37r), as well as the Crucifixion and descent from the Cross (fols. 71v–72r). In other words, these sequences show how facing images in the Sacramentary were designed as full-page pairs to be read together, as the book lay open.

The sequence concerning the Magi especially accentuates the visual relationships of reading across the pages of the Sacramentary. Here the motif of the city in the framing has returned, though with details distinct for joining these two folios together, and the ground-line of the two pages is again unified in the common registers. Furthermore, the two images

---

48 For images, see Ohlgren, *Anglo-Saxon Textual Illustration*, plates 5.1–28. On relationships between these manuscripts, see esp. Temple, *Anglo-Saxon Manuscripts, 900–1066*, nos. 23, 44, and 72.

contain the chiastic organization of enthroned royalty (Herod and Jesus) visited by the Magi at different points in the chronology of the gospel. Like the images of the Nativity and Flight into Egypt, these depictions of the Magi highlight the significance of reading visual arts as translations that capture the drama of Christian narratives, as well as evidence for biblical and apocryphal details mingling together within the pages of a single book.

The sequence of narrative illuminations for the Nativity and the Flight into Egypt, like the translation of *Pseudo-Matthew* in Vercelli 6, particularly highlights the miraculous nature of Jesus, even as a child. In one sense, the depiction of the Flight into Egypt in the Sacramentary preserves the episode of the palm tree's obedience to Jesus as a portion of the apocryphal narrative otherwise lost from Vercelli 6. While damage to the Vercelli Book has precluded the survival of this episode in the Old English sermon (from which it was excised at some point), this part of *Pseudo-Matthew* is attested in the Sacramentary's illuminations. The Sacramentary survives as a major witness for the general knowledge and circulation of episodes from *Pseudo-Matthew* in Anglo-Saxon England. Like Vercelli 6, the illuminations also preserve an interest in the miracles of Jesus. The episodes of this apocryphon, as well as the translations in Vercelli 6 and the images of the Sacramentary, point to miracles as key to Jesus' life. Foremost among these miracles is the universal salvation of humanity through Jesus' Crucifixion and Resurrection. As Hill notes about this type of scene, "the iconographic program of the *Benedictional of Æthelwold* Nativity scene and related illuminations associates the crib and the Nativity with the Passion and sacrifice of Jesus. The beginning and end of Jesus' earthly ministry are in effect conflated."[49] For Christian audiences, the Nativity cannot help but evoke this progression, since, in typological expectancy, Jesus' Crucifixion and Resurrection are the primary reasons for his birth in the first place.

Other than Jesus' childhood miracles, these illuminations also point forward to his future miracles. For example, Jesus' miracle with the palm tree points to his public miracles as an adult, narrated in the canonical gospels, especially the adoration that surrounds him. It even evokes Jesus' other botanical miracle, the cursing of the fig tree in Matthew 21:18–22:[50]

---

49 Thomas D. Hill, "The Baby on the Stone," 75.
50 Cf. Mark 11:12–14, 20–5.

mane autem revertens in civitatem esuriit et videns fici arborem unam secus
viam venit ad eam et nihil invenit in ea nisi folia tantum et ait illi numquam ex
te fructus nascatur in sempiternum et arefacta est continuo ficulnea et viden-
tes discipuli mirati sunt dicentes quomodo continuo aruit respondens autem
Iesus ait eis amen dico vobis si habueritis fidem et non haesitaveritis non
solum de ficulnea facietis sed et si monti huic dixeritis tolle et iacta te in mare
fiet et omnia quaecumque petieritis in oratione credentes accipietis

(And in the morning, returning into the city, he was hungry. And seeing a certain fig tree by the way side, he came to it and found nothing on it but leaves
only. And he saith to it: "May no fruit grow on thee henceforward for ever."
And immediately the fig tree withered away. And the disciples seeing it won-
dered, saying: "How is it presently withered away?" And Jesus answering,
said to them: "Amen, I say to you, if you shall have faith and stagger not, not
only this of the fig tree shall you do, but also if you shall say to this mountain,
'Take up and cast thyself into the sea,' it shall be done. And all things whatso-
ever you shall ask in prayer believing, you shall receive.")

While the gospel account leads to a moment of teaching – the expected
response from Jesus in his role as rabbi to his disciples – the episode in
Pseudo-Matthew is one of several that diverge from this model. Instead,
Jesus' power is on display, and this is taken over into both sermon and illumination in Vercelli 6 and the Sacramentary.

Mediating the Cult of the Virgin

There are also reasons to link the influences of *Pseudo-Matthew* in the
Sacramentary with the veneration of the Virgin Mary in Anglo-Saxon
England. For medieval readers, this apocryphon was related to the rise of
Marian devotion, particularly from the ninth century onward, and pos-
sibly even at its inception.[51] In the introduction to his edition of *Pseudo-
Matthew*, Jan Gijsel suggests that the author of this apocryphon was a
monk who was fascinated with the venerated depiction of Mary in the
Protevangelium of James, and who used this potential in the hopes of

---

51 On Marian devotion, see esp. Clayton, *The Cult of the Virgin Mary in Anglo-Saxon
England* and *The Apocryphal Gospels of Mary in Anglo-Saxon England*; Fulton, *From
Judgment to Passion*; Gambero, *Mary in the Middle Ages*, esp. 74–80; and Rubin,
Mother of God.

promoting the expansion of Benedictine ideals. Connections with Marian devotion may be seen in adaptations of *Pseudo-Matthew*, particularly *De nativitate Mariae*, which is often accompanied by an epistolary prologue spuriously attributed to Jerome.[52] This letter, purported to be a response to a request by Bishops Chromatius and Heliodorus for Jerome to translate *De nativitate Mariae* from Hebrew (which was not its actual original language), begins: "Petitis a me ut uobis rescribam quid mihi de quodam libello uideatur qui de natiuitate sanctae Mariae a nonnullis habetur" ("You ask of me that I write back about a little book that some have concerning the nativity of Saint Mary").[53] All of these texts related to *Pseudo-Matthew* made an impact on Anglo-Saxon culture, in which the cult of the Virgin Mary developed strong roots by the late tenth century.

The popularity and significance of translations of *Pseudo-Matthew* in Anglo-Saxon England are related also to the rise of the cult of Mary, which may be brought to bear on contextualizing the Sacramentary. Clayton claims that "At the very end of the Anglo-Saxon period we find the first artistic reflections of the *Pseudo-Matthew* legend," citing a troper containing supplemental liturgical texts for the mass and Office from around 1050.[54] With the foregoing examination in mind, the details in the Sacramentary's miniatures allow for acknowledging an earlier date for the emergence of artistic translations of *Pseudo-Matthew*, in the first quarter of the eleventh century. While not noting the connection to *Pseudo-Matthew*, Clayton does note the veneration afforded to the Virgin in the Sacramentary's visual art, particularly in the miniatures depicting the Nativity and the Ascension.[55] For instance, it is particularly noteworthy that "the angel's blessing is clearly directed at Mary" rather than the infant Jesus – a rare feature in Anglo-Saxon iconography for the Nativity.[56]

Other connections within the Sacramentary also add to these assessments. The two illuminations of the Nativity and Flight into Egypt closely follow the *temporale* entry for 8 January, listed as "Natale Domini ad Sanctam Mariam Maiorem," on folios 31r–31v. Part of the observation for this feast day, as given in the Sacramentary, includes honouring "gloriosae semper uirginis maria genitricis dei et domini nostri iesu

---

52 See Beyers, ed., *Libri de nativitate Mariae*, 272–7.
53 Ibid., 273, lines 1–3.
54 Clayton, *The Cult of the Virgin Mary in Anglo-Saxon England*, 172.
55 Ibid., 169–70.
56 Ibid., 170.

christi" (fol. 31v: "the glorious eternally virgin Mary, mother of our God and Lord Jesus Christ").[57] This entry certainly shares resonances with the declaration of Mary's perpetual virginity in *Pseudo-Matthew* (a long-standing tradition),[58] and it is notable that even the child Jesus afforded veneration to Mary when he commanded the palm tree to yield its fruit for her refreshment.

Moreover, associations with Marian devotion are substantiated by the manuscript's early reception, since the donation inscription on folio 228r reads:[59]

ego. Rotbertus abba gemmetesium prius postmodum uero sancte londoni-orum sedis presul factus dederim librum hunc sancte Mariae in hoc michi comisso monachorum sancti Petri cenobio ad honorem sanctorum quorum hic mentio agitur et ob memoriale mei ut hic in perpetuum habeatur.

(I, Robert, former abbot of Jumièges, afterward made bishop of the holy See of London, give this book of Saint Mary to this community of the monks of Saint Peter having been entrusted to me, in honour of the saints, whose mention is made here, and as a memorial for me to be held here forever.)

The Sacramentary images and the apocryphal narratives they translate thus evoke the significance of Marian veneration that developed from the very beginnings of Christianity. As a book specifically associated with Mary, the Sacramentary reflects the habits of the community to which it was given: they were meant to take the devotion between its covers and extend it into their world.

Understanding the Sacramentary as a close contemporary to audiences of Vercelli 6 allows for highlighting a number of features common to the two, as well as some key historical issues for considering Anglo-Saxon Christian beliefs. As already noted, one commonality is that Jesus' deeds are key in these intermedial translations. But both artefacts also highlight how the transmission and reception of *Pseudo-Matthew* fit into Anglo-Saxon mainstream religion. Indeed, the Sacramentary shares a number of features important for the contexts of preaching in late Anglo-Saxon England. After all, the intended use of the Sacramentary was in the mass itself. This

---

57 Henry A. Wilson, *The Missal of Robert of Jumièges*, 49.
58 Clayton, *The Cult of the Virgin Mary in Anglo-Saxon England*, 1–24.
59 Henry A. Wilson, *The Missal of Robert of Jumièges*, 316.

resonates with connections to *Pseudo-Matthew* already discussed, such as Latin and Old English sermons found in a range of Continental and Anglo-Saxon manuscripts – for example, those including extracts from and versions of the *Protevangelium*, *Pseudo-Matthew*, *De nativitate Mariae*, and *Trinubium Annae* (see chapter 1). These media all speak to the fact that part of the circulation and use of this apocryphon was closely linked to liturgy and preaching. The images of Jesus' early life in the Sacramentary, therefore, are closely linked with Vercelli 6 not only because of common content but also through their inclusion among the necessary media for Christian worship.

Also suggestive are the types of porous boundaries for preaching and belief exhibited when considering Anglo-Saxon sermons alongside the Sacramentary. While Latin and Old English sermons as well as the mass-book were created (and likely used) by elites in ecclesiastic or monastic communities, they illustrate the potential for a variety of people to be brought together in common belief and practice. Written in the vernacular, Old English sermons like Vercelli 6 (and other translations of *Pseudo-Matthew*) were accessible to a wide range of audiences, lay and ecclesiastical. Similarly, the visual illuminations of the Sacramentary could have been just as accessible to a priest as to an elite layperson, even if nuances of understanding existed for different viewers. Furthermore, intriguing associations exist between Marian devotion and versions of *Pseudo-Matthew* across media, in preaching texts as well as visual art, prompting consideration of audiences beyond ecclesiasts and elite laity. This facet of the apocryphon's intermedial afterlife is particularly relevant for the female religious who followed this cult, exposing porous boundaries between classes and genders. These cultural artefacts, then, demonstrate how a variety of social groups within Anglo-Saxon Christian communities were linked through a complex network of apocryphal media.

A Harrowing Web

As with Vercelli 6 and the illuminations in the Sacramentary of Robert of Jumièges, we see similar issues of multimedia translation in Anglo-Saxon representations of the Harrowing of Hell. This case, however, offers an even more expansive network of multimedia associations. The widely popular narrative of the Harrowing (also known as the "Descensus Christi ad Inferos") relates how Jesus, after his death, descended into hell to rescue the just Jews into heaven with him. As with many apocryphal traditions, this legend circulated widely, in countless versions, in an array of texts from the patristic and early medieval periods. In its fullest and most prominent narrative form, this legend was recounted in the *Gospel of Nicodemus* – composed and compiled from various earlier apocrypha sometime between the second and fifth centuries – which influenced later depictions either directly or through intermediary sources.[60] However, clear evidence for the circulation of that particular text in Anglo-Saxon England is elusive.[61] In addition to the *Gospel of Nicodemus*, the narrative was transmitted in a variety of forms throughout the medieval period, particularly in works attributed to patristic authors, which influenced myriad other media over the centuries.[62] No matter how this legend circulated, its impact on Anglo-Saxon culture is obvious from the surviving media.

One well-known example of the Harrowing of Hell that serves as a starting point is a visual depiction on folio 14r of the Tiberius Psalter (London, British Library, Cotton Tiberius C.vi; c.1050), which is representative of portrayals of the Harrowing of Hell in the early medieval period.[63] In this scene, Jesus has entered Hell rather violently, knocking the door off its hinges (upper left) and trampling atop the bound devil (lower left), and he gently bends to help the noble Jewish patriarchs (middle right) out of the open hellmouth (bottom right). William Noel has suggested that this image in the Tiberius Psalter is dependent on iconography in the ninth-century Utrecht Psalter (Utrecht, Universiteitsbibliotheek 32; c.816x840), situating this image among a range of visual translations of the Harrowing in the early medieval period.[64]

Iconography, however, is not the only translation undertaken in this image. More generally, the drama depicted is necessarily connected with the narrative of the Harrowing as it circulated in the larger network of media from the patristic period onward. Despite many references to the

---

60 *CANT*, 62.

61 See "Gospel of Nicodemus," *SASLC Apocrypha*, 29–31.

62 For a general overview, with special reference to medieval English literature, see Tamburr, *The Harrowing of Hell in Medieval England*, in which he discusses the theological framework behind some of the Anglo-Saxon literary depictions of the Harrowing.

63 *ASM*, 378. See esp. Fillitz, *Das Mittelalter I*, no. 76; Backhouse, Turner, and Webster, eds., *Golden Age of Anglo-Saxon Art*, 83 (no. 66) and colour plate XX; and Brantley, "The Iconography of the Utrecht Psalter and the *Old English Descent into Hell*," 56 n. 44, with further references there.

64 *ASM*, 939. For digital images, see *The Utrecht Psalter*. For detailed analyses, see esp. van der Horst, Noel, and Wüstefeld, eds., *The Utrecht Psalter in Medieval Art*.

Harrowing in early Christian texts, the earliest surviving visual representations were made around the eighth century,[65] well after the prominence of the most significant texts had been established. This emergence of visual representation was, in fact, several centuries after the doctrine of the Harrowing had achieved ecclesiastical acceptance, through creedal affirmation, in the fourth century.[66] When set within this chronology, visual and verbal depictions may be read as contemporary and analogous, intermedial translations from the same traditions, transferring narrative power into new forms of representation. For this, the specific sources used matter less than how coherent narratives were translated across media for new audiences. Also part of this type of translation is the significance of the narrative retaining its coherence and effectiveness through the drama of Jesus' actions. As with translations of *Pseudo-Matthew*, the Harrowing of Hell is not a story of Jesus' teachings but of his deeds.

The case of the Harrowing of Hell in Anglo-Saxon media also prompts rethinking transmission not as a linear, one-way occurrence, but instead as a dynamic process across multimedia. What the Harrowing of Hell presents as an apocryphal narrative is not a specific source that may be traced simply, but an accumulative tradition. This presents a complicated issue for source and translation studies, but it is a familiar concept in adaptation and media studies that may contribute to more nuanced investigations of the transmission of apocrypha. It is clear from the long history of adaptations through retellings, recombinations, and remixes of narratives that such traditions not only accumulate but also feed back into each other in a web of multidirectional influences. Similarly, a core finding of media studies is that new media do not leave the old behind to decay in obscurity, but that media continue to converge with, layer upon, and respond to each other.

Representations of the Harrowing of Hell extend to a wide array of media that all exist within the same system of intermedial relationships. Brantley suggests as much when discussing implications for considering representations of the Harrowing: "the mere translation of an idea from one medium to another requires more interaction than our common notion

---

65   Cartlidge and Elliot, *Art and the Christian Apocrypha*, 126–31.
66   See esp. Gatch, "The Harrowing of Hell"; Connell, "*Descensus Christi ad Inferos*"; and du Toit, "The Origin of the Christian Doctrine of the 'Descensus Christi ad Inferos.'"

of 'source' implies."[67] There is room to extend this observation further. I have previously suggested that the backgrounds of any given Anglo-Saxon literary motif need to be understood in a more nuanced manner, not related to a single, specific, identifiable source, but rather related to a "matrix of associations" that travel through various media.[68] As I have prompted throughout this book, the future of source studies should rest on examinations that move away from single-text source identifications in order to acknowledge the interrelated nature of media that cannot be understood without reference to the whole cultural network. One way to think about these relationships is through the concept of media ecology, in which the various artefacts coexist through related cultural currents. In the case of the Harrowing of Hell, the focal point at the centre of the media network remains the dramatic arc of the Descent narrative, with a system of related representations that translate it into various media to represent the apocryphal legend.

The numerous depictions of the Harrowing in visual images emphasize the drama of action, since they are not textual but pictorial. Such visual examples of the Harrowing that circulated in Anglo-Saxon England appear in many media such as manuscript illustrations like the Psalms in the Utrecht Psalter and Harley Psalter (London, British Library, Harley 603; s. x/xi or xi[1], Canterbury);[69] stone sculptures like a panel at Bristol Cathedral and another set above the church door at South Cerney;[70] and metal engraving like the mount of the so-called Crozier of St Heribert.[71]

---

67 Brantley, "The Iconography of the Utrecht Psalter and the *Old English Descent into Hell*," 62.

68 Hawk, "'Id est, crux Christi.'"

69 *ASM*, 422. For descriptions and images, see Ohlgren, *Anglo-Saxon Textual Illustration*; and "Detailed Record for Harley 603." For detailed analysis, see esp. Noel, *The Harley Psalter*.

70 See esp. Wizowaty, "The Iconography of Adam and Eve on Sculptured Stones in Anglo-Saxon England," 408–36; Cramp, *Corpus of Anglo-Saxon Stone Sculpture, Volume VII*, 145–6; and Bryant and Hare, *Corpus of Anglo-Saxon Stone Sculpture, Volume X*, 90–2, which contains a more detailed discussion with reference to other possible stone sculptures.

71 Description and digital photographs at "Stab des heiligen Heribert." See esp. no. 189 in Okasha, "A Second Supplement to *Hand-List of Anglo-Saxon Non-Runic Inscriptions*," 43–4 and plates IIa (i) and (ii); Hare, "Cnut and Lotharingia," 276–7; Okasha, "A Third Supplement to *Hand-List of Anglo-Saxon Non-Runic Inscriptions*," 267, and "A Fourth Supplement to *Hand-List of Anglo-Saxon Non-Runic Inscriptions*," with further references there. My thanks to Elisabeth Okasha for sharing her work before publication, via private correspondence.

The goal of this examination is not to enumerate the many multimedia translations of the Harrowing of Hell, but to seek out how they interrelate to each other, with particular attention to how they reveal contemporary contexts for the account in Blickling 7. Part of this task requires acknowledging the varieties of difference in Anglo-Saxon representations of the Harrowing of Hell. Brantley indicates this diversity in her discussion of the Old English poetic *Descent into Hell* along with the Utrecht and Harley psalters.[72] While there are certainly observable differences in modes of representation in different media – verbal texts, visual arts, as well as the varieties within them (poetry, prose, drawings, engravings) – examining cultural artefacts can reveal striking similarities and variations in the translations of narrative and the depictions of beliefs. Since all of these media help to contextualize Blickling 7, I begin with an examination of the widespread representations of the Harrowing before returning to address how the Old English sermon fits into this multimedia network.

The Fluid Harrowing

Like many apocrypha, the details of the Harrowing are not fixed. In her study of the Old English poem *Descent into Hell*, Brantley is particularly concerned with how the chronology of events is depicted for the Harrowing, Resurrection, and women's visit to the tomb, as well as what these chronologies reveal about theological beliefs in the corporeal or spiritual presence of Christ in Hell at the Harrowing. The central question, variously discussed by patristic and medieval theologians, is whether Jesus descended into hell in corporeal form, or only in spirit. In the *Descent into Hell*, it is unclear whether or not the women appear at the sepulchre – and, by implication, whether or not the Resurrection occurs – before the Harrowing. By exploring this question, Brantley gestures towards a spectrum of media, all translations of the Harrowing in different forms, some with radically different chronologies for the events surrounding Jesus' Crucifixion, Harrowing, and Resurrection. For example, both the *Descent into Hell* and the imagery for Psalm 15 in the Utrecht Psalter (Brantley's closest analogue) – a type of allegorical "visual exegesis" on verse 10 – seem to introduce the women at Jesus' tomb before the Harrowing.[73] Similar

---

72 Brantley, "The Iconography of the Utrecht Psalter and the *Old English Descent into Hell*."

73 Ibid., 54.

imagery also appears in the famous English copy of the Utrecht Psalter, the Harley Psalter, for Psalms 15 and 138.

The issue of chronology, while it is a detailed point for the overall arc of the narrative, provides one way of working through the diversity of representations as well as the coherence of the tradition as a network around a central narrative concept. After all, every example that might be brought to bear on this examination is, fundamentally, a representation of the general narrative of the Harrowing, drawn from the tradition as it developed from the core of biblical, apocryphal, and patristic writings. Yet the details morph from one version to another. Looking to Old English sermons, Brantley suggests, "These homilies demonstrate that passion-chronology was not absolutely fixed at this period."[74] There is, however, a question of what this "very unorthodox temporal sequence" means for considering the range of Harrowing translations.[75] Indeed, as I argue throughout this study, tensions between "orthodoxy" and "heterodoxy" are prevalent in discussions of Anglo-Saxon religious belief because modern scholars read apocryphal media through a lens of suspicion. In Brantley's examination of the varieties of chronology in representations of the Harrowing, these tensions have come to the fore even more. This notion of diversity affords an exaggerated case of fluidity often associated with apocryphal media that I address throughout this book. In what follows, I suggest some nuances to temper how we view orthodoxy, suggesting that if we think in terms of diversity rather than strict orthodoxy, we have a better chance of understanding the variance of Christian traditions.

In addition to the examples that Brantley cites, one more case study emphasizes these concepts: the depiction of the Harrowing of Hell engraved on the silver mount of the Crozier of St Heribert. Now held by the parish church of Neu-St-Heribert in Deutz (Cologne), this ecclesiastical staff includes a textual inscription that Elizabeth Okasha has identified as Anglo-Saxon.[76] Michael Hare has summarized the relevant scholarship,

---

74 Ibid., 53.

75 Although Brantley moves beyond a strict dichotomy of "orthodox" and "unorthodox" to discuss atemporal representations, she does use this phrase, referring to work by Izydorczyk (ibid., 54); see also Izydorczyk, "The Inversion of Paschal Events in the Old English *Descent into Hell*."

76 Okasha, "A Second Supplement to *Hand-List of Anglo-Saxon Non-Runic Inscriptions*," 43–4 and plates IIa (i) and (ii). This artefact was previously held in the Cologne Cathedral, on loan from the church of Neu-St-Heribert, but was returned in 1996; see Hare, "Cnut and Lotharingia," 276 n. 78.

particularly regarding the date and origin of this artefact (with special attention to the ivory-work and silver-work), concluding that the ivory cross for the top of the staff was crafted in the late tenth century, and the silver mount around 1020. It is even possible that this staff was a gift from King Cnut (c. 995–1035) to Archbishop Heribert of Cologne (c. 970–1021).[77] In any case, a crozier such as this was used by a high-ranking ecclesiast, and it is a prominent example of the Harrowing on a liturgical object closely contemporary with the compilation of the Blickling Book.

The crozier raises questions of chronology for Jesus' deeds after the Passion, which are narrated in the gospels as his Resurrection, forty days of further public ministry with believers, and Ascension into heaven. The sequence of images on the crozier, however, may be read in multiple ways, complicating notions of temporality as might be expected or assumed. The ivory cross and silver mount together include four main images in two registers: the Crucifixion (top) and Harrowing (bottom); and, obverse, Christ in Majesty (top) and the women at the empty tomb (bottom). A "correct" way to read this sequence is not readily apparent. For instance, a viewer might first see the Christ in Majesty and women at the tomb before the chronologically prior Crucifixion and Harrowing. Alternatively, a viewer might first view the Crucifixion and Christ in Majesty in the top register on the ivory cross before the Harrowing and women at the tomb in the lower register on the silver mount. Western standards of reading (textually and visually) from left to right and top to bottom are confounded. While Brantley rightly stresses that depictions of the Harrowing illustrating the Psalms are "radically atemporal,"[78] this crozier exhibits an even further exaggerated form of an atemporal visual sequence. Moreover, another complication to visual chronology is the fact that the crozier depicts the Harrowing, Resurrection, and Christ in majesty, but not the Ascension.

Such atemporality may be seen as demonstrating the limits of iconography for establishing chronology, but it also indicates a fluid account for the events derived from a mixture of tradition encompassing both canonical and apocryphal gospels. Perhaps atemporality in visual depictions of the Harrowing indicates that emphasis on salvation is more important than fluid details. A similar case appears in *The Dream of the Rood*, which

---

77 Hare, "Cnut and Lotharingia," 276–7.
78 Brantley, "The Iconography of the Utrecht Psalter and the *Old English Descent into Hell*," 54.

presents an extended meditation on the Crucifixion and Resurrection.[79] At the end of the poem, after a retelling of the gospel events, the poet relates:

Se Sunu wæs sigorfæst   on þam siðfate,
mihtig ond spedig,   þa he mid manigeo com,
gasta weorode,   on godes rice,
Anwealda ælmihtig,   englum to blisse
ond eallum ðam halgum   þam þe on heofonum ær
wunedon on wuldre,   þa heora Wealdend cwom,
ælmihtig God,   þær his eðel wæs.

(150–6: The son was victorious in the journey, mighty and powerful, when he came with many, a troop of spirits, into the kingdom of God, almighty Ruler, as a joy to the angels and all the saints who before lived in glory, when their Ruler came, almighty God, where his homeland was.)

Relating the Harrowing and Ascension,[80] the poem provides imprecise chronology, since it is unclear when the Resurrection and Jesus' forty days of further ministry took place. Yet, for the poet (the speaker for the majority of the poem), devotion to the Rood and the salvation narrative are the key themes of the poem, not a detailed temporal chronology of events. Taking the evidence together, non-traditional chronologies or atemporalities of the Harrowing and Resurrection were not all that uncommon after all. Blickling 7, another sermon in Cambridge, Corpus Christi College 41,[81] illustrations of psalms, the crozier of Heribert, and *The Dream of the Rood* provide substantial evidence for widespread fluidity. This evidence even indicates that such chronologies were not strictly considered "unorthodox" by medieval authors, even though they might be problematic for modern scholars who set them in relation to theological statements from normative patristic sources. It might be difficult to reconcile these media within a modern framework that strives for systematic theology, but this was not the case for Anglo-Saxon artists. The amount

---

79 References by line nos. are to Swanton, ed., *The Dream of the Rood.*
80 While I read these lines as representing the Harrowing and Ascension, Monica Brzezinski has claimed that they instead portray the Last Judgment; see "The Harrowing of Hell, the Last Judgment, and *The Dream of the Rood.*"
81 Discussed briefly in Brantley, "The Iconography of the Utrecht Psalter and the *Old English Descent into Hell,*" 53.

of evidence suggests that these non-traditional temporalities were just as viable as patristic models to some Anglo-Saxons.

Like the associations discussed between Vercelli 6 and the Sacramentary of Robert, the crozier also demonstrates the relevance of lived devotion for situating apocryphal sermons in Anglo-Saxon England. A textual engraving on the crozier mount speaks to the significance of this concept. The inscription reads, "+ RELIQVI . SANCTE: MARIE: ET: SANCTE CRISTOFORI": ("Relics of Saint Mary and of Saint Christopher")[82] – references to related relics which, Okasha notes, may have been kept inside the staff.[83] The cross, then, exhibits relationships between apocrypha and Marian devotion, as well as saints' cults in general. As already discussed, stories of Mary's life associated with her cult come from apocryphal gospels and adaptations of them.[84] Similarly, the roots of the legend of Saint Christopher are also apocryphal, ultimately derived from the apostolic acts of Andrew and Bartholomew – and the Latin *Passio sancti Christophori* is arguably as apocryphal as it is hagiographic, since these are, after all, blurred genre categories (as discussed in previous chapters).[85] Myriad intermedial associations could be evoked to follow this constellation further, since the Latin legend of Christopher is used for 28 April in both Bede's *Martyrology* and the *Old English Martyrology* (again, texts closely linked with the liturgy)[86] and translated into an Old English sermon in the famous Nowell Codex (London, British Library, Cotton Vitellius A.xv; s. x/xi).[87] Nevertheless, the significant point for the current argument is that the Harrowing of Hell in Blickling 7 sits firmly within a wider web of liturgical and devotional associations, through which it is closely linked with lived Anglo-Saxon religion.

---

82 I have adapted Okasha's transcription, silently expanding abbreviations, accepting her emendations, and providing spaces between words and punctuation; see "A Second Supplement to *Hand-List of Anglo-Saxon Non-Runic Inscriptions*," 44.

83 Ibid.

84 See Clayton, *The Cult of the Virgin Mary in Anglo-Saxon England* and *The Apocryphal Gospels of Mary in Anglo-Saxon England*.

85 For general discussions, see White, *Myths of the Dog-Man*, 34–6; and Friedman, *The Monstrous Races in Medieval Art and Thought*, 70–5. There is no discussion of Christopher legends in *SASLC Apocrypha*.

86 See Rauer, ed. and trans., *The Old English Martyrology*, 90–1 and 255.

87 See Whatley, "Christophorus," *SASLC 1*, 137–9.

Blickling 7

Sources for Blickling 7 further demonstrate the adaptive potential of the diverse and fluid traditions surrounding the Harrowing of Hell. While Blickling 7 shares verbal parallels with Pseudo-Augustine *Sermo* 160,[88] the version used by the Anglo-Saxon author is seemingly an adaptation of the Latin text as it survives elsewhere.[89] The second part of the Old English sermon shifts towards an eschatological focus, consisting of a translation of the *Apocalypse of Thomas* outlining the signs to come leading up to the Last Judgment.[90] Much of the Pseudo-Augustinian sermon used as a source for Blickling 7 is a catena of the Psalms, typologically linked to a narrative frame about the Harrowing, demonstrating the convergence of biblical, apocryphal, and patristic traditions within the transmission of the Harrowing of Hell legend. The author of Blickling 7 also combines a variety of sources, extending the combinatory process of adaptation to suit the needs of a tenth-century preacher.

The heart of the translation of the Pseudo-Augustinian sermon in Blickling 7 focuses on Jesus' post-Crucifixion descent into hell to rescue the just Jews. The dramatic action is summarized at the beginning of Blickling 7:

> & he þa onsende his þone wuldorfæstan gast to helle grunde, & þær þone ealdor ealra þeostra & þæs ecean deaþes geband & gehynde, & ealne his geferscipe swyþe gedrefde, & helle geatu & hire þa ærenan scyttelas he ealle tobræc, & ealle his þa gecorenan he þonon alædde, & þara deofla þeostro he oforgeat mid his þæm scinendan leohte.

> (85.3–9: And then he sent his glorious spirit into the abyss of hell, and there he bound and humbled the prince of all darkness, and greatly terrified all of his followers, and completely broke the gates of hell and their brass bolts, and from there he led all of his chosen ones, and he overcame the darkness of the devil with his shining light.)

---

88 *PL* 39.2059–61.

89 See Biggs and Morey, "Gospel of Nicodemus," *SASLC Apocrypha*, 33–5. No entry exists for Blickling 7 in *Fontes*.

90 See Biggs and Wright, "Apocalypse of Thomas," *SASLC Apocrypha*, 71–2; and Wright, "Vercelli Homily XV and *The Apocalypse of Thomas*," with further references there.

More specifically, much of the following narrative is taken up with dialogue from those in hell, terrified demons as well as hopeful Old Testament patriarchs. The dialogues of the inhabitants in hell as well as the direct actions of Jesus drive the drama of this sermon. In this respect, especially poignant is the distinct lack of Jesus' voice.

Furthermore, the speech of other characters – the demons as well as the righteous Jews who are rescued – continually emphasizes Jesus' deeds, before and during the Harrowing. For example, after Jesus has broken down the gates of hell, pulled his chosen out of the pit, and bound the devil to cast him into hell, those who have been saved cry out: "Astig nu, Drihten Hælend Crist, up, nu þu hafast helle bereafod, & þæs deaþes aldor on þyssum witum gebundenne. Gecyþ nu middangearde blisse þæt on þinum upstige geblissian & gehyhton ealle þine gecorenan" (87.22–5: "Now ascend, Lord Saviour Christ, now you have robbed hell, and have bound the prince of death in these torments. Now make bliss known to the world so that all your chosen may rejoice and trust in your Ascension"). Despite the dearth of Jesus' speech, the narrative is propelled by his actions, even when narrated through the voices of others. Jesus bursts into hell, rescues the just Jews, and ascends, while the demons remain passive in fearful speech, and the rescued souls remain passive in deference to Jesus' mercy. Jesus' words may be absent, but his actions are central.

Marian devotion is also conveyed in this sermon, through Eve's speech. After relating her sin in Paradise and repenting of it, she continues:

Ic þe halsige nu, Drihten, for þinre þeowene, Sancta Marian, þa þu mid heofonlicum wuldre geweorþodest; hire innoþ þu gefyldest nigon monaþ mid ealles middangeardes weorþe; þu wast þæt þu of minre dehter, Drihten, onwoce; & þæt hire flæsc is of minum flæsce, & hire ban of minum banum. Ara me nu, min Drihten, for hire wuldres weorþmyndum, ara me ungesæligost ealra wifa, & min Scyppend miltsa me, & genere me of þysses deaþes bendum.

(I implore you now, Lord, by your servant, Saint Mary, whom you honoured with heavenly glory. You filled her womb for nine months with the treasure of all the world. You know that you were born from my daughter, Lord, and that her flesh is from my flesh, and her bone from my bones. Have mercy on me now, my Lord, for the honour of her glory; have mercy on me, most wretched of all women, and my Maker pity me, and deliver me from the bonds of this death.)

Here, Marian devotion is folded directly into salvation history, typologically framed against Eve's first sin. Even more, Mary's role is made apparent through retelling the highlights of Mary's pregnancy, Jesus' Nativity, directly linking these with the present subjects of Jesus' Crucifixion, Harrowing, Resurrection, and Ascension. The liturgical centrality of the Virgin Mary that we have seen throughout this chapter is made manifest in Blickling 7 with this speech.

Situating Blickling 7 in direct relation to other liturgical associations is not difficult, since it shares a common source with ninth-century texts on the Harrowing of Hell in the *Old English Martyrology* (for 26 March)[91] and the *Book of Cerne* (Cambridge, University Library, Ll.1.10; 820x840, Mercia).[92] Like Blickling 7, both of these apparently rely on a reworked Latin adaptation of the Pseudo-Augustine *Sermo* 160. A collection of prayer texts compiled most likely for private devotion, the *Book of Cerne* contains a range of apocryphal materials, including a dramatic liturgical dialogue in Latin known as the *Harrowing of Hell* on folios 98v–99v (for a translation, see appendix 3).[93] Especially telling about this piece is its status as a dramatic dialogue, with speeches by Adam and Eve crying out for redemption from the soon to be resurrected Christ. David N. Dumville has suggested this reading of the text, noting that the narrative instructions (lines 1–4, 25, 34, 44–5, and 52) all appear in red ink in the manuscript, setting them apart from the speeches.[94] As a piece of liturgical dialogue, then, this *Harrowing of Hell* was meant for public performance, in a way that would have been accessible to an audience beyond private devotional reading. The same could be said for Blickling 7.

The payoff for situating Blickling 7 among the many representations of the Harrowing of Hell is that we also find the many resonances that Anglo-Saxon audiences would have brought with them to the reading of

---

91 Rauer, ed. and trans., *The Old English Martyrology*, 74–7 and 249–50.

92 NRK, 27; and *ASM*, 28. See Kuypers, ed., *The Prayer Book of Aedeluald the Bishop Commonly Called The Book of Cerne*. For extended analysis, see Michelle P. Brown, *The Book of Cerne*.

93 References by line nos. are to Dumville, "Liturgical Drama and Panegyric Responsory from the Eighth Century?," 376–7; cf. Kuypers, ed., *The Prayer Book of Aedeluald*, 196–8.

94 Dumville, "Liturgical Drama and Panegyric Responsory from the Eighth Century?," 380–1.

this sermon. As a popular, dramatic, performative narrative, the Harrowing pervaded Christian media. It is true that we cannot rely on speculation to explain what Anglo-Saxons across the spectrum of society might have known about the Harrowing, considering that the more learned (monks, priests, literate laity) were more likely to encounter the artefacts discussed than others. Yet depictions survive from much more public objects like crosses, architectural reliefs, and stone sculptures, which were accessible to a wider range of people. It is unlikely that the audience of Blickling 7 – whether it was read devotionally or in a mass – would learn about the Harrowing for the first time from this sermon. Nonetheless, an attentive audience could appreciate this specific adaptation, and its place in the larger network of related media, as a dramatic unfolding of the Harrowing prompting them to consider their own salvation before the subsequent exhortations about the Doomsday in the second part of the sermon.

Conclusions

Imagining the performance of Vercelli 6 and Blickling 7 in the liturgical setting of preaching – for example, mass or the monastic office – it is not difficult to understand the uses of apocrypha to emphasize Jesus' dramatic deeds. For Anglo-Saxon authors, the infancy miracles from the *Gospel of Pseudo-Matthew* and the redemption of the just Jews from the Harrowing of Hell presented compelling additions to the already performative setting of liturgical services. The deeds of Jesus, after all, are already enacted in such settings, such as in the dramatic liturgical moment of celebrating the Eucharist. By emphasizing Jesus' deeds further, through the narratives of apocryphal gospels, Vercelli 6 and Blickling 7 participate in this complex of performance for all involved in the service. Visual arts allow a glimpse into the multimedia experience of worship, in which verbal and visual elements were mixed for a fuller spiritual experience. The translation of apocryphal gospels, then, was not a simple matter of preaching, but a holistic adaptation of narratives to present them in many representative forms to the people. In this, apocryphal media pervaded the worship experiences of many Anglo-Saxons, including preachers and parishioners, monks and priests, elites and commoners, men and women. Far from the margins of belief, apocryphal gospel narratives suffused the religious experiences of Anglo-Saxons.

Chapter Five

A Network Microcosm in Bodley 343

In this chapter I trace the various connections between apocrypha and preaching within a single book: the twelfth-century preaching collection Oxford, Bodleian Library, Bodley 343. In studying this manuscript with a whole book approach,[1] I suggest that the codex is a representative in microcosm of the preaching network I discussed in chapter 1. As one of the most extensive compilations of Latin and Old English homilies and sermons from early England, Bodley 343 is a valuable representative of preaching in Latin and the vernacular, by named and anonymous Anglo-Saxon authors. Indeed, Bodley 343 is largely analogous to sermon collections examined in chapter 1 and demonstrates the continued vivacity of preaching apocrypha beyond the Norman Conquest, including materials that originated as early as the tenth century reused for late twelfth-century contexts.[2]

In tracing the threads of apocrypha in Bodley 343, I stress the notions of both book as medium and the network inside of it comprised of textual media. These concepts return to theoretical ideas previously posed about related layers of media, remediation, and intermediality between codex and individual texts. After all, the message may be found in both the whole book and the individual pieces of it. What brings together all of the texts in Bodley 343 as a coherent network is the fact that the compilers saw them as interrelated and included them in the codex. N.R. Ker indicates

---

1 See esp. Nichols and Wenzel, eds., *The Whole Book*; and, more recently, Johnston and Van Dussen, eds., *The Medieval Manuscript Book*.

2 See esp. Swan and Treharne, eds., *Rewriting Old English*; Treharne, *Living through Conquest*; and *PUEM*.

that "There is no obvious arrangement" other than one group of texts in liturgical order (fols. 65–128);[3] yet there is no reason to believe that the compilers did not have a plan in mind in bringing these texts together. More about this will be addressed in the next section, in which I describe the book and its contents.

I focus mainly on items included in this collection for their usefulness on certain specific feast days. All of these come from the part of the liturgical calendar known as the *sanctorale* (or Proper of Saints) that gathers together the fixed feast days of saints, in distinction from the *temporale* (or Proper of Time) that includes moveable feasts related to the life of Christ. Regarding Bodley 343 as a coherent, contained network, sermons for feast days of the *sanctorale* cycle may be treated as nodes, highlighted from the entire cycle of the liturgical year, connected to each other through common content, themes, subjects, and even the commonality that they are meant to be used for specific liturgical occasions. Since such feast days would have been celebrated in public worship across contexts (in the mass and Divine Office), these vernacular sermons present key points in the year with the potential to reach a wide range of those in the community. Bodley 343 provides a significant witness for the types of apocrypha used in these situations, bound together and related to each other within a single collection.

Bodley 343 as Book

The significance of Bodley 343, already established, is as a large, variegated collection of Latin and Old English preaching, with texts ranging from versions of the earliest surviving vernacular sermons to compositions from the twelfth century.[4] Bodley 343 is arguably the most representative extant witness to Anglo-Saxon preaching, since it contains ninety-six items in both Latin and Old English, ranging across the types of sermons available in Anglo-Saxon England from the tenth through twelfth centuries. These contents include selections from Ælfric's *Catholic Homilies*, *Lives*

---

3 NRK, 310.

4 For descriptions, see esp. NRK, 310; Irvine, ed., *Old English Homilies from MS Bodley 343*, xviii–liv; Conti and Da Rold, "Oxford Bodleian Library, Bodley 343"; and Conti, "Individual Practice, Common Endeavor," with further references there. I have also examined the manuscript on microfilm. I follow Conti and Da Rold's item numbers.

of Saints, and other pastoral texts; a cycle of anonymous Latin sermons identified as the Homiliary of Angers; versions of various anonymous vernacular sermons; sermons by Wulfstan; and two Latin dialogues between a student and master on the Lord's Prayer and the Creed. Notable additions in spaces originally left blank include a selection of Latin liturgical music; anonymous Latin sermons; the only extant version of the Old English poem *The Grave*; and two Latin texts attributed to Alan of Lille (c. 1122–1202/3) and Hildebert of Le Mans (c. 1055–1133).

The main production of this book seems to be the work of two scribes, one for folios xi^r–xxxix^v (including selections from Ælfric's *Catholic Homilies*, liturgical music, and the Homiliary of Angers) and another for folios 1r–170r (including mainly Old English sermons), plus other scribes for additions. Folios xi^r–xxxix^v and 1r–170r were perhaps written and compiled separately and bound together later, although it is difficult to determine the exact process or chronology. As Aidan Conti writes, "it seems reasonable to posit that the material written by scribes 1 and 2 was, if not physically bound together, used by one individual ... and therefore probably in the same repository at the end of the twelfth or beginning of the thirteenth century."[5] What is important, then, is that all of the contents were, at some point, bound together into a single codex.

My examinations and arguments rest on the notion that *selection* is a significant aspect of the production of Bodley 343. Suggesting that the work of the scribes who copied the contents was "archival in nature," Conti points out that this type of compilation "is an active process that involves selection, sifting and (within limited space) the promotion of some material over other matter."[6] In other words, the very contents of this manuscript demonstrate what was valuable to the compilers and ideas about preaching in the late twelfth century. For my argument, it is especially significant that apocryphal texts are included in this archival network. Furthermore, it is meaningful that apocryphal sermons are interleaved and interconnected in a variety of ways with the other contents of Bodley 343. Part of every network are the "architectonic shape" and the "values and motivations" that all contribute to the meaning of the larger collective.[7] To the scribes who worked on this manuscript, apocryphal texts were no

---

5 Conti, "Individual Practice, Common Endeavour," 260.

6 Ibid., 271.

7 See Galloway, "Networks," 282.

more outliers than any of the others – they selected and included all of the contents of this book because they viewed each item as significant. Even before examining the more specific connections between these contents, then, it is clear that all of the texts in Bodley 343 are interrelated, since those involved in the production – even over time, if the two sections were bound together at a later date – perceived them together as part of the archive they collectively created.

Peter, Paul, and Antichrist

I begin with items contained in the large group of Latin sermons (fols. xi^r– xxxix^v) that Conti has identified as a complete copy of a collection known as the Homiliary of Angers, based on previous work by Raymond Étaix.[8] The selection of sermons generally illustrates the diversity of materials used by early medieval preachers, such as biblical, apocryphal, patristic, and liturgical texts, and the collection may possibly have links with reform movements at the time of its compilation. In his preliminary identification and examination of the Homiliary of Angers in a number of Continental manuscripts, Étaix determined that the original collection was probably compiled in the tenth century, on the Continent or in England, and dispersed widely throughout Europe over the next several centuries.[9] Most recently, Winfried Rudolf has discovered what is (for now) the earliest identified fragment of the homiliary in some binding fragments in Bamberg, Staatsbibliothek, Msc.Bibl.30a, originally from a manuscript created in northern France in the early tenth century – based on one scribe's hand, datable not long after 900.[10] This new evidence, together with other identified witnesses, tips the scales in favour of a Continental origin for the Homiliary of Angers no later than the end of the ninth century.

Soon after its compilation, the Homiliary of Angers circulated in England. Since Conti's identification of the collection in Bodley 343,

---

8 Conti first identified the Homiliary of Angers in "Preaching Scripture and Apocrypha," and published his findings in "The Circulation of the Old English Homily in the Twelfth Century."

9 Étaix, "L'homéliaire carolingien d'Angers." I follow Étaix's numbering for the reconstructed contents.

10 Rudolf, "An Early Manuscript Witness of the Homiliaries of Angers and St. Père de Chartres in Bamberg, Staatsbibliothek, MS Msc.Bibl.30a." My thanks to Winfried Rudolf for allowing me to read a draft of his work.

studies of other manuscript fragments and textual associations have provided further evidence for its circulation in England as early as the tenth century.[11] Important for this study is the fact that some of the earliest witnesses to the homiliary were copied in England between the late tenth and mid-eleventh centuries: London, British Library, Sloane 280, fols. 1 and 286 (s. x², Kent) and Taunton, Somerset County Record Office, DD/SAS C/1193/77 (s. xi?med., ?2, ?3/3, SE England, Kent?).[12] The Taunton fragment presents Old English translations of the contents alongside a Latin portion of the homiliary, striking evidence of multilingual practices in Anglo-Saxon preaching.[13] Stephen Pelle has demonstrated that a Rogationtide sermon in the homiliary (item 22) incorporates the apocryphal motif of the "Seven Pains of Hell," and a version of this apocryphal subject was used by the authors of Vercelli 9 and another Old English sermon in Oxford, Bodleian Library, Hatton 115 (s. xi³/⁴ or xi²).[14] As Rudolf has asserted, "we may at least rely on the fact that this homiliary was disseminated and used in Anglo-Saxon England from the late tenth century on, if not earlier."[15] For its use from the tenth through twelfth centuries, the Homiliary of Angers is an important collection for considering preaching media used by Anglo-Saxon authors and intersections with vernacular texts.[16]

Previous work has already revealed some associations with apocrypha as sources for sermons included in the Homiliary of Angers. For example, Conti has highlighted a number of apocryphal sources in the Bodley 343 version of this homiliary, which inform the present examination.[17] In an extended examination of *Sermo x* in Bodley 343 (fols. xvi^r–xvii^r),[18] he has demonstrated that it contains a translation of the Greek *De Christi passione* spuriously attributed to Eusebius Alexandrinus, which likely shares a common source with the account of the Harrowing of Hell in the *Gospel*

---

11 See Conti, "The Taunton Fragment and the Homiliary of Angers"; Rudolf, "The Homiliary of Angers in Tenth-Century England"; and Pelle, "The Seven Pains of Hell."

12 *ASM*, 498.0 and 756.8.

13 Conti, "The Taunton Fragment and the Homiliary of Angers."

14 Pelle, "The Seven Pains of Hell." On Hatton 115, see NRK, 332; and *ASM*, 639.

15 Rudolf, "The Homiliary of Angers in Tenth-Century England," 183.

16 For Homiliary of Angers texts in Bodley 343, I rely on Conti's transcriptions in "Preaching Scripture and Apocrypha," confirmed by my own examination of the manuscript on microfilm; I have accepted Conti's emendations, though, in some cases, I have altered modernizations such as capitalization and punctuation.

17 Ibid.; and Conti, "The Circulation of the Old English Homily in the Twelfth Century."

18 This text is also extant in another witness to the Homiliary of Angers, Cambridge, St John's College C.12 (s. xiii), fol. 141b.

of Nicodemus.[19] Pelle's study of the Rogationtide sermon (item 22) has implications for looking towards the homiliary for not only sources of Old English literature but also the transmission of apocrypha: the "Seven Pains of Hell" motif that he identifies derives from certain versions of the *Apocalypse of Paul*, and the sermon must be a mediating text for the tradition in England. Furthermore, identified manuscripts containing the Homiliary of Angers besides Bodley 343 include apocryphal materials beyond the primary collection:[20] versions of the *Gospel of Pseudo-Matthew*,[21] *Gospel of Nicodemus*,[22] *Vindicta Salvatoris*,[23] Pseudo-Melito *Transitus Mariae*,[24] a text on the names of the wise men who visited Jesus titled *Nomina Magorum*,[25] *Martyrdom of Andrew*,[26] *Martyrdom of Thomas*,[27] Pseudo-Methodius *Revelationes*,[28] and *Three Utterances*.[29] These associations reveal how the Homiliary of Angers – the version in Bodley 343 as well as various iterations in other manuscripts – is interconnected with the media network discussed in chapter 1.

The first text I consider is an item assigned for the feast of Peter and Paul on 29 June (Étaix's item 32), *Sermo xxix* in Bodley 343 (folios xxiii[v]–xxiv[r]).[30] Examining this sermon and its apocryphal associations will provide a starting point for considering other related texts within Bodley 343, both in the Homiliary of Angers and more generally. It is useful, then, to understand *Sermo xxix* as the first node in the network to be explored in this chapter, with various other nodes in Bodley 343 connected through

---

19 Conti, "Preaching Scripture and Apocrypha," 147–212; on St John's College C.12, see 211–12.

20 See descriptions in Étaix, "L'homéliaire carolingien d'Angers," 158–64. Dates, origins, and provenances for identified manuscripts of this homiliary are provided in Rudolf, "The Homiliary of Angers in Tenth-Century England," 165–6.

21 Engelberg, Stiftsbibliothek 44 (s. xiii[1/2]), fols. 74v–77v.

22 Angers, Bibliothèque municipale 236 (s. xi, prov. St Aubin, Angers), fols. 39v–47r; Engelberg 44, fols. 97r–103r; and Grenoble, Bibliothèque municipale 278 (470) (s. xii, prov. Chartreuse of Pierre-Châtel), fols. 20r–25v (imperfect).

23 Grenoble 278, fols. 27r–30r (acephalous).

24 Budapest, Országos Széchényi Könyvtár, Clmae 481 (s. xi[2], prov. Northern Italy), fols. 128r–132v; and Grenoble 278, fols. 95r–99r (acephalous).

25 Engelberg 44, fol. 119r.

26 Budapest 481, fols. 152r–156v (acephalous).

27 Budapest 481, fols. 156v–end (incomplete).

28 Engelberg 44, fols. 103r–105r.

29 Engelberg 44, fol. 105v.

30 See Conti, "Preaching Scriptures and Apocrypha," 88–9, transcription at 279–81.

common associations. This sermon begins as a commentary on Peter's declaration of Jesus as Christ in Matthew 16 and ends with an exemplum about the confrontation between the apostles Peter and Paul with the magician Simon Magus and Emperor Nero in Rome. In tracing the network related to this sermon, the first relationship to highlight is the the apocryphal *Martyrdom of Peter and Paul* as a source for *Sermo xxix*.[31] To my knowledge, this source has not been previously identified, though it is possible to demonstrate based on both the general summary of the shared narrative and verbal correspondences between the two texts. As seen in chapters 1 and 2, evidence for the circulation and use of the *Martyrdom* in Anglo-Saxon England is well established, especially vernacular translations in Blickling 15, Ælfric's *Passio Apostolorum Petri et Pauli* (*CH* I.26), and Wulfstan's *De temporibus Antichristi*. *Sermo xxix* therefore stands as yet another witness within this tradition.

Sermo xxix provides the following account (verbal parallels with the *Martyrdom* to be discussed appear in bold):

Postea uenit beatus Petrus apostolus ad Romam et ibidem construxit ecclesias quinque et uiginti annos et ibidem conuinxit Antichristum, Simon Magus, **qui se dicebat filium Dei esse** et promittebat se **ascendere in celum cepitque uolare** per suas **magicas artes coram populo**. Sed beatus **Petrus** apostolus **orauit**. Antea uenit oratio quam Antichristi presumptio. Tunc per orationem Sancti Petri coram populo cecidit Antichristus cum cantatione fuitque sepultus in infernum cum diabolis cum corpore et anima. Expauescite, fratres karissimi, ut nulla superbia ueniat in uos. Qualem potestatem dedit Dominus apostolo suo qui alligauit Antichristum per suam sanctam orationem. Inde fuerunt postea passi sub Nerone Petrus et Paulus. Iunior uenit ad seniorem, senior Petrus, iunior Paulus. Petrus fuit crucifixus diuersis **pedibus** sicut ipse dixit: Ego **non sum dignus** sic crucifigi **sicut Dominus noster** fuit. **Paulus decollatus est** sed in uno momento uel in una hora uenerunt ante conspectum Domini cum angelis et archangelis cum leticia et exultatione.

(Afterward the blessed apostle Peter came to Rome, and there he established churches for twenty-five years, and there he conquered Antichrist, Simon Magus, who declared himself to be the son of God and promised to ascend

---

31 References by chapter numbers are to the Latin text in Lipsius and Bonnet, eds., *Acta Apostolorum Apocrypha*, 1:118–77. See further discussion and references in chapter 2.

into the heavens and by his magical arts began to fly in the presence of the people. But the blessed apostle Peter prayed. The prayer came before the presumption of the Antichrist. Then by the prayer of Saint Peter in the presence of the people the Antichrist fell with his spells and was buried in hell with the devils in body and soul. Be afraid, dearest brothers, so that no pride might come into you. The Lord gave such power to his apostle who bound Antichrist with his holy prayer. Thence, afterward, Peter and Paul were martyred under Nero. The younger came to the elder, the elder Peter, the younger Paul. Peter was crucified with feet upside-down, as he himself said: "I am not worthy to be crucified as our Lord was." Paul was beheaded, but in one moment, or in one hour, they came before the face of the Lord with angels and archangels, with gladness and joy.)

The most obvious correspondences with the *Martyrdom* exist in the general narrative of this exemplum, comprised of the major figures of the apostles Peter and Paul, the antagonists Simon Magus and Nero, and the central episodes of Simon Magus's magical flight and death, followed by the martyrdoms of the apostles at Nero's orders. Although narratives for the martyrdoms of Peter and Paul occur in other apocrypha, *Sermo xxix* includes the same characters and plot as that of the Pseudo-Marcellus *Martyrdom of Peter and Paul*. Comparing the range of other early Christian apostolic apocrypha reveals as much. In the *Actus Vercellenses* and the *Martyrdom of Peter*, the apostle Peter confronts Simon Magus and Nero, which leads to his execution, but he does so without Paul's support; in the Pseudo-Linus *Martyrdom of Peter*, Simon Magus is absent and Peter is martyred by the Roman prefect Agrippa (not Nero); and in the Pseudo-Linus *Martyrdom of Paul*, although Paul is executed by Nero, there is no confrontation with Simon Magus.[32] While various versions of these apocrypha circulated in Anglo-Saxon England,[33] *Sermo xxix* follows the Pseudo-Marcellus *Martyrdom* in pairing the two apostles in their conflict with Simon Magus as well as combining their executions by Nero.

More specifically, as indicated by the phrases in bold, *Sermo xxix* shares a number of verbal parallels with the Latin *Martyrdom*. For example, the *Martyrdom* contains parallel phrasing about Simon's claims to be the son of God. First, when Nero is tricked by the magic that Simon Magus

---

32 For various Petrine and Pauline acts, see esp. introductions, texts, and translations in Eastman, *The Ancient Martyrdom Accounts of Peter and Paul*.

33 For summaries of scholarship, see entries in *SASLC Apocrypha*, 50–3.

performs, the narrative relates, "uere hunc **esse dei filium** aestimabat" (14: "he thought that he [Simon] was truly the son of God"). Only a few lines later, in the very next chapter, Simon himself makes the claim: "Audi me, bone imperator: Ego **sum filius dei**" ("Hear me, good emperor: I am the son of God"). Again, *Martyrdom* 26 relates, "Petrus dixit: Tu ergo, **qui filium dei te esse dicis**, dic quid cogitem" ("Peter said: 'You, therefore, who declare yourself to be the son of God, say what I think'"). While this latter most closely parallels *Sermo xxix*, all of these passages taken together speak to the pervasive themes and consistent verbal similarities between these texts.

Two separate passages share parallels in the details about Simon Magus's flight. In *Martyrdom* 30, "Simon dixit: Iube mihi turrim altam fabricare ex lignis, et **ascendam** super eam, et uocabo angelos meos et praecipiam eis ut cunctis uidentibus **in caelum** perferant me ad patrem meum" ("Simon said: "Order a high tower of wood to be made, and I will climb up it, and I will summon my angels and command them to bear me into the heavens to my father before the sight of all"). Further along in the narrative, after some interludes, the finale of this episode occurs in *Martyrdom* 54, in which is related, "Tunc **ascendit** Simon in turrim **coram omnibus**, et extensis manibus coronatus lauro **coepit uolare**" ("Then Simon ascended the tower in the presence of all, and with hands extended and head crowned with laurel he began to fly"). The reference to Simon's "magicas artes" could be a general phrase, but the term "arte magica" occurs twice in the *Martyrdom*, in chapters 32 and 33. In addition, the remark about Peter's prayer is another instance that may be generally gleaned from the apocryphal narrative, but a more precise equivalent is found in a variant addition to the text in Munich, Bayerische Staatsbibliothek, Clm 4554 (s. viii/ix, Benediktbeuren).[34] In this manuscript, added to the end of chapter 55 is the remark, "Tunc stans in medio **Petrus orauit**" (folio 10v: "then standing in the middle Peter prayed"), followed by a prayer.[35] This observation is not meant to suggest that *Sermo xxix* is based directly on Munich 4554,

---

34 Digital facsimile at *MDZ: Münchener Digitalisierungs Zentrum Digitale Bibliothek*, http://daten.digitale-sammlungen.de/~db/0006/bsb00064009/images/index.html. See Glauche, *Katalog der lateinischen Handschriften der Bayerischen Staatsbibliothek München*, 80–2; available online at *Manuscripta Medievalia*, http://www.manuscripta-mediaevalia.de/hs/kataloge/HSK0448.htm.

35 See apparatus in Lipsius and Bonnet, eds., *Acta Apostolorum Apocrypha*, 1:166 (siglum M); I have also confirmed this reading based on the digital facsimile at *MDZ*.

but this manuscript does represent the types of parallels that circulated and could have informed similar accounts.

For information about the martyrdoms of the two apostles, chapters 59–60 in the *Martyrdom* are especially relevant:

> Et deducti sunt Petrus et Paulus a conspectu Neronis. **Paulus decollatus est** in uia Ostiensi.
>
> Petrus autem dum uenisset ad crucem ait: Quoniam dominus meus Iesus Christus de caelo ad terram descendens recta cruce sublimatus est, me autem quem de terra ad caelum euocare dignatur, crux mea caput meum in terra debet ostendere, et **pedes** ad caelum dirigere: ergo quia **non sum dignus** ita esse in cruce **sicut dominus meus**, girate crucem meam. At illi uerterunt crucem et **pedes** eius sursum fixerunt, manus uero deorsum.

> (And Peter and Paul were led away from the presence of Nero. Paul was beheaded on the Ostian Way.
>
> But when Peter had come to the cross he said: "Since my Lord Jesus Christ, who descended from heaven to earth, was raised upright on a cross, but he deemed me worthy to call me from earth to heaven, my cross should stretch my head towards the earth, and direct my feet to heaven: therefore, since I am not worthy to be on the cross as my Lord, turn my cross." So they turned the cross and fixed his feet upward, his hands downward.)

Concerning Peter's feet, *Sermo xxix* is not as clear, perhaps even confusing the meaning while losing the wordplay without Peter's longer explanation. However, Peter's speech and the brief statement about Paul's execution are direct echoes of the *Martyrdom*. It is also worth noting the close proximity of these parallels in both texts, since the statement about Paul's execution in chapter 59 of the *Martyrdom* is followed closely by Peter's speech about his death in chapter 60.

These verbal parallels establish the close relationship that *Sermo xxix* shares with the Latin *Martyrdom of Peter and Paul*, suggesting that the apocryphon is the ultimate source for the sermon. The evidence for this identification does not preclude the possibility of an intermediary that might explain the condensed nature of the Latin sermon and its differences in language. Nonetheless, an intermediary would only add yet another node, and multiple edges, to the network, presenting a more complex intertextual system. The significance of this identification is that *Sermo xxix* in the Bodley 343 version of the Homiliary of Angers contributes yet another substantial witness to the transmission and circulation of the apocryphal *Martyrdom of Peter and Paul* in Anglo-Saxon England. Unfortunately, given their incomplete nature, there is no way to know if it would have been included in other witnesses known in Anglo-Saxon England like Sloane 280 or the Taunton fragment. Since the sermon appears in five other versions of the homiliary, however, chances are good that it was known to Anglo-Saxon preachers earlier than the twelfth century.[36] What may be taken away from verbal correspondences between these two texts, even beyond source identification, is the notion that individual words and phrases – often the playground of philology – help us to understand networks of intertextuality between discrete texts.

In order to gain a greater appreciation of the types of network associations that *Sermo xxix* shares in Bodley 343, we can look beyond its source to other preaching texts within the Homiliary of Angers. Within this collection of Latin sermons, *Sermo xxix* most directly relates to *Sermo v* (folios xiii^r–v), assigned to the third Sunday in Lent (Étaix's item 13).[37] In this commentary on Jesus' exorcism of a mute demon in Luke 11, Simon Magus is mentioned as an example of one who receives baptism but continues in a sinful life: "**Simon Magus** postquam baptizatus fuit, deuenit **Antichristus. Dicebat se esse** Deum et cecidit cum ruina et **in infernum cum corpore et anima**" ("Simon Magus, when he was baptized, became Antichrist. He declared himself to be God and fell with destruction and into hell in body and soul"). Like *Sermo xxix*, a common connection may be traced to the apocryphal legends of Simon Magus (related to the *Martyrdom*), as well as the commonplace typological association with Antichrist. Moreover, the verbal parallels support the notion of common authorship for at least some of the Homiliary of Angers items.

Looking towards the contents of Bodley 343 outside of the version of the Homiliary of Angers, comprised mainly of vernacular texts, reveals further associations within the network being discussed. Closely related,

---

36 The sermon is also included in Angers 236, fols. 72v–74v; Grenoble 278, fols. 47r–49r; Madrid, Biblioteca de la Real Academia de la Historia, Aem. 39 (s. xi^1?, Spain), fols. 29v–30v; Toledo, Archivo y Biblioteca Capitular 33–1 (s. xii, Spain), fols. 60r–63v; and Uppsala, Universitetsbibliotek, C 148 (s. xii^2), fols. 102v–105v.

37 See Conti, "Preaching Scriptures and Apocrypha," 76, transcription at 235–38.

since the *Martyrdom* is a mutual source, is Ælfric's *Passio Apostolorum Petri et Pauli* (*CH* I.26). In this sermon, Ælfric directly translates some of the same selections of the *Martyrdom* that the author of *Sermo xxix* found to be important. A few examples suffice to draw parallels. Describing Simon Magus, Ælfric explains: "Ðes dry wæs mid þam awyriedum gaste to þam swiðe afylled þæt he cwæð þæt he wære crist godes sunu ⁊ mid his drycræfte þæs folces geleafan amyrde" (107–9: "This magician was filled with the evil spirit so much that he said that he was Christ the son of God, and with his magic craft he corrupted the belief of the people"). This passage does not directly correlate to any wording in the Latin source, but it does summarize both the character and the magical trickery that he performs throughout the narrative. When Nero expresses astonishment at Simon Magus's tricks, "ða wende he ðæt he godes sunu wære" (175: "then he thought that he was the son of God"), which is a close translation of *Martyrdom* 14 ("uere hunc esse dei filium aestimabat"). Ælfric also translates passages relating Simon's flight, with the emphasis on ascension ("astigan" and "astah" in lines 231 and 235) before the people ("ætforan eallum folce" in line 235); and he retains the wordplay surrounding Peter's feet ("fet" and "fotwelmas" in lines 257–63) at his crucifixion. Like the author of *Sermo xxix*, Ælfric condenses his source, placing these two moments – in chapters 30 and 54 of the *Martyrdom* – in close succession in the Old English narrative.

Besides a shared source in the *Martyrdom*, typological associations of Simon Magus with Antichrist present several intertexts between *Sermo xxix* and other materials in Bodley 343.[38] The development of legends about the Antichrist stretching from early Christianity into the Middle Ages had built up a complex legend surrounding this figure, and a number of Anglo-Saxon texts participated in this tradition.[39] While developments around the figure of Antichrist are not necessarily apocryphal, the few concrete references in the New Testament are ambiguous compared to the detailed picture created over the next millennium. In fact, characterizations and lore about Antichrist demonstrate the fluidity of biblical and

---

38 Conti generally notes thematic relationships, though they are not the focus of his examination, in "Revising Wulfstan's Antichrist in the Twelfth Century," 640–1.

39 See esp. Emmerson, *Antichrist in the Middle Ages*; McGinn, *Antichrist*; Hughes, *Constructing Antichrist*; and Palmer, *The Apocalypse in the Early Middle Ages*; and my discussion in chapter 2.

extra-biblical traditions, since they accumulated over time as various writers expanded on previous authors' ideas.

Decidedly significant for the Antichrist tradition is a treatise titled *De ortu et tempore Antichristi*, by the French Abbot Adso of Montier-en-Der (d. 992).[40] This text clearly made an impact on Anglo-Saxon literature, since it circulated in both Latin and Old English versions[41] and influenced Old English works by Ælfric, Wulfstan, and at least one anonymous translator.[42] One text in Bodley 343 indebted to Adso's work appears as an Old English composite sermon made up of material by Wulfstan, though it was likely compiled by a later, anonymous author.[43] This sermon, *De temporibus Anrichristi* (folios 141v–143v), brings together material from Wulfstan's *Secundum Marcum* (Bethurum V), *De Antichristo* (Bethurum Ib), and *De temporibus Antichristi* (Bethurum IV).[44] In association with *Sermo xxix*, content concerned with the Antichrist is clear, even though no reference to Simon Magus is made in this particular text.

Specific textual associations in the Wulfstanian sermon appear in a passage based on Adso's treatise evoking Elijah and Enoch.[45] As the two Old Testament prophets who did not experience death (related in Genesis 5:24 and 2 Kings 2:11), these figures stand in a fascinating relationship to eschatological concepts. Adso draws on the tradition of the two prophets living

---

40 References are to Verhelst, ed., *Adso Dervensis*; translations from McGinn, *Apocalyptic Spirituality*, 89–96. On Adso and his work on Antichrist, see esp. Palmer, *The Apocalypse in the Early Middle Ages*, 194–8, with further references there.

41 The Latin text survives in two manuscripts associated with Anglo-Saxon England: Cambridge, Corpus Christi College 190 (s. xi¹, Worcester?) and London, British Library, Cotton Vespasian D.ii (s. xi/xii, Normandy, England by 1100?); see NRK, 45; and *ASM*, 59 and 388.

42 See entries for "Adso" in *Fontes*.

43 On Wulfstan and his works, see esp. Bethurum, ed., *The Homilies of Wulfstan*; Gatch, *Preaching and Theology in Anglo-Saxon England*; Townend, ed., *Wulfstan, Archbishop of York*; and Lionarons, *The Homiletic Writings of Archbishop Wulfstan*.

44 References by line numbers are to Conti, "Revising Wulfstan's Antichrist in the Twelfth Century," 650–63, confirmed by my own examination of the manuscript on microfilm; in quotations, I have silently expanded abbreviations and adopted modernized capitalization and punctuation. See also Jonathan Wilcox, "Wulfstan and the Twelfth Century"; and Lionarons, *The Homiletic Writings of Archbishop Wulfstan*, 16–17 and 43–74.

45 See notes in Bethurum, ed., *The Homilies of Wulfstan*, 292.

outside of time, with God, waiting to be sent back to earth to finish God's will for them in facing Antichrist. The Old English translation of Adso's work presents the following passage:

> La, hwylc wundor bið þeah ðe mennisce deofol synfullum mote derian heardlice, ðone God iðafæð þæt he mot on his agene halgum swylc wundor gewurcan þæt Enoc ⁊ Helias þurh ðone ðeodfeond imartyrode wurðaþ, þe God sylfe fela hund wintræ mid sawla ⁊ lichoman geheold ær to þam anum ...

> (158–68: Alas, what a wonder it is though the human devil might be allowed to injure the sinful severely, when God allows that he might work on his own saints such a wonder that Enoch and Elijah, through this archfiend, will be martyred, whom God himself kept many hundreds of winters before with soul and body for that one thing ...)

This conjunction of Elijah and Enoch with Antichrist during the Last Judgment follows Adso's conception of a sequence of necessary events during Antichrist's tyranny. In the signs leading to the Final Judgment, these figures will face Antichrist directly: "Sed ne subito et improuise Antichristus ueniat et totum humanum genus suo errore decipiat et perdat, ante eius exordium duo magni prophete mittentur in mundum, Enoch scilicet et Helias" ("Lest the Antichrist come suddenly and without warning and deceive and destroy the whole human race by his error, before his arrival the two great prophets Enoch and Elijah will be sent into the world").[46] The place of the prophet and patriarch, in this scheme, is necessary for the chronology of events leading up to the defeat of Antichrist and the Last Judgment. Still later, Adso writes, "Postquam Heliam et Enoch interfecerit et ceteros in fide permanents martyrio coronauerit, ad ultimum ueniet iudicium Dei super eum" ("After he has killed Elijah and Enoch and crowned with martyrdom the others who persevere in the faith, at last God's judgment will come upon him [Antichrist]").[47]

In relation to Wulfstan's eschatology in his sermon on Peter and Paul (based on the *Martyrdom of Peter and Paul*), Joyce Tally Lionarons has observed "two sets of holy men as examples of steadfastness in Christian

---

46 Verhelst, ed., *Adso Dervensis*, 27–8, lines 151–4; McGinn, trans., *Apocalyptic Spirituality*, 94.

47 Verhelst, ed., *Adso Dervensis*, 28, lines 176–9; McGinn, trans., *Apocalyptic Spirituality*, 96.

faith and opposition to the enemy, Peter and Paul against Simon Magus, and Enoch and Elias against Antichrist."[48] This same evocation is established in the intertextual relationships between the Latin *Sermo xxix* and the composite Wulfstanian sermon, linked by the common subjects of Antichrist and martyrdom. Furthermore, the parallel of the Old English phrase "mid sawla ꝛ lichoman" with Latin "cum corpore et anima" also emphasizes a resonance across the texts. These two details – referring to martyrdom ("imartyrode wurðaþ") and the soul and body ("sawla ꝛ lichoman") – are not, in fact, explicitly mentioned in the Latin text, but are part of Wulfstan's adaptations of his source, which were subsequently retained by the author of the composite sermon.

The figure of Antichrist also makes an appearance in Bodley 343 in the Lenten sermon Irvine 6 (item 85), containing part of an exposition about the Last Judgment.[49] In this amalgamation of descriptions from Bede, biblical sources, and other motifs from a variety of sources in the Christian tradition, the sermon turns to an allegorical explanation of the significance of Moses and Elijah (lines 141–70). About Elijah, the author relates:

Eliæs næfre gyt deaþ ne þolode, ac he is gyt on lichame libbende on þam stowe þe God him hæfð isæt; and he sceal þær abidæn sundfullice his martyrdoms oððet Drihten asende hine æft hider on middænearde ær worldes ende, þæt he sceal þenne secgæn and cuþæn moncynne Godes lare, and his martyrdom for Cristes lufæ þrowæn on Antecristes dagum.

(159–64: Elijah still never suffered death, but he is still living in body in the place where God has set him; and there he shall safely await his martyrdom until the Lord sends him back to middle-earth before the end of the world, so that he shall then tell and teach God's lore to humankind, and suffer his martyrdom for the love of Christ in the days of Antichrist.)

Again, the echo of Adso is apparent, as Elijah is presented as living with God before his future opposition to Antichrist during the final countdown to the Last Judgment. While it is difficult to establish a direct reliance on Adso's treatise in this passage (since this tradition about Elijah

---

48 Lionarons, *The Homiletic Writings of Archbishop Wulfstan*, 67.
49 References by line numbers for Irvine texts are to Irvine, ed., *Old English Homilies from MS Bodley 343*, 146–78.

was so widespread), there is nonetheless a close connection between these texts in their common formulations about Doomsday.

While Irvine 6 contains only a brief reference to Antichrist, the Doomsday exposition multiplies associations that range across the preaching media of Bodley 343. Most immediately, it is linked to the sermons directly preceding and following it, Irvine 5 and 7 (items 85 and 87). As these three items are collected together in Bodley 343 as a sequence for Lent and Rogationtide,[50] there is a logical thematic progression between them – particularly since Irvine 6 ends with a Judgment Day exposition and Irvine 7 is almost wholly concerned with this subject. In this sequence, Antichrist and Judgment Day are embedded in preaching traditions as subjects of Christian history, leading from the gospels (Irvine 5) to contemporary applications for Christian living and an eschatological outlook (Irvine 6 and 7). Similarly, the Judgment Day exposition in Irvine 6 evokes similar imagery to a Doomsday sermon titled *Larspell* (item 71), which includes translations of parts of the *Apocalypse of Paul* and the *Three Utterances*.[51] Considering media networks and the evidence of these associations, the degrees of separation between biblical narratives, apostles, Antichrist, and apocrypha are practically negligible; they are ineluctably connected.

While following the trail of Antichrist through Bodley 343 has seemingly led away from a focus on the *Martyrdom of Peter and Paul*, intertextual parallels continue to proliferate, demonstrating the ways in which the texts are connected through a network of associations. Significantly, the central figure of Antichrist links the various narratives discussed so far through its thematic emphasis on martyrdom. In the Latin *Martyrdom*, the execution of the apostles is celebrated as a victory just as is the death of their opponent the sorcerer. In Adso's treatise, the Wulfstanian sermon based on it, and Irvine 6, the martyrdoms of Elijah and Enoch are celebrated for their perseverance and as portents of the soteriological victory in the Last Judgment. Their deaths must occur before Antichrist is defeated, just as all of these signs (and the many others leading up to this moment) must take place before Christ's final eschatological return. These suggestions are only possible while looking across the pages of this codex, not only reading each text in its own right but also considering the topical

---

50 Irvine, ed., *Old English Homilies from MS Bodley 343*, 179–204; on intended occasions, see xlix, 116, 146–9, and 181–2.
51 Napier, ed., *Wulfstan*, 232–42.

and thematic relationships that constitute the network of ideas between these sermons.

Jesus' Apostles, Brothers, and Mary

Sermons on Peter and Paul make up only a small portion of preaching texts based on apocryphal acts of apostles within the media network within Bodley 343. In fact, this codex includes five of Ælfric's *Catholic Homilies* based on various martyrdom accounts for apostles: *Passio Sancti Bartholomei Apostoli* (*CH* I.31, item 18) based on the *Martyrdom of Bartholomew*; *Natale Sancti Mathei Apostoli et Evangelistae* (*CH* II.32, item 20) based on the *Martyrdom of Matthew*; *Natale Sancti Andreae Apostoli* (*CH* I.38, item 33) based on the *Martyrdom of Andrew*; the previously addressed *Passio Apostolorum Petri et Pauli* (*CH* I.26, items 51–2) based on the *Martyrdom of Peter and Paul*; and *Natale Sancti Iacobi Apostoli* (*CH* II.27, item 66) based on the *Martyrdom of James the Great*. In this section, I discuss interconnections between Ælfric's *Catholic Homilies* on Bartholomew and James with other anonymous sermons in Bodley 343, as examples of the ways in which these all participate within the overall network of this codex. Common to all of these sermons are a few features that link them within the larger network under discussion. First, most obviously, all of these sermons concern apostles, composed for their specific feast days. In this sense, they are all linked via common intentions for veneration and commemoration, part of the larger, growing popularity of saints' cults in late Anglo-Saxon England. These cultural currents were clearly much more widespread than the confines of Bodley 343, but the *temporale* sermons for apostles present individual nodes that anchor the network of cultic interest in this specific codex.

Ælfric's *Passio Sancti Bartholomei Apostoli* (*CH* I.31) presents one node with subtle associations in anonymous sermons that previously have been noticed only in passing, but significant implications for the notion of selection and the network of media in Bodley 343. As discussed in chapter 3, in this sermon Ælfric relates the narrative about Bartholomew before moving on to exempla and exhortations equating physical and spiritual health, emphasizing the role of God as the "true doctor" ("soða læce"). Ælfric is able, within this framework, to relate the *Martyrdom of Bartholomew* to physical and spiritual health, folk superstition about cures, biblical and apostolic examples for the true faith, and the nature of sin and suffering through a discussion of theodicy. As a text for Bartholomew's feast day, this particular sermon is a sophisticated piece that moves beyond the apocryphal narrative to address issues of doctrine and belief. It is this wide-ranging nature of Ælfric's sermon, in fact, that allows for finding associations with other preaching media in Bodley 343.

Among the various examples that Ælfric uses in his sermon on Bartholomew, as Susan Irvine notes, "he offers a catalogue of the reasons for which men are afflicted by God," summarizing the episode of Jesus healing a blind man in John 9.[52] As he says there, "Sume men beoð geuntrumode for Gode's tacnum, swa swa Crist cwæð be sumum blindan men" (288: "Some men are afflicted for God's miracles, just as Christ said about certain blind men"), signalling that theodicy must take account of God allowing suffering for miracles. This same episode is the focus of Ælfric's exposition of the gospel account in Irvine 3 (item 61), for Wednesday in the fourth week of Lent.[53] Although this sermon was not formally included in any of his preaching collections, it has been recognized as part of Ælfric's general project while composing the *Catholic Homilies*, and belongs to a cycle of texts for the Proper of the Season (*temporale*) often referred to as the Temporale Homilies.[54] In her edition of Old English sermons in Bodley 343, Irvine mentions the connection between Ælfric's sermon on Bartholomew and an anonymous sermon on Matthew 18:23–35 (Irvine 2, item 13), concerning Jesus' parable about the kingdom of heaven and a servant's failure to forgive.[55] As Irvine notes, both Ælfric and the anonymous author make a "comparison of the relationship between one who must chastise and a wrongdoer and that of doctor to his patient" – a trope that ultimately "derives from Augustine."[56]

The common thread between these connected sermons is a concern for physical and spiritual health related to theodicy. Ælfric's explanation in the sermon on Bartholomew sidesteps a clear answer to the problem of suffering: while afflictions are allowed for the sake of miracles, he leaves the issue open about whether these afflictions come from God, the devil, sin, or natural causes. Relying on common tropes about God as physician and links between physical and spiritual health or illness, Ælfric and the anonymous

---

52 Irvine, ed., *Old English Homilies from MS Bodley 343*, 49.
53 Ibid., 48–76.
54 See ibid., xv–lxxviii, esp. xviii–xxii.
55 Ibid., 29–47.
56 Ibid., 34.

author of Irvine 2 are able to exhort audiences about contemporary concerns, updating Augustine's theology for situational preaching to Anglo-Saxon audiences. While the apostles may be presented as models, they may also be perceived as difficult models for the laity to follow. After all, how can common Anglo-Saxons be expected to live up to the standards of Jesus' first disciples? Rather than posing Bartholomew as vague exemplum, however, Ælfric uses the apocryphal narrative of his missionary work to address questions about physical suffering and pain. Indeed, as this common thread throughout the related Ælfrician and anonymous sermons demonstrates, questions about physical health and spiritual well-being were more than just passing concerns; they were teaching moments embedded in a long history of Christian doctrine, encompassing biblical, apocryphal, and patristic sources. Within the pages of Bodley 343, these three sermons and their teachings on health form a significant matrix of associations for emphasizing the doctrine of theodicy throughout the liturgical year. They fit together nicely within the collection, particularly because of the diversity of their sources and means of approaching these theological themes.

Ælfric's sermon on James the Great (*CH* II.27) highlights the relevance of further considering notions of selection that I have invoked in this chapter. As I discussed in chapter 3, Ælfric is clearly judicious when considering his sources, avoiding certain apocrypha, embracing others, and combining some with known authorities for further weight to his exhortations. This is the case with his sermon on James. While he relies on the *Martyrdom of James the Great*, he also characteristically adds his own introduction:

> On þisum dæge we wurðiað on urum lofsangum and on freolse ðone mæran apostol Iacobum. Iohannes broðor þæs godspelleres; Hi begen sind cristes moddrian suna. þas he genam oftost. and petrum to his sunderspræce. swa swa we on cristesbec gehwær rædað

> (1–5: On this day we honour in our hymns and in festival the great apostle James, the brother of John the Evangelist. They both are sons of Christ's maternal aunt. These he took most often, and Peter, to his private speech, just as we read everywhere in the book of Christ.)

In the details about James and John the Evangelist, Ælfric draws on traditions seeking to reconcile the virginity of Mary with the fact that the canonical gospels refer to Jesus' siblings.

The issue with James the Great is twofold. First, in Galatians 1:19 appears a statement that he was "the brother of the Lord" ("Iacobum fratrem Domini"), which raises the question of their relationship. Yet this issue is complicated by many references throughout the gospels and Acts to multiple men named James and a mother named Mary.[57] Second, besides the name James, cryptic references to Jesus' "brothers" ("fratres") appear in Matthew 12:46–7, Acts 1:14, and 1 Corinthians 9:4–5. In addressing these issues (however briefly), Ælfric deals with the problem that the gospels often omit biographical information about the apostles and with the subsequent traditions that emerged to fill these gaps in early Christian literature. The results present an instance in the transmission of apocryphal details as they circulated in narratives about the apostle James, even in authoritative writings, that Ælfric faces head-on in this sermon.

The sources to which Ælfric could have turned for explanations about the relationship between James, John, and Jesus would have been many and complicated. While the gospels are ambiguous, the P-recension of the *Gospel of Pseudo-Matthew* includes a prologue attributing the apocryphon to "Iacobus filius Ioseph" ("James, the son of Joseph the carpenter"), which is a holdover from the epilogue of the Greek *Protevangelium of James*.[58] In this tradition, James is Joseph's child from a previous marriage, before Mary. John C. Pope lays out several possibilities available to Ælfric, including texts by Augustine, Jerome, Gregory, and Bede, who all participated in attempts to understand the relationship between James and Jesus, and none of whom Ælfric followed.[59] The predominant view in the medieval period was Jerome's, that James the Less and Joseph were Jesus' cousins by the sister of the Virgin Mary, also named Mary (Cleophas), and her husband Alphaeus, while James the Great was the son of Zebedee – though he does not address this James's mother, nor his brother.[60]

In the ninth century, Jerome's ideas were expanded in an anonymous sermon that circulated in the Homiliary of Haymo of Auxerre (d. c. 878) – which Ælfric certainly knew and used – as well as in Haymo's own synthesis

---

57   Matthew 4:21, 10:3, 13:55, 17:1, and 27:56; Mark 1:19, 3:17–18, 5:37, 6:3, 9:1, 10:35, 10:41, 13:3, 14:33, 15:40, and 16:1; Luke 5:10, 6:14–16, 8:51, 9:28, 9:54, and 24:10; and Acts 1:13, 12:2, 12:17, 15:13, and 21:18.

58   Gijsel, ed., *Libri de nativitate Mariae*, 277.

59   Pope, *Homilies of Ælfric*, 1:217–20.

60   *Adversus Helvidium de Mariae virginitate perpetua* 11–14, in *PL* 23.194–216, at 205–8. See Hall, "The Earliest Anglo-Latin Text of the *Trinubium Annae* (*BHL* 505zl)."

of several separate traditions in his *Historiae sacrae epitome*. The passage from the *Epitome* began circulating individually by the end of the eleventh century, in a text now known as the *Trinubium Annae*.[61] Significant for English literary history, a vernacular rendering of the *Trinubium Annae* is appended to an Old English translation of a sermon on the Assumption of the Virgin Mary by Ralph d'Escures (1114–22) in London, British Library, Cotton Vespasian D.xiv (s. xii[med.]).[62] Thomas N. Hall has shown how such developments in late Anglo-Saxon England, and continuing into the Norman period, were closely linked with the rise in devotion to Mary and her mother Anna – indeed, related to the same currents explored in chapter 4.[63] Clearly the Anglo-Saxons turned to apocrypha to establish these traditions, since the Bible was largely silent about them.

In Ælfric's brief introduction to his sermon on James, it is clear that he invokes not only the *Martyrdom* but also the larger tradition of attempting to understand biblical knowledge about the apostle. The beginning of his source begins, "Apostolus domini nostri Iesu Christi Iacobus frater beati Iohannis apostoli et euangelistae omnem Iudaeam et Samariam uisitabat" ("The apostle of our Lord Jesus Christ, James, the brother of the blessed John the apostle and evangelist, visited all of Judea and Samaria").[64] From this, Ælfric could have gleaned the fraternal relationship between the two apostles, although this detail is present in the gospels. Yet even the *Martyrdom of James the Great* does not include in one single text all of the information I have laid out so far. What is important is the fact that only a few sources include both details about James and John as brothers and their mother as Jesus' maternal aunt. The first source to synthesize all of these details is Haymo's *Epitome*, followed by the independent text known as the *Trinubium Annae*. It is possible that Ælfric knew the general traditions and synthesized the beginning of the *Martyrdom* with his other knowledge about James, but it is also equally possible that he turned to Haymo's text or a version of the *Trinubium Annae*.

---

61 Hall prints the earliest identified version from the eleventh-century Cambridge, St John's College 35, in ibid., 115.

62 NRK, 209. See Warner, ed., *Early English Homilies from the Twelfth Century MS. Vesp. D. xiv*, 134–9. See also Hall, "The Earliest Anglo-Latin Text of the *Trinubium Annae* (*BHL* 505zl)," 133.

63 Ibid.

64 Mombritius, *Sanctuarium seu Vitae Sanctorum*, 2:37, lines 18–19. See Godden, *CH Introduction*, 577–8.

Ælfric's *Natale Sancti Iacobi Apostoli* is not his only work in which apocryphal Marian traditions feature, although it is the only one in Bodley 343. Frederick M. Biggs has demonstrated the variety of ways in which Ælfric might have encountered information about the Virgin Mary's parents and family – namely their names and details about them living according to the Mosaic law – including apocrypha (like *Pseudo-Matthew*, discussed in chapter 4), martyrologies (like the *Old English Martyrology*), sermons (like those in the Pembroke Homiliary, discussed in chapter 1), liturgy (like texts for the Nativity or Assumption of Mary), and the same sources used in Haymo's *Epitome* and the *Trinubium Annae*.[65] Even more curiously, as Pope notes, the details surrounding Anna and Joachim, the various Marys, the apostles, and their relations form "a notion that recurs several times in Ælfric's writings, always, so far as I have observed, without warrant from whatever Latin author Ælfric is following for the surrounding details."[66] When taken together, the evidence of the Jamesian material and Ælfric's whole preaching corpus points to the fact that he made recourse to apocryphal Marian traditions on several occasions. Furthermore, as Pope's claim indicates, he did so intentionally, beyond the scope of his immediate sources, in order to supplement his sermons with details about biblical subjects from well beyond the canonical Vulgate.

Looking outward at the contents of Bodley 343 from the starting point of Ælfric's sermon on James, a number of associations may be traced to other related texts. Most directly related is a unique Latin genealogy of James in the Homiliary of Angers (folios xix[v]–xx[r]).[67] This short genealogical text (not included in other identified versions of the homiliary) relates that "Iste Iacobus filius Alphei fuit quia et frater Domini nominator, Tres enim sorores fuerunt, Maria mater Domini et Maria Iacobi et Ioseph mater, et Maria mater filiorum Zebedei" ("This James was the son of Alpheus and is therefore called brother of the Lord. For there were three sisters, Mary the mother of the Lord, and Mary the mother of James and Joseph, and Mary the mother of the sons of Zebedee"). As Conti shows, this passage draws on the same tradition of texts already described, derived in this instance from the *Historiae sacrae epitome* by Haymo of Auxerre.[68] By the time Bodley 343 was compiled, the *Trinubium Annae* was in heavy circulation both in England and on the Continent, so there is no way ultimately

---

65 Biggs, "'Righteous People According to the Old Law.'"
66 Pope, *Homilies of Ælfric*, 217.
67 See Conti, "The Circulation of the Old English Homily in the Twelfth Century," 392–4.
68 Ibid.

to know the direct source on which the anonymous author of this Jamesian genealogy relied. What is clear is that this Latin author turned to the same types of materials as Ælfric, and that later scribes included these types of texts in their collections regardless of having an authorial name attached to them.

In addition to texts about the apostle James, the Marian traditions discussed so far have clear associations with an Old English sermon rubricated as "Natiuitas sancte Marie" (fols. 30r–33v).[69] This anonymous sermon comprises a translation of chapters 1–12:5 of the *Gospel of Pseudo-Matthew* – about Mary's parents, childhood, marriage to Joseph, and early pregnancy with Jesus – with a homiletic beginning and exhortation at the end, presumably (as Mary Clayton suggests) "to make it suitable reading for the feast of the nativity of Mary on 8 September."[70] Besides genealogy, this sermon is concerned with Mary's biography writ large. This larger point is related in the very first lines of the sermon: "Men ða leofestan, weorþian we nu on andweardnysse þa gebyrdtide þære eadigan fæmnan Sancta Marian, seo wæs cennystre ures Drihtnes Hælendes Cristes" ("Most beloved people, now at the present time let us honour the birth of the blessed virgin Saint Mary, who was the mother of our Lord the Saviour Christ").[71] The sermon, then, is meant as a feast-day celebration of Mary, not only as the mother of Christ but also as a holy virgin saint in her own right.

The sermon "Natiuitas sancte Marie" continues with extra-biblical exegesis on Mary's name, further establishing her sanctity and the reason for the celebration. The etymology is given as follows:

Nu is hyre nama gereht hlæfdige oððe cwen oððe sæsteorra. Heo is hlæfdige gecweden forðan þe heo cende þone hlaford heofonas and eorðan. And heo is cwen gecweden forðan þe heo com of ðam æðelan cynne and of ðam cynelican sæde Dauides cynnes. Sæsteorra heo is gecweden forðan þe se sæsteorra on niht gecyþeð scypliðendum mannum hwyder bið east and west, hwyder suð and norð. Swa þonne wearð þurh ða halgan fæmnan Sancta Marian gecyþed se rihte siðfæt to ðam ecan life þam ðe lange ær sæton on þeostrum and on deaþes scuan and on þam unstillum yðum þære sæ þises middaneardes …

---

69 Edited (collated with two other witnesses) in Clayton, *The Apocryphal Gospels of Mary in Anglo-Saxon England*, 153–91, with commentary at 196–209.

70 Ibid., 196.

71 Ibid., 164.

(Now her name is explained as "lady" or "queen" or "sea-star." She is called "lady" because she birthed the Lord of heaven and earth. And she is called "queen" because she came from the noble kin and from the royal family of the people of David. She is called "sea-star" because at night the sea-star shows to seafaring people where east and west, and where south and north are. So also through the holy virgin Saint Mary is shown the right path to eternal life to those who for a long time sat in darkness and in the shadow of death and in the restless waves of the sea of this middle-earth ...)[72]

Ideas in this introduction ultimately derive from Isidore of Seville, who gives the supposed etymologies of Mary's name and her titles in his *Etymologiae* VII.x, a section titled "De reliquis in Evangelio nominibus" ("Other names in the Gospel"). "Maria," he says at the start of this section, "inluminatrix, sive stella maris. Genuit enim lumen mundi. Sermone autem Syro Maria domina nuncupatur; et pulchre; quia Dominum genuit" ("Mary, 'she who illuminates,' or 'star of the sea.' She gave birth to the light of the world. Further, in Syrian speech, 'Mary' means 'mistress'; and 'beautiful'; for she gave birth to the Lord").[73] The etymological notes at the start of the sermon therefore derive from biblical and patristic learning, transmitted into the Middle Ages even as they accumulated meaning with the development of the cult of Mary from the ninth century onward. When considering how to introduce a sermon derived from *Pseudo-Matthew*, the author of "Natiuitas sancte Marie" found an appropriate beginning by turning to this biblical lore.

This explanation of Mary's name certainly addresses her familial relationships, but in a much more general, typological connection with the line of David. Genealogy is quickly brought to bear again, once the sermon author moves to a translation of the *Pseudo-Matthew* in the very next section: "We habbað geræd on bocum þæt wære sum swiðe æþele wer on Israheliscum folce, þæs nama wæs Ioachim, of Iudan cynne" ("We have read in books that there was a certain very noble man among the people of Israel, whose name was Joachim, from the people of Judah").[74] Only several lines later, we are also told about a woman "gehaten Anna ... of ðam æþelan cynne Dauides þæs cynincges" ("named Anna ... from the noble people of

---

72 Ibid., 164.

73 Lindsay, ed., *Isidori Hispalensis Episcopi Etymologiarum sive Originum Libri XX*, n.p.; translation adapted from Barney, Lewis, Beach, and Berghof, trans., *The Etymologies of Isidore of Seville*, 170.

74 Clayton, *The Apocryphal Gospels of Mary in Anglo-Saxon England*, 166.

David the King").[75] In this text, genealogical concerns move outward from immediate family to the long line of Israelite family, stretching back to the nobility of the Old Testament. In the earliest Christian writings, of course, this appeal to Israelite heritage is part of the authority that the authors of the gospels give to Jesus and his family. In *Pseudo-Matthew*, and adopted into this sermon on "Natiuitas sancte Marie," the same may be said, as the genealogical connections establish a typological thread running through the canonical Bible. Thus, this is a double gesture towards authority: the apocryphal sermon aligns with the authority of Jesus' heritage just as it seeks to align its own textual heritage with the canonical gospels.

Again, the issue of selection in the contents of Bodley 343 is significant with the sermon on the "Natiuitas sancte Marie." Especially curious is the fact that this sermon is included in a series of selections from Ælfric's *Catholic Homilies* for other saints' days. Directly preceding the sermon for the Nativity of Mary are sermons for the feast days of Laurence (*CH* I.29, item 17) and Bartholomew (*CH* I.31, item 18), and directly following is the sermon for Matthew (*CH* II.32, item 20). As Irvine writes about the sermon for the Nativity of Mary, "This is not, as one might have expected, Ælfric's First Series homily for the occasion, but rather a post-Ælfrician piece," possibly because of the choices of the compiler of the source exemplar for this section of Bodley 343; given what can be known about the First Series source for the Ælfrician texts in this section of the manuscript, she notes that "it is particularly strange that the anonymous homily drawing on the apocryphal gospel appears in preference to it."[76] In many ways, this selection is parallel to the choice to include the *History of the Holy Rood Tree* for the feast of the Exaltation of the Cross instead of Ælfric's sermon for the occasion (discussed in chapter 3). Irvine also suggests that this sermon appealed to the compiler of the source collection "because it was pure narrative not exegesis."[77] Nonetheless, we cannot be sure exactly what the Bodley 343 compilers' source manuscripts contained in them, nor whether the choice to include the sermon on the Nativity of Mary was one of preference or of materials at hand. Still, the selection to include it at all speaks to the importance accorded to the text, as do the immediate contexts among other saints' lives as models for the Christian faith.

---

75 Ibid.
76 Irvine, ed., *Old English Homilies from MS Bodley 343*, xxiv.
77 Ibid., xxxv.

Finally, tracing connections through the genealogy of Mary and Jesus' extended family in Bodley 343 leads to a note on folio 154v, in a space originally left blank. After the compilation of the main contents, a scribe from around the turn of the thirteenth century added a note about the ages of the Virgin Mary at different points in her and Jesus' lives. The brief addition relates, "Sancta Maria wes ðreo & sixti winter ða heo of middenærde ferde. And heo wes fiftene æld ða heo crist acende. And heo wes mid him ðreo & ðritti winter on middenærde. And heo wes efter him sixtene gær on ðissere worlde" ("Saint Mary was sixty-three winters old when she went from the earth. And she was fifteen years old when she gave birth to Christ. And she was with him thirty-three winters on the earth. And after him she was in this world for sixteen years").[78] While the details of these claims are gleaned from apocrypha like the *Gospel of Pseudo-Matthew* or Pseudo-Melito *Transitus Mariae*, the note in Bodley 343 is not unique within the Anglo-Saxon corpus, as Heide Estes has shown that it survives in several manuscripts ranging from the eleventh through twelfth centuries, and is also part of the lore included in the prose *Solomon and Saturn* dialogue.[79] It seems that this note is part of the circulation of commonplace knowledge about biblical figures discussed in chapter 1 (particularly notes copied into Tiberius A.iii). As seen in the manuscripts examined at the start of this study, this addition of a note about Mary and Jesus is neither uncommon nor inappropriate in a collection of preaching texts combining biblical, apocryphal, patristic, and early medieval teaching about Christian subjects. Furthermore, it is not all that different from the beginning of the sermon "Natiuitas sancte Marie," since it is compiled from the same types of sources and forges similar connections between canonical and apocryphal knowledge about a central biblical figure.

Apocrypha and Beyond

In addition to the associations already examined, tracing the network in Bodley 343 demonstrates how the circulation and use of apocrypha in Anglo-Saxon England is fundamentally intermedial in relation to other traditional media like the Bible. The texts included in this collection indicate the necessary interconnections between canonical and extra-biblical

---

78 Printed in Estes, "Anglo-Saxon Biblical Lore," 646 n. 105.

79 On other versions of this note, see Cross and Hill, *The Prose Solomon and Saturn and Adrian and Ritheus*, 80–1; Hall, "The Ages of Christ and Mary in the Hyde Register and in Old English Literature"; and Estes, "Anglo-Saxon Biblical Lore," passim.

materials. Of course, this should already be apparent in the preceding examinations, considering how closely entwined the biblical gospels are with apocryphal stories of Jesus, his disciples, and Mary. In many of these cases, it is apparent that the apocryphal materials emerged or were viewed by medieval authors as supplementing sparse or ambiguous information in the Bible. This is the case especially with stories of the apostles' missions and passions, and eschatological conceptions about Antichrist and the Last Judgment, as well as lore about Mary and genealogies of Jesus' family. As W.J.T. Mitchell and Mark B.N. Hansen write, media "do not remain static, but constitute a dynamic, historically evolving environment or ecosystem" – that is, media and their uses morph along with culture.[80] As knowledge about the Bible developed, so too did related apocrypha, as well as the complex relationships between these media in the growing apparatus of Christian tradition inherited by Anglo-Saxons.

In terms of network theory, one of the characteristic features is the notion of "six degrees of separation" between distinct elements, or that every network constitutes within itself a "small world" of interconnectivity.[81] To return to the notion of sermons for saints' feast days as nodes connected by the conceptual network running through the liturgical year, we see this small world at work. Viewing the network of Bodley 343 with this line of thinking in mind exemplifies the types of close connections that theorists have found in all networks through the "six degrees" or "small world" concept. Following this line of thinking also allows us to see how the network encompasses not only apocrypha but the whole apparatus of Christian tradition built into the manuscript. As indicated throughout this study, biblical and apocryphal media are intimately linked, inseparable from each other, and the network of texts in Bodley 343 typifies this point.

Interconnectivity is apparent even in the gospel readings that serve as pericopes for certain sermons in Bodley 343. By way of common pericopes, seventeen links are shared between the Latin sermons in the version of the Homiliary of Angers and Ælfric's *Catholic Homilies* included in the manuscript (see appendix 4). The most striking of these, regarding apocrypha, is the common reading for the feast of Peter and Paul (29 June) and Matthew 16:13–19, used for both *Sermo xxix* and Ælfric's *Passio Apostolorum Petri et Pauli* (*CH* I.26). Since these texts have featured largely already in this study, little more needs to be said, but the intersection

---

80 Mitchell and Hansen, "Introduction," xiv.
81 See Watts, *Six Degrees*, 38–43; and Barabási, *Linked*, 25–40.

of apocryphal and biblical common sources in both of these sermons is a notable case to highlight to demonstrate my point. For both the anonymous author of the Latin sermon and Ælfric, the connection was logical, since the gospel reading was a customary passage for the feast day, and the apocryphal narrative was a fitting story for exhortation. Likewise, the integration of these sermons into Bodley 343 was also logical, since both represent the need for various types of preaching media related to liturgical feasts in late Anglo-Saxon England.

The links do not stop with apocryphal sermons, however. Biblical sources and exegesis sit comfortably beside the apocrypha discussed throughout this chapter. Since both the Homiliary of Angers and Ælfric's *Catholic Homilies* are designed to cover the liturgical year, there is a significant amount of overlap in the customary gospel readings covered in both. These associations present a small world indeed. Thus, the sermons cover common ground including Easter Sunday, Rogationtide, feast days for Peter and Paul and the Common of a Confessor, Circumcision, Septuagesima, and Sexagesima. By far the most commonality between the cycles is in sermons for Ordinary Time: eight for various Sundays after Pentecost and one for the third Sunday after Epiphany.

Each sermon for each occasion, then, is a connected node within the larger liturgical cycle that covers the church year, as each contributes to the overall network of preaching across time, and all are connected through mutual associations. These common threads also cross the boundaries of the specific cycle (in this case, the Homiliary of Angers or the two series of *Catholic Homilies*) to create links with other related texts. These notions about sermons for specific liturgical occasions as nodes within cycles of preaching also emphasize the ways in which media and networks can encompass smaller forms within themselves. We might thus consider the version of the Homiliary of Angers in Bodley 343 as one coherent, self-contained network, and the *Catholic Homilies* that are included as another, both contributing to the larger, more comprehensive network comprising all of the texts in this collection. Even as it contains these smaller networks, Bodley 343 remediates them, posing them with fresh representations of the contents, and with subsequently fresh associations in a new, integrated network.

Conclusions

With the accumulation of these examples, Bodley 343 may be seen as a collective network within a single codex. Moreover, the examples discussed here are only representative, not comprehensive; no doubt further associations between the texts of this codex could be enumerated – and, indeed, the idea of the small world of network interconnectivity seems to encourage such associative proliferations. Tracing this network, in fact, follows only one set of associations that holds these various texts together; other associations could also be traced to find other ways of connecting the contents of Bodley 343 as a coherent network. More generally, associative connections are also accumulative, not only linking together the contents within this collection but also creating threads that might be traced to further connections, to other cultural artefacts beyond this single bound book. Some of the discussions in this chapter indicate such prospects, since it is impossible to discuss many of the texts in Bodley 343 without gesturing to other social contexts.

As more nodes of the network are added – in this case, texts – more edges may be adduced, stretching further outward from the focal point of this examination. As Michel Foucault observes: "The frontiers of a book are never clear-cut: beyond the title, the first lines, and the last full stop, beyond its internal configuration and autonomous form, it is caught up in a system of references to other books, other texts, other sentences: it is a node within a network."[82] Keeping in mind the broad-ranging issue of how networks grow with ever-expanding associative accretions, we might return to the materials discussed in chapter 1, to trace links with other preaching collections. From a different perspective, following some of the gestures I have made throughout this book, we might look beyond preaching to consider how apocryphal sources in sermons intersect with Old English literature more generally, such as in the corpus of Old English poetry.

To present one instance, the Old English poem *The Grave* added to folio 170r of Bodley 343 poses further possible links, such as the *ubi sunt* motif of the address of the soul to the body.[83] This topos is found most prominently in the vernacular poems *Soul and Body I* in the Vercelli Book and *Soul and Body II* in the Exeter Book, but also a number of Old English sermons.[84] All of these texts have thematic relationships with the

---

82 Foucault, *The Archaeology of Knowledge and the Discourse on Language*, 23.

83 Buchholz, ed., *Die Fragmente der Reden der Seele an den Leichnam in zwei Handschriften zu Worcester und Oxford*, 18–19.

84 The sermons are Vercelli 4; item 2 in Cambridge, Corpus Christi College 201 (s. xi³/⁴, Exeter), pp. 222–30 (NRK, 50; and *ASM*, 66); Assmann 14 in Cambridge, Corpus Christi College 302 (s. xi/xii, SE England?), pp. 73–8 (NRK, 56; and *ASM*, 86) and

Apocalypse of Paul,[85] and following up on each one multiplies associations with sources, parallels, and other intermedial relationships that expand the network radically.[86] *The Grave* also shares the image of a burial site as a house with a roof lying on the dead's chest with the eschatological sermon Vercelli 9.[87] These are only a few of the possibilities available when we consider apocryphal sermons as part of a larger media ecology. This study generally, and Bodley 343 in particular, pose only starting points.

Texts collected in Bodley 343 are most explicitly associated with each other because they are useful for preaching, but exploring connections via sources, themes, and verbal elements reveals other associations in a network of intertextuality. Parallels between such diverse texts do not diminish the significance of networks in Bodley 343 or more generally, but emphasize all the more the fundamental interrelatedness of Anglo-Saxon preaching. Such associations span across anonymous, Ælfrician, and Wulfstanian preaching, forging connections between a vast array of texts and revealing more similarities in concerns than differences sometimes highlighted in modern scholarship. In this way, the apparatus of Christian tradition used for preaching – including biblical, apocryphal, patristic, and early medieval sources – reveals that scholars can only benefit from examining both the differences and similarities, and how the transmission of these texts together contributes to a nuanced picture of the wide world of preaching in Anglo-Saxon England.

London, British Library, Cotton Faustina A.ix (s. xii[1]), fols. 23v–27v (NRK, 153); and Fadda 7 in Cambridge, University Library, Ii.1.33 (s. xii[2]), fols. 207r–211r (NRK, 18). See Di Sciacca, "The *Ubi Sunt* Motif and the Soul-and-Body Legend in Old English Homilies," 365–87, and *Finding the Right Words*, 105–48.

85 See Healey, "Apocalypse of Paul," *SASLC Apocrypha*, 67–70.

86 Di Sciacca traces many of these associations, assessing the complex *ubi sunt* tradition, in "The *Ubi Sunt* Motif and the Soul-and-Body Legend in Old English Homilies" and *Finding the Right Words*, 105–48.

87 See Wright, *The Irish Tradition in Old English Literature*, 99.

Mediating Tradition

One of my goals in *Preaching Apocrypha in Anglo-Saxon England* has been to show how extra-biblical narratives saturated Anglo-Saxon Christianity in a variety of media related to sermons. The title of the book is meant to evoke a twofold meaning: as a verb phrase signalling how Anglo-Saxons broadcast apocrypha in their sermons, and as a noun phrase signalling how apocrypha were part of the tools for teaching in a variety of media. In other words, I have sought to show that the influences of Christian apocrypha permeated Anglo-Saxon culture. These claims confront a number of modern assumptions about categories that have previously hindered the study of medieval apocrypha and preaching texts. In the modern world, we have a propensity to categorize, organize, and structure knowledge in ways that make it seemingly easier to understand and compartmentalize. Yet culture often resists categorization, blurs boundaries, disrupts organization and structure – particularly concerning media and their roles in our lives.

As I have highlighted throughout this book, one way to acknowledge and consider the significance of sermons is as media. Returning to Marshall McLuhan's magnum opus on the subject, a cogent expression is found in what he says about games as technological tools of human communication, which may also be said about preaching if we replace "sermons" for "games":

> That [sermons] are extensions, not of our private but of our social selves, and
> that they are media of communication, should now be plain. If, finally, we
> ask, "Are [sermons] mass media?" the answer has to be "Yes." [Sermons] are

situations contrived to permit simultaneous participation of many people in some significant pattern of their own corporate lives.[1]

For authors, preachers, scribes, monks, nobles, commoners, men, and women – anyone who might have read preaching texts directly from books, or heard them in the Office, masses, or other public addresses – sermons were tools of mass communication. While they survive only in written expression, sermons were prevalent media, and potent forces for the communication of cultural currents in medieval culture. About literature, McLuhan writes in the same chapter, "Any play or poem or novel is, also, rigged *to produce an effect*."[2] With this perspective, all texts are media, all pieces of literature cultural artefacts and communication technologies situated within wider social contexts. In this conclusion, then, I offer some reflections on what the preceding study has added to our understanding of sermons as media and their remediation of apocryphal narratives. I begin by considering the types of modern categories that apocryphal sermons challenge, before turning to the key intersections between definitions of media as such and the role of preaching in Anglo-Saxon culture.

On the one hand, there is a tendency in modern scholarship about the history of Christianity to view apocrypha as culturally marginal, attributed only to heretical voices, in opposition to orthodox teachings. The pervasiveness of apocrypha in Anglo-Saxon England, and the interweaving of various sources in similar ways throughout Old English sermons, disrupts binary notions of Bible/apocrypha or orthodox/heterodox. Here it is useful to invoke Marjorie Garber's notion of "category crisis" in culture, which she defines as "a failure of definitional distinction, a borderline that becomes permeable, that permits of border crossings from one (apparently distinct) category to another."[3] Garber claims that, by deconstructing definitions, the function of a category crisis is in "disrupting and calling attention to cultural, social, or aesthetic dissonances," and, furthermore, such disruption "is not the exception but rather the ground for culture itself."[4] This notion may also be conceived of through the imagery of

---

1 McLuhan, *Understanding Media*, 327. This passage could similarly be used in relation to a host of other media, as it encompasses many of McLuhan's arguments and subsequent theorizations in media studies; see references in my Introduction, nn. 68–71.
2 McLuhan, *Understanding Media*, 326.
3 Garber, *Vested Interests*, 16.
4 Ibid.

"moving boundaries," as we find and resituate transgressions of definitional borders based on new understandings of cultural contexts.

On the other hand, there is also a tendency in modern scholarship about the Middle Ages to separate "high culture" (the world of educated ecclesiasts) from "popular culture" (the world of illiterate commoners). Considering that so many sermons survive in the vernacular, and that various other media discussed could reach more than just highly literate audiences, the preaching apocrypha examined in this study cut across the grain of such constructed categories. So too do the associations of so many apocryphal artefacts with religious devotion by women, who are often relegated to a lower class of society. In addition to Garber's notion of "category crisis," it is useful to return to the formulation by Mikita Brottman mentioned in the introduction to this book: "popular and 'high' culture are virtually interchangeable – or at least, the distinction between them is blurred."[5] These domains are inseparable, as they inform each other and cohere. In the words of cultural critic Raymond Williams, "every available version of high culture is always … local and selective, and … in the process of being made available in a real society, it includes (whether these are noticed or not) elements of the popular culture, in the widest sense, of its own society."[6] The works of scholars like David L. d'Avray, Aaron Gurevich, Jacques Le Goff, and Siegfried Wenzel have exhibited the same back and forth between social strata in medieval literature, often regarding sermons as the bearers of interrelations.[7] In terms of media, "high" and "popular" culture are unrealistic categories, since the effects of media spiral outward to potentially affect the far reaches of society, even when the impact is not directly felt or even acknowledged explicitly. This is evident even in McLuhan's attention to language, electricity, roads, numbers, clothing, housing, money, clocks, comics, wheels, photographs, film, among many other media – all permeating diverse social strata.

All of this relates to how we view the relationships between apocrypha, sermons, and media explored throughout this book. Famously, McLuhan's goal (to paraphrase his now familiar dictum) was to emphasize the medium

---

5 Brottman, *High Theory/Low Culture*, xxvi.

6 Raymond Williams, "On High and Popular Culture."

7 See, for example, d'Avray, *Medieval Marriage Sermons* and *Medieval Marriage*; Gurevich, *Medieval Popular Culture*; Le Goff, *The Medieval Imagination*; Wenzel, *Preachers, Poets, and the Early English Lyric* and *Latin Sermon Collections from Later Medieval England*. On popular culture more generally, see Somerset and Watson, eds., *Truth and Tales*, esp. Somerset, "Introduction," with further references there.

as the message: effects, forms, and processes of technology, not just the content (the communication of information) that it carries. In the preceding chapters, I have navigated between these ideas, taking sermons as media containers for the apocryphal content I have analysed. At times, as in chapters 1 and 5, sermons themselves have come to the fore as media deserving of attention for the messages they send about the permeating role of apocrypha in culture. At other times, as in chapters 2 through 4, apocrypha have remained the focus, as the messages embedded in the sermons examined have informed how and why Anglo-Saxons turned to extra-biblical narratives for teaching. Along the way, other media and the messages of their forms have been important for contextualizing apocryphal sermons, as in taking account of manuscript codices as collections (chapters 1, 3, and 5), ecclesiastical and legal texts (chapter 2), visual arts (chapter 4), and vernacular poetry (throughout). After all, McLuhan suggests, "Since all media are extension of ourselves, or translations of some part of us into various materials, any study of one medium helps to understand all the others."[8]

But we might also use McLuhan's formulation about the medium as the message in another manner, to consider how apocrypha as content actually force us also to confront the role of Anglo-Saxon preaching as the basic message – the root of the ways in which apocrypha are transmitted. What, in other words, do apocrypha tell us about sermons? From this perspective, a sermon ("the medium") may transmit apocrypha, which can be regarded as the content, but that content turns us back to reflect upon the message of *preaching* worth remembering in the first place. The transmission of apocrypha in early England is technologically facilitated because the media of vernacular sermons and preaching collections became major developments within the English literary tradition. Preaching texts and collections comprise a large part of the literary output during the tenth, eleventh, and twelfth centuries, and as the surviving manuscripts attest (and as discussed in chapters 1, 3, and 5), they continued to be used, copied, and adapted well after the Norman Conquest, as part of the legacy of the English in the face of colonialism.[9] It is no accident that the majority of surviving apocrypha come down to us as translations in sermons, since preaching collections remain one of the most significant repositories for understanding Christianity in Anglo-Saxon literary culture. As recent

---

8 McLuhan, *Understanding Media*, 189.
9 See esp. Swan and Treharne, eds., *Rewriting Old English in the Twelfth Century*; Treharne, *Living through Conquest*; and Yeager, *From Lawmen to Plowmen*.

studies by Samantha Zacher, Joyce Tally Lionarons, Hiroshi Ogawa, Elaine Treharne, and Stephen Yeager argue, sermons deserve attention in their own right.[10]

Another key characteristic of media that brings us closer to Old English sermons and the transmission of apocrypha I have traced is that every new medium replaces some older technology, reforming the old and sending previous forms into obsolescence. Echoing McLuhan's many comments on this matter, W.J.T. Mitchell and Mark B.N. Hansen write, "media have always been entangled in cycles of innovation and obsolescence, innovation and renovation – from the invention of writing, printing, and artificial perspective to the invention of photography, television, and the Internet."[11] As a new medium in early England, what did vernacular preaching replace? In one sense, Old English sermons arose out of Latin sermons, making antecedents obsolete since they could reach a wider audience. This is not to say (as media theorists remind us) that obsolescence brought about the disappearance of previous forms. While vernacular sermon authors did not wholly exile Latin preaching, they did usher in a tradition of preaching in English, unbroken from at least the tenth century onward to the present day. In this, vernacular sermons became the perfect receptacles for the apocrypha already part of the Latin preaching tradition.

Conceptually, sermons mediate and remediate the apparatus of Christian tradition to fit present, local, ideological needs.[12] While medieval sermons always survive to us in the medium of text written on the page, they carry within them cultural mores beyond only this single form. They are hybrid media, bringing together oral performance (the original intent of preaching, despite later appropriations) and textual record (the survival in manuscripts) even as they mediate their content to various audiences medieval and modern. We must acknowledge that some sermons may have found life first as written texts, and perhaps some never had afterlives through the utterances of spoken voices; indeed, some sermons might be completely lost to us now because they had only oral lives and not textual afterlives in writing. Without contemporary records about oral performances, we

---

10 Zacher, *Preaching the Converted*; Lionarons, *The Homiletic Writings of Archbishop Wulfstan*; Ogawa, *Language and Style in Old English Composite Homilies*; Treharne, *Living through Conquest*; and Yeager, *From Lawmen to Plowmen*.
11 Mitchell and Hansen, "Introduction," xviii.
12 On mediation and remediation, see Bolter and Grusin, *Remediation*; and Grusin, "Radical Mediation."

will never know. But the basic purpose of sermons, from biblical times onward, is oral delivery in public address and, later, worship services. As McLuhan continually emphasizes, "characteristic of all media," and even more so for hybrid media, "the 'content' of any medium is always another medium"; for example, "The content of writing is speech, just as the written word is the content of print, and print is the content of the telegraph."[13] Media beget media, and they always coexist in proliferations of communication best suited to the needs at hand. For preaching texts, oral and textual forms meet, inextricably combined in their manifestations on manuscript pages.

Yet mediation and remediation constitute not only the transmission of information or media in distinct, tangible forms but also ideological manifestations through translation, in Richard Grusin's words, "generating, refashioning, and transforming *experiences* as well as connecting them."[14] Ideas travel across sermons, between oral and written expressions, as contents and media coincide. Sermons represent what matters to culture. Some examples related to Old English sermons may be gleaned from this study, as preaching media have been shown to remediate ecclesiastical concerns about Trinitatian theology during the tenth century (chapter 2); Ælfric's anxieties about correct doctrine in light of apostolic examples (chapter 3); and the rise of the Marian cult as well as concerns about Christ's actions (chapter 4).

Captured as they are in Old English sermons, these concerns of contemporary Anglo-Saxon culture show the power of preaching texts as hybridized media. Their authors take on content as they translate and adapt, turning antecedents into new means of communication for new audiences under new circumstances. In turn, later authors, scribes, and compilers continued to perceive the cultural potential of sermons, remediating them in their own ways as they reused them in new composite forms (as with adapted Ælfrician and Wulfstanian sermons discussed in chapters 3 and

---

13 McLuhan, *Understanding Media*, 20.

14 Grusin, "Radical Mediation," 147, emphasis added. Cf. McLuhan, *Understanding Media*, 85: "All media are active metaphors in their power to translate experience into new forms ... Words are a kind of information retrieval that can range over the total environment and experience at high speed. Words are complex systems of metaphors and symbols that translate experience into our uttered or outered senses. They are a technology of explicitness. By means of translation of immediate sense experience into vocal symbols the entire world can be evoked and retrieved in any instant"; and, more generally, ibid., 83–90.

5), or situating them within new contexts in preaching collections (as discussed in chapters 1, 3, and 5). In view of these processes, sermons act as exemplary media within "a densely resonating network of carefully differentiated media forms"[15] that "do[es] not remain static, but constitute[s] a dynamic, historically evolving environment or ecosystem."[16] Sermons are powerful media for understanding ideologies at the heart of mainstream Anglo-Saxon Christianity.

In preaching texts, narratives from the canonical Bible and non-canonical apocrypha, patristic and early medieval works, and the hermeneutics of exegesis are incontrovertibly related in a continual process of remediating the apparatus of Christian tradition inherited from the past through mass media. To borrow the words of Maximilian Diesenberger, "sermons and sermon collections were not accidental gatherings of unrelated material. They were designed and adapted to suit particular needs and circumstances."[17] For some Anglo-Saxon authors, their particular needs and circumstances led them to seek out gold in the mud of the sources at hand. What they found were apocryphal narratives just right for preaching to the people.

---

15 Foys, "Media," 136.
16 Mitchell and Hansen, "Introduction," xiv.
17 Diesenberger, "Introduction," 14.

Excursus on Terminology

Although not often acknowledged in scholarship on early medieval preaching, the terminology used to talk about surviving texts continues to pose significant questions. For all the distinctions that modern scholars may make in categorizing preaching texts (a phrase I use generally to refer to texts for or closely related to preaching), medieval witnesses present rather ambiguous cases.[1] This makes navigating between terminology difficult not only because certain choices lead to privileging some terms over others but also because using specific terms may seem like either casually accepting tradition or fully flying in the face of it. Some explanatory remarks for the terms I use in this book, therefore, are in order.

Two main terms dominate both medieval and modern classifications: homily (*omelia*), an extended exegesis on a single passage of scripture, often the gospel reading for the day; and sermon (*sermo*), a general address on a subject, such as a doctrinal theme, a moral exhortation, or a saint's life, often for a specific occasion like a feast day. It is significant, however, that distinctions between terms like "homily" and "sermon" are often blurry in medieval contexts.[2] J.E. Cross summarizes the issue: "Scholars in the past have had no difficulty distinguishing homilies from sermons, although

---

1 Generally, see Kienzle, ed., *The Sermon*; as well as studies by Muessig: "What Is Medieval Monastic Preaching?," "Preacher, Sermon and Audience in the Middle Ages," "Sermon, Preacher and Society in the Middle Ages," and "Medieval Preaching." Like many studies of medieval preaching, Muessig's discussions focus largely on late medieval examples.

2 Cf. discussion of distinctions between "biblical" and "apocryphal" materials imposed by modern categories in the Introduction.

they have used these terms interchangeably, as sometimes did mediaeval scribes."[3] In addition to the Latin terms, Anglo-Saxons also used the Old English terms *spel(l)*, *larspel(l)*, and *cwide/cwyde* (and variants of these terms), with meanings like story, narration, account, relation, discourse, saying, remark, statement, speech, and utterance.[4] A host of other terms also apply, such as *narratio* (narration), *tractatus* (treatise), and *sententia* (discourse) – each dependent on the idiosyncratic use of the particular author or scribe. In her "Introduction" to a volume on *The Sermon* as medieval genre, Beverly Mayne Kienzle, like Cross, highlights "the ambiguity and interchangeability of the terms" used for preaching texts by examining medieval terminology and definitions.[5]

Perhaps it is because of ambiguities that recent scholarship has largely side-stepped addressing the terminology of Anglo-Saxon preaching texts while mostly preferring use of the term *homily*. This is clear even from the titles of recent books on the subject.[6] To be sure, such use is in accordance with traditional title designations for major texts in editions, such as *The Vercelli Homilies*, *The Blickling Homilies*, *Ælfric's Catholic Homilies*, *The Homilies of Wulfstan*, and *Old English Homilies from MS Bodley 343*.[7] This term is also found in older printings of Old English preaching texts, such as Benjamin Thorpe's *The Sermones Catholici or Homilies of Ælfric* and Arthur Napier's massive collection titled *Wulfstan: Sammlung der ihm Zugeschriebenen Homilien nebst Untersuchungen über ihre Echtheit*;[8] farther back in time, these terms appear in early editions of Ælfric's works published in the sixteenth and seventeenth centuries.[9]

We find some specific examples of contemporary Anglo-Saxon terminology in titles from the main Old English preaching collections discussed in this book. In many cases, preaching texts with titles often indicate only

---

3 Cross, "Vernacular Sermons in Old English," 563.

4 Momma, ed., *Dictionary of Old English*, s.v. *cwide*; and Toller, ed., *An Anglo-Saxon Dictionary, Based on the Manuscript Collections of the Late Joseph Bosworth*, s.v. *spell*, *larspell*, and *cwide*.

5 Kienzle, "Introduction," 160–4.

6 See, for example, Kleist, ed., *The Old English Homily*; Zacher, *Preaching the Converted*; Lionarons, *The Homiletic Writings of Archbishop Wulfstan*; and Ogawa, *Language and Style in Old English Composite Homilies*.

7 *VH*; *BH*; *CH* I; *CH* II; Bethurum, ed., *The Homilies of Wulfstan*; and Irvine, ed., *Old English Homilies from MS Bodley 343*.

8 Thorpe, ed. and trans., *The Homilies of the Anglo-Saxon Church*; and Napier, ed., *Wulfstan*.

9 See Magennis, "Ælfric Scholarship"; and Brackmann, *The Elizabethan Invention of Anglo-Saxon England*.

the occasion or subject matter, not a specific heading for the piece. In the Vercelli Book, ten of the sermons have proper titles, and only six of these indicate some sort of genre: Vercelli 6, 7, and 8 are all titled *spel*, Vercelli 14 is titled *larspel*, while Vercelli 15 and 16 are both titled *omelia* – even though only the latter offers a formal exegetical exposition.[10] In the Blickling Book, eleven of the sermons have titles, and only Blickling 15 includes a genre label, *spel*.[11] Similarly, in his *Catholic Homilies* Ælfric often supplies a title indicating the occasion or subject matter without generic terms, with a few exceptions, in which he uses *sermo*: I.1, II.1, II.2, II.15, and II.16.[12] In the Latin Preface to his First Series of the *Catholic Homilies*, he uses *sententiae* to describe preaching texts in the collection;[13] while in the Second Series Latin Preface he uses *sermones*, which he renders as *cwyda* in the Old English Preface.[14] The titles of Wulfstan's preaching texts are also instructive, as he prefers the term *sermo* for six of his preaching texts.[15] The most famous of these is titled *Sermo Lupi ad Anglos*, although two manuscripts containing a variant version give the title as *Larspell*.[16]

More generally, searching the surviving corpus of Old English literature yields some statistical data.[17] The term *omelia* appears only eight times, of which five are in glossaries accompanied by the glosses *folclic lar*, *locutiones*, *spræce* (twice), and *uerba folclare*. The term *sermo(nes/num/nibus)* appears 463 times, of which many instances appear to be in the general sense of speech or discourse, rendered with Old English glosses such as *word* and *(ge)spræc*. Limiting the search only to prose texts (excluding glosses and poetry) yields forty-two instances of *sermo* and variants, twenty-one of which are specific titles of or references to preaching texts. One telling instance is found in Ælfric's *Grammar*, where he together provides the Latin and English terms "*sermo* oþþe *locutio* spræc"[18] – an indicator of

---

10 *VH*, passim.

11 *BH*, 171.

12 *CH* I and *CH* II, passim.

13 *CH* I, 173, line 20.

14 *CH* II, 1, line 17 and 2, line 37.

15 Bethurum, ed., *The Homilies of Wulfstan*, passim.

16 Ibid., 255. The two manuscripts with the variant title are Cambridge, Corpus Christi College 419 (s. xi¹, prob. SE England); and Oxford, Bodleian Library, Bodley 343 (s. xii², West Midlands).

17 Searches were performed in the *Web Corpus* of Momma, ed., *The Dictionary of Old English*.

18 Zupitza, ed., *Ælfrics Grammatik und Glossar*, 305, line 18.

the interchangeability of terms. For Old English terms, *larspel(l)* appears in titles for five sermons, and *spel* in titles for eight sermons. As a further complication, the Latin terms only appear in the *Dictionary of Old English Web Corpus* because of their place in direct relation to vernacular texts, so these numbers do not account for the larger multilingual corpus of Anglo-Saxon literature including Anglo-Latin texts. Nonetheless, of the Latin generic labels, *sermo* is more integrated into the terminology concerning Old English preaching texts than *omelia*. In terms of statistics from the surviving vernacular corpus, in other words, Anglo-Saxon authors and scribes preferred *sermo* as the more popular term for preaching texts in Old English.[19]

The various preceding examples and statistical findings go a long way towards representing how medieval authors and scribes labelled preaching materials with variant terms, confounding the boundaries of modern genre classifications. "The varied application of nomenclature, and often the change of purpose in individual items," Cross concludes, "suggests that Anglo-Saxon authors were more concerned about the effectiveness of their writings for the faith than about echoing models or conforming to strict rules of genre."[20] In the service of effective writing, however, modern scholarship demands closer scrutiny and attention to terminology. For that reason, I err on the side of generality, rather than weighing down readers in muddy prose attempting to distinguish between generic types with each new reference to a preaching text. As a guide, I follow Kienzle's observation: "The terms sermon, homily, *tractatus*, and so on, fall within the bounds of that genre, and the generic term, sermon, encompasses them."[21] Adhering to this loose hierarchy of classification, then, I generally use *sermon* and *preaching texts* as inclusive terms – the former for specific items and the latter to evoke the broader category of compositions generally related to preaching. For the purposes of this book, the term *sermon* is all the more appropriate regarding preaching texts that incorporate apocrypha, since they do not constitute occasions of systematic exegesis but narratives that extend beyond biblical sources, further defying the boundaries of modern classifications.

---

19 Unfortunately, without a searchable database for the corpus of Latin texts from Anglo-Saxon England (comparable to the *Web Corpus* of Momma, ed., *The Dictionary of Old English*), it is difficult to come to broader conclusions about the use of Latin terms.
20 Cross, "Vernacular Sermons in Old English," 565.
21 Kienzle, "Introduction," 161.

The Pseudo-Marcellus *Martyrdom of Peter and Paul* in the Earliest Manuscripts of the *Virtutes apostolorum*

The following provides a list of the earliest complete manuscripts of the *Virtutes apostolorum* that include the Pseudo-Marcellus *Martyrdom of Peter and Paul* (*BHL* 6657). This list is meant to demonstrate the early transmission of this narrative, and to suggest that the widespread dissemination helps to explain its use by Anglo-Saxon authors. While this list focuses only on the *Virtutes apostolorum*, in which the *Martyrdom* circulated widely, it does not account for the large number of manuscripts that also contain the narrative independent of the apostolic collection; it is hoped that further work (especially by Alberto D'Anna) will shed more light on this issue.[1]

For the present list, the manuscript corpus surveyed – a total of twenty-five complete manuscripts, dated from the eighth to the thirteenth century – was selected by the Utrecht University research team, led by Els Rose, for the critical edition of the *Virtutes apostolorum* in the Corpus Christianorum Series Apocryphorum.[2] In general, I have relied on Rose's descriptions of each manuscript, though I have examined and confirmed (via digital images online) the contents of Graz, Universitätsbibliothek 412, St Gall, Stiftsbibliothek 561, and Wolfenbüttel, Herzog August Bibliothek, Weissenburg 48. Following the shelf-mark for each manuscript, I include the date and (when known) place of origin; in some cases, I provide notes that elucidate the relevant contents.

---

1 I would like to thank Alberto D'Anna for discussing this issue with me, via private correspondence.

2 See Rose, "*Abdias scriptor vitarum sanctorum apostolorum?*," esp. for a list of all twenty-five manuscripts, contents for each, as well as justification and discussion of the team's manuscript selection.

1. Angers, Bibliothèque municipale 281 (s. xi, Angers, St Aubin)
2. Graz, Universitätsbibliothek 412 (s. ix, Aquileia or Bavaria)[3]
3. Montpellier, Bibliothèque universitaire, École de médicine 55 (s. viii$^{ex.}$/ix$^{in.}$, Metz? North Burgundy?)
4. Paris, Bibliothèque St Geneviève 547 (s. xii, ?)
5. Paris, Bibliothèque St Geneviève 558 (s. xiii, Paris)
6. Paris, Bibliothèque nationale de France, lat. 5273 (s. xiii, ?)
7. Paris, Bibliothèque nationale de France, lat. 9737 (s. xii, ?)
8. Paris, Bibliothèque nationale de France, lat. 12602 (s. xii, ?)[4]
9. Paris Bibliothèque nationale de France, lat. 12604 (s. xiii, ?)[5]
10. St Gall, Stiftsbibliothek 561 (s. ix^2, add. x, xi, Northeast France)
11. Wolfenbüttel, Herzog August Bibliothek, Weissenburg 48 (s. ix$^{2/3}$, Weissenburg/St Gall)

---

3 The title on folio 74v is given as "Gesta sanctorum apostolorum et martirum Christi Petri et Pauli."
4 This manuscript also includes separate accounts for Peter (*BHL* 6655) and Paul (*BHL* 6570), and sermons on Peter and Paul.
5 The Pseudo-Marcellus *Martyrdom* (*BHL* 6658) is included not as part of the *Virtutes apostolorum*, but afterward, on folios 78v–85r.

Apostolic Apocrypha in Ælfric's Corpus

Apostle(s)	Ælfric's Use	Source[1]	BHL (closest to Ælfric)	Cotton-Corpus Legendary[2]	Virt. apost.[3]	Other Extant MSS (ASM)[4]
Andrew	*CH* I.38	*Martyrdom of Andrew*	428	139 (later mss)	X	–
Bartholomew	*CH* I.31	*Martyrdom of Bartholomew*	1002	89	X	–
James the Great	*CH* II.27	*Martyrdom of James the Great*	4057	74	X	898
John	*CH* I.4	*Ps-Mellitus Martyrdom of John*	4320	–	X	131
Mark	*LS* 15	*Martyrdom of Mark*	5276	43	Some mss[5]	344 625

1 For specifics on Ælfric's sources, see various entries by Godden in *Fontes*; and *CH Introduction*, passim.

2 Item nos. correspond to the reconstructed contents; there exists the problem of reconstructing the contents from later manuscripts (s. xii), and I have noted where this is particularly the case.

3 Based on comparison of *BHL* item numbers (esp. those versions used by Ælfric) with versions included in the earliest manuscripts of the *Virtutes apostolorum*; for the former, see *CH Introduction*; and entries in *SASLC Apocrypha*; for the latter, see Rose, "*Abdias scriptor vitarum sanctorum apostolorum?*"

4 References are not exhaustive, and further study would potentially reveal a greater number of apostolic apocrypha circulating independently.

5 Some manuscripts include this text following the *Virtutes apostolorum*, although it is not part of the collection proper.

Apostle(s)	Ælfric's Use	Source	BHL (closest to Ælfric)	Cotton-Corpus Legendary	Virt. apost.	Other Extant MSS (ASM)
Matthew	*CH* II.32	*Martyrdom of Matthew*	5690	104	X	–
Peter and Paul	*CH* I.26	Ps-Marcellus *Martyrdom of Peter and Paul*	6657	–	X	–
Philip and James the Less	*CH* II.17	*Martyrdom of Philip;* and *Martyrdom of James the Less*	6814 4093	4645	XX	130 898
Simon and Jude	*CH* II.33	*Martyrdom of Simon and Jude*	7749–51	121(later mss)	X	–
Thomas	*LS* 36	*Martyrdom of Thomas*	8136	146	X	–

Translation of the *Book of Cerne* *Harrowing of Hell*

This piece of dramatic liturgy retelling the Harrowing of Hell survives in the ninth-century *Book of Cerne* (Cambridge, University Library, Ll.1.10; 820x840, Mercia), on folios 98v–99v. This verse text is based on the Latin Pseudo-Augustine *Sermo* 160, with parts of the Roman Psalter added to form a type of catena of biblical material. A.B. Kuypers printed the text in his diplomatic transcription of the *Book of Cerne*,[1] and David N. Dumville provided a critical edition, with notes on the text and its sources.[2] This translation (based on Dumville's edition) is, to my knowledge, the first full translation to appear in print. References in brackets are to sources in the Psalms. When biblical passages have been used as a source, I have generally followed the Douay-Rheims translation, with some modernizations for style.

> *This is the prayer of the innumerable crowd of saints*
> *who were held in the captivity of hell.*
> *With mournful voice and supplication they call to the Saviour,*
> *saying, when he descends into hell:*
> You have come, Redeemer of the world;
> you have come, you whom we longingly have hoped for daily;
> you have come, you who the prophets have announced would be a light for us;
> you have come, giving in living flesh forgiveness for the sins of the world.

---

1 Kuypers, ed., *The Prayer Book of Aedeluald*, 196–8.
2 Dumville, "Liturgical Drama and Panegyric Responsory from the Eighth Century?," 376–7.

Save the lost captives of hell:
Descend before us to hell;
do not abandon us when you return above!
You set the pillar of glory on the world;
set the sign of victory in hell!
Now, O Lord, let your mercy be upon us, just as we have hoped in you.
  [32:22]
For with you is the fountain of life [35:10]
and in your light we shall see light. [35:10]
Show us, O Lord, your mercy [84:8]
and grant us your salvation! [84:8]
Remember your congregation, which you created from the beginning; [73:2]
remember not our former iniquities; [78:8]
let your mercies speedily prevent us, for we are become exceedingly poor.
  [78:8]
Help us, O God, our Saviour, [78:9]
and for the honour of your name, O Lord, deliver us, [78:9]
and forgive us our sins for the sake of your name! [78:9]
But after the request and supplication of the innumerable captives is heard,
steadily all, by the decree of the Lord, the ancient just ones,
without any delay to the authority of the Lord Saviour for the loosened bonds,
grasping the knees of the Lord Saviour,
in humble supplication with inexpressible joy, crying:[3]
You have broken, O Lord, our bonds; [115:16; cf. 106:14]
we will sacrifice to you the sacrifice of praise, [115:17]
He has not dealt with us according to our sins [102:10]
nor rewarded us according to our iniquities. [102:10]
But Adam and Eve were not yet freed from the bonds.
Then Adam, with mournful and miserable voice, cried to the Lord, saying:[4]
Have mercy on me, O Lord, have mercy on me in your great mercy, [50:3]
and in the multitude of your tender mercies, blot out my iniquity, [50:3]
for to you only have I sinned and done evil before you. [50:6]

---

3 See Dumville, "Liturgical Drama and Panegyric Responsory from the Eighth Century?,"
   378–9 n. i, for discussion of the textual issues of this passage.
4 The phrase reads, "adhuc non sunt desoluti"; for discussion of temporal problems raised
   in these lines, see Dumville, "Liturgical Drama and Panegyric Responsory from the
   Eighth Century?," 379 n. j.

I have gone astray like a sheep. [118:176]
Loosen my bonds, because your hands have made me and formed me. [118:73]
You will not leave my soul in hell, [15:10]
but deal with me in mercy [118:124]
and bring me out of the bonds of this prison and the shadow of death.
   [106:14; cf. 141:8]
Then, the Lord showing mercy, Adam was loosed out of the bonds,
grasping the knees of Jesus Christ:
Bless the Lord, O my soul, [102:1]
and let all that is within me bless his holy name. [102:1]
Who forgives all my iniquities? [102:3]
Who heals all my weariness? [102:3]
Who redeems my life from destruction? [102:4]
Who satisfies my desire with good things? [102:5]
Yet Eve persists in weeping, saying:
You are just, O Lord, and your judgment is right [118:137]
for I deserve to suffer these things, [Gen. 42:21]
for I, when I was in honour, did not understand: [48:13]
I am compared to senseless beasts [48:13]
and am become like to them. [48:13]
But you, O Lord, do not remember the sins of my youth and my ignorance.
   [24:7]
Turn not the face of your mercy from me, [26:9]
and decline not in your wrath from your handmaiden. [26:9]

Common Pericopes in the Homiliary of Angers and Ælfric's *Catholic Homilies* in Bodley 343

HA sermon	CH in Bodley 343	Pericope	Occasion
xii	I.15	Mark 16:1–7	Easter Sunday
xx	I.18	Luke 11:5–13	Rogationtide
xxvii	I.24	Luke 15:1–7	4th Sunday after Pentecost
xxix	I.26	Matt. 16:13–19	Feast of Sts Peter and Paul
xxx	II.25	Mark 8:1–9	8th Sunday after Pentecost
xxxi	II.26	Matt. 7:15–21	9th Sunday after Pentecost
xxxiv	I.28	Luke 19:41–47	11th Sunday after Pentecost
xxxv	II.28	Luke 18:9–14	12th Sunday after Pentecost
xxix	II.31	Matt. 6:24–33	16th Sunday after Pentecost
xl	I.33	Luke 7:11–16	17th Sunday after Pentecost
xlvi	I.35	Matt. 22:1–14	21st Sunday after Pentecost
liii	I.40	Luke 21:25–33	2nd Sunday in Advent
liv	II.38	Matt. 25:14–30	Feast of St Nicholas/ Common of a Confessor
lix	I.6	Luke 2:21	Feast of Circumcision (Octave of Christmas)
lxiii	I.8	Matt. 8:1–13	3rd Sunday after Epiphany
lxv	II.5	Matt. 20:1–16	Septuagesima
lxvi	II.6	Luke 8:4–15	Sexagesima

Bibliography

Acland, Charles R. *Screen Traffic: Movies, Multiplexes, and Global Culture.*
  Durham, NC: Duke University Press, 2003.

Allen, Michael J.B., and Daniel G. Calder. *Sources and Analogues of Old English
  Poetry: The Major Latin Texts in Translation.* Cambridge: D.S. Brewer, 1976.

Amara, Souad Hamerlain. "Towards a Model of *Tradaptation.*" In *IDEA:
  Studies in English*, ed. Evrim Dogan Adanur, 458–68. Newcastle upon Tyne:
  Cambridge Scholars, 2011.

Atherton, M. "The Sources of Vercelli 5 (Cameron B.3.2.1)." In *Fontes Anglo-
  Saxonici: A Register of Written Sources Used by Anglo-Saxon Authors.* 1996.

– "The Sources of Vercelli 6 (Cameron B.3.4.10)." In *Fontes Anglo-Saxonici:
  A Register of Written Sources Used by Anglo-Saxon Authors.* 1996.

Auerbach, Erich. *Mimesis: The Representation of Reality in Western Thought.*
  Princeton: Princeton University Press, 1953.

Backhouse, Janet, D.H. Turner, and Leslie Webster, eds. *The Golden Age
  of Anglo-Saxon Art.* London: British Museum Publications, 1984.

Backus, Irena. *Historical Method and Confessional Identity in the Era of the
  Reformation (1378–1615).* Studies in Medieval and Reformation Traditions 94.
  Leiden: Brill, 2003.

Baldwin, Matthew C. *Whose Acts of Peter? Text and Historical Context of the
  Actus Vercellenses.* Wissenschaftliche Untersuchungen Zum Neuen Testament
  196. Tübingen: Mohr Siebeck, 2005.

Barabási, Albert-László. *Linked: How Everything Is Connected to Everything
  Else and What It Means for Business, Science, and Everyday Life.* New York:
  Basic Books, 2014.

Barney, Stephen A., W.J. Lewis, J.A. Beach, and Oliver Berghof, trans. *The
  Etymologies of Isidore of Seville.* Cambridge: Cambridge University Press,
  2006.

Bassnett, Susan. "Culture and Translation." In *A Companion to Translation Studies*, ed. Piotr Kuhiwczak and Karin Littau, 13–23. Topics in Translation 34. Clevedon: Multilingual Matters, 2007.

– *Translation Studies*. 3rd ed. London: Routledge, 2002.

– "Translation Studies at a Cross-Roads." *Target* 24 (2012): 15–25.

Batt, Catherine. "Introduction." In *Translating the Middle Ages*, ed. Karen L. Fresco and Charles D. Wright, 1–10. Farnham: Ashgate, 2012.

Bauer, Walter. *Orthodoxy and Heresy in Earliest Christianity*. Ed. and trans. Robert A. Kraft and Gerhard Krodel. Philadelphia: Fortress, 1971.

– *Rechtgläubigkeit und Ketzerei im ältesten Christentum*. Ed. Georg Strecker. 2nd ed. Tübingen: Mohr, 1964.

Bedingfield, M. Bradford. *The Dramatic Liturgy of Anglo-Saxon England*. Anglo-Saxon Studies 1. Woodbridge: Boydell Press, 2002.

Benjamin, Walter. "La tâche du traducteur." In *Mythe et violence*, trans. Maurice de Gandillac, 261–75. Paris: Denoël, 1971.

– "The Task of the Translator." In *Selected Writings, Volume 1: 1913–1926*, ed. Marcus Bullock and Michael W. Jennings, trans. Harry Zohn, 253–63. Cambridge, MA: Harvard University Press, 1996.

Berry, David M., ed. *Understanding Digital Humanities*. New York: Palgrave, 2012.

Bethurum, Dorothy, ed. *The Homilies of Wulfstan*. Oxford: Oxford University Press, 1957.

Beyers, Rita. "The Transmission of Marian Apocrypha in the Latin Middle Ages." *Apocrypha* 23 (2012): 117–40.

Beyers, Rita, ed. *Libri de nativitate Mariae: Libellus de nativitate Sanctae Mariae, textus et commentarius*. CCSA 10. Turnhout: Brepols, 1997.

Bibliotheca Hagiographica Latina Antiquae et Mediae Aetatis. 2 vols. Subsidia Hagiographica 6. Brussels: Société des Bollandistes, 1898–1901.

Bibliotheca Laureshamensis Digital. Heidelberg: Universitätsbibliothek, 2014. http://bibliotheca-laureshamensis-digital.de/.

Bibliothèque virtuelle des manuscrits médiévaux. 2013. http://bvmm.irht.cnrs.fr/.

Biggs, Frederick M. "Ælfric's Andrew and the Apocrypha." *JEGP* 104 (2005): 473–94.

– "Ælfric's Comments about the *Passio Thomae*." *N&Q* n.s. 52 (2005): 5–8.

– "Ælfric's Mark, Other Things, and Apostolic Authority." *Studies in Philology* 104 (2007): 227–49.

– "A Further Quotation of Columbanus in Alchfrid's Letter to Hygelac." *N&Q* n.s. 53 (2006): 12–14.

– "An Introduction and Overview of Recent Work." In *Apocryphal Texts and Traditions in Anglo-Saxon England*, ed. Kathryn Powell and Donald G.

Scragg, 1–25. Publications of the Manchester Centre for Anglo-Saxon Studies 2. Cambridge: D.S. Brewer, 2003.

– "A Picture of Paul in a Parker Manuscript." In *Intertexts: Studies in Anglo-Saxon Culture Presented to Paul E. Szarmach*, ed. Virginia Blanton and Helene Scheck, 169–89. MRTS 334. Tempe: Arizona Center for Medieval and Renaissance Studies, 2008.

– "'Righteous People According to the Old Law': Ælfric on Anne and Joachim." *Apocrypha* 17 (2006): 151–78.

Biggs, Frederick M., ed. *Sources of Anglo-Saxon Literary Culture: The Apocrypha*. Instrumenta Anglistica Mediaevalia 1. Kalamazoo: Medieval Institute Publications, 2006.

Biggs, Frederick M., and Thomas N. Hall. "Traditions Concerning Jamnes and Mambres in Anglo-Saxon England." *ASE* 25 (1996): 69–89.

Biggs, Frederick M., Thomas D. Hill, and Paul E. Szarmach, eds. *Sources of Anglo-Saxon Liteerary Culture: A Trial Version*. MRTS 74. Binghamton, NY: Center for Medieval and Early Renaissance Studies, 1990.

Biggs, Frederick M., Thomas D. Hill, Paul E. Szarmach, and E. Gordon Whatley, with the assistance of Deborah A. Oosterhouse, eds. *Sources of Anglo-Saxon Literary Culture, Volume One: Abbo of Fleury, Abbo of Saint-German-des-Prés, and Acta Sanctorum*. Kalamazoo: Medieval Institute Publications, 2001.

Billett, Jesse D. *The Divine Office in Anglo-Saxon England, 597–c. 1000*. Henry Bradshaw Society Subsidia 7. London: Boydell Press, 2014.

Bischoff, Bernhard. *Katalog der festländischen Handschriften des neunten Jahrhunderts (mit Ausnahme der wisigotischen)*. Ed. Birgit Ebersperger. 3 vols. Wiesbaden: Harrassowitz, 1998–2014.

– *Manuscripts and Libraries in the Age of Charlemagne*. Trans. and ed. Michael M. Gorman. Cambridge Studies in Palaeography and Codicology 1. Cambridge: Cambridge University Press, 1994.

– *Mittelalterliche Studien: Ausgewählte Aufsätze zur Schriftkunde und Literaturgeschichte*. 3 vols. Stuttgart: A. Hiersemann, 1966–81.

– *Die südostdeutschen Schreibschulen und Bibliotheken in der Karolingerzeit, I: Die bayrischen Diözesen*. 3rd ed. Wiesbaden: Harrassowitz, 1974.

– "Turning-Points in the History of Latin Exegesis in the Early Middle Ages." Trans. Colm O'Grady. In *Biblical Studies: The Medieval Irish Contribution*, ed. Martin McNamara, 74–160. Proceedings of the Irish Biblical Association 1. Dublin: Irish Biblical Association, 1975.

– "Wendepunkte in der Geschichte der lateinischen Exegese im Frühmittelalter." *Sacris Erudiri* 6 (1954): 189–279.

Bischoff, Bernhard, and Virginia Brown. "Addenda to *Codices Latini Antiquiores*." *Mediaeval Studies* 47 (1985): 317–66.

Bischoff, Bernhard, Virginia Brown, and James J. John. "Addenda to *Codices Latini Antiquiores* (II)." *Mediaeval Studies* 54 (1992), 286–307.

Blair, John. *The Church in Anglo-Saxon Christianity*. Oxford: Oxford University Press, 2005.

Boenig, Robert, trans. *The Acts of Andrew in the Country of the Cannibals: Translations from the Greek, Latin, and Old English*. Garland Library of Medieval Literature 70. New York: Garland, 1991.

Bolter, Jay David, and Richard Grusin. *Remediation: Understanding New Media*. Cambridge, MA: MIT Press, 1999.

Bovon, François. "Beyond the Canonical and the Apocryphal Books, the Presence of a Third Category: The Books Useful for the Soul." *Harvard Theological Review* 105 (2012): 125–37.

– "Canonical and Apocryphal Acts of Apostles." In *New Testament and Christian Apocrypha: Collected Studies II*, ed. Glenn E. Snyder, 197–222. Wissenschaftliche Untersuchungen Zum Neuen Testament 237. Tübingen: Mohr Siebeck, 2009.

– "Canonical, Rejected, and Useful Books." In *New Testament Christian Apocrypha: Collected Studies II*, ed. Glenn E. Snyder, 318–22. Wissenschaftliche Untersuchungen Zum Neuen Testament 237. Tübingen: Mohr Siebeck, 2009.

Bovon, François, and Eric Junod. "Reading the Apocryphal Acts." In *The Apocryphal Acts of Apostles*, ed. Dennis Ronald McDonald, 161–71. Decatur, GA: Scholars Press, 1986.

Brackmann, Rebecca. *The Elizabethan Invention of Anglo-Saxon England: Laurence Nowell, William Lambarde, and the Study of Old English*. Studies in Renaissance Literature 30. Cambridge: D.S. Brewer, 2012.

Brant, Jo-Ann A., Charles W. Hedrick, and Chris Shea, eds. *Ancient Fiction: The Matrix of Early Christian and Jewish Narrative*. Society of Biblical Literature Symposium Series 32. Atlanta: Society of Biblical Literature, 2005.

Brantley, Jessica. "The Iconography of the Utrecht Psalter and the *Old English Descent into Hell*." *ASE* 28 (1999): 43–63.

Bredehoft, Thomas A. "Filling the Margins of CCCC 41: Textual Space and a Developing Archive." *RES* 57 (2006): 721–32.

– *The Visible Text: Textual Production and Reproduction from "Beowulf" to "Maus."* Oxford: Oxford University Press, 2014.

Bremmer, Jan N. "The Five Major Apocryphal Acts: Authors, Place, Time and Readership." In *The Apocryphal Acts of Thomas*, ed. Jan N. Bremmer, 149–70. Studies on Early Christian Apocrypha 6. Leuven: Peeters, 2011.

Bremmer, Rolf H., Jr. "The Anglo-Saxon Continental Mission and the Transfer of Encyclopedic Knowledge." In *Foundations of Learning: The Transfer of*

Encyclopedic Knowledge in the Early Middle Ages, ed. Rolf H. Bremmer, Jr and Kees Dekker, 19–50. Mediaevalia Groningana New Series 9. Leuven: Peeters, 2007.

Brooks, Kenneth R. *Andreas and the Fates of the Apostles*. Oxford: Clarendon Press, 1961.

Brottman, Mikita. *High Theory/Low Culture*. New York: Palgrave, 2005.

Brown, Michelle P. *The Book of Cerne: Prayer, Patronage, and Power in Ninth-Century England*. London: British Library, 1996.

Brown, Peter. *The Cult of the Saints: Its Rise and Function in Latin Christianity*. The Haskall Lectures on History of Religions, New Series 2. Chicago: University of Chicago Press, 1981.

Bryant, Richard, and Michael Hare. *Corpus of Anglo-Saxon Stone Sculpture, Volume X: The Western Midlands*. Oxford: Oxford University Press, for the British Academy, 2012.

Brzesinski, Monica. "The Harrowing of Hell, the Last Judgment, and *The Dream of the Rood*." *Neuphilologische Mitteilungen* 89 (1988): 252–65.

Buchholz, Richard, ed. *Die Fragmente der Reden der Seele an den Leichnam in zwei Handschriften zu Worcester und Oxford*. Erlanger Beiträge zur Englischen Philologie 2.6. Erlangen: A. Deichert, 1890.

Burdick, Anne, et al., eds. *Digital_Humanities*. Cambridge, MA: MIT Press, 2012. https://mitpress.mit.edu/sites/default/files/titles/content/9780262018470_Open_Access_Edition.pdf.

Buringh, Eltjo. *Medieval Manuscript Production in the Latin West: Explorations with a Global Database*. Global Economics History Series 6. Leiden: Brill, 2011.

Burke, Tony. *Secret Scriptures Revealed: A New Introduction to the Christian Apocrypha*. Grand Rapids, MI: Eerdmans, 2013.

Burke, Tony, ed. *Forbidden Texts on the Western Frontier: The Christian Apocrypha in North American Perspectives, Proceedings from the 2013 York University Christian Apocrypha Symposium*. Eugene, OR: Cascade, 2015.

Camargo, Martin. *Ars Dictaminis/Ars Dictandi*. Typologie des Sources du Moyen Âge Occidental 60. Turnhout: Brepols, 1991.

Cameron, Averil. *Christianity and the Rhetoric of Empire*. Sather Classical Lectures 55. Berkeley: University of California Press, 1991.

Campbell, Emma, and Robert Mills. "Introduction: Rethinking Medieval Translation." In *Rethinking Medieval Translation: Ethics, Politics, Theory*, ed. Emma Campbell and Robert Mills, 1–20. Cambridge: D.S. Brewer, 2012.

Cartlidge, David R. *ApocIcon*. http://apocicon.maryvillecollege.edu/.

Cartlidge, David R., and J. Keith Elliott. *Art and the Christian Apocrypha*. London: Routledge, 2001.

Cataldi, Claudio. "St Andrew in the Old English Homiletic Tradition." In *Hagiography in Anglo-Saxon England: Adopting and Adapting Saints' Lives into Old English Prose (c. 950–1150)*, ed. Loredana Lazzari, Patrizia Lendinara, and Claudia Di Sciacca, 293–308. Textes et Études du Moyen Âge 73. Barcelona: Féderation Internationale des Instituts d'Études Médiévales, 2014.

Charlesworth, James H., ed. *The Old Testament Pseudepigrapha*. 2 vols. Garden City, NY: Doubleday, 1983.

Clayton, Mary. "Ælfric and the Nativity of the Blessed Virgin Mary." *Anglia* 104 (1986): 286–315.

– *The Apocryphal Gospels of Mary in Anglo-Saxon England*. CSASE 26. Cambridge: Cambridge University Press, 1998.

– *The Cult of the Virgin Mary in Anglo-Saxon England*. CSASE 2. Cambridge: Cambridge University Press, 1990.

– "Delivering the Damned: A Motif in OE Homiletic Prose." *Medium Ævum* 55 (1986): 92–102.

– "Homiliaries and Preaching in Anglo-Saxon England." *Peritia* 4 (1985): 207–42. Repr. in *Old English Prose: Basic Readings*, ed. Paul E. Szarmach, 151–98. New York: Garland, 2000.

Clemoes, Peter A.M. "The Chronology of Ælfric's Works." In *The Anglo-Saxons: Studies in Some Aspects of Their History and Culture Presented to Bruce Dickens*, ed. Peter A.M. Clemoes, 212–47. London: Bowes & Bowes, 1959.

Clemoes, Peter A.M., ed. *Ælfric's Catholic Homilies: The First Series, Text*. EETS ss 17. Oxford: Oxford University Press, 1997.

Colgrave, Bertram, and Ann Hyde. "Two Recently Discovered Leaves from Old English Manuscripts." *Speculum* 37 (1962): 60–78.

Collins, J.J. *The Apocalyptic Imagination: An Introduction to Jewish Apocalyptic Literature*. 2nd ed. Grand Rapids, MI: Eerdmans, 1998.

– "Sibylline Oracles." In *The Old Testament Pseudepigrapha*, ed. James H. Charlesworth, 1:317–472. 2 vols. Garden City, NY: Doubleday, 1983–5.

Connell, Martin F. "*Descensus Christi Ad Inferos*: Christ's Descent to the Dead." *Theological Studies* 62 (2001): 262–82.

Constable, Giles. *Letters and Letter Collections*. Typologie des Sources du Moyen Âge Occidental 17. Turnhout: Brepols, 1976.

Conti, Aidan. "The Circulation of the Old English Homily in the Twelfth Century: New Evidence from Oxford, Bodleian Library, MS Bodley 343." In *The Old English Homily: Precedent, Practice, and Appropriation*, ed. Aaron J Kleist, 365–402. Turnhout: Brepols, 2007.

– "Individual Practice, Common Endeavor: Making a Manuscript and Community in the Second Half of the Twelfth Century." In *Producing and*

Using English Manuscripts in the Post-Conquest Period, ed. Elaine Treharne, Orietta Da Rold, and Mary Swan, 253–72. Special Issue of *New Medieval Literatures* 13 (2011).

– "Preaching Scripture and Apocrypha: A Previously Unidentified Homiliary in an Old English Manuscript, Oxford, Bodleian Library, MS Bodley 343." Unpublished PhD diss., University of Toronto, 2004.

– "Revising Wulfstan's Antichrist in the Twelfth Century: A Study of Medieval Textual Re-appropriation." *Literature Compass* 4 (2007): 638–63.

– "The Taunton Fragment and the Homiliary of Angers: Context for New Old English." *RES* 60 (2009): 1–33.

Conti, Aidan, and Orietta Da Rold. "Oxford Bodleian Library, Bodley 343." In Orietta Da Rold, Takako Kato, Mary Swan, and Elaine Treharne, *The Production and Use of English Manuscripts 1060 to 1220*. University of Leicester, 2010. http://www.le.ac.uk/english/em1060to1220/mss/EM.Ox.Bodl.343.htm.

Copeland, Rita. *Rhetoric, Hermeneutics, and Translation in the Middle Ages: Academic Traditions and Vernacular Texts*. Cambridge Studies in Medieval Literature 11. Cambridge: Cambridge University Press, 1991.

Cramp, Rosemary. *Corpus of Anglo-Saxon Stone Sculpture, Volume VII: South-West England*. Oxford: Oxford University Press, for the British Academy, 2006.

Crawford, S.J. "The Worcester Marks and Glosses of the Old English Manuscripts in the Bodleian, Together with the Worcester Version of the Nicene Creed." *Anglia* 52 (1928): 1–25.

Cross, J.E. *Cambridge Pembroke College MS. 25: A Carolingian Sermonary Used by Anglo-Saxon Preachers*. King's College London Medieval Studies 1. Exeter: Short Run Press, for King's College London, 1987.

– "Hiberno-Latin Commentaries in Salisbury Manuscripts Before 1125 A.D." *Hiberno-Latin Newsletter* 2 (1988): 8–9.

– "Portents and Events at Christ's Birth: Comments on Vercelli V & VI and the Old English Martyrology." *ASE* 2 (1973): 209–20.

– "Towards the Identification of Old English Literary Ideas – Old Workings and New Seams." In *Sources of Anglo-Saxon Culture*, ed. Paul E. Szarmach and Virginia D. Oggins, 77–101. Studies in Medieval Culture 20. Kalamazoo: Medieval Institute Publications, 1986.

– "Vernacular Sermons in Old English." In *The Sermon*, ed. Beverly Mayne Kienzle, 561–96. Typologie des Sources du Moyen Âge Occidental 81–3. Turnhout: Brepols, 2000.

Cross, J.E., ed. *Two Old English Apocrypha and Their Manuscript Source: The Gospel of Nicodemus and The Avenging of the Saviour*. CSASE 19. Cambridge: Cambridge University Press, 1996.

Cross, J.E., and Thomas D. Hill, eds. *The Prose Solomon and Saturn and Adrian and Ritheus*. McMaster Old English Studies and Texts 1. Toronto: University of Toronto Press, 1982.

Cubitt, Catherine. "Images of St Peter: The Clergy and the Religious Life in Anglo-Saxon England." In *The Christian Tradition in Anglo-Saxon England: Approaches to Current Scholarship and Teaching*, ed. Paul Cavill, 41–54. Woodbridge: D.S. Brewer, 2004.

– "Review Article: The Tenth-Century Benedictine Reform in England." *Early Medieval Europe* 6 (1997): 77–94.

Curtius, Ernst Robert. *European Literature and the Latin Middle Ages*. Trans. R.W. Trask. Princeton: Princeton University Press, 1953.

D'Anna, Alberto. "The Relationship between the Greek and Latin Recensions of the *Acta Petri Et Pauli*." *Studia Patristica* 39 (2006): 331–8.

D'Avray, David L. *Medieval Marriage: Symbolism and Society*. Oxford: Oxford University Press, 2005.

– *Medieval Marriage Sermons: Mass Communication in a Culture without Print*. Oxford: Oxford University Press, 2001.

– "Printing, Mass Communication, and Religious Reformation: The Middle Ages and After." In *The Uses of Script and Print, 1300–1700*, ed. Julia Crick and Alexandra Walsham, 50–70. Cambridge: Cambridge University Press, 2004.

Da Rold, Orietta, Takako Kato, Mary Swan, and Elaine Treharne. *The Production and Use of English Manuscripts 1060 to 1220*. University of Leicester, 2010. http://www.le.ac.uk/ee/em1060to1220/.

Dalbey, Marcia A. "Patterns of Preaching in the Blickling Easter Homily." *American Benedictine Review* 24 (1973): 478–92.

DeGregorio, Scott. "Þegenlic or Flæsclic: The Old English Prose Legends of St. Andrew." *JEGP* 102 (2003): 449–69.

Dekkers, Eligius. *Clavis Patrum Latinorum*. 3rd ed. Turnhout: Brepols, 1995.

Derrida, Jacques. "Des Tours de Babel." In *Difference in Translation*, ed. and trans. Joseph F. Graham, 165–207. Ithaca: Cornell University Press, 1985.

– "Living On/Border Lines." In *Deconstruction and Criticism*, trans. James Hulbert, 75–176. New York: Continuum, 1979.

Deshman, Robert. *The Benedictional of Æthelwold*. Studies in Manuscript Illumination 9. Princeton: Princeton University Press, 1995.

– "Servants of the Mother of God in Byzantine and Medieval Art." *Word & Image* 5 (1989): 36–42.

"Detailed Record for Harley 603." In *Catalogue of Illuminated Manuscripts*. British Library. http://www.bl.uk/catalogues/illuminatedmanuscripts/record. asp?MSID=18402&CollID=8&NStart=603.

Di Sciacca, Claudia. *Finding the Right Words: Isidore's Synonyma in Anglo-Saxon England*. Toronto Old English Series 18. Toronto: University of Toronto Press, 2008.

– "The *Ubi Sunt* Motif and the Soul-and-Body Legend in Old English Homilies: Sources and Relationships." *JEGP* 105 (2006): 365–87.

Diesenberger, Maximilian. "Introduction: Compilers, Preachers, and Their Audiences in the Early Medieval West." In *Sermo doctorum: Compilers, Preachers and Their Audiences in the Early Middle Ages*, ed. Maximilian Diesenberger, Yitzhak Hen, and Marianne Pollheimer, 1–24. SERMO 9. Turnhout: Brepols, 2013.

Diesenberger, Maximilian, Yitzhak Hen, and Marianne Pollheimer, eds. *Sermo doctorum: Compilers, Preachers and Their Audiences in the Early Middle Ages*. SERMO 9. Turnhout: Brepols, 2013.

DigiPal: Digital Resource and Database of Manuscripts, Palaeography and Diplomatic. London: King's College London, 2011–14. http://www.digipal. eu/.

Digitised Manuscripts. British Library. http://www.bl.uk/manuscripts/.

DiNapoli, Robert. *An Index of Theme and Image to the Homilies of the Anglo-Saxon Church: Comprising the Homilies of Ælfric, Wulfstan, and the Blickling and Vercelli Codices*. Hockwold cum Wilton: Anglo-Saxon Books, 1995.

DiTommaso, Lorenzo. "Apocalypses and Apocalypticism in Antiquity (Part I)." *Currents in Biblical Research* 5 (2007): 35–286.

– "Apocalypses and Apocalypticism in Antiquity (Part II)." *Currents in Biblical Research* 5 (2007): 367–432.

Dobschütz, Ernst von. *Das Decretum Gelasianum de libris recipiendis et non recipiendis in Kritischem Text herausgegeben und untersucht*. Texte und Untersuchungen zur Geschicte der altchristlichen Literatur 38.4. Leipzig: J.C. Hinrichs'sche, 1912.

Dodwell, C.R. *Anglo-Saxon Gestures and the Roman Stage*. CSASE 28. Cambridge: Cambridge University Press, 2000.

Du Toit, Marietjie. "The Origin of the Christian Doctrine of the 'Decensus Christi Ad Inferos'." *Ekklesiastikos Pharos* 89 (2007): 102–20.

Dumville, David. "Biblical Apocrypha and the Early Irish: A Preliminary Investigation." *Proceedings of the Royal Irish Academy (C)* 73 (1973): 299–338.

– "Liturgical Drama and Panegyric Responsory from the Eighth Century? A Re-examination of the Origin and Contents of the Ninth-Century Section of the Book of Cerne." *Journal of Theological Studies* 23 (1972): 374–406.

Dzon, Mary, and Theresa M. Kennedy, eds. *The Christ Child in Medieval Culture: Alpha es et O!* Toronto: University of Toronto Press, 2012.

e-Clavis: Christian Apocrypha. The North American Society for the Study of Christian Apocryphal Literature. http://www.nasscal. com/e-clavis-christian-apocrypha/.

Early English Laws. University of London, Institute of Historical Research/ King's College London. http://www.earlyenglishlaws.ac.uk.

Eastman, David L. *The Ancient Martyrdom Accounts of Peter and Paul.* Writings from the Greco-Roman World 39. Atlanta: Society of Biblical Literature, 2015.

– *Paul the Martyr: The Cult of the Apostle in the Latin West.* Writings from the Greco-Roman World, Supplements 4. Atlanta: Society of Biblical Literature, 2011.

Ehrman, Bart D. *Forgery and Counterforgery: The Use of Literary Deceit in Early Christian Polemics.* Oxford: Oxford University Press, 2013.

– *Lost Christianities: The Battles for Scripture and the Faiths We Never Knew.* Oxford: Oxford University Press, 2003.

Ehrman, Bart D., and Zlatko Pleše. *The Apocryphal Gospels: Texts and Translations.* Oxford: Oxford University Press, 2011.

Elliott, J.K. *The Apocryphal New Testament: A Collection of Apocryphal Christian Literature in an English Translation.* Oxford: Clarendon Press, 1999.

Emmerson, Richard K. *Antichrist in the Middle Ages: A Study of Medieval Apocalypticism, Art, and Literature.* Seattle: University of Washington Press, 1981.

– "From *Epistula* to *Sermo*: The Old English Version of Adso's *Libellus De Antichristo.*" *JEGP* 82 (1983): 1–10.

Estes, Heide. "Anglo-Saxon Biblical Lore: An Edition." *English Studies* 93 (2012): 623–51.

Étaix, Raymond. "L'homéliaire Carolingien d'Angers." *Revue Bénédictine* 104 (1994): 148–90.

– *Homéliaires patristiques latins: Recueil d'études de manuscrits médiévaux.* Série Moyen-Âge et Temps Modernes 29. Paris: Institut d'études augustiniennes, 1994.

Fadda, Anna Maria Luiselli. "'De descensu Christi ad inferos': una inedita omelia anglosassone." *Studi medievali* 13 (1972): 989–1011.

Faerber, Robert. "Les *Acta apocrypha apostolorum* dans le corpus homilétique vieil-anglais (x^e–xie s.). Ælfric: *De passione apostolorum Petri et Pauli* et *Cathedra Petri.*" *Apocrypha* 15 (2004): 259–92.

– "Les *Acta apocrypha apostolorum* dans le corpus littéraire vieil-anglais: *Aca Andreae.*" *Apocrypha* 16 (2005): 199–228.

Farmer, David. "The Monastic Reform of the Tenth Century and Sherborne."
In *St Wulfsige and Sherborne: Essays to Celebrate the Millennium of the
Benedictine Abbey, 998–1998*, ed. Katherine Barker, David A. Hinton, and
Alan Hunt, 24–9. Bournemouth University School of Conservation Sciences,
Occasional Paper 8. Oxford: Oxbow, 2005.

Fell, Christine E. "Introduction to Anglo-Saxon Letters and Letter-Writers."
In *"Lastworda Betst": Essays in Memory of Christine E. Fell, with Her
Unpublished Writings*, ed. Carole Hough and Kathryn A. Lowe, 278–98.
Donington: Shaun Tyas, 2002.

Ferreiro, Alberto. *Simon Magus in Patristic, Medieval, and Early Modern
Traditions*. Studies in the History of Christian Traditions 125. Leiden: Brill,
2005.

Fillitz, Hermann. *Das Mittelalter I*. Propyläen Kunstgeschichte 5. Berlin:
Propyläen Verlag, 1969.

Flint, Valerie I.J. *The Rise of Magic in Early Medieval Europe*. Princeton:
Princeton University Press, 1991.

*Fontes Anglo-Saxonici: A Register of Written Sources Used by Anglo-Saxon
Authors*. http://fontes.english.ox.ac.uk.

Forbes, Helen Foxhall. *Heaven and Earth in Anglo-Saxon England: Theology
and Society in an Age of Faith*. Farnham: Ashgate, 2013.

Foucault, Michel. *The Archaeology of Knowledge and the Discourse on
Language*. Trans. A.M. Sheridan Smith. New York: Pantheon Books, 1972.

Foys, Martin K. "Media." In *A Handbook of Anglo-Saxon Studies*, ed. Jacqueline
Stodnick and Renée R. Trilling, 133–48. Malden, MA: Wiley-Blackwell, 2012.

– "Medieval Manuscripts: Media Archaeology and the Digital Incunable." In
The Medieval Manuscript Book: Cultural Approaches, ed. Michael Johnston
and Michael Van Dussen, 119–39. Cambridge: Cambridge University Press,
2015.

– *Virtually Anglo-Saxon: Old Media, New Media, and Early Medieval Studies in
the Late Age of Print*. Gainesville: University Press of Florida, 2007.

Fresco, Karen L., and Charles D. Wright, eds. *Translating the Middle Ages*.
Farnham: Ashgate, 2012.

Friedman, John Block. *The Monstrous Races in Medieval Art and Thought*.
Cambridge, MA: Harvard University Press, 1981. Repr. Syracuse: Syracuse
University Press, 2000.

Friesen, Bill. "Legends and Liturgy in the Old English Prose *Andreas*." ASE 43
(2014): 209–29.

– "The Sources and Analogues of the Old English *Andreas*." Unpublished PhD
diss., University of Toronto, 2008.

Fulk, R.D., and Christopher M. Cain. *A History of Old English Literature.* Oxford: Blackwell, 2003.

Fulton, Rachel. *From Judgment to Passion: Devotion to Christ and the Virgin Mary, 800–1200.* New York: Columbia University Press, 2002.

Gallagher, Edmon L. *Hebrew Scripture in Patristic Biblical Theory: Canon, Language, Text.* Supplements to Vigiliae Christianae 114. Leiden: Brill, 2012.

Galloway, Alexander R. "Networks." In *Critical Terms for Media Studies,* ed. W.J.T. Mitchell and Mark B.N. Hansen, 280–96. Chicago: University of Chicago Press, 2010.

Gambero, Luigi. *Mary in the Middle Ages: The Blessed Virgin Mary in the Thought of Medieval Latin Theologians.* San Francisco: Ignatius Press, 2005.

Gameson, Richard. *The Manuscripts of Early Norman England (c. 1066–1130).* Oxford: Oxford University Press, for the British Academy, 1999.

Garber, Marjorie. *Vested Interests: Cross-Dressing and Cultural Anxiety.* New York: Routledge, 1992.

Gatch, Milton McC. "Eschatology in the Anonymous Old English Homilies." *Traditio* 21 (1965): 117–65.

– "The Harrowing of Hell: A Liberation Motif in Medieval Theology and Devotional Literature." *Union Seminary Quarterly Review* 36 (1981): 75–88.

– *Preaching and Theology in Anglo-Saxon England: Ælfric and Wulfstan.* Toronto: University of Toronto Press, 1977.

– "The Unknowable Audience of the Blickling Homilies." *ASE* 18 (1989): 99–115.

Geerard, Maurits. *Clavis Apocryphorum Novi Testamenti.* Turnhout: Brepols, 1992.

Gerry, Sarah S. "An Edition with Commentary of the Latin/Anglo-Saxon *Liber Scintillarum.*" Unpublished PhD diss., University of Pennsylvania, 1969.

Gijsel, Jan, ed. *Libri de nativitate Mariae: Pseudo-Matthaei Evangelium, textus et commentarius.* CCSA 9. Turnhout: Brepols, 1997.

Gitelman, Lisa. *Always Already New: Media, History, and the Data of Culture.* Cambridge, MA: MIT Press, 2006.

– *Paper Knowledge: Toward a Media History of Documents.* Durham, NC: Duke University Press, 2014.

Gitelman, Lisa, and Geoffrey B. Pingree, eds. *New Media, 1740–1915.* Cambridge, MA: MIT Press, 2004.

Gittos, Helen, and Marvin Bradford Bedingfield, eds. *The Liturgy of the Late Anglo-Saxon Church.* Henry Bradshaw Society Subsidia 5. Woodbridge: Boydell Press, for the Henry Bradshaw Society, 2005.

Glauche, Günter. *Katalog Der Lateinischen Handschriften Der Bayerischen Staatsbibliothek München: Die Pergamenthandschriften Aus Benediktbeuern,*

Clm 4501–4663. Catalogus Codicum Manu Scriptorum Bibliothecae Monacensis Tomus III, Series Nova, pars 1. Wiesbaden: Harrassowitz, 1994.

Gneuss, Helmut, and Michael Lapidge. *Anglo-Saxon Manuscripts: A Bibliographical Handlist of Manuscripts and Manuscript Fragments Written or Owned in England up to 1100*. Toronto Anglo-Saxon Series 15. Toronto: University of Toronto Press, 2014.

Goddard, Michael. "Opening Up the Black Boxes: Media Archaeology, 'Anarchaeology' and Media Materiality." *New Media & Society* (2014): 1–16.

Godden, Malcolm. "Ælfric and the Vernacular Prose Tradition." In *The Old English Homily and Its Backgrounds*, ed. Paul E. Szarmach and B.F. Huppé, 99–118. Albany: SUNY Press, 1978.

– *Ælfric's Catholic Homilies: Introduction, Commentary and Glossary*. EETS ss 18. Oxford: Oxford University Press, 2000.

– "*Ælfric's Saints' Lives and the Problem of Miracles*." *Leeds Studies in English* n.s. 16 (1985): 83–100. Repr. in *Old English Prose: Basic Readings*, ed. Paul E. Szarmach, 287–309. New York: Garland, 2000.

– "The Sources of Catholic Homilies 1.26 (Cameron B.1.1.28)." In *Fontes Anglo-Saxonici: A Register of Written Sources Used by Anglo-Saxon Authors*. 1998.

– "The Sources of Catholic Homilies 1.31 (Cameron B.1.1.33)." In *Fontes Anglo-Saxonici: A Register of Written Sources Used by Anglo-Saxon Authors*. 1998; updated 2002.

– "The Sources of Catholic Homilies 2.19 (Cameron B.1.2.24)." In *Fontes Anglo-Saxonici: A Register of Written Sources Used by Anglo-Saxon Authors*. 1998.

– "The Sources of Catholic Homilies 2.27 (Cameron B.1.2.34)." In *Fontes Anglo-Saxonici: A Register of Written Sources Used by Anglo-Saxon Authors*. 1998.

– "The Sources of Catholic Homilies 2.32 (Cameron B.1.2.40)." In *Fontes Anglo-Saxonici: A Register of Written Sources Used by Anglo-Saxon Authors*. 1998.

Godden, Malcolm, ed. *Ælfric's Catholic Homilies: The Second Series, Text*. EETS ss 5. Oxford: Oxford University Press, 1979.

Gold, Matthew K., ed. *Debates in the Digital Humanities*. Minneapolis: University of Minnesota Press, 2012. http://dhdebates.gc.cuny.edu.

Goossens, Louis. *The Old English Glosses of MS. Brussels, Royal Library 1650 (Aldhelm's De Laudibus Virginitatis)*. Brussels Verhandelingen Van De Koninklijke Academie Voor Wetenschappen, Lettern En Schone Kunsten Van Belgie, Klasse Der Letteren 36. Brussels: Paleis der Academiën, 1974.

Gorman, Michael. "The Myth of Hiberno-Latin Exegesis." *Revue Bénédictine* 110 (2000): 42–85.

Gounelle, Rémi. "Actes apocryphes des apôtres et Actes des apôtres canoniques: État de la recherche et perspectives nouvelles (I)." *Revue d'histoire et de philosophie religieuses* 84 (2004): 3–30.

– "Actes apocryphes des apôtres et Actes des apôtres canoniques: État de la recherche et perspectives nouvelles (II)." *Revue d'histoire et de philosophie religieuses* 84 (2004): 419–41.

Gounelle, Rémi, and Zbigniew Izydorczyk. "Thematic Bibliography of the *Acts of Pilate*." In *The Medieval "Gospel of Nicodemus": Text, Intertexts, and Contexts in Western Europe*, ed. Zbigniew Izydorczyk, 419–519. MRTS 158. Tempe: Arizona Center for Medieval and Renaissance Studies, 1997.

– "Thematic Bibliography of the *Acts of Pilate*: Addenda and Corrigenda." *Apocrypha* 11 (2000): 259–92.

Gradon, P.O.E., ed. *Cynewulf's "Elene."* Rev. ed. Exeter: University of Exeter Press, 1977. Repr. 1996.

Grant, Raymond J.S. *Cambridge, Corpus Christi College 41: The Loricas and the Missal*. Amsterdam: Rodopi, 1979.

Grant, Raymond J.S., ed. *Three Homilies from Cambridge, Corpus Christi College 41: The Assumption, St Michael and the Passion*. Ottawa: Tecumseh Press, 1982.

Greenfield, Stanley B., and Daniel G. Calder. *A New Critical History of Old English Literature*. New York: New York University Press, 1986.

Grégoire, Réginald. *Homéliaires Liturgiques Médiévaux: Analyse De Manuscrits*. Biblioteca Degli Studi Medievali 12. Spoleto: Centro Italiano di studi sull'alto medioevo, 1980.

Grüll, Tibor. "The Legendary Fate of Pontius Pilate." *Classica Et Mediaevalia* 61 (2010): 151–76.

Grundy, Lynne. *Books and Grace: Ælfric's Theology*. King's College London Medieval Studies 6. London: King's College, 1991.

Grusin, Richard. "Radical Mediation." *Critical Inquiry* 42 (2015): 124–48.

Gurevich, Aron. *Medieval Popular Culture: Problems of Belief and Perception*. Trans. Janos M. Bak and Paul A. Hollingsworth. Cambridge Studies in Oral and Literate Culture 14. Cambridge: Cambridge University Press, 1988.

Haines, Dorothy. *Sunday Observance and the Sunday Letter in Anglo-Saxon England*. Anglo-Saxon Texts 8. Cambridge: D.S. Brewer, 2010.

Hall, Thomas N. "Ælfric and the Epistle to the Laodicians." In *Apocryphal Texts and Traditions in Anglo-Saxon England*, ed. Kathryn Powell and Donald G. Scragg, 65–83. Publications of the Manchester Centre for Anglo-Saxon Studies 2. Cambridge: D.S. Brewer, 2003.

– "The Ages of Christ and Mary in the Hyde Register and in Old English Literature." *N&Q* 233 (1988): 4–11.

– "The Earliest Anglo-Latin Text of the *Trinubium Annae* (*BHL* 505zl)." In *Via Crucis: Essays on Early Medieval Sources and Ideas in Memory of J.E. Cross*, ed. Thomas N. Hall, with assistance from Thomas D. Hill and Charles D.

Wright, 104–37. Medieval European Studies 1. Morgantown: West Virginia University Press, 2002.

– "The *Euangelium Nichodemi* and *Vindicta Saluatoris* in Anglo-Saxon England." In *Two Old English Apocrypha and Their Manuscript Source: The Gospel of Nicodemus and The Avenging of the Saviour*, ed. J.E. Cross, 36–81. CSASE 19. Cambridge: Cambridge University Press, 1996.

– "Latin Sermons for Saints in Early English Homiliaries and Legendaries." In *The Old English Homily: Precedent, Practice, and Appropriation*, ed. Aaron J Kleist, 227–63. Turnhout: Brepols, 2007.

– "The Portents at Christ's Birth in Vercelli Homilies V and VI: Some Analogues from Medieval Sermons and Biblical Commentaries." In *New Readings in the Vercelli Book*, ed. Samantha Zacher and Andy Orchard, 62–97. Toronto Anglo-Saxon Series 4. Toronto: University of Toronto Press, 2009.

Hare, Michael. "Cnut and Lotharingia: Two Notes." *ASE* 29 (2000): 261–78.

Hartog, Paul A., ed. *Orthodoxy and Heresy in Early Christian Contexts: Reconsidering the Bauer Thesis*. Eugene, OR: Pickwick, 2015.

Hawk, Brandon W., "The *Fifteen Signs before Judgment* in Anglo-Saxon England: A Reassessment." *JEGP*, forthcoming.

– "A Fragment of Colossians with Hiberno-Latin Glosses in St. Gall, Stiftsbibliothek, Cod. Sang. 1395." *Sacris Erudiri* 51 (2012): 233–56.

– "'Id est, crux Christi': Tracing the Old English Motif of the Celestial Rood." *ASE* 40 (2011): 43–73.

– "Preaching Apocrypha in Anglo-Saxon England." https://brandonwhawk.net/preaching-apocrypha/.

– "Psalm 151 in Anglo-Saxon England." *RES* 66 (2015): 805–21.

– "Pseudo-Bede." Sources of Anglo-Saxon England. Amsterdam: Amsterdam University Press, forthcoming.

Hawk, Brandon W., trans. *The Gospel of Pseudo-Matthew*. Salem, OR: Polebridge Press, forthcoming.

Hayles, N. Katherine. *My Mother Was a Computer: Digital Subjects and Literary Texts*. Chicago: University of Chicago Press, 2005.

Hayward, Paul Anthony. "Saints and Cults." In *A Social History of England, 900–1200*, ed. Julia Crick and Elisabeth van Houts, 309–20. Cambridge: Cambridge University Press, 2011.

Hen, Yitzhak. "The Content and Aims of the So-Called Homiliary of Burchard of Würzburg." In *Sermo doctorum: Compilers, Preachers and Their Audiences in the Early Middle Ages*, ed. Maximilian Diesenberger, Yitzhak Hen, and Marianne Pollheimer, 127–52. SERMO 9. Turnhout: Brepols, 2013.

Henderson, George. "The Representations of the Apostles in Insular Art, with Special Reference to the New Apostles Frieze at Tarbat, Ross-shire." In *Text,

Image, Interpretation: Studies in Anglo-Saxon Literature and Its Insular Context in Honour of Éamonn Ó Carragáin, ed. Alastair Minnis and Jane Roberts, 473–94. Studies in the Early Middle Ages 18. Turnhout: Brepols, 2007.

Hennecke, Edgar, and Wilhelm Schneemelcher, eds. *New Testament Apocrypha*. Translated by R. McL. Wilson. Rev. ed. 2 vols. Louisville: Westminster/John Knox Press, 1991.

Hessels, J.H. *An Eighth-Century Latin-Anglo-Saxon Glossary*. Cambridge: Cambridge University Press, 1890.

Higgitt, John. "The Iconography of St. Peter in Anglo-Saxon England, and St. Cuthbert's Coffin." In *St. Cuthbert, His Cult and His Community to A.D. 1200*, ed. Gerald Bonner, David Rollason, and Clare Stancliffe, 267–85. Woodbridge: Boydell and Brewer, 1989.

Hildberg, Isidore, ed. *Sancti Eusebii Hieronymi Epistulae*. 2nd ed. Corpus Scriptorum Ecclesiasticorum Latinorum 54–6. Vienna: F. Tempsky, 1996.

Hill, Joyce. "Ælfric: His Life and Works." In *A Companion to Ælfric*, ed. Hugh Magennis and Mary Swan, 35–65. Companions to the Christian Tradition 18. Leiden: Brill, 2009.

– "Ælfric and Haymo Revisited." In *Intertexts: Studies in Anglo-Saxon Culture Presented to Paul E. Szarmach*, ed. Virginia Blanton and Helene Scheck, 331–47. MRTS 334. Tempe: Arizona Center for Medieval and Renaissance Studies, 2008.

– "Ælfric and Smaragdus." *ASE* 21 (1992): 203–37.

– "Ælfric's Authorities." In *Early Medieval English Texts and Interpretations: Studies Presented to Donald G. Scragg*, ed. Elaine Treharne and Susan Rosser, 51–65. MRTS 252. Tempe: Arizona Center for Medieval and Renaissance Studies, 2002.

– "Ælfric's Manuscript of Paul the Deacon's Homiliary: A Provisional Analysis." In *The Old English Homily: Precedent, Practice, and Appropriation*, ed. Aaron J Kleist, 67–96. Turnhout: Brepols, 2007.

– "Ælfric's Sources Reconsidered: Some Case Studies from the *Catholic Homilies*." In *Studies in English Language and Literature: "Doubt Wisely": Papers in Honour of E.G. Stanley*, ed. M.J. Toswell and E.M. Tyler, 362–86. London: Routledge, 1996.

– "Authority and Intertextuality in the Works of Ælfric." *Proceedings of the British Academy* 131 (2005): 157–81.

– "The Context of Ælfric's Saints' Lives." In *Hagiography in Anglo-Saxon England: Adopting and Adapting Saints' Lives into Old English Prose (c. 950–1150)*, ed. Loredana Lazzari, Patrizia Lendinara, and Claudia Di Sciacca, 1–27. Textes et Études du Moyen Âge 73. Barcelona: Féderation Internationale des Instituts d'Études Médiévales, 2014.

– "Reform and Resistance: Preaching Styles in Late Anglo-Saxon England."
In *De l'homélie au sermon: Histoire de la predication medievale*, ed. Jacqueline
Hamesse and Xavier Hermand, 15–46. Publications de l'Institut d'Études
Médiévales: Texts, Études, Congrés 14. Louvain-la-Neuve: Institut d'Études
Médiévales de l'Université Catholique de Louvain, 1993.

– "Translating the Tradition: Manuscripts, Models, and Methodologies in the
Composition of Ælfric's *Catholic Homilies*." In *Textual and Material Culture
in Anglo-Saxon England: Thomas Northcote Toller and the Toller Memorial
Lectures*, ed. Donald Scragg, 241–59. Publications of the Manchester Centre
for Anglo-Saxon Studies 1. Cambridge: D.S. Brewer, 2003.

Hill, Thomas D. "The Baby on the Stone: Nativity as Sacrifice (The Old English
Christ III, 1414–1425)." In *Intertexts: Studies in Anglo-Saxon Culture Presented
to Paul E. Szarmach*, ed. Virginia Blanton and Helene Scheck, 69–77. MRTS 334.
Tempe: Arizona Center for Medieval and Renaissance Studies, 2008.

– "The Conversion of Sibilla in the *History of the Holy Rood Tree*." *Studies in
Philology* 105 (2008): 123–43.

– "Introduction." In *Sources of Anglo-Saxon Literary Culture: A Trial Version*,
ed. Frederick M. Biggs, Thomas D. Hill, and Paul E. Szarmach, xv–xxix.
Binghamton, NY: Center for Medieval and Early Renaissance Studies, 1990.

– "The Seven Joys of Heaven in 'Christ III' and Old English Homiletic Texts."
N&Q 214 (1969): 165–6.

Hoffman, Eva R. "Pathways of Portability: Islamic and Christian Interchange
from the Tenth to the Twelfth Century." *Art History* 24 (2001): 17–50.

The Holy Bible: Douay Version Translated from the Latin Vulgate. London:
Catholic Truth Society, 1956.

Hughes, Kevin L. *Constructing Antichrist: Paul, Biblical Commentary, and the
Development of Doctrine in the Early Middle Ages*. Washington, DC: Catholic
University of America Press, 2005.

Huhtamo, Erkki, and Jussi Parikka. "Introduction: An Archaeology of Media
Archaeology." In *Media Archaeology: Approaches, Applications, and Implica-
tions*, ed. Erkki Huhtamo and Jussi Parikka, 1–21. Berkeley: University of
California Press, 2011.

Huhtamo, Erkki, and Jussi Parikka, eds. *Media Archaeology: Approaches,
Applications, and Implications*. Berkeley: University of California Press, 2011.

Hurst, D., and J. Fraipont, eds. *Bedae Venerabilis opera, pars III: opera homiletica,
pars IV: opera rhythmica*. CCSL 122. Turnhout: Brepols, 1955.

Hutcheon, Linda. *A Theory of Adaptation*. New York: Routledge, 2006.

Irvine, Susan. "The Compilation and Use of Manuscripts Containing Old English
in the Twelfth Century." In *Rewriting Old English in the Twelfth Century*,

ed. Mary Swan and Elaine Treharne, 41–61. CSASE 30. Cambridge: Cambridge University Press, 2000.

Irvine, Susan, ed. *Old English Homilies from MS Bodley 343*. EETS os 302. Oxford: Oxford University Press, 1993.

Izydorczyk, Zbigniew. "The *Evangelium Nicodemi* in the Latin Middle Ages." In *The Medieval "Gospel of Nicodemus": Text, Intertexts, and Contexts in Western Europe*, ed. Zbigniew Izydorczyk, 43–101. MRTS 158. Tempe: Arizona Center for Medieval and Renaissance Studies, 1997.

– "The Inversion of Paschal Events in the Old English *Descent into Hell*." *Neuphilologische Mitteilungen* 91 (1990): 439–47.

Jackson, Peter, and Michael Lapidge, "The Contents of the Cotton-Corpus Legendary." In *Holy Men and Holy Women: Old English Prose Saints' Lives and Their Contexts*, ed. Paul E. Szarmach, 131–46. Albany: SUNY Press, 1996.

James, Montague Rhodes. *The Ancient Libraries of Canterbury and Dover*. Cambridge: Cambridge University Press, 1903.

– *The New Testament Apocrypha*. Oxford: Oxford University Press, 1924.

Jenkins, Philip. *The Many Faces of Christ: The Thousand-Year Story of the Survival and Influence of the Lost Gospels*. New York: Basic Books, 2015.

Jeremias, Joachim. *Unknown Sayings of Jesus*. Trans. Reginald H. Fuller. 2nd English ed. London: SPCK, 1964.

Jockers, Matthew L. *Macroanalysis: Digital Methods and Literary History*. Urbana: University of Illinois Press, 2013.

Johnson, Richard F. "Archangel in the Margins: St Michael in the Homilies of Cambridge, Corpus Christi College 41." *Traditio* 53 (1998): 63–91.

Johnson, Sara Raup. *Historical Fictions and Hellenistic Jewish Identity: Third Maccabees in Its Cultural Context*. Berkeley: University of California Press, 2004.

Johnston, Michael, and Michael Van Dussen, eds. *The Medieval Manuscript Book: Cultural Approaches*. Cambridge: Cambridge University Press, 2015.

Jolly, Karen Louise. *Popular Religion in Late Saxon England: Elf Charms in Context*. Chapel Hill: University of North Carolina Press, 1996.

Jolly, Karen Louise, Catherine E. Karkov, and Sarah Larratt Keefer, eds. *Cross and Culture in Anglo-Saxon England: Studies in Honor of George Hardin Brown*. Medieval European Studies 9. Morgantown: West Virginia University Press, 2007.

Junod, Eric. "'Apocryphes du Nouveau Testament': une appellation erronée et une collection artificielle." *Apocrypha* 3 (1992): 17–46.

– "Apocryphes du Nouveau Testament ou apocryphes chrétiens anciens? Remarques sur la désignation d'un corpus et indications bibliographiques sur les instruments de travail reécents." *Etudes théologiques et religieuses* 58 (1983): 409–21.

Junod, Eric, and Jean-Daniel Kaestli, eds. *Acta Iohannis*. 2 vols. CCSA 1–2. Turnhout: Brepols, 1983.

Kabir, Ananya Jahanara. *Paradise, Death and Doomsday in Anglo-Saxon Literature*. CSASE 32. Cambridge: Cambridge University Press, 2001.

Karkov, Catherine E. *The Art of Anglo-Saxon England*. Woodbridge: Boydell Press, 2011.

– *Text and Picture in Anglo-Saxon England: Narrative Strategies in the Junius 11 Manuscript*. CSASE 31. Cambridge: Cambridge University Press, 2001.

Karkov, Catherine E., Sarah Larratt Keefer, and Karen Louise Jolly, eds. *The Place of the Cross in Anglo-Saxon England*. Publications of the Manchester Centre for Anglo-Saxon Studies 4. Woodbridge: D.S. Brewer, 2006.

Keefer, Sarah Larratt. "Margin as Archive: The Liturgical Marginalia of a Manuscript of the Old English Bede." *Traditio* 51 (1996): 147–77.

Keefer, Sarah Larratt, Karen Louise Jolly, and Catherine E. Karkov, eds. *Cross and Cruciform in the Anglo-Saxon World: Studies to Honor the Memory of Timothy Reuter*. Medieval European Studies 11. Morgantown: West Virginia University Press, 2010.

Kelly, J.N.D. *Early Christian Creeds*. New York: David Kay, 1972.

Kennedy, Kathleen E. *Medieval Hackers*. Brooklyn, NY: Punctum, 2014.

Ker, N.R. *Catalogue of Manuscripts Containing Anglo-Saxon*. Oxford: Clarendon Press, 1957.

– "An Eleventh-Century Old English Legend of the Cross before Christ." *Medium Ævum* 9 (1940): 84–5.

– *English Manuscripts in the Century after the Norman Conquest*. Oxford: Oxford University Press, 1960.

Kienzle, Beverly Mayne. "Introduction." In *The Sermon*, ed. Beverly Mayne Kienzle, 143–74. Typologie des Sources du Moyen Âge Occidental 81–3. Turnhout: Brepols, 2000.

Kienzle, Beverly Mayne, ed. *The Sermon*. Typologie des Sources du Moyen Âge Occidental 81–3. Turnhout: Brepols, 2000.

Kirschenbaum, Matthew G. *Mechanisms: New Media and the Forensic Imagination*. Cambridge, MA: MIT Press, 2012.

– *Track Changes: A Literary History of Word Processing*. Cambridge, MA: Harvard University Press, 2016.

Kittler, Friedrich A. *Gramophone, Film, Typewriter*. Trans. Geoffrey Winthrop-Young and Michael Wutz. Stanford: Stanford University Press, 1999.

Kleist, Aaron J. "Ælfric's Corpus: A Conspectus." *Florilegium* 18 (2001): 113–64.

– "An Annotated Bibliography of Ælfrician Studies: 1983–1996." In *Old English Prose: Basic Readings*, ed. Paul E. Szarmach, 503–52. New York: Garland, 2000.

– "Appendix: Anglo-Saxon Homiliaries as Designated by Ker." In *The Old English Homily: Precedent, Practice, and Appropriation*, ed. Aaron J Kleist, 493–506. Turnhout: Brepols, 2007.

Kleist, Aaron J, ed. *The Old English Homily: Precedent, Practice, and Appropriation*. Turnhout: Brepols, 2007.

Krapp, George Philip, and Elliott van Kirk Dobbie, eds. *Anglo-Saxon Poetic Records*. 6 vols. New York: Columbia University Press, 1931–53.

Kuypers, A.B., ed. *The Prayer Book of Aedeluald the Bishop Commonly Called the Book of Cerne*. Cambridge: Cambridge University Press, 1902.

Lang, James. "The Apostles in Anglo-Saxon Sculpture in the Age of Alcuin." *Early Medieval Europe* 8 (1999): 271–82.

Lapidge, Michael. *The Anglo-Saxon Library*. Oxford: Oxford University Press, 2006.

– "The Saintly Life in Anglo-Saxon England." In *The Cambridge Companion to Old English Literature*, ed. Michael Lapidge and Malcolm Godden, 243–63. Cambridge: Cambridge University Press, 1991.

Lapidge, Michael, and Rosalind C. Love. "The Latin Hagiography of England and Wales (600–1550)." In *Hagiographies: Histoire internationale de la littérature hagiographique latine et vernaculaire, en Occident, des origines à 1500*, ed. Guy Philippart, 3:203–25. 7 vols. Turnhout: Brepols, 1994–.

Lazzari, Loredana, Patrizia Lendinara, and Claudia Di Sciacca, eds., *Hagiography in Anglo-Saxon England: Adopting and Adapting Saints' Lives into Old English Prose (c. 950–1150)*. Textes et Études du Moyen Âge 73. Barcelona: Féderation Internationale des Instituts d'Études Médiévales, 2014.

Le Goff, Jacques. *The Medieval Imagination*. Trans. Arthur Goldhammer. Chicago: University of Chicago Press, 1988.

Lees, Clare A. "Theme and Echo in an Anonymous Old English Homily for Easter." *Traditio* 42 (1986): 115–42.

– *Tradition and Belief: Religious Writing in Late Anglo-Saxon England*. Medieval Cultures 19. Minneapolis: University of Minnesota Press, 1999.

– "Working with Patristic Sources: Language and Context in Old English Homilies." In *Speaking Two Languages: Traditional Disciplines and Contemporary Theory in Medieval Studies*, ed. Allen J. Frantzen, 157–80. Albany, NY: SUNY Press, 1991.

Leneghan, Francis. "Teaching the Teachers: The Vercelli Book and the Mixed Life." *English Studies* 94 (2013): 627–58.

Leuven Database of Ancient Books, Trismegistos. http://www.trismegistos.org/ldab/.

Levine, Caroline. *Forms: Whole, Rhythm, Hierarchy, Network*. Princeton: Princeton University Press, 2015.

Levison, Wilhelm. *England and the Continent in the Eighth Century*. Oxford: Clarendon Press, 1947.

Lewis, Charlton T., and Charles Short, eds. *A Latin Dictionary*. Oxford: Clarendon Press, 1879.

Liebermann, Felix. *Die Gesetze der Angelsachsen*. 3 vols. Halle: Max Niemeyer, 1903–16.

Lifshitz, Felice. *Religious Women in Early Carolingian Francia: A Study of Manuscript Transmission and Monastic Culture*. New York: Fordham University Press, 2014.

Lindsay, Wallace M., ed. *Isidori Hispalensis Episcopi Etymologiarum sive Originum Libri XX*. 2 vols. Oxford: Oxford University Press, 1911.

Lionarons, Joyce Tally. *The Homiletic Writings of Archbishop Wulfstan: A Critical Study*. Anglo-Saxon Studies 14. Woodbridge: D.S. Brewer, 2010.

Lipsius, Richard Adelbert. *Die Apokryphen Apostelgeschichten Und Apostellegenden: Ein Beitrag Zur Altchristlichen Literaturgeschichte*. 2 vols. Brunswick: C.A. Schwetschke and Son, 1883–7.

– *Die Quellen Der Römischen Petrus-Saga*. Kiel: Schwers'sche Buchhandlung, 1872.

Lipsius, Richard Adelbert, and Max Bonnet, eds. *Acta Apostolorum Apocrypha*. 2 vols. Leipzig: Hermann Mendelssohn, 1891.

Liuzza, Roy M., ed. *The Old English Version of the Gospels*. EETS os 304, 314. Oxford: Oxford University Press, 1994–2000.

Lowe, E.A. *Codices Latini Antiquiores*. 11 vols. and Supplement. Oxford: Oxford University Press, 1934–71.

Lucas, Peter J., and Angela M. Lucas. *Anglo-Saxon Manuscripts in Microfiche Facsimile, Volume 18: Manuscripts in France*. MRTS 381. Tempe: Arizona Center for Medieval and Renaissance Studies, 2012.

Magennis, Hugh. "Ælfric Scholarship." In *A Companion to Ælfric*, ed. Hugh Magennis and Mary Swan, 5–34. Companions to the Christian Tradition 18. Leiden: Brill, 2009.

Magennis, Hugh, and Mary Swan, eds. *A Companion to Ælfric*. Companions to the Christian Tradition 18. Leiden: Brill, 2009.

Maniaci, Marilena. "Quantificare la produzione manoscritta del passato. Ambizioni, rischi, illusioni di una 'bibliometria storica globale'." *IASLonline*. 4 February 2013. http://www.iaslonline.de/index.php?vorgang_id=3567.

Manovich, Lev. *Software Takes Command*. International Texts in Critical Media
    Aesthetics 5. New York: Bloomsbury, 2013.
Manuscripta Medievalia. 2010. http://www.manuscripta-mediaevalia.de/.
Marsden, Richard, ed. *The Old English Heptateuch and Ælfric's Libellus de
    Veteri Testamento et Novo, Volume 1: Introduction and Text*. EETS os 330.
    Oxford: Oxford University Press, 2008.
Martin, Josef, and Klaus D. Daur, eds. *Sancti Aurelii Augustini: De doctrina
    Christiana, de vera religione*. CCSL 32. Turnhout: Brepols, 1962.
Martin, Lawrence T., and David Hurst, trans. *Bede the Venerable: Homilies
    on the Gospels, Book One, Advent to Lent*. Cistercian Studies Series 110.
    Kalamazoo: Cistercian Publications, 1991.
McCoy, Adam Dunbar. "The Use of the Writings of English Authors in Old
    English Homiletic Literature." Unpublished PhD diss., Cornell University,
    1973.
McCune, James. "The Preacher's Audience, c. 800–c. 950." In *Sermo doctorum:
    Compilers, Preachers, and Their Audiences in the Early Medieval West*, ed.
    Maximilian Diesenberger, Yitzhak Hen, and Marianne Pollheimer, 283–338.
    SERMO: Studies on Patristic, Medieval, and Reformation Sermons and
    Preaching 9. Turnhout: Brepols, 2013.
McEntire, Sandra. "The Devotional Context of the Cross before A.D. 1000."
    In *Old English Literature: Critical Essays*, ed. Roy M. Liuzza, 392–403. New
    Haven: Yale University Press, 2002.
McGinn, Bernard. *Antichrist: Two Thousand Years of the Human Fascination
    with Evil*. San Francisco: HarperCollins, 1994.
McGinn, Bernard, trans. *Apocalyptic Spirituality: Treatises and Letters of
    Lactantius, Adso of Montier-en-Der, Joachim of Fiore, the Franciscan Spirituals,
    Savonarola*. Mahwah, NJ: Paulist Press, 1979.
McKitterick, Rosamond. "Anglo-Saxon Missionaries in Germany: Reflections
    on the Manuscript Evidence." *Transactions of the Cambridge Bibliographical
    Society* 9 (1989): 291–329.
– "The Diffusion of Insular Culture in Neustria between 650 and 850: The
    Implications of the Manuscript Evidence." *La Neustrie. Les pays au nord de la
    Loire de 650 à 850*, ed. Hartmut Atsma, 2:395–432. 2 vols. Beihefte der Francia
    16. Sigmaringen: Jan Thorbecke Verlag, 1989.
– "Nuns' Scriptoria in England and Francia in the Eighth Century." *Francia* 19
    (1992): 1–35.
– "Women and Literacy in the Early Middle Ages." In *Books, Scribes and
    Learning in the Frankish Kingdoms, 6th–9th Centuries*, chapter 13. Variorum
    Collected Studies Series 452. Aldershot: Ashgate, 1994.

McLuhan, Marshall. *Understanding Media: The Extensions of Man, Critical Edition*. Ed. W. Terrence Gordon. Berkeley: Gingko Press, 2003.

McNamara, Martin. *Apocrypha in the Irish Church*. Dublin: Dublin Institute for Advanced Studies, 1975.

McNamara, Martin, ed. *Biblical Studies: The Medieval Irish Contribution*. Proceedings of the Irish Biblical Association 1. Dublin: Irish Biblical Association, 1976.

MDZ: Münchener Digitalisierungs Zentrum Digitale Bibliothek. 2016. https://www.digitale-sammlungen.de/.

Meens, Rob. "Christianization and the Spoken Word: The Sermons Attributed to S. Boniface." In *Zwischen Niederschrift und Wiederschrift: Hagiographie und Historiographie im Spannungsfeld von Kompendienüberlieferung und Editionkstechnik*, ed. Richard Corradini, 211–22. Vienna: Österreichische Akademie der Wissenschaften, 2010.

Migne, J.-P. *Patrologia Cursus Completus, Series Latina*. 221 vols. Paris: Migne, 1844–64.

Mitchell, W.J.T. *Iconology: Image, Text, Ideology*. Chicago: University of Chicago Press, 1986.

– "Image." In *Critical Terms for Media Studies*, ed. W.J.T. Mitchell and Mark B.N. Hansen, 35–48. Chicago: University of Chicago Press, 2010.

– *Picture Theory: Essays on Verbal and Visual Representation*. Chicago: University of Chicago Press, 1994.

Mitchell, W.J.T., and Mark B.N. Hansen. "Introduction." In *Critical Terms for Media Studies*, ed. W.J.T. Mitchell and Mark B.N. Hansen, vii–xxii. Chicago: University of Chicago Press, 2010.

Mitchell, W.J.T., and Mark B.N. Hansen, eds. *Critical Terms for Media Studies*. Chicago: University of Chicago Press, 2010.

Mombritius, Boninus. *Sanctuarium seu Vitae Sanctorum*. 2nd ed. 2 vols. Paris: Fontemoing and Socios, 1910.

Momma, Haruko, ed. *The Dictionary of Old English*. Toronto: University of Toronto Press. https://www.doe.utoronto.ca.

Mommsen, Theodor, ed. *Historia Ecclesiastica in Eusebius Werke*. Vol. 2. in 2 parts. Leipzig: J.C. Heinrichs'sche Buchhandlung, 1903–8.

Moretti, Franco. *Distant Reading*. London: Verso, 2012.

– *Graphs, Maps, Trees: Abstract Models for Literary History*. London: Verso, 2005.

Morin, Germain. "L'homéliaire de Burchard de Würzburg: Contribution à la critique des sermons de saint Césaire d'Arles." *Revue Bénédictine* 13 (1896): 97–111.

Morris, Richard, ed. *The Blickling Homilies.* EETS os 58, 63, 73. London: Oxford University Press, 1874–80; repr. in 1 vol. 1967.

– ed. *Legends of the Holy Rood; Symbols of the Passion and Cross-Poems.* EETS os 46. London: N. Trübner & Co., 1871.

Mostert, Marco. "Reading Images and Texts: Some Preliminary Observations Instead of an Introduction." In *Reading Images and Texts: Medieval Images and Texts as Forms of Communication*, ed. Mariëlle Hegeman and Marco Mostert, 1–7. Utrecht Studies in Medieval Literacy 8. Turnhout: Brepols, 2005.

Muessig, Carolyn. "Medieval Preaching." In *A Handbook for Catholic Preaching*, ed. Edward Foley, 62–73. Collegeville, MN: Liturgical Press, 2016.

– "Preacher, Sermon and Audience in the Middle Ages: An Introduction." In *Preacher, Sermon and Audience in the Middle Ages*, ed. Carolyn Muessig, 3–9. A New History of the Sermon 3. Leiden: Brill, 2002.

– "Sermon, Preacher and Society in the Middle Ages." *Journal of Medieval History* 28 (2002): 73–91.

– "What Is Medieval Monastic Preaching? An Introduction." *Medieval Monastic Preaching*, ed. Carolyn Muessig, 3–16. Studies in Intellectual History 90. Leiden: Brill, 1998.

Muessig, Carolyn, ed. *Preacher, Sermon and Audience in the Middle Ages.* A New History of the Sermon 3. Leiden: Brill, 2002.

Napier, Arthur S., ed. *History of the Holy Rood-Tree: A Twelfth-Century Version of the Cross-Legend.* EETS os 103. London: Kegan Paul, Trench, Trübner & Co., 1894.

– ed. *Old English Glosses, Chiefly Unpublished.* Anecdota Oxoniensia, Mediaeval and Modern Series 11. Oxford: Clarendon Press, 1900. Repr. Hildesheim: Wiedmann, 1969.

– ed. *Wulfstan: Sammlung Der Ihm Zugeschriebenen Homilien Nebst Untersuchungen Über Ihre Echtheit.* Berlin: Weidmann, 1883.

Nichols, Stephen G., and Siegfried Wenzel, eds. *The Whole Book: Cultural Perspectives on the Medieval Miscellany.* Ann Arbor: University of Michigan Press, 1996.

Noel, William. *The Harley Psalter.* Cambridge Studies in Palaeography and Codicology 4. Cambridge: Cambridge University Press, 1995.

Noss, Philip A. *A History of Bible Translation.* History of Bible Translation 1. Rome: Edizioni di storia e letteratura, 2007.

Ó Cróinín, Dáibhi. "Bischoff's Wendepunkte Fifty Years On." *Revue Bénédictine* 110 (2000): 204–37.

O'Brien, Bruce R. *Reversing Babel: Translation among the English during an Age of Conquests, C. 800 to C. 1200.* Newark: University of Delaware Press, 2011.

O'Brien O'Keeffe, Katherine. "Source, Method, Theory, Practice: On Reading Two Old English Verse Texts." In *Textual and Material Culture in Anglo-Saxon England: Thomas Northcote Toller and the Toller Memorial Lectures*, ed. D.G. Scragg, 161–81. Publications of the Manchester Centre for Anglo-Saxon Studies 1. Cambridge: D.S. Brewer, 2003.

O'Leary, Aideen. "Apostolic *Passiones* in Early Anglo-Saxon England." In *Apocryphal Texts and Traditions in Anglo-Saxon England*, ed. Kathryn Powell and Donald G. Scragg, 103–19. Publications of the Manchester Centre for Anglo-Saxon Studies 2. Cambridge: D.S. Brewer, 2003.

– "By the Bishop of Babylon? The Alleged Origins of the Collected Latin Apocryphal Acts of the Apostles." In *The Legacy of M.R. James: Papers from the 1995 Cambridge Symposium*, ed. Lynda Dennison, 128–38. Donnington: Shaun Tyas, 2001.

– "An Orthodox Old English Homiliary? Ælfric's Views on the Apocryphal Acts of the Apostles." *Neuphilologische Mitteilungen* 100 (1999): 15–26.

O'Sullivan, Tomás. "*Predicationes Palatinae*: The Sermons in Vat. Pal. lat. 220 as an Insular Resource for the Christianization of Early Medieval Germany." Unpublished PhD diss., Saint Louis University, 2011.

Ogawa, Hiroshi. "Hagiography in Homily: Theme and Style in Ælfric's Two-Part Homily on SS Peter and Paul." *RES* 61 (2009): 167–87.

– *Language and Style in Old English Composite Homilies*. MRTS 361. Tempe: Arizona Center for Medieval and Renaissance Studies, 2010.

Ohlgren, Thomas H. *Anglo-Saxon Textual Illustration: Photographs of Sixteen Manuscripts with Descriptions and Index*. Kalamazoo: Medieval Institute Publications, 1992.

Okasha, Elizabeth. "A Fourth Supplement to *Hand-List of Anglo-Saxon Non-Runic Inscriptions*." *ASE*, forthcoming.

– "A Second Supplement to *Hand-List of Anglo-Saxon Non-Runic Inscriptions*." *ASE* 21 (1992): 37–85.

– "A Third Supplement to *Hand-List of Anglo-Saxon Non-Runic Inscriptions*." *ASE* 33 (2004): 225–81.

Oliphant, Robert T. *The Harley Latin–Old English Glossary*. Janua Linguarum, Series Practica 20. The Hague: Mouton, 1966.

Oxford English Dictionary Online. Oxford: Oxford University Press, 2016.

Page, R.I., Mildred Budny, and Nicholas Hadgraft. "Two Fragments of an Old English Manuscript in the Library of Corpus Christi College, Cambridge." *Speculum* 70 (1995): 502–29.

Palladio. Humanities + Design at Stanford University. 2016. http://hdlab.stanford.edu/palladio/.

Palmer, James T. *Anglo-Saxons in a Frankish World*. Studies in the Early Middle Ages 19. Turnhout: Brepols, 2009.

– *The Apocalypse in the Early Middle Ages*. Cambridge: Cambridge University Press, 2014.

Parikka, Jussi. *What Is Media Archaeology?* Cambridge: Polity, 2012.

Pelikan, Jaroslav, and Valerie Hotchkiss, eds. *Creeds and Confessions of Faith in the Christian Tradition, Volume I*. New Haven: Yale University Press, 2003.

Pelle, Stephen. "The Seven Pains of Hell: The Latin Source of an Old English Homiletic Motif." *RES* 62 (2011): 167–80.

Pervo, Richard I. "Direct Speech in Acts and the Question of Genre." *Journal for the Study of the New Testament* 28 (2006): 285–307.

– "Rhetoric in the Christian Apocrypha." In *A Handbook of Classical Rhetoric in the Hellenistic Period 330 B.C.–A.D. 400*, ed. Stanley E. Porter, 793–805. Leiden: Brill, 1997.

Pfaff, Richard W. *The Liturgy in Medieval England: A History*. Cambridge: Cambridge University Press, 2009.

– "Massbooks: Sacramentaries and Missals." In *The Liturgical Books of Anglo-Saxon England*, ed. Richard W. Pfaff, 7–34. Old English Newsletter Subsidia 23. Kalamazoo: Medieval Institute Publications, 1995.

Piovanelli, Pierluigi. "What Is a Christian Apocryphal Text and How Does It Work? Some Observations on Apocryphal Hermeneutics." *Nederlands Theologisch Tijdschrift* 59 (2005): 31–40.

Pope, John C. *Homilies of Ælfric: A Supplementary Collection*. 2 vols. EETS os 259–60. London: Oxford University Press, 1967–8.

Poster, Carol, and Linda C. Mitchell. *Letter-Writing Manuals and Instruction from Antiquity to the Present: Historical and Bibliographic Studies*. Columbia: University of South Carolina Press, 2007.

Powell, Kathryn, and Donald G. Scragg, eds. *Apocryphal Texts and Traditions in Anglo-Saxon England*. Publications of the Manchester Centre for Anglo-Saxon Studies 2. Cambridge: D.S. Brewer, 2003.

Prendergast, Christopher. *The Triangle of Representation*. New York: Columbia University Press, 2000.

Prescott, Andrew, ed. *The Benedictional of St Æthelwold: A Masterpiece of Anglo-Saxon Art, A Facsimile*. London: British Library, 2001.

Proud, Joanna. "The Sources of the ANON (OE) St James the Greater (Cameron B.3.3.11)." In *Fontes Anglo-Saxonici: A Register of Written Sources Used by Anglo-Saxon Authors*. 2001.

Randle, Jonathan T. "The 'Homiletics' of the Vercelli Book Poems: The Case of *Homiletic Fragment I*." In *New Readings in the Vercelli Book*, ed. Samantha

Zacher and Andy Orchard, 185–224. Toronto Anglo-Saxon Series 4. Toronto: University of Toronto Press, 2009.

Rauer, Christine, ed. and trans. *The Old English Martyrology*. Cambridge: D.S. Brewer, 2013.

Raw, Barbara C. *Trinity and Incarnation in Anglo-Saxon Art and Thought*. CSASE 21. Cambridge: Cambridge University Press, 1997.

Reed, Annette Yoshiko. "The Afterlives of New Testament Apocrypha." *Journal of Biblical Literature* 133 (2015): 401–25.

– "The Modern Invention of 'Old Testament Pseudepigrapha'." *Journal of Theological Studies* 60 (2009): 403–36.

– "Pseudepigraphy, Authorship, and the Reception of 'the Bible' in Late Antiquity." In *The Reception and Interpretation of the Bible in Late Antiquity*, ed. Lorenzo DiTommaso and Lucian Turcescu, 467–90. Bible in Ancient Christianity 6. Leiden: Brill, 2008.

Reifferscheid, August. *Bibliotheca patrum latinorum Italica*. 2 vols. in 1. Vienna: K. Gerold's Sohn, 1865–71. Repr. Hildesheim: Georg Olms, 1976.

Remley, Paul G. "The Vercelli Book and Its Texts: A Guide to Scholarship." In *New Readings in the Vercelli Book*, ed. Samantha Zacher and Andy Orchard, 318–416. Toronto Anglo-Saxon Series 4. Toronto: University of Toronto Press, 2009.

Richards, Mary P. *Texts and Their Traditions in the Medieval Library of Rochester Cathedral Priory*. Transactions of the American Philological Society 78.3. Philadelphia: American Philological Society, 1988.

Rikhardsdottir, Sif. *Medieval Translations and Cultural Discourse: The Movement of Texts in England, France and Scandinavia*. Cambridge: D.S. Brewer, 2012.

Robertson, D.W., Jr, trans. *Saint Augustine: On Christian Doctrine*. Indianapolis: Library of the Liberal Arts, 1958.

Robertson, Nicola. "Review: The Benedictine Reform: Current and Future Scholarship." *Literature Compass* 3 (2006): 282–99.

Robertson, Owen, and Orietta Da Rold. "London, British Library, Cotton Tiberius A. iii." In Orietta Da Rold, Takako Kato, Mary Swan, and Elaine Treharne, *The Production and Use of English Manuscripts 1060 to 1220*. University of Leicester, 2010. http://www.le.ac.uk/english/em1060to1220/mss/EM.BL.Tibe.A.iii.htm.

Robinson, Cynthia. "Arthur in Alhambra? Narrative and Nasrid Courtly Self-Fashioning in The Hall of Justice Ceiling Paintings." *Medieval Encounters* 14 (2008): 164–98.

Robinson, Pamela. "Self-Contained Units in Composite Manuscripts of the Anglo-Saxon Period." *ASE* 7 (1978): 231–8. Repr. in *Old English Manuscripts:*

Basic Readings, ed. Mary P. Richards, 25–35. Basic Readings in Anglo-Saxon England 2. New York: Garland, 1994.

Rollason, David. *Saints and Relics in Anglo-Saxon England*. Oxford: Blackwell, 1989.

Rose, Els. "*Abdias Scriptor Vitarum Sanctorum Apostolorum*? The 'Collection of Pseudo-Abdias' Reconsidered." *Revue d'histoire des textes* 8 (2013): 227–68.

– "The Apocryphal Acts of the Apostles in the Latin Middle Ages: Context of Transmission and Use." In *The Apocryphal Acts of the Apostles in Latin Christianity: Proceedings of the First International Summer School on Christian Apocryphal Literature (ISCAL), Strasbourg, 24–27 June 2012*, ed. Els Rose, 31–52. Turnhout: Brepols, 2014.

– *Ritual Memory: The Apocryphal Acts and Liturgical Commemoration in the Early Medieval West (c.500–1215)*. Leiden: Brill, 2009.

– "*Virtutes apostolorum*: Editorial Problems and Principles." *Apocrypha* 23 (2012): 11–45.

– "*Virtutes apostolorum*: Origin, Aim and Use." *Traditio* 68 (2013): 111–50.

Rosen, Rebecca J. "The Last Time a Pope Resigned Mass Media Was Called … Mass." *The Atlantic*. 13 February 2013. https://www.theatlantic.com/technology/archive/2013/02/the-last-time-a-pope-resigned-mass-media-was-called-mass/273098/ i.

Rubin, Miri. *Mother of God: A History of the Virgin Mary*. New Haven: Yale University Press, 2009.

Rudolf, Winfried. "An Early Manuscript Witness of the Homiliaries of Angers and St. Père de Chartres in Bamberg, Staatsbibliothek, MS Msc.Bibl.30a." *Journal of Medieval Latin* 27 (2017): 1–40.

– "The Homiliary of Angers in Tenth-Century England." *ASE* 29 (2010): 163–92.

Rushforth, Rebecca. *Saints in English Kalendars before A.D. 1100.* Henry Bradshaw Society 117. Woodbridge: Boydell and Brewer, 2008.

Sabatier, Pierre, ed. *Bibliorum Sacrorum Latinae Versiones Antiquae, Seu Vetus Italica*. 3 vols. Rheims, 1743–9. Repr. Turnhout: Brepols, 1976.

Sanders, Julie. *Adaptation and Appropriation*. New York: Routledge, 2006.

Schaefer, K.G. "An Edition of Five Old English Homilies for Palm Sunday, Holy Saturday, and Easter Sunday." Unpublished PhD diss., Columbia University, 1972.

Scharer, Anton. "Insular Mission to the Continent in the Early Middle Ages." In *Changing Perspectives on England and the Continent in the Early Middle Ages*, 55–62. Variorum Collected Studies Series 1042. Farnham: Ashgate, 2014.

Scheil, Andrew P. *The Footsteps of Israel: Understanding Jews in Anglo-Saxon England*. Ann Arbor: University of Michigan Press, 2004.

Scragg, D.G. "Cambridge, Corpus Christi College 162." In *Anglo-Saxon Manuscripts and Their Heritage*, ed. Philip Pulsiano and Elaine Treharne, 71–83. Aldershot: Ashgate, 1998.

– *A Conspectus of Scribal Hands Writing English, 960–1100*. Publications of the Manchester Centre for Anglo-Saxon Studies 11. Cambridge: D.S. Brewer, 2012.

– "The Corpus of Anonymous Lives and Their Manuscript Context." In *Holy Men and Holy Women: Old English Prose Saints' Lives and Their Contexts*, ed. Paul E. Szarmach, 209–30. Albany: SUNY Press, 1996.

– "The Corpus of Vernacular Homilies and Prose Saints' Lives before Ælfric." *ASE* 8 (1979), 223–77. Repr. in *Old English Prose: Basic Readings*, ed. Paul E. Szarmach, 73–150. New York: Garland, 2000.

– *Dating and Style in Old English Composite Homilies*. H.M. Chadwick Memorial Lectures 9. Cambridge: Department of Anglo-Saxon, Norse and Celtic, 1999.

– "'The Devil's Account of the Next World' Revisited." *American Notes and Queries* 24 (1986): 107–10.

– "The Homilies of the Blickling Manuscript." In *Learning and Literature in Anglo-Saxon England: Studies Presented to Peter Clemoes on the Occasion of His Sixty-fifth Birthday*, ed. Michael Lapidge and Helmut Gneuss, 299–316. Cambridge: Cambridge University Press, 1985.

– "A Late Old English Harrowing of Hell Homily from Worcester and Blickling Homily VII." In *Latin Learning and English Lore: Studies in Anglo-Saxon Literature for Michael Lapidge*, ed. Katherine O'Brien O'Keeffe and Andy Orchard, 2:197–211. 2 vols. Toronto Anglo-Saxon Series 14. Toronto: University of Toronto Press, 2005.

– "Source Study." In *Reading Old English Texts*, ed. Katherine O'Brien O'Keeffe, 39–58. Cambridge: Cambridge University Press, 1997.

– "The Vercelli Homilies and Kent." In *Intertexts: Studies in Anglo-Saxon Culture Presented to Paul E. Szarmach*, ed. Virginia Blanton and Helene Scheck, 369–80. MRTS 334. Tempe: Arizona Center for Medieval and Renaissance Studies, 2008.

Scragg, D.G., ed. *The Vercelli Homilies and Related Texts*. EETS os 300. Oxford: Oxford University Press, 1992.

Sharpe, Richard. "The Dating of *Quadripartitus* Again." In *English Law before Magna Carta: Felix Liebermann and "Die Gesetze Der Angelsachsen"*, ed. Stefan Jurasinski, Lisi Oliver, and Andrew Rabin, 81–93. Medieval Law and Its Practice 8. Leiden: Brill, 2010.

Shepherd, William H. "Early Christian Apocrypha: A Bibliographic Essay." *Theological Librarianship: An Online Journal of the American Theological Library Association* 3 (2010): 40–7.

Singer, Samuel, et al., eds. *Thesaurus Proverbiorum Medii Aevi/Lexikon der Sprichwörter des romanisch-germanischen Mittelalters*. 14 vols. Berlin: Walter de Gruyter, 1995–2002.

Skeat, Walter W., ed. *Ælfric's Lives of Saints*. EETS os 76, 83, 94, 114. London: Oxford University Press, 1881–1900.

Smetana, Cyril L. "Aelfric and the Early Medieval Homiliary." *Traditio* 15 (1959): 165–80.

– "Paul the Deacon's Patristic Anthology." In *The Old English Homily and Its Backgrounds*, ed. Paul E. Szarmach and B.F. Huppé, 75–97. Albany: SUNY Press, 1978.

Smith, Kathryn A. "Chivalric Narratives and Devotional Experience in the Taymouth Hours." In *Negotiating Secular and Sacred in Medieval Art: Christian, Islamic, and Buddhist*, ed. Alicia Walker and Amanda Luyster, 17–54. Farnham: Ashgate, 2009.

Somerset, Fiona. "Introduction." In *Truth and Tales: Cultural Mobility and Medieval Media*, ed. Fiona Somerset and Nicholas Watson, 1–16. Columbus: Ohio State University Press, 2015.

Somerset, Fiona, and Nicholas Watson, eds. *Truth and Tales: Cultural Mobility and Medieval Media*. Columbus: Ohio State University Press, 2015.

Speyer, Wolfgang. "Neue Pilatus-Apokryphen." *Vigiliae Christianae* 32 (1978): 53–9.

"Stab des heiligen Heribert." *Kulturelles Erbe Köln*. https://www.kulturelles-erbe-koeln.de/documents/obj/20365285.

Stansbury, Mark. *Earlier Latin Manuscripts*. NUI Galway. https://elmss.nuigalway.ie/.

Stanton, Robert. *The Culture of Translation in Anglo-Saxon England*. Cambridge: D.S. Brewer, 2002.

– "The (M)other Tongue: Translation Theory and Old English." In *Translation Theory and Practice in the Middle Ages*, ed. Jeanette Beer, 33–46. Studies in Medieval Culture 38. Kalamazoo: Medieval Institute Publications, 1997.

Starr, Rebecca I. "Raising John's Body: Ælfric's Homily for the Assumption of John." *Medieval and Early Modern English Studies* 18 (2010): 317–40.

Stephenson, Rebecca. *The Politics of Language: Byrhtferth, Ælfric, and the Multilingual Identity of the Benedictine Reform*. Toronto Anglo-Saxon Series 18. Toronto: University of Toronto Press, 2015.

Stevens, William O. *The Cross in the Life and Literature of the Anglo-Saxons.* Yale Studies in English 22. New York: Henry Holt, 1904. Repr. Hamden, CT: Yale University Press, 1977.

Stevenson, Henry, ed. *Codices Palatini latini Bibliothecae Vaticanae descripti praeside I.B. cardinali Pitra.* Vol. 1. Rome: Vatican, 1886.

Stock, Brian. *The Implications of Literacy: Written Language and Models of Interpretation in the Eleventh and Twelfth Centuries.* Princeton: Princeton University Press, 1983.

– *Listening for the Text: On the Uses of the Past.* Baltimore: Johns Hopkins University Press, 1990.

Stone, Michael E. *Ancient Judaism: New Visions and Views.* Grand Rapids: Eerdmans, 2011.

Striphas, Ted. *The Late Age of Print: Everyday Book Culture from Consumerism to Control.* New York: Columbia University Press, 2009.

Stroker, William D. *Extracanonical Sayings of Jesus.* Society of Biblical Literature, Resources for Biblical Study 18. Atlanta: Scholars Press, 1989.

Stryker, W.G. "The Latin–Old English Glossary in MS. Cotton Cleopatra A.III." Unpublished PhD diss., Stanford University, 1951.

Swan, Mary. "Identity and Ideology in Ælfric's Prefaces." In *A Companion to Ælfric*, ed. Hugh Magennis and Mary Swan, 247–69. Companions to the Christian Tradition 18. Leiden: Brill, 2009.

Swan, Mary, and Helen Foxhall Forbes. "Oxford, Bodleian, Hatton 114." In Orietta Da Rold, Takako Kato, Mary Swan, and Elaine Treharne, *The Production and Use of English Manuscripts 1060 to 1220.* University of Leicester, 2010. http://www.le.ac.uk/english/em1060to1220/mss/EM.Ox. Hatt.114.htm.

Swan, Mary, and Elaine Treharne, eds. *Rewriting Old English in the Twelfth Century.* CSASE 30. Cambridge: Cambridge University Press, 2000.

Swanton, Michael, ed. *The Dream of the Rood.* Rev. ed. Exeter: University of Exeter Press, 1987.

Szarmach, Paul E. "The Vercelli Prose and Anglo-Saxon Literary History." In *New Readings in the Vercelli Book*, ed. Samantha Zacher and Andy Orchard, 12–40. Toronto Anglo-Saxon Series 4. Toronto: University of Toronto Press, 2009.

Szarmach, Paul E., ed. *Old English Prose: Basic Readings.* New York: Garland, 2000.

Szarmach, Paul E., and B.F. Huppé, eds. *The Old English Homily and Its Backgrounds.* Albany: SUNY Press, 1978.

Szarmach, Paul E., and Virginia D. Oggins, eds. *Sources of Anglo-Saxon Culture.* Studies in Medieval Culture 20. Kalamazoo: Medieval Institute Publications, 1986.

Tamburr, Karl. *The Harrowing of Hell in Medieval England.* Cambridge: D.S. Brewer, 2007.

Temple, Elżbieta. *Anglo-Saxon Manuscripts, 900–1066.* A Survey of Manuscripts Illuminated in the British Isles 2. London: Harvey Miller, 1976.

Terras, Melissa, Julianne Nyhan, and Edward Vanhoutte, eds. *Defining Digital Humanities.* Farnham: Ashgate, 2013.

Thacker, Alan. "In Search of Saints: The English Church and the Cult of Roman Apostles and Martyrs in the Seventh and Eighth Centuries." In *Early Medieval Rome and the Christian West: Essays in Honour of Donald A. Bullough*, ed. Julia M.H. Smith, 247–77. The Medieval Mediterranean 28. Leiden: Brill, 2000.

Thomas, Christine M. *The Acts of Peter, Gospel Literature, and the Ancient Novel: Rewriting the Past.* Oxford: Oxford University Press, 2003.

Thompson, Nancy M. "Anglo-Saxon Orthodoxy." In *Old English Literature in Its Manuscript Context*, ed. Joyce Tally Lionarons, 37–65. Medieval European Studies 5. Morgantown: West Virginia University Press, 2004.

– "The Carolingian *De festiuitatibus* and the Blickling Book." In *The Old English Homily: Precedent, Practice, and Appropriation*, ed. Aaron J Kleist, 97–119. Turnhout: Brepols, 2007.

– "'Hit Segð on Halgum Bocum': The Logic of Composite Old English Homilies." *Philological Quarterly* 81 (2002): 383–419.

Thorpe, Benjamin, ed. and trans. *The Homilies of the Anglo-Saxon Church: The First Part, Containing the Sermones Catholici, or Homilies of Ælfric.* 2 vols. London: Ælfric Society, 1844–6.

Thurn, Hans. *Die Handschriften der Universitätsbibliothek Würzburg.* Vol. 3, part 1. Wiesbaden: Otto Harrassowitz, 1984.

Tite, Philip L. *The Apocryphal Epistle to the Laodiceans: An Epistolary and Rhetorical Analysis.* Texts and Editions for New Testament Study 7. Leiden: Brill, 2012.

Toller, T. Northcote, ed. *An Anglo-Saxon Dictionary, Based on the Manuscript Collections of the Late Joseph Bosworth.* Oxford: Oxford University Press, 1898. Repr. 1954.

Toswell, M.J. "The Codicology of Anglo-Saxon Homiletic Manuscripts, Especially the Blickling Homilies." In *The Old English Homily: Precedent, Practice, and Appropriation*, ed. Aaron J Kleist, 209–26. Turnhout: Brepols, 2007.

Townend, Matthew, ed. *Wulfstan, Archbishop of York: The Proceedings of the Second Alcuin Conference*. Studies in the Early Middle Ages 10. Turnhout: Brepols, 2004.

Treharne, Elaine. "The Architextual Editing of Early English." *Poetica* 71 (2008): 1–13.

– "Fleshing Out the Text: The Transcendent Manuscript in the Digital Age." *postmedieval* 4 (2013): 465–78.

– "The Form and Function of the Vercelli Book." In *Text, Image, Interpretation: Studies in Anglo-Saxon Literature and Its Insular Context in Honor of Éamonn Ó Carragáin*, ed. Alastair J. Minnis and Jane Annette Roberts, 253–66. Turnhout: Brepols, 2007.

– *Living through Conquest: The Politics of Early English, 1020–1220*. Oxford: Oxford University Press, 2012.

– "London, British Library, Cotton Vespasian D. xiv." In Orietta Da Rold, Takako Kato, Mary Swan, and Elaine Treharne, *The Production and Use of English Manuscripts 1060 to 1220*. University of Leicester, 2010. http://www.le.ac.uk/english/em1060to1220/mss/EM.BL.Vesp.D.xiv.htm.

– "Making Their Presence Felt: Readers of Ælfric, C. 1050–1350." In *A Companion to Ælfric*, ed. Hugh Magennis and Mary Swan, 399–422. Companions to the Christian Tradition 18. Leiden: Brill, 2009.

– "Producing a Library in Late Anglo-Saxon England: Exeter, 1050–1072." *RES* 54 (2003): 155–72.

– "Scribal Connections in Late Anglo-Saxon England." In *Texts and Traditions of Medieval Pastoral Care: Essays in Honour of Bella Millett*, ed. Catherine Gunn and Catherine Innes-Parker, 29–46. York: York Medieval Press, 2009.

Treharne, Elaine, Orietta Da Rold, and Mary Swan. *Producing and Using English Manuscripts in the Post-Conquest Period*. Special Issue of *New Medieval Literatures* 13 (2011).

Turner, D.H. "Illuminated Manuscripts." In *The Golden Age of Anglo-Saxon Art, 966–1066*, ed. Janet Backhouse, D.H. Turner, and Leslie Webster, 46–87. London: British Museum Publications, 1984.

Universitätsbibliothek Würzburg. 2015. http://vb.uni-wuerzburg.de/ub/index.html.

The Utrecht Psalter. Universiteitsbibliotheek Utrecht, 2013. http://bc.library.uu.nl/node/599.

Van der Horst, Koert, William Noel, and Wilhelmina C.M. Wüstefeld, eds. *The Utrecht Psalter in Medieval Art: Picturing the Psalms of David*. Utrecht: HES, 1996.

Venuti, Lawrence. "Adaptation, Translation, Critique." *Journal of Visual Culture* 6 (2007): 25–43.

– *The Translator's Invisibility: A History of Translation*. 2nd ed. New York: Routledge, 2008.

Venuti, Lawrence, ed. *The Translation Studies Reader*. 3rd ed. New York: Routledge, 2012.

Verhelst, D. *Adso Dervensis: De ortu et tempore Antichristi, necnon et tractatus qui ab eo dependunt*. CCCM 45. Turnhout: Brepols, 1976.

Von Tischendorf, Constantin, ed. *Evangelia Apocrypha*. 2nd ed. Leipizg: Hermann Mendelssohn, 1876.

Walker, Alexander. *Apocryphal Gospels, Acts, and Revelations*. Ante-Nicene Christian Library 16. Edinburgh: T. & T. Clark, 1890.

Warner, Rubie D-N., ed. *Early English Homilies from the Twelfth Century MS. Vesp. D. XIV*. EETS os 152. Oxford: Oxford University Press, 1917 for 1915.

Watts, Duncan J. *Six Degrees: The Science of a Connected Age*. New York: W.W. Norton, 2004.

Webb, Jen. *Understanding Representation*. London: SAGE, 2009.

Weber, Robert., ed. *Biblia sacra iuxta vulgatam versionem*. 5th ed. Stuttgart: Deutsche Bibelgesellschaft, 2007.

Webster, Leslie. *Anglo-Saxon Art: A New History*. Ithaca: Cornell University Press, 2012.

Wenzel, Siegfried. *Latin Sermon Collections from Later Medieval England: Orthodox Preaching in the Age of Wyclif*. Cambridge Studies in Medieval Literature 53. Cambridge: Cambridge University Press, 2005.

– *Preachers, Poets, and the Early English Lyric*. Princeton: Princeton University Press, 1986.

Westwood, J.O. *Facsimiles of the Ornaments of Anglo-Saxon and Irish Manuscripts*. London: Bernard Quaritch, 1868.

Whatley, E. Gordon. "Acta Sanctorum." In *Sources of Anglo-Saxon Literary Culture, Volume One: Abbo of Fleury, Abbo of Saint-German-des-Prés, and Acta Sanctorum*, ed. Frederick M. Biggs, Thomas D. Hill, Paul E. Szarmach, and E. Gordon Whatley, with the assistance of Deborah A. Oosterhouse, 22–486. Kalamazoo: Medieval Institute Publications, 2001.

– "An Introduction to the Study of Old English Prose Hagiography: Sources and Resources." In *Holy Men and Holy Women: Old English Prose Saints' Lives and Their Contexts*, ed. Paul E. Szarmach, 3–32. Albany: SUNY Press, 1996.

White, David Gordon. *Myths of the Dog-Man*. Chicago: University of Chicago Press, 1991.

Whitelock, Dorothy. "Bishop Ecgred, Pehtred and Niall." In *Ireland in Early Mediaeval Europe: Studies in Memory of Kathleen Hughes*, ed. Dorothy

Whitelock, Rosamond McKitterick, and David Dumville, 47–68. Cambridge: Cambridge University Press, 1982.

Wilcox, Jonathan. *Ælfric's Prefaces*. Durham Medieval Texts 9. Durham: Durham Medieval Texts, 1994.

– "The Blickling Homilies Revisited: Knowable and Probable Uses of Princeton University Library, MS Scheide 71." In *The Genesis of Books: Studies in the Scribal Culture of Medieval England in Honour of A.N. Doane*, ed. Matthew T. Hussey and John D. Niles, 97–115. Turnhout: Brepols, 2011.

– "Wulfstan and the Twelfth Century." In *Rewriting Old English in the Twelfth Century*, ed. Mary Swan and Elaine Treharne, 83–97. CSASE 30. Cambridge: Cambridge University Press, 2000.

Wilcox, Miranda. "Creeds and Confessions of Faith." Sources of Anglo-Saxon England. Amsterdam: Amsterdam University Press, forthcoming.

Willard, Rudolph, ed. *The Blickling Homilies*. EEMF 10. Copenhagen: Rosenkilde & Bagger, 1960.

– *Two Apocrypha in Old English Homilies*. Beiträge Zur Englischen Philologie 30. Leipzig: B. Tauchnitz, 1935.

Williams, Mark. *Fiery Shapes: Celestial Portents and Astrology in Ireland and Wales, 700–1700*. Oxford: Oxford University Press, 2010.

Williams, Raymond. *Culture and Society, 1780–1950*. New York: Columbia University Press, 1958. Repr. 1983.

– *Marxism and Literature*. Oxford: Oxford University Press, 1977.

– "On High and Popular Culture." *The New Republic*. 22 November 1974. https://newrepublic.com/article/79269/high-and-popular-culture.

Wilson, Henry A., ed. *The Missal of Robert of Jumièges*. Henry Bradshaw Society 11. London: Henry Bradshaw Society, 1896. Repr. Woodbridge: Boydell Press, 1994.

Wilson, Rita, and Brigid Maher, eds. *Words, Images and Performances in Translation*. New York: Continuum, 2012.

Wilson, Stephen. "Annotated Bibliography." In *Saints and Their Cults: Studies in Religious Sociology, Folklore, and History*, ed. Stephen Wilson, 309–417. Cambridge: Cambridge University Press, 1983.

Witherington, Ben, III. *New Testament Rhetoric: An Introductory Guide to the Art of Persuasion in and of the New Testament*. Eugene, OR: Cascade, 2009.

Wizowaty, Judith Vaughan. "The Iconography of Adam and Eve on Sculptured Stones in Anglo-Saxon England." Unpublished PhD diss., University of Texas at Austin, 1989.

Wolfenbütteler Digitale Bibliothek. Herzog August Bibliothek. http://www.hab.de/de/home/bibliothek/digitale-bibliothek-wdb.html.

Woodfin, Warren T. "An Officer and a Gentleman: Transformations in the Iconography of a Warrior Saint." *Dumbarton Oaks Papers* 60 (2006): 111–42.

Wormald, Francis, ed. *English Kalendars before A.D. 1100*. Henry Bradshaw Society 72. London: Harrison & Sons, 1934. Repr. Woodbridge: Boydell and Brewer, 1988.

Wormald, Patrick. *The Making of English Law: King Alfred to the Twelfth Century, Volume I: Legislation and Its Limits*. Oxford: Blackwell, 2001.

Wright, Charles D. "*The Apocalypse of Thomas*: Some New Latin Texts and Their Significance for Old English Versions." In *Apocryphal Texts and Traditions in Anglo-Saxon England*, ed. Kathryn Powell and Donald G. Scragg, 27–64. Publications of the Manchester Centre for Anglo-Saxon Studies 2. Cambridge: D.S. Brewer, 2003.

– "Bischoff's Theory of Irish Exegesis and the Genesis Commentary in Munich clm 6302: A Critique of a Critique." *Journal of Medieval Latin* 10 (2000): 115–75.

– "Hiberno-Latin and Irish-Influenced Biblical Commentaries, Florilegia, and Homily Collections." In *Sources of Anglo-Saxon Literary Culture: A Trial Version*, ed. Frederick M. Biggs, Thomas D. Hill, and Paul E. Szarmach, 87–123. MRTS 74. Binghamton, NY: Center for Medieval and Early Renaissance Studies, 1990.

– "Hiberno-Latin Writings in *Sources of Anglo-Saxon Literary Culture*." OEN 3 (1992): 21–3.

– *The Irish Tradition in Old English Literature*. CSASE 6. Cambridge: Cambridge University Press, 1993.

– "Latin Analogue for *The Two Deaths: The Three Utterances of the Soul*." In *The End and Beyond: Medieval Irish Eschatology*, ed. John Carey, Emma Nic Cárthaigh, and Caitríona Ó Dochartaigh, 113–37. Oxford: Oxbow, 2014.

– "More Latin Sources for the Old English 'Three Utterances' Homilies." *Mediaeval Studies* 77 (2015): 45–79.

– "More Old English Poetry in Vercelli Homily XXI." In *Early Medieval English Texts and Interpretations: Studies Presented to Donald G. Scragg*, ed. Elaine Treharne and Susan Rosser, 245–62. MRTS 252. Tempe: Arizona Center for Medieval and Renaissance Studies, 2002.

– "A New Latin Source for Two Old English Homilies (Fadda I and Blickling I): Pseudo-Augustine, *Sermo* App. 125 and the Ideology of Chastity in the Anglo-Saxon Benedictine Reform." In *Source of Wisdom: Old English and Early Medieval Latin Studies in Honour of Thomas D. Hill*, ed. Charles D. Wright, Frederick M. Biggs, and Thomas N. Hall, 239–65. Toronto Old English Series 16. Toronto: University of Toronto Press, 2007.

– "Old English Homilies and Latin Sources." In *The Old English Homily: Precedent, Practice, and Appropriation*, ed. Aaron J Kleist, 15–66. Turnhout: Brepols, 2007.

– "Vercelli Homilies XI–XIII and the Benedictine Reform: Tailored Sources and Implied Audiences." In *Preacher, Sermon and Audience in the Middle Ages*, ed. Carolyn Muessig, 203–27. A New History of the Sermon 3. Leiden: Brill, 2002.

– "Vercelli Homily XV and *The Apocalypse of Thomas*." In *New Readings in the Vercelli Book*, ed. Samantha Zacher and Andy Orchard, 150–84. Toronto Anglo-Saxon Series 4. Toronto: University of Toronto Press, 2009.

Yeager, Stephen M. *From Lawmen to Plowmen: Anglo-Saxon Legal Tradition and the School of Langland*. Toronto Anglo-Saxon Series 17. Toronto: University of Toronto Press, 2014.

Zacher, Samantha. "Circumscribing the Text: Views on Circumcision in Old English Literature." In *Old English Literature and the Old Testament*, ed. Michael Fox and Manish Sharma, 89–118. Toronto Anglo-Saxon Series 10. Toronto: University of Toronto Press, 2012.

– *Preaching the Converted: The Style and Rhetoric of the Vercelli Homilies*. Toronto Anglo-Saxon Series 1. Toronto: University of Toronto Press, 2009.

– *Rewriting the Old Testament in Anglo-Saxon Verse: Becoming the Chosen People*. London: Bloomsbury, 2013.

Zacher, Samantha, and Andy Orchard, eds. *New Readings in the Vercelli Book*. Toronto Anglo-Saxon Series 4. Toronto: University of Toronto Press, 2009.

Zanoletti, Margherita. "Marinetti and Buvoli: A Translation Studies Approach to Italian Art and Culture." In *Shaping an Identity: Adapting, Rewriting and Remaking Italian Literature*, ed. Pamela Arancibia et al., 175–91. Media and Education Studies 63. New York: Legas, 2012.

Zettel, Patrick H. "Saints' Lives in Old English: Latin Manuscripts and Vernacular Accounts: Ælfric." *Peritia* 1 (1982): 17–37.

Zupitza, Julius, ed. *Ælfrics Grammatik und Glossar*. 3rd ed. Introduction by Helmut Gneuss. Hildesheim: Weidmann, 2003.

Index of Manuscripts

Page numbers followed by f indicate references to figures.

General Index

Page numbers followed by f indicate references to figures.

Toronto Anglo-Saxon Series

General Editor
ANDY ORCHARD

Editorial Board
ROBERTA FRANK
THOMAS N. HALL
ANTONETTE DIPAOLO HEALEY
MICHAEL LAPIDGE
KATHERINE O'BRIEN O'KEEFFE